THE WORLD'S CLASSICS

LANCELOT OF THE LAKE

CORIN CORLEY was educated at Bedales School and
Edinburgh University, where he went on to do a doctoral
thesis on Old French Arthurian romance, published as
'The Second Continuation of the Old French *Perceval*: a
critical and lexicographical study' (London, 1987). He is
currently working as a freelance translator.

ELSPETH KENNEDY, Emeritus Fellow of St Hilda's
College, Oxford, has edited *Lancelot do Lac: The non-cyclic
Old French Prose Romance* (Oxford, 1980) and written
Lancelot and the Grail: A Study of the Prose Lancelot (Oxford,
1986).

CORIN CORLEY was educated at Bedales School and Edinburgh University, where he went on to do a doctoral thesis on Old French Arthurian romance, published as The Second Continuation of the Old French Perceval, a critical and lexicographical study (London, 1987). He is currently working as a freelance translator.

ELSPETH KENNEDY, Emeritus Fellow of St Hilda's College, Oxford, has edited Lancelot do Lac: The non-cyclic Old French Prose Romance (Oxford, 1980) and written Lancelot and the Grail: A Study of the Prose Lancelot (Oxford, 1986).

THE WORLD'S CLASSICS

Lancelot of the Lake

Translated with Notes by
CORIN CORLEY

and an Introduction by
ELSPETH KENNEDY

Oxford   New York
OXFORD UNIVERSITY PRESS

Oxford University Press, Great Clarendon Street, Oxford OX2 6DP

Oxford New York
Athens Auckland Bangkok Bogota Bombay
Buenos Aires Calcutta Cape Town Dar es Salaam
Delhi Florence Hong Kong Istanbul Karachi
Kuala Lumpur Madras Madrid Melbourne
Mexico City Nairobi Paris Singapore
Taipei Tokyo Toronto Warsaw

and associated companies in
Berlin Ibadan

Oxford is a trademark of Oxford University Press

Translation, translator's note, select bibliography, explanatory notes
© Corin Corley 1989
Introduction © Elspeth Kennedy 1989

This edition first published 1989 as a World's Classics paperback

British Library Cataloguing in Publication Data
Data available

Library of Congress Cataloging in Publication Data
Lancelot du Lac. English.
Lancelot of the Lake / translated with notes by Corin Corley; and
an introduction by Elspeth Kennedy.
p. cm. - (The World's classics)
Translation of: Lancelot du Lac.
Bibliography: p.
1. Lancelot (Legendary character) - Romances.
I. Corley, Corin F. W. II. Title.
PQ1489..2E5 1989 843'.1–dc19 88-17845
ISBN 0-19-281756-6

5 7 9 10 8 6

Printed in Great Britain by
Caledonian International Book Manufacturing Ltd, Glasgow

CONTENTS

CONTENTS

INTRODUCTION

The romance translated here tells the story of Lancelot of
the Lake, one of the most famous and best loved of all
Arthurian knights. It was written in French and in prose,
early in the thirteenth century, by an unknown and unnamed
author; it begins with Lancelot's childhood in the Lake and
ends with the death of Lancelot's friend Galehot, but it was
not the first nor indeed the last medieval French romance to
have this particular knight as its main hero. As we shall see,
it represents the first stage in the development of the great
Lancelot–Grail prose cycle (or *Vulgate* cycle as it used to be
called), one of the French books known to Malory, but it also
has its roots in twelfth-century Arthurian tradition.

Lancelot first makes his appearance in the surviving texts
in the romances of Chrétien de Troyes (second half of the
twelfth century): his name occurs in a list of good knights in
Erec et Enide, he is defeated by the main hero in a tournament
in *Cligés*, and finally establishes his reputation as greatest
knightly lover in the *Chevalier de la Charrette* (*The Knight of
the Cart*). This last romance already contains the main
elements of the tradition lying behind the prose romance,
which makes a number of implicit allusions to the earlier
work and appears to expect its readers to be familiar with it.
Chrétien's romance combines an old tradition of the abduction and rescue of Guinevere (including a few resonances of
a journey into an otherworld) with an attempt to translate into
narrative terms the concept of *fin' amor*, celebrated in the
lyrics of the *troubadours* and *trouvères*. Guinevere is carried off
by a knight called Meleagant to the land of Gorre, of which
the chief town is Bath, where many of Arthur's men are held
captive. Anyone seeking to deliver the prisoners of Gorre
must cross one of two strange and perilous bridges—an

underwater bridge and a sword bridge. Gawain sets off to rescue the queen and meets an unnamed knight whom he does not recognize and whose identity as Lancelot of the Lake is only revealed by Guinevere herself to the other characters and to the reader or listener half-way through the poem. The two knights pursue the abductor, and Lancelot has a series of adventures which test his quality as humble and obedient lover. Absorbed in thoughts of his beloved, he falls into trances from which he can be aroused to perform great deeds; he is prepared to endure humiliation for the sake of his love and only hesitates a few steps before getting on to a shameful cart on which the knight must ride who is to rescue the queen. Gawain, faced with the same choice, decides to continue his journey on horseback, but when he tries to cross the underwater bridge, he fails and nearly drowns. Lancelot's other adventures prove not only his fidelity to the queen when he refuses a damsel's advances, but also his quality as a knight. He deals calmly with a perilous bed in which he is threatened by flaming lances and establishes his identity as the hero destined to deliver the prisoners of Gorre when he alone can raise a slab in a perilous cemetery. He crosses the sword bridge, defeats the queen's abductor, but, at the very moment when he expects to be welcomed as her deliverer, is rejected (he learns later that this is because of his momentary hesitation in mounting the cart). It is only after he disappears into prison and false rumours of his death reach the queen that she forgives him on his return and grants him one night of love. Yet even here the obstacles in the way of pursuing this love further outside the strange kingdom of Gorre are hinted at through echoes of the Tristan story, reminders of the potential threat to society and the possible tragic fate of those involved in a love which binds together a knight and the wife of a king. Tragedy and destruction are kept at arms' length in Chrétien's poem, but are banished from our thoughts in this first Lancelot prose romance, where, as we shall see, the love saves Arthur and his kingdom and poses no threat.

Another important element of the Lancelot story, as it is to be told in the prose romance, is already hinted at in Chrétien in the name of the hero, Lancelot *of the Lake*, and in a brief allusion to his upbringing in a lake by a fairy who has given him a magic ring able to lay bare enchantment. A more detailed account of Lancelot's childhood in a lake, where he is taken after the death of his father Pant, is to be found in a German version of a lost French romance, the *Lanzelet* of Ulrich von Zatzikhoven, where Lancelot is not the lover of Guinevere; it would seem likely that some such romance was one of the sources of the prose *Lancelot*. In Ulrich's poem, Lanzelet is brought up in isolation from the world and ignorant of his name and of knightly combat on a horse, much as is Perceval in Chrétien's *Conte del Graal*. Both these romances have marked similarities with the *Tale of the Fair Unknown*, a tale which has survived in an early thirteenth-century version, *Le Bel Inconnu*, by Renaut de Beaujeu, but of which there are traces in a number of twelfth-century romances, including those of Chrétien. In this tale an unnamed youth comes to court and insists on undertaking the first adventure which offers itself; on the way to the task undertaken, he goes through a series of tests and, after achieving a certain adventure, discovers his own identity. In the prose *Lancelot* this quest for identity intertwines with the theme of love for Guinevere, and interplay with earlier romances, in particular with Chrétien's *Chevalier de la Charrette* and his Perceval romance, the *Conte del Graal*, helps to bring out the thematic structure of the work.

The romance can be divided into phases, each corresponding to a particular stage in the development of the identity theme. The introductory phase, which serves as a kind of historical prologue, describes the circumstances which lead to Lancelot's loss as a baby of name, family and inheritance, and to his removal to the Lake. Phase I of his story proper describes his education in the Lake, his progress spurred on by his uncertainty over his birth and his determination to prove himself worthy through his own efforts of aspiring to knighthood; the Lady of the Lake's careful preparation of the youth for chivalry leads up to his departure for Camelot, where he learns a little about his noble origins, meets and falls in love with the queen, and is knighted. Phase II recounts Lancelot's first adventures as White Knight, culminating in his conquest of the Dolorous Guard, a conquest in which he learns his own name. Phases III to V deal with Lancelot, under various arms, making a name for himself as a great knight, or rather a series of great knights, in the kingdom of Logres, and with the efforts of Arthur and his knights to discover the name of these unknown knights. In phase III Gawain sets off alone to discover the name of the conqueror of the Dolorous Guard and bring it back to court. Lancelot completes the adventure of the castle by putting an end to its enchantments, and this stage in the story ends with Gawain returning to court with the name of the White Knight (Lancelot, son of King Ban) while Lancelot slips quietly away. Phase IV recounts Lancelot's exploits as Red Knight and Black Knight in Arthur's battles against Galehot; it tells of the hero's friendship with Galehot, who, at Lancelot's request, surrenders to Arthur at the moment of victory and then arranges Lancelot's first secret meeting with Guinevere. It describes Gawain's undertaking of an unsuccessful quest for the Red Knight (Lancelot) together with thirty-nine knights of the Round Table, in the interval between Arthur's two wars with Galehot. After Guinevere has persuaded Lancelot to admit to his exploits and his love, has discovered who he is, has shared her knowledge with Galehot, and has granted her lover his first kiss, this part ends with Lancelot leaving secretly with Galehot for Sorelois. Phase V deals with another quest for the hero (here as Black Knight), with the physical consummation of Lancelot's love, and with Arthur's wars against the Saxons. Gawain, now accompanied by a young knight, Hector (sent out in quest of him), completes his search for the unknown hero when he presents Lancelot by name and in person to Arthur as the knight who saved him from Galehot and from the Saxons. The phase ends with Lancelot's installation as a Knight of the Round Table. Phase VI deals with the defence of a name: Lancelot proves by battle the queen's right to her own name when she is accused of being an impostor in the False Guinevere episode. Galehot's death is also foretold through dreams and portents and foreshadowed when Lancelot agrees to remain with Arthur as a member of his household. Lancelot's name has been made as the greatest knight in the world, a noble son of a high lineage; the identity of the woman he loves has been questioned and established as the true queen. The last two episodes provide an epilogue: Lancelot's cousin Lionel is knighted and, in a telescoped version of the hero's career, proves his right to his own name when he kills the Crowned Lion of Libya; Lancelot's love for Guinevere has its tragic consequence in the death of Galehot, caused by his separation from his friend and companion and a false rumour of Lancelot's death.

The progress of Lancelot's love, as can be seen, is closely linked with the making of his name; his inability to explain who he is when he arrives at court stems from his ignorance of his name, but could also be interpreted as the silence of the lover, overwhelmed by the sight of the beloved, as the queen herself suspects. The deeds which establish his knightly reputation under various disguises are all inspired by his love for Guinevere, as is made clear in the key episode in which Guinevere discovers his name through his admission of his exploits.

The relation of Lancelot and Guinevere is, indeed, presented in very positive terms throughout these adventures of the young Lancelot; the potentially destructive aspect of their love in terms of conflict with loyalty to king and with a Christian society is avoided. The conflict lies rather between friendship with a companion in arms and love of a man for a woman. Galehot sacrifices his greatest ambition when he surrenders to Arthur and knowingly prepares the way for his own separation from Lancelot by arranging for the secret meeting between his friend and the queen. His love for his companion, based on his admiration for his quality as a knight, brings him no gain, whereas Lancelot, inspired by his love to prove himself worthy, saves the king and Logres, and becomes the greatest of all knights. Lancelot, however much he may feel for his friend, must place his love for Guinevere above everything else, so Galehot dies.

These two central themes of the making of a name and love are also reflected in the adventures (summarized in this book) of the other two knights whose narrative threads are followed through in their quests, that is Gawain and Hector. Gawain represents the knight who has already established his reputation and now has to show himself worthy of it when he fights as an unnamed champion for a lady who doubts his prowess, the Lady of Roestoc. Hector embodies the lover and young knight with a reputation still to make, as he fulfils the role of Lancelot while the latter has been withdrawn from the action and lies hidden in Sorelois, except that Hector's damsel has a more negative attitude towards the relationship between love and prowess than does the queen. Their adventures and the couples they meet present different aspects of the tension, whether positive or negative, between the demands of love and those of chivalry. Their experiences appear as variations on the main themes, echoing as they do the adventures of earlier tradition; the tale of Lancelot is thus woven into the web of Arthurian literature.

The narrative structure consists mainly of a series of adventures encountered, apparently by chance, as the individual knights proceed on their quests, their paths crossing at intervals, and the accounts of their adventures interlacing as the tale switches from one narrative thread to another according to a certain formulaic pattern. The organization of the romance on the narrative level is far more subtle and complex than it might first appear to a twentieth-century reader unfamiliar with medieval literary techniques. It is designed to appeal to a sophisticated public; in addition to the thematic coherence explored above, various means are used to bind these narrative threads into a firm and rich texture. In this Arthur and his court play an important role. The court performs its traditional function in romance as the centre of chivalry throughout the whole of Christendom; it is also the centre of Arthur's feudal kingdom within which it is his responsibility to protect his vassals and to see that justice is done. Many of the adventures undertaken by his knights are concerned with the defence of his vassals. For example, Lancelot's first adventure is to serve as champion for a lady who holds her land from Arthur. The great courts held by the king in celebration of the main religious festivals, according to the custom of the medieval kings of history, bring the knights back from their adventures and thus draw the marriage threads together; a similar function is performed by the armed encounters or assemblies, whether they be tournaments at which prizes can be won, or the great battles (against Galehot or the Saxons) where the fate of a kingdom is at stake.

A number of events, even some of those which, at first sight, appear strange and mysterious, are, therefore, provided with a motivation on the human level, and indeed the *merveilleux*, the wonders and enchantments characteristic of Arthurian romance, are used with discretion. Contact with the *merveilleux* is mainly reserved for the hero and serves to mark important stages in his career: for example, the discovery of his name at the Dolorous Guard. The supernatural is usually linked with a place or an object rather than a being from another world: for example, the magic ring possessed by Lancelot which, like that in Chrétien's poem, lays bare enchantment, the three shields used by him to conquer the Dolorous Guard, or the split shield which draws together as the love progresses. All these come from the Lady of the Lake. She is described as a fairy, but even here an explanation is given for her knowledge of magic: she does not know it of her nature as some strange being, but, as a lady born of human parents, she learned it from Merlin, the son of a devil; she then imprisoned him so that the dangerous element of such knowledge is neutralized, and her magic is purely beneficent. Even the Lake is not a real lake but the semblance of one: a land with houses (and horses) lies beneath the misleading appearances. Thus the Lady of the Lake is presented as a suitable protectress for Lancelot, one who can give him the right preparation for chivalry in terms of providing him with the appropriate tuition in all the knightly skills (unlike the mother of Perceval or the fairy in the *Lanzelet*, where horses could not live in the more fully magic lake). There is no clear conflict between this magic, rational-ized in thirteenth-century terms, and Christian society; thus the abbey, founded by Lancelot's mother on the spot where his father died, can quite properly be situated beside the Lake where Lancelot lives unseen as a child; similarly, the Lady of the Lake is presented as an appropriate person to give Lancelot a detailed explanation of the role of the knight in Christian society as the defender of the Church and the people, the maintainer of justice. Although, on one level, the *merveilleux* element can serve to interrupt the natural sequence of events in terms of a normal system of cause and effect, it can also provide a framework for future events in terms of predictions and prophecies. Some events can indeed be motivated on two levels: the great military encounters or assemblies may be prepared for by agreements between kings, announcements of tournaments, or by an ultimatum from an invader, but they are also fitted into the pattern of predictions made by the damsels of the Lady of the Lake. Repeated sequences of events can also serve to provide landmarks within this vast romance: some of these may stem from the need to fulfil a promise, such as the oath sworn by Lancelot to avenge the wounded knight, a promise made on his arrival at Camelot; others may be associated with a recurring use of shields, such as those used by Lancelot during and after the conquest of the Dolorous Guard. A series of imprisonments or withdrawals from the action for recovery from wounds or for other reasons also serves to provide a broad pattern or rhythm to the narrative within the thematic framework.

This first prose *Lancelot*, ending with the death of Galehot, has, therefore, a coherent structure of its own in medieval terms, but it is also presented as part of a wider Arthurian tradition. This is done through the inclusion of episodes or other elements, echoing similar adventures or motifs in other romances, and through allusions to events taking place outside the story and contemporary with it (as, for example, Arthur's activities as king, particularly during the childhood of Lancelot, or the wars between barons encountered by Gawain or Hector on their quests). The allusions to the past serve to provide a depth in time and set this tale of Lancelot within the context of the three main Arthurian traditions: the so-called 'historical' tradition of Geoffrey of Monmouth and his adaptors, that is of Arthur, great and active king, defender of Britain against the pagan Saxons and against the dissensions of his barons; the magical tradition, characteristic of Arthurian romance and here usually evoked by references to Merlin and the time when the adventures began; the Christian supernatural and the more spiritual aspirations of knighthood as embodied by the Grail. Both Merlin and the Grail belong to the past: at this stage there is no preparation for a Grail Quest yet to come; indeed, there is an allusion early in the text (p. [33]) to Perceval as Grail-winner and achiever of the adventure of the Perilous Seat, thus looking back to the romances of Chrétien de Troyes and of Robert de Boron, not forward to a Galahad Quest.

The time has now come to set these early adventures of Lancelot within a new framework, that in which they would have been placed for most medieval readers. Probably about 1220, there began the transformation of this pre-cyclic prose *Lancelot*, ending with the death of Galehot and without a Grail Quest, into a branch of a romance cycle. The text of Lancelot's adventures up to his installation as Knight of the Round Table was taken over unchanged, including the reference to Perceval mentioned above, but the episode of Lancelot's journey to the lands of Galehot, the False Guinevere episode, and those leading up to the death of Galehot were rewritten to prepare the way for the inclusion in one great romance of the twelfth-century themes of the abduction and rescue of Guinevere, the Grail Quest, and the death of Arthur and end of the Round Table. The Grail theme was linked to the tale of Lancelot in the person of a new Grail-winner, Galahad, his son, the pure and virgin knight, who was to surpass his father, sit in the Perilous Seat, and achieve the greatest adventure of all—that of the Grail. A few scribes, at a later stage, noticed the contradiction with the Perceval allusion early in the text and tried to modify that reference. This introduction of the Grail theme into the Lancelot story entailed a re-evaluation of the hero's earlier adventures and of the nature and consequences of his love for Guinevere, now presented as sinful. Both Lancelot and the reader are, in the cyclic romance, forced to reinterpret past events. The theme of making a name and that of the love of Lancelot for Guinevere as a source of his greatness are thus transformed. His winning of the name Lancelot at the Dolorous Guard becomes the loss of his baptismal name, Galahad, a loss which his son makes good. The love becomes an obstacle to greatness, not a source of it: Lancelot fails at the Grail Quest because of it, and the adulterous passion of Lancelot and Guinevere sets in train the events which bring about the death of Arthur in the last branch of the cycle, the *Mort Artu*. However, in the prose *Lancelot* as presented here, no shadow has yet been cast over Lancelot's early achievements, inspired by his love for the queen, achievements which win him a seat at the Round Table, the respect and the admiration of the king, and the title of the greatest knight, surpassing even Arthur's nephew Gawain.

The adventures of the young Lancelot, as related here, but set in the context of the cyclic romance, continued to be read for more than three centuries; they were also translated or adapted into other languages. The *Lancelot* was one of the earliest and the most influential of the French prose romances, and it clearly had a wide appeal amongst the nobility and gentry. It also found an eager audience in the rich merchants of towns like Arras, where Adam de la Halle, in one of his plays (*Le Jeu de la Feuillée*) mocks the unsuccessful attempts of a wealthy burgher, Robert Sommeillon, to ape the deeds of a Lancelot. The 'Matter of Britain',[1] with its wonders and marvels, its great deeds of chivalry and celebrated lovers, evidently held a considerable fascination for the medieval public, but not just as escape literature. The structure of the Arthurian kingdom, as presented in this work, creates a link with the world outside romance. Problems concerning kingship, feudal relations, and the law are explored, and some of the concerns and aspirations of both great barons and more humble gentry are reflected, both in the Lady of the Lake's discourse on chivalry and the advice given to Arthur on kingship, and in the important role given to knights in the maintenance of order and justice in the

---

[1] This is the term used for the subject-matter of romances dealing with the Arthurian themes of Britain as opposed to classical or French themes.

kingdom; of particular interest is the way that the relationship of individual effort to inherited qualities and lineage is explored. Thirteenth-century nobles and jurists, as well as poets and writers of romance, such as Philippe de Novare and Philippe de Beaumanoir, quote from the text or use it as a source for their didactic or legal works. Ramon Lull, also writing in the thirteenth century, uses the explanation of the origins of chivalry as a source of his *Libre del ordre de cavayleria*, translated in the fifteenth century by Caxton (the *Book of the Ordre of Chyvalry*). Perhaps the most famous allusion of all is to be found in Canto 5 of Dante's *Inferno*, a reference, not this time to a passage on law or on chivalry, but to the kiss granted by Guinevere to Lancelot at the request of Galehot. The lovers, Paolo and Francesca, were reading together the description of that episode; their passions were so inflamed that they sinned and were killed before they had time to repent. This scene of the kiss is central to the whole structure of the first prose *Lancelot* and is so regretfully and reluctantly reinterpreted by Lancelot in the *Quest* and so maliciously distorted by Morgan le Fay in the *Mort Artu* of the *Lancelot–Grail* cycle. In the manuscript illuminations, ivories, and wallpaintings illustrating the story of Lancelot, it provides one of the key visual images of Arthurian romance and of one of the world's great love-stories.

ELSPETH KENNEDY

TRANSLATOR'S NOTE

The translation is based on Elspeth Kennedy's edition of the prose *Lancelot*. As the dimensions of this book did not permit translation of the text in its entirety, I decided to translate only those parts of the story directly concerned with Lancelot, although this meant skating over, in the summaries, large sections of richly interesting and well-written material.

Any translator sails a narrow line between the Scylla of paraphrasing in pursuit of a readable version and the Charybdis of producing a text which is faithful to the original, but unreadable. The translation of Old French presents its own special problems, not least the constant repetition of certain phrases, the extensive use of pronouns instead of names, and the presence of expressions which would best be rendered by corresponding but archaic English expressions. A tendency to indulge in almost routine hyperbole and to begin every sentence with 'And' poses further problems, while the distinction between singular and plural 'you' is inevitably lost, and I have chosen to rationalize the very varied mixture of tenses which is a feature of Old French.

Broadly speaking, I have attempted to be as faithful as possible to the original, while producing a readable, unambiguous text and avoiding an excessive use of archaisms. Where possible, I have left the sentence construction unchanged, and I have always tried to preserve the flavour of the text. In the final analysis, though, my priority has been to convey the sense, rather than reproduce the wording of the original.

In general, I have followed the punctuation of Kennedy's edition. I have made no attempt to be consistent over proper names: most have been left as they appear in the text, but for some I have used the accepted English forms (Arthur, Gawain, Kay, Camelot, etc.), and the modern names of places and rivers have been used where appropriate (Humber, Northumberland, etc). I have generally capitalized pronouns relating to God (You, His, etc.), as it helps to eliminate ambiguities. Arabic numerals in square brackets refer to the page numbers of Kennedy's text. Roman numerals in square brackets, prefixed by the letter M., refer to the chapter divisions of Micha's edition (see Select Bibliography).

My heartfelt thanks go to Shian, to Hans-Peter and Cornelia, to Tony Holden, and especially to Martin. The extensive glossary and notes of Elspeth Kennedy's edition were invaluable, and I have used both freely. Finally, I should like to thank George, Michael, and Jenni for their friendship.

CORIN CORLEY

SELECT BIBLIOGRAPHY

The text of the translation is based on *Lancelot do Lac: The Non-Cyclic Old French Prose Romance*, ed. E. Kennedy, 2 vols (Oxford, 1980). Reference is also made to the text of the cyclic version, *Lancelot: roman en prose du XIIIe siécle*, ed. A. Micha, 9 vols. (Paris and Geneva, 1979–83).

For the general background of the text, *Arthurian Literature in the Middle Ages: A Collaborative History*, ed. R. S. Loomis (Oxford, 1959), will prove invaluable, and pp. 295–318 are devoted specifically to the prose *Lancelot*. For the text itself, the reader could not do better than turn to Elspeth Kennedy's excellent work *Lancelot and the Grail* (Oxford, 1986). The latter work contains an extensive bibliography; it will suffice here to mention F. Lot's *Étude sur le Lancelot en prose* (Paris, 1954) and the chapter by Jean Frappier in J. Frappier and R. R. Grimm, *Grundriss der romanischen Literaturen des Mittelalters*, iv. 2 (Heidelberg, 1978), 536–89.

To
BEATRICE

Et sachiez que vos porriez bien compaig-
nie avoir de plus riche home que ge ne
sui; mais vos ne l'avroiz ja mais a home
qui tant vos aint.

Lancelot do Lac. p. 324, ll. 35–7

Lancelot of the Lake

Lancelot of the Lake

[1] [M. Ia] In the marches of Gaul and Brittany, long ago, there were two kings. They were brothers, and their wives were sisters. One of them was called King Ban of Benwick, and the other was called King Bors of Gaunes. King Ban was an old man, while his wife was young and very beautiful, a very good woman who was loved by everyone. She had only had one child by him, a son, who was called Lancelot, although his baptismal name was Galahad.* The story will explain later* why he was called Lancelot, for this is not the right time or place; instead the story goes straight on, and says that King Ban had a neighbour, whose lands bordered with his in the direction of Berry,* which was then known as the Waste Land. This neighbour was called Claudas, and was lord of Bourges and the surrounding lands.

Claudas was a king, and an excellent knight, very clever and very treacherous; he was a vassal of the King of Gaul, which is now called France. Claudas's kingdom was called the Waste Land because it had been completely laid waste by Uther Pendragon and Aramont, who at that time was lord of Brittany, and whom people called Hoel. Aramont was overlord of Gaunes and Benwick, and all the land as far as the marches of Auvergne and Gascony; he should have been lord over the kingdom of Bourges, but Claudas did not recognize this, and would not pay him feudal service:* instead he had taken the King of Gaul as his overlord. At that time Gaul was subject to Rome, and paid tribute, and all the kings were elected.

When Aramont saw that Claudas, with the backing of the Romans, had rejected his dominion, he made war on him. Claudas was aided by the King of Gaul and all his forces, so that Aramont suffered heavy losses in the war, which lasted a very long time. Then he went to Uther Pendragon, who was king of Britain, and became his man,* on condition that he put an end to the war for him. Uther Pendragon crossed the sea with his forces, and heard news that the nobility of Gaul had joined with Claudas against Aramont, who was coming with Uther Pendragon. Then the two of them attacked Claudas, defeated him and took away his land and drove him out. And the land was everywhere so [2] utterly devastated that no fortress was left with one stone standing on another, except for the city of Bourges, which was saved from destruction by order of Uther Pendragon, because he remembered that he was born there. After that Uther Pendragon returned to Brittany, and when he had stayed there as long as he wished, he crossed into Britain. From then on Brittany was subject to the kingdom of Logres.*

When Aramont and Uther Pendragon were dead, and the kingdom of Logres was in King Arthur's hands, wars sprang up in many parts of Britain, and most of the barons made war on King Arthur. This was at the beginning of his reign, when he had only just married Queen Guinevere, and he had much to deal with on all sides. Then Claudas once more took up the war which had been interrupted for so long, for he had recovered all his land as soon as King Aramont died. Then he also began to make war on King Ban of Benwick, because they were neighbours, and because he[1] had been a vassal of Aramont, who had deprived him[2] of his lands for so long, and because he[1] had done him[2] great harm while he was at a disadvantage.

At that time a consul of great renown, Pontius Antonius, had come from Rome: he helped Claudas, backing him with all the forces of Gaul and its subject countries, and they reduced King Ban to such a state that they took from him the

---

[1] i.e. Ban.   [2] i.e. Claudas.

city of Benwick, and all the rest of his land except for one castle, called Trebe, which was at the edge of his land and was so strong that at that time it was safe from everything except starvation and treachery. One day, however, his enemies stormed a castle of his which was less than three leagues* from Trebe, and he went to the rescue, intending to go in. When he saw that the besiegers had already forced their way in, he and his knights rushed in among their army; he had many valorous knights with him, and he himself had been renowned for his marvellous prowess. They killed many of the attackers there, and caused them so much trouble that the assault stopped, and the whole army hurried to deal with King Ban and all his men. They began to withdraw, but they had delayed too long, for Pontius Antonius, with his men, had come from the forest,* and came in front of them. They had such a weight of numbers that King Ban and his men could not withstand them, and all but three of his companions were killed or captured. However, King Ban had some revenge, in that he killed Pontius Antonius, their leader, and he did such deeds of arms, when he [3] had only three men left, that he put all the Romans to flight, and chased them a long way, until Claudas came galloping at full speed ahead of the others. When King Ban saw him, he said something truly fitting for a man who had been dispossessed.

'Ha! Lord,' he said, 'I see there my mortal enemy. Lord God, You who have given me so much honour, grant that I kill him. And I would rather die with him, dear Lord God, than that he get away, for then all my sorrows would be eased.'

Then they jousted, and King Ban knocked Claudas down so violently that everyone thought he was dead. Then King Ban went away, delighted, for he believed that his prayer had been answered; he plied his spurs until he reached Trebe. Within four days, the castle to which Claudas was laying siege was captured, and he came to besiege King Ban in

Trebe. When King Ban discovered that he was not dead, he felt such distress in his heart that he was never again free of it, as was apparent afterwards.

Claudas laid siege to Trebe for a long time. King Ban had often sent to King Arthur for help, but he had so much to deal with on all sides that he could not easily concern himself with someone else's needs. And King Bors, his brother, who had been of great help to him, lay mortally ill, and every day the foragers* roamed over his land, which bordered with Benwick in the direction of Trebe. When Claudas saw that he would not take the castle easily, he arranged a parley with King Ban, and each guaranteed that the other might come and go in safety. King Ban went to the parley with just two others: his seneschal and one of his knights. Claudas, likewise, went with only two companions. The parley was right outside the castle gate. The castle stood on a hill, and the army[1] was encamped down below; and the slope was very steep and hard to climb.

When Claudas saw King Ban, he complained first about Pontius Antonius, whom he had killed, while Ban complained about his land, which he had taken from him without reason.

'I did not take it from you,' Claudas said, 'because of anything you have done to me, or out of any enmity towards you, but because of King Arthur, who is your lord, for his father, Uther Pendragon, drove me from my land. If you wish, though, I shall offer you good terms: give me possession of this castle, and I shall hand it straight back to you, on condition that you immediately become my man, and hold all your land from me.'

[4] 'I will not do that,' King Ban replied, 'for I should be breaking my oath to King Arthur, whose liege man I am.'

'Then I shall tell you', Claudas said, 'what to do. Send word to King Arthur asking him to come to your aid within

---

[1] i.e. Claudas's army.

forty days, and if he has not come within that time, surrender the castle to me and hold all your land from me, and I shall increase it with rich fiefs.'

The king said that he would consider it, and in the morning he would be able to tell him, or send him word, which he was going to do, surrender the castle, or defend it.

Thereupon King Ban left; but his seneschal stayed behind a little, and Claudas spoke to him.

'Seneschal,' he said, 'I am certain that wretch is ill-fated, for he will never have any help from King Arthur, and he will lose everything through foolishly waiting. I am very sorry that you are attached to a man from whom no good can come to you, for I have heard many good things said about you: therefore I advise you to join me. Let me tell you what I shall do for you: I shall promise faithfully to give you this kingdom as soon as I have conquered it, and all my power will be at your disposal. However, if I capture you in battle, I shall be sorry to have to do you great harm, for I have sworn on holy relics that anyone who is taken in battle in this war will be killed, or imprisoned without hope of release.'

They spoke together until the seneschal promised to help him as much as he could, short of betraying or selling his lord's person. Claudas then promised that as soon as he had Trebe he would give him the whole country, and he would become his man.

Thereupon they parted, and Claudas returned to his troops, while King Ban's seneschal went back to Trebe and told King Ban that Claudas had talked to him for a long time, and was anxious to have his friendship.

'So what do you advise me to do?' asked King Ban.

'What, sire?' he said; 'the best that I can see is for you yourself to go and implore King Arthur's help, for that which you have to guard[1] will be well guarded until your return.'

---

[1] i.e. the castle.

Then the king went to the queen, and told her how Claudas had called on him to surrender the castle.

'And he will swear to me that as soon as he has it, he will invest me with it, and with all the rest of my land. But I know he is so treacherous that if he once had this castle, he would never give it or the rest of the land back to me. However, I must tell him tomorrow what I am going to do, for he has called on me to send to [5] my lord King Arthur, and he will give me a truce in respect of this castle for forty days, and if my lord the king comes to my aid within forty days, well, Lord! so much the better; and if he does not, I shall give the castle to Claudas.'

The queen, who greatly feared being dispossessed, advised him to do that:

'For if King Arthur fails you, who is going to help you?'

'My lady,' he said, 'since you favour the idea, I shall do it. And do you know what I have decided to do? I myself shall go to my lord the king, to implore his help in the matter of my dispossession. He will be more sympathetic than if I were not there, for he will see me in person; it would be useless if I sent some other messenger, for the best way to be believed concerning bad news is to bring clear evidence* of it. Now, get ready, for you are to come with me, and we shall take no one with us but my son and one squire, who will attend to our needs, for I wish my lord the king to be greatly moved when he sees my great distress. Now, we shall set out this very night: make sure that you bring all the valuables that you can find here, both jewellery and plate, and put everything in my big chests; I do not know what may become of my castle before I come back, and I should not wish for anything that you be left unprovided for—not that I have any fear of this castle being taken by storm, but no one is safe from treachery.'

The queen made ready, as the king had specified, and when she had prepared for the journey, she told him that she

was all ready. Then the king chose from among his squires
the one he most trusted, and told him to make sure that his
hack was quite ready, as he would have to ride that very
night. The squire, who loved his lord dearly, quickly did as
he ordered; and he had a big, strong hack, swift and fully
equipped. Then the king went to his seneschal, and revealed
to him his intention to go to King Arthur's court:

'I trust you more than any other man, for I have already
held you in great affection, and I entrust my castle to you:
guard it like the heart in my breast. Tomorrow, tell Claudas
on my behalf that I have sent to my lord King Arthur, and
give him whatever guarantees he wants that, if I receive no
help from my lord King Arthur within forty days, I shall give
him the castle at his pleasure. Make sure, though, that he
does not discover that I have left here, for he would care little
for the defence of the castle, once I was gone.'

[6] 'Sire,' said the traitor, 'you need not worry, for I shall
see to it.'

That night the king went to bed quite early, for the nights
were short. It was, the story says, a Friday evening, the night
of the Assumption.* The king was anxious about the journey
he had to make, which was very much on his mind, and he
rose at least three leagues* before daylight. When the horses
were saddled and everything was ready, he commended his
seneschal and all the others to God. Then the king went out
by a little wattle bridge, over the little river which ran past
the castle. The castle was only besieged on one side, and the
besiegers were the best part of three bowshots away, at the
nearest point, for near the castle rock there were hills and
valleys and awkward approaches, while no one could lay siege
on the other side because of the river, for the marsh there
was wide and deep, and the only way across was a narrow
little causeway, which stretched for more than two leagues.

The king left by the causeway, taking with him his wife, on
a fine, big, smooth-paced palfrey, and a squire, worthy* and

competent, who was carrying the baby in front of him on a big hack, in a cot. The king was riding a palfrey which he had found to be a good ride, and he had a footservant* bringing an excellent horse for him. The squire was carrying his shield, and the servant who was riding the horse was driving a pack-horse in front of him, and carrying the king's lance. The pack-horse was heavily laden with jewellery and plate and money. The king was wearing mail leggings and his hauberk, with his sword belted on and his rain-cape over the top, and he brought up the rear of the party.

He rode until he was out of the marshes, and went into a forest. After riding about half a league through the forest, he came out into a beautiful stretch of open country, where he had often been before. He and his party rode until they came to a lake at the edge of the open country, and at the foot of a very high hill, from the top of which you could survey the whole country. Then it was daybreak.

The king said that he would not move from there until it was a little bit lighter, and dismounted, for he intended to go up to the top of the hill to look at his castle, which he loved more than any other in the world. The king waited until it was somewhat lighter, then mounted his horse, and left the queen and his company down by the lake, which was very large.

[7] The lake had been called the lake of Diana, since pagan times. Diana was queen of Sicily and reigned in the time of the good author Virgil, and the foolish pagan people of that time believed that she was a goddess. She loved the pleasures of the forest[1] more than any woman in the world, and would go hunting all day long, and for that reason the pagans called her the goddess of the woods.

The forest where the lake was was the smallest forest in Gaul and Brittany, for it was no more than ten English

[1] i.e. hunting.

leagues long and six or seven wide, and it was called the Wood in the Valley. The king went up the hill, for he was eager to see the castle he so loved. Now, though, the story stops speaking of him for a while, and speaks of his seneschal.

[M. IIa] The story says that when King Ban had left Trebe castle the seneschal, who had not forgotten what was agreed between him and Claudas, went out of the town to Claudas, and said to him:

'My lord, I bring you good news, and you are the most fortunate of men, if you will fulfil your promise to me, for you can take this castle at once without any resistance.'

'What?' said Claudas; 'where is King Ban, then?'

'Indeed,' said the other, 'he has left the castle and gone away, with my lady the queen and just one squire.'

'Now, surrender the castle to me, then,' said Claudas, 'and I shall hand the castle, and then all the land, over to you, and after mass on Sunday, which will be the day of the Assumption, you will become my man, in front of all my barons.'*

The seneschal was delighted about this, and said:

'My lord, I shall go back and leave the gates unbarred for you. And I shall tell them that we have a proper truce: they will be glad to rest, for they have suffered severely. And when you and your men are inside, keep quiet until you reach the main castle: that way you will be able to take the whole town without delay.'

Thus the traitor spoke to Claudas, and then went back to the castle. When he was inside, he met a knight, who was a godson of King Ban, and very valiant. He kept watch every night, in full armour; and when he saw the seneschal coming in from outside, he asked him where he had come from, and why he had gone out at such an hour.

'I have just come,' the traitor said, 'from Claudas, from agreeing a truce which he has granted to our lord the king.'

[8] When the other heard him, he shuddered inwardly, for he greatly feared treachery, and he said:

'Truly, seneschal, this is no hour for a man who wishes to act loyally to come from making a truce with his lord's mortal enemy.'

'What?' said the seneschal, 'do you believe I am disloyal?'

'God forbid', said the knight, whose name was Banin, 'that you should do, or have done, anything disloyal.'

He said that much, and would have said more if he dared, but the seneschal had force on his side, and could quickly have had him killed, so he left it at that. The seneschal told the men on watch that, by the grace of God, they had a proper truce, and sent them all to bed; and they were very glad to rest, for they were very tired. Banin, however, had no wish to go and sleep: instead he set himself to watch, and went up into a turret to see what the besiegers would do, and whether the defenders would go and open the gates for them. He did not realize, though, that the gates were already unbarred. When he looked around, he saw as many as twenty knights coming, their helms laced on, and after them another twenty, and so on, two hundred of them in twenties. Then he guessed that the town would be betrayed, and he went down the steps inside the walls, crying loudly: 'Betrayed! Betrayed!' throughout the castle. He was not yet aware that the gates were unbarred.

The alarm was raised throughout the castle, and the men, who were unprepared, ran to their weapons. At once, though, Claudas's knights came in through the first gate. When Banin saw them, he was so distressed that he was nearly distracted. He went towards them, on foot, and struck the front man so hard, through shield and hauberk, that he put his lance clean through his body, and hurled him down dead.* Then the others charged forward, on foot and on horseback, and he saw that if he ran to the main castle, they could knock him down two or three times before he got there, because they were mounted, while he was on foot. Then he rushed back up the steps to the walls, and went around the alures* until he reached the door of the great tower. He raised a draw-bridge* behind him, and inside he found men-at-arms, one of whom had opened the door for him, while the others were down in the bailey asleep, for they all thought there was no danger.

There was a party of Claudas's knights coming after him around the walls, for they wished to capture him. When they saw that he had escaped them, they turned back again. Meanwhile, the others had captured the small castle* before those inside could assemble. The clamour was so great that you could not have heard God's thunder.

[9] At this noise and clamour the seneschal rushed out and made a show of defending himself, as though he knew nothing of what was happening, and began to lament his lord's absence. And Banin, up in the tower he had taken possession of, began to call to him:

'Hey! whore's son, murderer! you have brought all this upon us, and you have betrayed your liege lord, who raised you from nothing to high estate, and you have taken from him all hope of recovering his land. But may you have as much goodwill from it in the end as Judas did, who betrayed Him who had come to earth to save him and the other sinners, if he had not prevented it, for you have certainly done Judas's work.'

Thus Banin spoke to the traitor from the tower. The small castle was taken at once, as were all the other strong points except the tower. However, Claudas was very upset about one thing: some man of his set fire to the town, and the rich, beautiful houses were burned down. After this the men in the tower stood firm and put up a good defence, although there were only four of them, three men-at-arms and Banin; and they killed Claudas's men in great numbers as they defended themselves.

After five days, Claudas had a perrier set up in front of the

tower; there was not room for more than one. However, they
would never have been captured because of the perrier, but
they had nothing to eat; even so, they defended themselves
manfully. Banin, though, put up a stouter resistance than any
of the others, killing many of Claudas's men with sharpened
stakes and jagged stones, which he threw at them. Banin
resisted so vigorously, and withstood so much, that everyone
was quite astonished by it; and Claudas said, when he heard
people talk about him and his great deeds of prowess, that if
he had such a valorous knight, and one who was so loyal to
him, he would cherish him more than his own self.

After they had completely run out of proper food, the men
in the tower held out for three whole days, by which time
they were very weak from the pangs of hunger. On the third
night they happened to catch an owl in a crack in the tower:
there were no other birds there because the blows from the
perrier had driven them away. They were greatly heartened
by this stroke of fortune. And the perrier had shaken them
up severely, and shattered and shaken the walls.

One day Claudas called to Banin, and said:

'Banin, do surrender, because if you do not, you cannot
hold out for long. And I shall give you plenty of horses and
arms and enough provisions to go wherever you wish. If you
will remain in my service, as [10] God and the saints of that
church'—and he stretched out his hand towards a chapel—
'are my witnesses, I shall cherish you more than any knight I
ever had, because of your great prowess and loyalty.'

Claudas appealed to him in this way several times, and one
day Banin said to him, very distressed and worried:

'My lord Claudas, my lord Claudas, understand this: when
I surrender to you, I shall have such clear, compelling reasons
that no one can reproach me for it; and when I surrender, to
you or anyone else, it will not be as a traitor.'*

Banin held out in the tower until he and his companions
were very weak from hunger, and every day Claudas entreated

him to surrender, for he was very anxious to have him in his service, as he held him in high esteem because of the great prowess which he had seen in him. When Banin saw that he could not hold out, and would have to surrender because of lack of food and because of the perrier, which had shaken them up badly, he began to grieve bitterly. His companions, who could no longer endure their hunger, told him that they were going to surrender, for there was no question of holding out longer. And he said to them:

'Now, do not be dismayed, for I shall surrender the tower, and it will be done with such honour that we shall never be reproached for it. I am just as weary and starving as any of you, but even when a man is under great pressure, and must make a sacrifice, he should still preserve his honour.'

That day Claudas spoke again to him and asked him what he intended to do, surrender or hold out.

'My lord,' he replied, 'I have discussed it with my companions, and they advise holding this tower, for we have nothing to fear yet awhile from any perrier or other siege-engine. However, I no longer wish to bear the burden, since worthier and more powerful men than I have relinquished it. So, I have decided to surrender the tower and myself and my companions to you, for it seems to me that I could not surrender it to a worthier man, and you will take us into your service. First, though, you must give us your assurance that you will protect us from all men, and maintain our rights in your household against everyone, so that if anyone wishes to accuse us of anything, we can settle the matter through you, and if we have any accusation to make against any man in your service, you will give us justice.'

Claudas agreed to these conditions, and had holy relics brought to the foot of the tower, and swore it to them. Then they came out of the tower, and Claudas put his garrison in. And he honoured Banin greatly, and [11] cherished him in his heart, because he had seen that he was very valiant.

Within three days it happened that the seneschal asked for what he had been promised; Claudas said that he would gladly give it to him, and began to look for ways to delay. With all the talk about it, Banin heard something of the matter. Then he went to Claudas, who was with his barons, and said:

'My lord, I wish all these barons to know that I surrendered to you so that you would guarantee me against all men and maintain my rights against anyone who might wish to accuse me of anything, and that you would give me proper justice against any man in your service whom I might accuse of something.'*

Claudas admitted that this was so.

'Then, my lord,' he said, 'I now ask and call on you to do justice to the seneschal here, who has treacherously broken his oath to God and his earthly lord. And if he dares deny that he has treacherously broken his oath to God and to his liege lord,* I am ready to prove it in combat against him, here and now, or at such time as you please.'

'Hear, seneschal,' Claudas said, 'what this knight has said about you. I should be very badly served if I cherished you and raised you up as far as I could, and you were a traitor to me.'

'Sire,' he said, 'there is no knight under the sun, however valiant or renowned, against whom I would not defend myself, if he wished to prove that I had betrayed you.'

'Accept my gage,' Banin said, 'to prove in combat against him that I have seen and heard his treachery against his earthly liege lord.'

Now what Claudas heard pleased and suited him, for he himself detested the seneschal because of his treachery, and he was delighted to find a good reason for him to forfeit the fiefs* which he had promised him. He asked him what he meant to do.

'Sire,' said the seneschal, 'you advise me, for this man has a mortal hatred of me because of you, and that is the only reason he is accusing me.'

'I shall advise you', Claudas said, 'at once. If you are innocent of the charge, then do not hesitate to defend yourself, for you are no less strong or well built than he, nor are you less renowned as a warrior. If he accused me as he has you, then I should be [12] disgraced if I did not defend myself. And rest assured that you have only him to deal with, and he has only you;* and if you do not defend yourself, then you will indeed seem like a man who feels himself guilty of treachery.'

Following what Claudas said to them, they both put their gages in his hands, and he called the seneschal, and said:

'Seneschal, I have always thought you very loyal, and King Ban, your lord, said that you were. Come forward and take this.* I invest you with the kingdom of Benwick, the rents and the revenues and all that belongs to it, except the fortresses, which I shall entrust to no one. If you can defend yourself against Banin in this matter, you will do fealty and homage to me, and if he proves you guilty of his charge, I shall give him the lands, and he will become my loyal man.'

Thus Claudas invested the seneschal with the kingdom of Benwick, because he did not wish to break the oath he had made to him. And he suspected that he would not hold it for long, for he knew Banin to be imbued with prowess and loyalty.* Why should I tell you any more? Four days later, the combat was fought on the meadows of Benwick, between the Loire and the Arsie. There Banin cut off the seneschal's head. Then Claudas offered him the land of Benwick in fief and heritage, and Banin said:

'My lord, I joined your service on condition that I should not stay in it any longer than I wished, and now I wish to leave. So I ask your leave, in front of all your barons, for, by the grace of God, I have achieved what I joined your service to do. And you should know that I would not take any land

from you, for God never made a land so rich that I should
like to have it, if I could not use it against you: my heart,
which commands me, would not allow it to be otherwise.'

With that he left; and Claudas was most put out, for he
would have made any effort to keep him, if he could, as he
had never seen a knight whose prowess and loyalty were so
much to his liking. The story says no more at this point about
Banin or Claudas and his companions, though, returning
instead to King Ban, about whom it has been silent for a long
time.

[M. IIIa] King Ban, the story says, went up the hill to
look at the castle which he loved so dearly. It began to get
really light, and he looked, and saw the walls shining white,
the high tower and the bailey around it. He had only been
looking for a moment, though, when he saw thick smoke
inside the castle, and shortly afterwards he saw [13] flames
spring up all over the castle, and in a short time he saw the
fine halls collapse to the ground, and churches and minsters
crumble, with the fire leaping from place to place, and the
terrible flames soaring towards the sky, so that the air glowed
red, and all the ground was lit up round about.

King Ban saw his castle burning, the castle which he loved
more than any other, for it was his comfort, his only hope of
recovering all his land. He had put all his faith in it, and
when he saw that he had lost it, there was nothing in the
world to give him any hope, for he felt old and broken, while
his son was not able to help him, and his wife was a young
lady, brought up in great comfort, and a very noble lady with
respect to God and the world, descended as she was from
the noble line of King David. He was saddened to think that
his son must grow up in poverty and sorrow, and his wife
be in someone else's power, and under the protection of
many people, and he himself would be poor and old, and
spend the rest of his life in great poverty, he who had been
so rich and powerful, and who in his youth had so loved

pleasant company and a joyful household. The king thought of all these things and pictured them in his mind, and such great sorrow pierced his heart that his tears were stopped up* and his heart wrung within him, and he fainted, and fell from his palfrey to the ground, so hard that his neck was nearly broken, and the red blood spurted from his nose and mouth, and from his two ears.

The king lay like that for a long while, and when he came to, he spoke as well as he could and, looking towards the sky, said:

'Ah! Lord God, I give thanks to You, dear sweet Father, because You are pleased that I should die in poverty, for You came poor and needy to suffer death on earth. Lord, since I cannot have remained in the world without sinning, I ask You for mercy, for I can see that my time has come. And You, dear Father, who came to redeem me with Your blood, do not let the soul which You put in me be lost; but on this last day, when my end is at hand, receive me, having confessed to You the burden of my sins, which are so great and terrible that I cannot list them all. And if my body has done wrong on earth, where no man can be without sin, dear Lord, take Your vengeance on me in such a way that, however the soul is tormented after the body, it may eventually join the company of those who will share eternally in the everlasting brightness of Your joyful house. Dear, merciful Father, [14] take pity on my wife Helen, who is descended from the noble line that You established in the Kingdom of Adventures* to glorify Your name and the dignity of Your faith, and to hold Your great secrets, which have given them victory over the foreign peoples. Lord, help her in her need, she who is descended from such a noble line, and who has so cherished Your faith, and kept Your commandments. And do not forget, Lord, my wretched son, who is orphaned so young, for the poor are in Your hands, and Your help should support the orphans.'

When the king had said these words, he looked up to the
sky and confessed himself and wept for his sins in the sight
of Our Lord, then picked three blades of grass in the name
of the Holy Trinity, and used them in the name of the Holy
Creed. Then his heart was wrung, and his grief for his wife
and son was so great that he could not speak, and his eyes
glazed, and he fell full length so hard that the veins of his
heart burst, and his heart broke in his breast, and he lay dead
on the ground, his hands outstretched in a cross and his face
towards the sky and his head pointing straight towards the
east.

His horse was startled by his fall, and bolted away down
the hill, straight to the other horses. And when the queen
saw it, she told the squire who had come with them to catch
it. He put the baby down on the ground, and ran to catch the
horse. Then he went up to the top of the hill, and found the
king lying as you have heard. He dismounted, when he found
the king dead, and let out such a loud cry that the queen
heard it clearly, and was so taken aback that she left her son
on the ground in front of the horses' hooves. Then she
gathered up her skirts, and ran up the hill, and found the
squire lying over the king and grieving as bitterly as he could.
When she saw her husband dead, she fainted over the body.
And when she came to, she lamented and bewailed her great
and numerous sorrows. She tore her beautiful, long, blond
hair, and rent her clothes and threw them away, and scratched
her soft face, so that the red blood ran down her cheeks in
streams, and she lamented the loss of her husband's great
prowess and graciousness, and cried so loudly that the hill
and the valley and the great lake beside it echoed.

She cried until she could cry no longer, and was tired and
hoarse, and she could not speak for the great grief which
wrung her heart, and often she fainted [15] for a long time,
and when she came to she wailed and lamented. When she
had lamented the loss of her husband's great prowess, and

thoroughly wept over and bewailed her great misfortunes, she just wanted to die, and greatly reproached Death for delaying so long. When she had been like this for a long time, she remembered about her son—nothing else could have comforted her—and, terribly afraid that the horses, in front of which she had left him, might have killed him, she cried out as loud as she could; then she leapt up like a madwoman, and ran towards where she had left her son. She was so tormented by her great fear that he might be dead, however, that she fell down in a faint before she began to go down the hill. When she came to, she wailed and lamented bitterly. Then she leapt up again and went running down the hill, her hair dishevelled and her clothes torn. When she approached the horses, beside the lake, she saw her son, unswaddled and out of the cot, and saw a damsel holding him stark naked in her lap, clasping and pressing him very gently to her bosom, and kissing his eyes and mouth repeatedly—and she was quite right to do so, for he was the most beautiful little boy in the whole world.

The morning was cold, and it was only just after daybreak. And the queen said to the damsel:

'Dear, sweet friend, for the Lord's sake, put the child down, for he will have hardship and sorrow enough from now on, for he has today become an orphan, and lost all joy, for his father has just now died, and he has lost his land, which would have been extensive, had God kept it for him as he should have had it.'

The damsel did not say a word in response to anything the queen said, and when she saw her approaching, she stood up, holding the child in her arms, and went straight to the lake and jumped in with her feet together. When the queen saw her son in the lake, she fainted; and when she came to, she could see neither the child nor the damsel. Then she began to grieve as bitterly as anyone could, and would have jumped into the lake, if the squire had not held her back: he had left the king on the hilltop, and come to comfort her, because he was very much afraid that she would despair.

No one could tell you how the queen grieved. And while she was lamenting, an abbess happened to pass by with two nuns, and with them her chaplain, [16] a monk, and two squires; she had no one else with her. She heard the queen grieving, and was very much moved; and she went over to the queen and said, God give her joy.

'Indeed, madam,' the queen replied, 'I have great need of it, for I am the most helpless creature in the world, since I have today lost all honour and all joy, of which I have had a good deal in the past.'

'Ah! madam,' said the abbess, who saw that she would have been very beautiful, were it not for her great distress, 'who are you?'

'As God is my witness, madam,' she said, 'it scarcely matters to me now who I am, only that I have lived too long.'

Then the chaplain looked at her, and said to the abbess:

'My lady, in God's name, never believe me again, if this is not my lady the queen.'

Then the abbess began to weep bitterly, and said to her:

'My lady, for the Lord's sake, at least tell us if you are the queen.'

The queen promptly fainted; and when she came to, the abbess again said to her:

'For the Lord's sake, my lady, do not conceal your identity from me, for I am certain that you are the queen.'

'As God is my witness, madam, I am truly the Queen of Great Sorrows.'

The first part of this story is known by that name, which she gave herself: the story of the Queen of Great Sorrows.

Then she said to the abbess:

'Madam, for the Lord's sake, whoever I may be, make me a nun, for I desire that more than anything.'

'Indeed, my lady,' the abbess said, 'most willingly, but, for the Lord's sake, tell me about your trouble, for I am very anxious about it.'

The queen told her about her misfortunes: about losing her land, and about her husband who was dead up on the hill, and about the way in which her son had been carried off by a devil incarnate in the form of a damsel. Then the abbess asked her what had killed the king, but she could not tell her.

'My lady,' she said, 'perhaps it was grief over Trebe being burned?'

'What?' said the queen; 'has it been burned, then?'

'Yes, my lady; I thought you would know all about it.'

'As God is my witness,' she said, 'I did not know. But now I am sure that it is that sorrow which killed him, and from now on, whatever thoughts I may have, I no longer wish to stay in the world.* But, for [17] the Lord's sake, madam, give me the veil and take this great wealth, gold and plate, and jewellery, and have a little minster built here, where masses can be sung for the soul of my husband for ever more.'

'Indeed, my lady,' the abbess said, 'you have no idea what a great burden it is keeping the rule of a religious order, for it involves all the hardships of the body, and all the perils of the soul. But come to our abbey now, my lady, and be mistress there, as you should, for my lord the king's forebears founded and established it.'

'Madam, for the Lord's sake,' the queen said, 'I call on you, for the sake of the Lord and as you value your soul, to make me a nun, for I have no more interest in the world, and the world has no more use for me. And if you will not do this for me, I shall go away into the wild forests, wretched and abandoned, and then I may soon be lost, body and soul.'

'My lady,' the abbess said, 'since you are so set on it, then God be thanked and praised, for we are delighted that God is giving us the company of such a good lady and a noble queen.'

Then and there the queen's lovely tresses were cut off—

and she had the most beautiful hair in the whole world. Then the habit was brought to her, and they veiled her on the spot. And when the squire who was with her saw her veiled, he said that he would no longer stay in the world, since his lady had left it, and he became a monk, and the habit was put on him before he left that place. Then they took the king's body, and carried it to the abbey, which was not far from there, where they performed a service fitting for a dead king, and he was given a noble burial, interred in the abbey itself until a minster could be built on the spot where he died.

When the body was buried, the queen stayed in the abbey, and the abbess had a beautiful minster built where the king died, with beautiful work-buildings, and it was all done within the year. When the minster had been dedicated, the king was taken there. And then the queen went there with two nuns and two chaplains and three monks.

Every new day the queen's custom was that, as soon as she had heard the mass that was sung for the king, she would go to the lake and, at the spot where she had lost her son, she would sometimes read her psalter, and would say what prayers she knew and weep bitterly. And it became known throughout the country that Queen Helen of Benwick had become a nun, and the place was called Royal Minster. [18] The minster grew in size and importance, and the noble-women of the area became nuns there in great numbers, both for the Lord's sake, and because of the queen. With that, though, the story falls silent about the queen and her company and returns to King Claudas of the Waste Land.

{Summary of pp. [18–38].}
[18–19] [M. IVa] Heartbroken at the news of Ban's death, King Bors dies, leaving two sons, Lionel (aged twenty-one months) and Bors (nine months). Claudas takes over the kingdom of Gaunes, except for the castle of Montlair. When

he besieges the castle, Bors's widow, Evainne, flees, intending to join her sister at Royal Minster.

She encounters Pharien, one of Claudas's knights who once served King Bors. He agrees to let her go free, and takes her to safety, but keeps the two young princes, saying that he will look after them until they are old enough to reclaim their land from Claudas.

[20] [M. Va] Evainne joins her sister in the minster, where they comfort one another in their sorrow.

[21–4] [M. VIa] The lady who took Lancelot, whose name is Niniane, is a fairy, by which is meant a woman with a knowledge of magic. She learned her magic from the prophet Merlin, who was the offspring of a woman and a devil, and then used the knowledge to imprison him for ever. She lives with knights and damsels in the lake, which is in fact a magic illusion.

She adores Lancelot, for whom she arranges a nurse, and then a tutor. Only she knows his name, while everyone else calls him the Handsome Foundling, King's Son, or the Rich Orphan. Lancelot thinks of her as his mother. After three years in the lake, he has grown more than most children would in five.

[25–9] [M. VIIa] Pharien looks after the young princes, Lionel and Bors, intending that they should one day reclaim their inheritance. He keeps them for three years, only his wife knowing their true identity. Then an affair between Claudas and Pharien's wife leads to her telling him about them.

Claudas arranges for an enemy of Pharien to accuse him of treachery towards Claudas, promising him the office of seneschal, which he had previously bestowed on Pharien. Pharien is duly accused, and refuses the offer of his nephew, Lambegue, to fight in his place.* Lambegue then argues that Pharien has not been guilty of treachery, since he is still technically a vassal of the late King Bors.* Claudas persuades the accuser to fight in spite of this, but Pharien kills him.

Claudas swears to look after Lionel and Bors until they are full-grown, and then give them Gaunes and Benwick.* Should he die in the meantime, Pharien would assume control of these lands for them. Pharien agrees to this, and brings the boys to him. Claudas puts them and Pharien and Lambegue in a tower, where they have whatever they desire.

[30–8] [M. VIIIa] Claudas has one son, Dorin, who is nearly fifteen. He is strong, brave, and generous—so much so that Claudas, who is extremely mean, dares not make him a knight, for fear of his life.* Claudas himself has a mixed character, combining good qualities with bad. He has re-nounced love, arguing that no man who loves can hope to live long, for he should strive to surpass all other men, and the body could not endure what the heart would dare undertake. Were this not the case, Claudas says, he would have been a lover, and surpassed the prowess of all others, for only a man who loves truly can be a great warrior.

When he has held Benwick and Gaunes for over two years,* Claudas decides that even King Arthur must fear him, since he has left him for so long in undisputed control of lands which rightfully belong to his[1] vassals. He decides that Arthur must become his vassal, and goes incognito to Arthur's court, to assess for himself the reality behind his reputation.

At this time, Arthur has not been ruling for long, and is at war with many of his vassals. He married Guinevere a short time previously. Guinevere's beauty can only be compared with that of two other women, Helen the Peerless, and Heliabel,* while no one can match her qualities.

Arthur is at war with King Yon of Little Ireland,* with his own cousin, King Aguissant of Scotland, with the King from

---

[1] i.e. King Arthur's.

Over the Borders of Galone,* and with others. He overcomes them all, with the help of God and warriors from all over the world. Claudas stays more than nine months at Arthur's court, and is very impressed by what he sees.

He returns to Bourges, where, told of his son's excesses, he replies that a king's son should not be restricted in his generosity, and tells his men of King Arthur's great largesse.

The story returns to Lancelot, in the lake.

[M. IXa] When Lancelot had been in the damsel's care for three years, as you have heard, he was so comely that anyone who saw him would have thought he was a third as old again. And besides being big for his age, he was sensible and intelligent, quick and agile—and all more than a child of his age should be. The damsel gave him a tutor,* who taught him, and showed him how to conduct himself as a nobleman. None the less, of all those in the household, no one knew who he was, with the exception of the damsel and one of her maidens, and they called the boy by the names which the story has already mentioned.

As soon as he was strong enough, his tutor made a bow the right size for him, with lightweight arrows, which he made him shoot at a target. Once he knew how to use the bow, he made him shoot at small forest birds. [39] And as he grew, and his body and limbs became stronger, his tutor increased the size of his bow and arrows, and he began to shoot at hares and other small animals, and at large birds when he could find them. And as soon as he could ride a horse, one was ready for him—a fine, good-quality horse, well-equipped with saddle and bridle and everything—and he rode around the lake, up and down, though always nearby, never far away. He was not alone, but had a fine com ıy of youths, some older, some younger, and most of them ɔble He conducted himself so well in their company that all who saw him thought he must be one of the world's greatest noblemen, and, in truth, so he was. He learned chess and tables, and every game he could watch being played, so readily that by the time he was a young knight, no one could teach him anything about them.

He was, the story says, the fairest child in the world and had the most shapely body and limbs, while his face should not be forgotten, but should be described for everyone who would like to hear about a beautiful child.

He had a beautiful complexion, not too white or brown, but a mixture of the two; you might call it light brown. His face glowed with a natural ruddiness, in such just proportion that evidently God had put the white and the brown and the red there: for the white was not spoiled or overshadowed by the brown, nor the brown by the white; instead they were tempered by one another, and the ruddiness, which was overlaid in moderation, gave a glow both to itself and to the mixture of the other two colours, so that there was nothing there too white or too brown or too red, just an equal mixture of the three together. His mouth was reasonably small and becoming, his lips red and quite full, and his teeth small and shining white and close together; his chin was well made, with a small dimple, his nose reasonably long, slightly prominent in the middle; his eyes were bright and laughing, and full of joy, as long as he was happy; but when he was truly angry, he looked like a burning coal, and it was as if drops of red blood started from his cheek-bones, and in his fury he snorted like a horse, and gnashed his teeth together, so that they grated terribly, and it was as if his breath came red from his mouth, and he spoke so fiercely that it sounded like a trumpet, [40] and he shattered anything he had in his hands or between his teeth. Finally, in his fury, he forgot everything except what had made him angry, as was later apparent in many affairs.

His forehead was high and comely, and his eyebrows were brown and well spaced. His hair was fine, and so naturally blond and lustrous, when he was a child, that no hair could be a better colour; but when he was old enough to bear arms, as you will hear, it changed from natural blond to a real chestnut. It was always shining, though, quite curly and very attractive. There is no need to ask about his neck: had it been that of a beautiful woman, it would have been becoming enough, comely and well in proportion with his body and shoulders, neither too slender nor too thick, nor disproportionately long or short. And his shoulders were reasonably broad and square. His chest, though, was such that you would never find one so big and broad and deep on such a body; in fact, that was the one thing about him that anyone ever found to criticize, and everyone who observed him said that if he had had a little less chest, he would have been more pleasing and attractive. Later on, though, the person who observed him more closely than anyone—that is, the excellent Queen Guinevere—said that God had not given him too much chest, however big or broad or deep it was, for his heart was just as big, proportionately, and it would surely have burst, if it had not had a space that size to reside in. 'And if I were God,' she said, 'I should have made Lancelot just as he is.'

Such were his shoulders and chest. And his arms were long and straight and well muscled, well endowed with sinew and bone, but moderately spare of flesh. His hands would have been just like a lady's, if the fingers were a little smaller. As for his loins and hips, no one could tell you that any knight could have better. His thighs and calves were straight, and his feet arched, and no one ever stood straighter. And he sang wonderfully well when he wanted to, but that was not often, for no one was ever so little given to rejoicing without good reason; when he had a reason, though, no one could be nearly as merry and jolly as he. And he often said, when he was full of joy,* that there was nothing his heart would dare undertake that he could not achieve, such was his faith in the great joy which made him succeed in many great tasks. And because he said that so confidently, many people held it against him, thinking that he said it [41] to brag and boast; but he did not: rather, he said it because he had such great confidence in the source* of all his joy.

Such were Lancelot's limbs and his appearance: his face, body, and limbs were well made. The qualities of the heart were not forgotten in him, for he was the gentlest and most gracious of children, when he met with graciousness, but you would find him utterly pitiless when faced with cruelty. No child was ever so generous, for he distributed everything to his companions as readily as he accepted it. He honoured noble men so wholeheartedly that he devoted all his attention to it. Nor was any child ever like him, for no one ever saw him show displeasure unless he had a good reason, such that no one could rightly blame him; but when he was angry about some wrong which had been done to him, then it was no easy matter to placate him. He was so sensible and well inten-tioned that from the age of ten he rarely did anything which a good child should not do; and if he meant to do something which seemed good and reasonable to him, it was not easy to dissuade him, while he would never heed his tutor in anything.

It happened one day that he was hunting a roe-deer, his tutor and his companions behind him. And they had galloped a long way, so that they all began to lag behind, while he and his tutor were better mounted, and outstripped all the others. Quite soon his tutor's hack fell, and broke its neck. The boy never looked back, but spurred after his quarry until he killed it with an arrow, on a broad paved road. Then he dismounted and loaded the deer behind his saddle, while in front of him he carried his bratchet, which had followed the deer all day, ahead of the other dogs.

As he was returning in this way to his companions, who were very worried about him, he met a man on foot, leading an exhausted hack. He was a very handsome young man, with his first beard. He was wearing only a tunic, kilted up, with a cape round his shoulders and his spurs on, all bloody from the hack, which he had galloped until it could do no more. When he saw the boy, he was very embarrassed and hung his head, and began to weep bitterly. The boy waited for him a little way off the track, and [42] asked him who he was, and where he was going in that way. The other thought that the boy must be of very high estate, and said:

'Sir, God give you honour. Who I am need not concern you, for indeed I am poor enough, and I shall have still less within three days, unless God helps me more than he has until now. Yet in the past I have been better off than I am at present; and however things turn out, well or badly, I am nobly born on my father's and my mother's side, and I am therefore the more distressed by the misfortunes which have befallen me, for if I were low-born, my heart could more easily endure whatever hardships befell me.'

The boy was very much moved, and yet he said:

'What? you are of noble birth, and yet you weep over some misfortune which has befallen you? Unless it is because you have lost a friend,* or some dishonour has been done to you which you cannot avenge, no noble heart should be dismayed by a loss which can be made good.'

Then the surprised youth wondered who this boy could be, who was so young and yet had spoken to him so nobly, and he replied:

'Indeed, sir, I am not weeping over the loss of a friend or of land, but I am due to appear in the morning at King Claudas's court, to prove guilty of treachery a man who some time ago killed my godfather, a very valorous knight, in his bed, so that he could have his wife. And yesterday evening, as I was coming here, he set an ambush for me, on the way through the forest. So I was attacked as I passed through the forest, and my horse was mortally wounded under me, though it did carry me to safety. This one was given to me by a

worthy man—God give him honour!—but I have driven it so
hard to escape from death that it is now of no real use to me
or anyone else. So I am sorrowing over the friends I have
lost, who were killed or wounded when I was attacked; and
on the other hand I am very upset that I shall not arrive in
time for my appointed day at King Claudas's court, for if I
could be there, I should lighten my heart of part of my grief,
since right is on my side; but now I shall be disgraced* by my
delay.'

'Now, tell me,' the boy said, 'if you had a strong, fast horse,
could you be there in time?'

'Indeed, yes, sir,' he said, 'easily, if I only went a third of
the remaining way on foot.'

'Then, in God's name,' the boy said, 'you will not be
disgraced for want of a horse, as long as I have one—neither
you nor any noble man that I may meet.'

[43] Then he dismounted, and gave him the hunter that
he was riding, while he mounted the horse that the youth was
holding, loaded his venison behind his saddle, and put the
bratchet on a leash. When he had gone a little way, he had to
dismount, for the hack could only walk with great distress.
So he dismounted, and drove it in front of him. He had not
gone far, though, when he met a vavasour on a palfrey, a
switch in his hand, and with him two greyhounds and a
bratchet. The vavasour was elderly, and as soon as he saw
him, the boy greeted him. And he replied, God grant him
betterment. Then he asked the boy where he was from, and
he said that he was from a country nearby.

'Indeed,' the vavasour said, 'whoever you are, you are very
handsome and well mannered. And where have you been like
this, my boy?'

'Sir,' he said, 'I have been hunting, as you can see. I have
taken this venison, and you can have some if you would like
it, for I think that would be a good use for it.'

'Many thanks, dear boy,' said the vavasour. 'And I shall

not refuse it, since you have offered it to me good-naturedly and graciously. I think your lineage must be as noble as your nature. And, truly, I have great need of the venison, for I have today married my daughter, and I came hunting for something to please those at the wedding, but I have failed to take anything.'

The vavasour dismounted, and took the deer and asked the boy how much he wished him to take.

'Sir,' the boy said, 'are you a knight?' And he said that he was. 'Then take it all, for I could not find a better use for it, since it will be eaten at the wedding of a knight's daughter.'

When the vavasour heard that, he was delighted, and took the deer, and loaded it behind his saddle; he urged the boy to accept his hospitality for the night, and offered him some of his own venison and other things. However, the boy said that he would not stop for the night yet, for 'my company,' he said, 'is not very far from here. Now, I commend you to God.'

Thereupon the vavasour left and began to think about who the boy could be, for it seemed to him that he strongly resembled someone, but he did not know whom. He thought about it for a long time, until he realized that, more than anyone, he was like the King of Benwick. Then he set spurs to his palfrey and galloped swiftly back after the boy until he caught up with him: he was only going at a walk, and had just then mounted [44] the hack, which was relieved by having had the deer taken off it. And he said to him, with a sigh:

'Dear boy, could you possibly tell me who you are?'

And he replied that he could not, at the moment, 'but what is it to do with you?'

'Indeed,' he said, 'you are like my lord, who was one of the most worthy men in the world. And if you had need of me, I would risk life and land for you. I and forty knights like me, who are less than four leagues from here.'

'Who', said the boy, 'was this worthy man whom I resemble?'

And the vavasour replied, weeping:

'Indeed, he was King Ban of Benwick. All of this country was his, and he was wrongfully dispossessed, and his son was lost, who was the fairest child of his age in the world.'

'And who dispossessed him?' the boy asked.

'My friend,' the vavasour said, 'a rich and powerful king named Claudas of the Waste Land, which borders with this kingdom. And if you are his[1] son, for the Lord's sake, tell me, for everyone in this land would be overjoyed. And I should look after you as I do myself—and much better, for I should lay down my life to save and protect yours.'

'Truly, sir,' the boy said, 'I am no king's son, as far as I know. Yet I have often been called "King's Son", and I like you the better for what you have said, for you speak like a loyal man.'

The vavasour saw that he would get no more out of him, yet he could not stop thinking about it, and he felt sure that the boy was his lord's son. And he said:

'Sir, whoever you are, you certainly seem very noble, from your looks and behaviour. And I have here two of the finest greyhounds I have ever seen, and I beg you to take one of them. God grant you growth and betterment, and protect our lord[2] for us if he is alive, and have mercy on the soul of the worthy man who fathered him.'

When the boy heard about the quality of the greyhounds, he was delighted; and he said that he would not refuse the hound, and he would be very pleased to repay the gift if he had the opportunity. 'But give me the better one,' he said. And the other gave it to him by its chain, which was very fine and light. Thereupon they commended one another to God; the boy went on his way, [45] and the vavasour went in the other direction, but he did not stop thinking about the boy.

---

[1] i.e. Ban's.   [2] i.e. Ban's son.

Shortly afterwards the boy met his tutor and three of the others, who were looking for him. They were all amazed to see him on the gaunt hack, the two dogs on leash, his bow slung around his neck, and his quiver at his belt; and by now he had spurred the hack so much that he was all bloody up to his calves. Then his tutor asked him what he had done with his hack, and he said that he had lost it.

'And where', he said, 'did you get this one?'

'It was given to me.'

His tutor, though, did not believe him, and charged him, by the loyalty he owed his lady, to tell him what he had done with it. And the boy, who would not lightly have been false to her, admitted the truth to him, both about the hack and about the deer which he gave to the vavasour.

'What?' said the other, who wished to dominate him: 'so you have given away your hack—and you will not find one under the sun which will suit you as well—and my lady's venison, without my permission?'

Then his tutor stepped forward and threatened him direly. And the boy said to him:

'Sir, do not be angry, for this greyhound which I have acquired is worth two such hacks.'

'By the Holy Cross,' said the tutor, 'you will regret the very thought. You will never do such a foolish thing again, when you are finished with this.'

Then he raised his hand, and gave him such a slap that he knocked him off the hack to the ground. The boy did not cry out or weep because of the blow he gave him; and in spite of it he said that he still preferred the greyhound to two hacks. When his tutor heard him still speaking against his wishes, he raised a stick he was holding and struck the greyhound across the flank; the stick was thin and cutting, and the hound delicate, and it began to howl terribly. Then the boy was very angry, and he let go of both the dogs and pulled his bow from around his neck, and took hold of it in both hands. His tutor saw him coming, and tried to catch and hold him, but he was quick and nimble, and leapt to one side and struck him with the edge of the bow on his bare head, so that he cut through his hair and split skin and flesh right down to the skull. And he stunned him so badly that he knocked him to the ground, and the bow flew into pieces. And when he saw his bow broken, he was furious, and swore that the other would regret breaking his bow. [46] Then he gathered himself and struck him again on the head and the arms and all over the body, until there was not enough left of the whole bow for him to strike a blow with, for it was completely shattered and in pieces. Then the other three ran to seize him; and since he had nothing with which to defend himself, he drew the arrows from his quiver and threw those at them, and tried to kill them all. They ran away; and his tutor fled as fast as he could, and dashed on foot into the thickest part of the forest.

And the boy took the hack of one of the three youths, from which he had knocked his tutor; he mounted and rode off, carrying his greyhound and his bratchet, one in front of him and one behind, until he came to a great valley. Then he saw a large herd of hinds grazing, and he reached up to take his bow, thinking it was still hanging around his neck. When he remembered that he had broken it, striking his tutor, he was so angry that he was nearly distracted; and he swore to himself that, if he found him, he would make him pay dearly for the fact that, because of him, he had not got one of the hinds, for, he said, he could not have failed to get one, as he had the best greyhound and the best bratchet in the world.

So he rode, very angry, until he reached the lake, and he went through the gate into the courtyard. Then he dismounted, and took his hound, which was very beautiful, for his lady to see. And when he went to her, he found his tutor, all bloody, who had already complained about him. He greeted the lady, and she, who loved him as much as anyone can love a child who is not his own, returned his greeting. However, she pretended to be extremely angry, and said:

'King's Son, why have you behaved so outrageously as to beat and injure the man I had given you to teach you and to be your tutor?'

'Indeed, my lady,' he said, 'he was not my tutor or my teacher, when he beat me, when I had done nothing wrong. And I did not care about my beating, but he struck my hound here—which is one of the best in the world—so hard that he nearly killed it before my eyes, because he knew that I loved it. And he has caused me further annoyance, for he prevented me from killing one of the finest hinds in the world, and one that I had the best chance of killing.'

Then he told her how he gave away his hack and the deer, and how he came across the hinds, and could have shot one if he had had his bow.

'And you should know, my lady,' he said, 'that if I find him anywhere other than here, I shall kill him.'

[47] When the lady heard him speak so fiercely, she was delighted, for she saw that he could not fail to be a man of valour, with God's help, and her own, for she expected to be of great help in the process. None the less, she pretended to be very angry. And when he saw that, he left her, very upset and direly threatening the man who had made her so angry with him. And she called him back, and said:

'What? so you think you can give away your hack and my property like that, and beat the tutor I put in charge of you to keep you from foolishness and teach you how to behave properly? I do not want you to do either of those things.'

'In that case, my lady,' he said, 'I shall have to refrain from doing them, as long as I wish to be in your care and in the charge of a servant; and when I no longer wish it, then I shall go where I please and obtain what I need. But before I go, I want you to know that a man cannot achieve great happiness if he is under someone else's authority for too long, for he will often be afraid. And for my part, I do not wish to have a tutor any longer—a lord or a lady is a different matter; but a curse on any king's son who does not dare give away someone else's property, when he is not afraid to give away his own.'*

'What?' said the lady, 'do you think you are a king's son, because I call you that?'

'My lady,' he said, 'I am called King's Son, and I have been taken for a king's son.'

'Now, let me tell you,' she said, 'that whoever took you for a king's son was mistaken, for you are not one.'

'My lady,' he said, with a sigh, 'I am sorry to hear it, for my heart would have dared to be one.'

Then he turned away, so upset that he could not say a single word. Then the lady jumped up, and took him by the hand and led him back, and began to kiss him very tenderly on the eyes and the mouth, so that anyone who saw her would have thought he was her son. Then she said:

'Dear son, do not worry for, as God is my witness, I want you to give away hacks and other things, and you will have plenty to give. And if you were forty years old, you would deserve praise for giving away the hack and the venison. And from now on I want you to be your own lord and master, since you know for yourself how a good child should behave. [48] And whoever's son you are, you truly have the heart of a king's son, and in fact you are the son of a man who, through prowess of heart and body, would have dared to challenge the noblest king in the world.'

Thus the Lady of the Lake comforted and reassured Lancelot. And the story only relates this incident because of the noble things he said. At this point, though, the story leaves him for the present, returning instead to his mother and his aunt, the Queen of Gaunes, who were grieving and helpless in Royal Minster.

{Summary of pp. [48–138].}

[48–56] [M. Xa] The Queen of Benwick goes every day to the hill where her husband died, and to the lake where her son disappeared, and prays for them. One day, a monk meets her there. He has been a knight, and has turned to religion. The queen explains her distress, whereupon the monk tells her that her son is still alive and well cared-for, safe from his enemies. He recalls a kindness she once did him, and says that, in return, he will go to King Arthur to plead her cause, and that of Lancelot. Also that of the Queen of Gaunes, to whom he gives spiritual comfort. He will tax the king with this dispossession of his vassals, but says that he is not surprised Arthur has done nothing: he has problems of his own, and may not even have heard of Ban's dispossession.

The monk reaches Arthur's court in London on a Sunday in the first week of September. The king has just returned from Scotland, having made peace with his cousin, King Aguissant. He also has a truce with the King from Over the Borders, until Easter. The monk upbraids Arthur, telling him of Ban's death, of his widow left abandoned, her son stolen. Arthur replies that he knows of the matter, but has heard no formal complaint. He will deal with it when he can. The monk returns to the Queen of Benwick with this reply.

[57–60] [M. XIa] Hearing that Lionel and Bors are prisoners in Gaunes, the Lady of the Lake calls Saraide,* one of her damsels, and tells her to go to Gaunes at the feast of Mary Magdalene,* when Claudas will be holding court there, and bring the princes away. She tells her how, and gives her the necessary things.

Saraide goes into the city with two squires, each leading a greyhound. Hearing that the princes are still in prison, she goes to Claudas, who is at table, celebrating, as he is about to knight his son, Dorin. She accuses him of lacking good sense, graciousness, and courtesy; otherwise the princes would be present, and well treated, rather than in prison. Claudas has to agree, and sends for the boys and their tutors.

[61–8] [M. XIIa] Lionel is the most headstrong child imaginable, very like Lancelot in temperament, but lacking his unusual maturity of judgement. He has given everyone an uneasy night: having discovered from Pharien that he is a prisoner, while Claudas holds court in what should be his capital, he declared that he would not eat until he had taken vengeance on Claudas. Pharien has persuaded him to wait, though Lionel says he will not be restrained if he sees Claudas or his son.

Claudas's seneschal arrives to fetch the princes. Lionel is delighted, and goes to get a knife, but is persuaded by Pharien to leave it behind. The four of them go to court, and the townspeople turn out to see their rightful lords, weeping and praying for them.

The two boys are brought before Claudas, at table. Saraide comes forward and puts chaplets of herbs on the boys' heads, which excite them, and gold clasps around their necks, which make them immune to weapons.

Lionel takes Claudas's proferred cup, and strikes him with it, stunning him. He also knocks down Claudas's regalia, which stand on display. Dorin leaps up to avenge his father, who lies stunned. Lionel takes the sword, and Bors the sceptre, from the regalia, and they strike out on all sides. Many of those present, natives of Gaunes, help rather than hinder them. Saraide leads them towards the door, but Dorin springs after them. Lionel strikes him with the sword, and Bors with the sceptre, and they kill him.

Claudas comes after them, whereupon Saraide's enchantment makes the boys look like greyhounds, and the two hounds like the boys. Claudas is about to strike them when she jumps forward in the way. The hilt of his sword splits her face open, scarring her for life. She remonstrates with Claudas, who is astonished to find that he was apparently trying to kill a pair of dogs. He seizes the false princes, and has them locked up.

[69–70] [M. XIIIa] Saraide takes the boys to the Lady of the Lake, telling them their tutors will soon join them. Lancelot welcomes them, treating them like nephews of the Lady. They become his close friends, whereas his other companions are like his servants.

[70–97] [M. XIVa] Claudas laments the death of Dorin, his only child. The city of Gaunes is up in arms, because of his treatment of the princes. Pharien and Lambegue, and many others, decide they would rather die than let Claudas kill the boys, and they take over the tower in which they were being held. They decide to attack Claudas, who is still grieving, in the palace, and rescue the boys.

Claudas refuses their demand that he give up the princes, and battle is joined. In the fighting, Lambegue twice wounds Claudas, who is rescued before he can kill him. Then Pharien saves Lambegue from being killed by Claudas, but falls out with him when he refuses to allow him to kill Claudas.

Claudas begs Pharien for mercy, and surrenders his sword, agreeing to hand over the princes. Despite criticism from many of his party, including Lambegue, who wish to deal with Claudas once and for all, Pharien puts a stop to the fighting, and goes with Claudas to get the boys. They all return to the tower, happy to have the princes safely back.

At dusk, the enchantment wears off, and the 'boys' become hounds again. The people assume that Claudas has killed the real princes, and once again take up arms. They find Claudas about to leave, with Dorin's body. Although distraught, Pharien wishes to avoid bloodshed, partly for fear that Claudas might kill Lambegue. He talks with Claudas, who realizes that the damsel has taken the real boys. He offers to swear he has not harmed them, and to place himself in Pharien's custody until this can be verified.

Pharien consults the others, who wish him to agree, so that

they can then kill Claudas. Pharien wants Claudas's safety guaranteed, and lectures them on their feudal duty to their lord. No man should attack his lord unless he has first duly renounced his homage, and even then he should not kill him, unless terribly provoked. Pharien offers to take Claudas into his custody if they will guarantee his safety, and agree that he will not be killed without prior trial at King Arthur's court. They refuse.

Claudas swears to Pharien that he has not harmed the boys, and that he will surrender himself to him whenever he wishes, if his safety is assured. As a result, Pharien takes no part in the ensuing fighting, hoping to effect a peaceful solution in due course.

In the fighting, Claudas, with the wind at his back, sets fire to the street. The fight moves outside the city, and continues all night. The townspeople suffer heavier losses than do Claudas's men, and at dawn they appeal to Pharien, and decide to accept Claudas's original offer. Lambegue and a certain Graier, a cousin of King Ban and King Bors, decide to kill Claudas once he is Pharien's prisoner.

Pharien talks with Claudas, who accepts the proposals. Worried about his safety, Pharien suggests a decoy. Three of Claudas's barons, one of whom wears Claudas's armour, are handed over, and taken to the tower.

Lambegue promptly attacks the supposed Claudas, and wounds him. Pharien leaps to his defence, and wounds Lambegue. He also wounds Graier, but is prevented from killing him by the other Gaunes barons. He is also persuaded not to kill Lambegue, by his wife, although she and Lambegue detest one another. A further attempt to kill Graier leads to the angry barons attacking Pharien, at which Lambegue rushes to his rescue. The whole affair is settled without loss of life, and Pharien is reconciled both with Lambegue and with his wife.*

[98–111] [M. XVa] The princes are missing their tutors,

after three days in the lake. The Lady finds this out, through Lancelot, and promises to send for them. Lionel also tells Lancelot who he is, and how he struck Claudas, and killed Dorin. Lancelot likes him the more for it.

The Lady sends a damsel to Gaunes, with the boys' belts as token of recognition. There, the damsel finds out that Pharien and the others are besieged in the tower by the townspeople, who had discovered that Claudas is not there. She speaks to one of the chief barons, a cousin of King Bors, called Leonce of Paerne, telling him that the princes are alive, and that she wishes to see their tutors. By passing the good news on to the townspeople, Leonce persuades them to relax their siege, thus allowing the damsel into the tower.

She shows the belts to Pharien and Lambegue, who are delighted to hear that the princes are all right. The townspeople, however, wish actually to see the boys before they will believe Pharien and let him go. He suggests that the damsel take Lambegue to the boys, which she does, also taking Leonce, as the representative of the townspeople.

When they reach the lake, the damsel tells Leonce to wait there, and she and a surprised Lambegue go into the lake. Bors is delighted to see Lambegue, but Lionel goes off in a sulk, because Pharien has not come. He comes across Saraide, who is having the wound on her face dressed, and asks how she came by it. When she tells him, he says that she is kinder to him than Pharien, and from now on she, and no one else, will be his 'tutor'.

Lionel then asks Lambegue how Dorin is, and is delighted to hear confirmation of his death. Now, he says, he will certainly recover his land, and he hopes Claudas will live long enough for him to teach him not to steal someone else's land.

They arrange that the Lady will go with Lambegue and the boys to see Leonce. Lancelot comes in, and Lambegue wonders who he is. The next morning, they go to meet

Leonce. Lambegue asks Bors who Lancelot is, but he does not know: he thinks, the Lady's son.

Leonce is delighted to see the two boys, and tells the Lady to take good care of them, since they are the sons of King Bors, who was a great man (although his brother was a better knight). More than that, though, they are descended on their mother's side from the line of King David: it is common knowledge that someone from that line is to free Britain from its wonders and adventures, and it might be one of the boys.

Lionel weeps at the thought of his father's land in someone else's hands. Lancelot upbraids him, saying that he should not weep about it, but concentrate on becoming valiant, so as to win it back and keep it. Everyone is amazed at this noble advice. The Lady is also struck by the fact that Lancelot calls Lionel 'cousin'.

She tells Leonce not to worry: she will keep the princes safe, and love them. He can go back and reassure the people of Gaunes. She sends a squire with Lambegue, to guide him and Pharien back to the lake. Leonce continually stares at Lancelot, and suspects that he knows who he is.

On the way home, the Lady asks Lancelot why he called Lionel 'cousin'. Rather embarrassed, he explains that he said it instinctively. When she asks whether he thinks he is more noble than the princes, or the reverse, he replies that he does not really know who he is; all men are descended from one man and one woman, though, and how would one become noble, except through prowess? If a great heart can make a nobleman, he says, he feels he can be as noble as anyone. The Lady reassures him that, if his heart does not let him down, he need have no other fears on that score.

His spirit makes her love him more than ever, but she is saddened to see him growing up so fast, aware that he will soon become a knight, and leave her. She decides that keeping the princes with her will help to cushion the blow;

similarly, she will still have Bors with her when Lionel grows up and leaves.

[112–13] [M. XVIa] Leonce and Lambegue go back to Gaunes. On the way, Leonce reveals that he is positive that Lancelot is King Ban's son.

On hearing that the princes are alive and well, the townspeople raise the siege on Pharien, in the tower. However, they wish to have Pharien's three prisoners as hostages, to prevent reprisals: when he brings the prisoners out, by night, intending to take them to his own castle, they attack and capture his party.

[114–30] [M. XVIIa] Claudas assembles his troops, intent on punishing the rebellious people of Gaunes. Some of the barons, who were not involved in abducting the prisoners, free Pharien, and ask for his help. He goes to Claudas alone, and appeals to him for leniency. When Claudas will not listen, Pharien renounces his homage to him. Stating that he is now his mortal enemy, he calls on him to give himself up as his prisoner, as he swore to do. Claudas denies swearing the oath, and refuses Pharien's offer to prove it in combat. Pharien leaves his camp, uttering dire threats.

He is pursued by some of Claudas's knights and, goaded by the watching Lambegue, turns and attacks them. Claudas comes after them, and orders his men back. Seeing him, Lambegue charges out from the city, calling on him to fight or run away. Despite being without shield, lance, or helm, Claudas turns to meet Lambegue, who knocks him to the ground, in a daze. Before he can dismount and finish him off, however, Lambegue is attacked by Claudas's men. Pharien goes to help him, and they make a fighting withdrawal.

Pharien refuses to allow Lambegue to kill the three prisoners. Claudas comes, alone, to speak to Pharien. He asks after the prisoners, and offers to surrender to Pharien, if he will protect him, and swear that he[1] has heard nothing of

---

[1] i.e. Pharien.

the princes. He then asks to see ten barons from the city, and offers them peace, on two conditions. They must swear that they had nothing to do with his son's death, and they must give Lambegue up to him. Otherwise it will be war, and he will put every man he captures to death. The barons refuse, and go to tell Pharien of the offer.

Lambegue happens to overhear Pharien wishing he were in Lambegue's position: he would certainly sacrifice himself to save the city. Lambegue says that he will do so, and no one can dissuade him.

The agreement is made the next day, and the three prisoners are returned to Claudas. Then Lambegue rides out to Claudas's tent, where he throws down his helm, sword, and shield. Claudas picks up the sword and threatens him with it, but Lambegue does not flinch. His fiercely courageous replies, in their conversation, so impress Claudas that he decides not to kill him.*

Claudas asks Lambegue and Pharien to become his men, but they refuse. Pharien does, however, promise not to enter anyone else's service without first informing Claudas.

[130–1] [M. XVIIIa] The squire takes the two men to the lake. Lionel is still angry with Pharien, and is hardly mollified by his explanations. He accuses Pharien of rescuing his arch-enemy, Claudas, to which Pharien replies that he would do the same again. After a long period in the lake, Pharien dies.

[132–4] [M. XIXa] In Royal Minster, the two queens lead a holy and ascetic life, especially Helen. Evainne is very worried at not knowing what has become of her sons. Her health declines, while Helen's flourishes, despite her austere regime. Evainne prays for news of the boys, if they are still alive. In a vision, she sees three boys together, and guesses that two are her sons, because Pharien and Lambegue are with them. She does not know who the third is. Waking from her vision, she finds the names, Lionel, Bors, and Lancelot written on her hand. She tells her sister this, then makes confession and dies.

[134–8] [M. XXa] King Arthur is at dinner at Carhaix, holding his Easter court. This is the greatest of his five main courts, the others being Ascension, Pentecost, All Saints, and Christmas. After dinner, the young men who are not part of Arthur's retinue hold games, including mock jousts and a quintain. The victor in these martial games is Banin, freshly arrived from some successful fighting against Claudas.

Tradition has it that the victor of the afternoon's sport sits at King Arthur's own table, at supper. The king asks Banin who he is, and on hearing that he is from Benwick, falls into a profound reverie, from which he is only roused by Kay blowing a horn. Gawain upbraids him for neglecting his duties as a host, and Arthur explains that he is ashamed that he has not yet done anything about Claudas's dispossession of Ban. Gawain replies that this is not the time to worry about it. When the time comes, then he should exert himself to do something about it.

In due course, Banin becomes one of the knights of the Watch.* The story returns to Lancelot and the Lady of the Lake.

[M. XXIa] Now the story says that Lancelot had been in the charge of the Lady of the Lake for so long that he was eighteen. And he was such a handsome youth that you could not have found one more handsome in the whole world, [139] and so sensible that there was nothing, in whatever he did, for which he could rightly be reproached or criticized. When he was eighteen, he was remarkably big and robust; and the lady who had brought him up saw that it was the right time for him to receive the order of knighthood, and that if she put it off any longer it would be a sinful shame; for she knew, from the lots which she had often cast, that he would achieve great things. If she could have put off his becoming a knight any longer, she would gladly have done so, for she could scarcely do without him, having given him all the love which stems from tenderness and nurture; but if she kept and prevented him from being a knight beyond the proper age, she would be committing a great and mortal sin, a betrayal, for she would deprive him of something which he could not readily recover.

At the end of his eighteenth year, a little after Pentecost, he went hunting, and found a stag, so big that he had never seen a bigger one in his life. And, so that he could display this wonder, he shot at it and killed it. When he had killed it, he found it was very fat, as though it was August; and all his companions looked at it in amazement. He sent two squires to his lady with the stag; and she wondered how it could possibly be so fat at that time of year, and was quite astonished by its size.

Everyone looked at the stag in amazement, and the lady was delighted with it. Lancelot had remained in the forest, and he lay for a long time under an oak-tree on the green grass, because it was very hot. When it grew less hot, he mounted his hunter and went back to the lake. And he certainly looked like a man coming back from the hunt, for he was wearing a green hunting-tunic, quite short, with a chaplet of leaves on his head to keep the heat off, and his quiver hanging at his belt, for he was never without it, wherever he went. However, one of the squires carried his bow as soon as he was near home.* He was riding his big hunter, straight and firm in the saddle.

He went into the courtyard, where he was seen by his lady, who was waiting for him; and when she saw him, the tears came to her eyes. She stood up and left, without waiting for him, and went into the great hall, where she leaned her head in her hands, and was thoughtful for a long time. Lancelot went after her, but as soon as she saw him, she rushed into a chamber. He saw her go, and wondered what could possibly be the matter, and went after her and found her in her principal chamber, lying face down on a great bed. [140] He strode over to her, and saw that she was sighing and weeping bitterly. He greeted her, but she did not say a word to him, or look at him. He was very surprised, for he was used to her running to meet him, kissing and embracing him, whenever he arrived. Then he said:

'Ha! my lady, tell me what is the matter, and if anyone has upset you, do not hide it from me: I should not have thought anyone would dare upset you while I am alive.'

When she heard that, she burst out weeping again, and was in such a state that she could not say a word to him, her sobs interrupted her speech so much. After a while, however, she said, so that he heard her quite clearly:

'Ah! King's Son, go away, or my heart will break in my breast.'

'My lady,' he said, 'I should prefer to go away, for it would not be pleasant to stay, since I offend you so.'

Then the youth left, and went to get his bow, and hung it around his neck, and belted his quiver on again. Then he went to his hack, and bridled it himself, and led it out into the courtyard. However, the lady, who loved him above all else, realized that she had said too much, and that he was going away very angry; and she knew he was so proud and vigorous that no hardship would weigh with him at all, compared with his feelings. She sprang up, and wiped her eyes, which were red and swollen, and went swiftly into the yard, and saw the youth, who was about to mount, and looked extremely angry. She sprang forward, and seized his bridle and said:

'What is this, young sir? Where are you going?'

'My lady,' he said, 'I am going into those woods.'

'Get down at once,' she said, 'for you are not going there now.'

He dismounted, and she took his horse, and had it stabled.

Then she led him by the hand to her chambers, and sat down on a bed again and made him sit beside her; and she charged him, by the great loyalty he owed her, to tell her truthfully where he had meant to go.

'My lady, he said, 'it seemed to me that you were angry with me, when you did not wish to speak to me; and if I was on bad terms with you, I had no desire to stay here.'

'And what did you mean to do,' the lady said, 'dear King's Son?'

'What, my lady?' he said; 'by my faith, I should have gone somewhere where I could obtain my livelihood.'

[141] 'Where would you have gone,' she asked, 'by the loyalty you owe me?'

'Where, my lady?' he said; 'indeed, I should have gone straight to King Arthur's court, and there served some man of valour until he made me a knight, for they say that all the men of valour are in King Arthur's household.'

'What?' she said, 'King's Son, do you then aspire to be a knight? Tell me.'

'Indeed, my lady,' he said, 'the order to knighthood is the thing I should most like in the world.'

'Really,' she said; 'so you would dare take it on? I think that if you knew what a great burden knighthood entails, you would not be inclined to shoulder it.'

'Why, my lady?' he asked; 'do all knights have stronger bodies and limbs than other men, then?'

'No, King's Son,' she said, 'but a knight needs some things which other men do not need. And if you heard what they are, you would tremble, however bold-hearted you are.'

'My lady,' he said, 'these things which a knight needs, can they be found in the heart and body of a man?'

'Yes,' the lady said, 'certainly, for God has made some men worthier than others, more valiant, and more gracious.'

'In that case, my lady,' he said, 'a man must feel very cowardly and devoid of good qualities, if fear of that prevents him from becoming a knight, for everyone should always aim to increase and improve his good qualities; and a man should hate himself terribly, if he forfeits, through his indolence, something which everyone can have, that is, the virtues of the heart, which are a hundred times more easily come by than those of the body.'

'What difference is there, then,' the lady asked, 'between the virtues of the heart and those of the body?'

'My lady,' he said, 'I shall tell you what I think. It seems to me that a man can have the qualities of the heart even if he cannot have those of the body, for a man can be courteous and wise and gracious and loyal and valorous and generous and courageous—all these are virtues of the heart—though he cannot be big and robust and agile and handsome and attractive; all these things, it seems to me, are qualities of the body, and I believe that a man brings them with him out of his mother's womb when he is born. But I think that anyone can have the qualities of the heart, if indolence does not prevent him, for anyone [142] can have courtesy and graciousness and the other good qualities which stem from the heart, it seems to me. So I believe that it is only indolence which prevents a man from being valorous, for I have often heard you yourself say that it is the heart alone which makes a man of valour. None the less, if you would tell me about the great burden of knighthood, because of which no one should be so bold as to become a knight, I should be pleased to hear it.'

'Then I shall tell you', the lady said, 'the burdens of knighthood, those that I know—which is not all of them, for my knowledge is not that great. Even so, listen to them carefully. When you have heard them, then apply your heart and reason to what you have heard, for, just because you wish to be a knight, you should not press forward with that wish without first considering reason, for reason and understanding were given to man so that he could consider what is right before embarking on anything.

'And understand this, that knighthood was not created and set up light-heartedly, nor because some men were originally more noble or of higher lineage than the others, for all people are descended from one father and one mother. But when envy and greed began to grow in the world, and force began to overcome justice, at that time all men were still equal in lineage and nobility. And when the weak could no longer withstand or hold out against the strong, they established protectors and defenders over themselves, to protect the weak and the peaceful and to maintain their rights, and to deter the strong from their wrongdoing and outrageous behaviour.

'To provide this protection, they established those who were most worthy in the opinion of the common people. These were the big and the strong and the handsome and the nimble and the loyal and the valorous and the courageous, those who were full of the qualities of the heart and of the body. However, knighthood was not given to them frivolously, or for nothing, but with it a great burden was placed on their shoulders. And do you know what that was? Originally, when the order of knighthood began, a man who wished to be a knight, and who was accorded that privilege by right of election, was told he should be courteous without baseness, gracious without cruelty, compassionate towards the needy, generous and prepared to help those in need, and ready and prepared to confound robbers and killers; he should be a fair judge, without love or hate, without love to help wrong against right, without hate to hinder right in order to further wrong. A knight should not, for fear of death, do anything [143] which can be seen as shameful: rather, he should be more afraid of shame than of suffering death.

'The knight was established wholly to protect the Holy Church, for she should not avenge herself by arms, or give back evil for evil; and for that reason the knight was established to protect the Church, who turns the left cheek, when she is struck on the right. And you should know that originally, as the Scriptures reveal, no one was so bold as to mount a horse, if he was not a knight; and that is why they were called knights.* And the arms* which the knights carried, and which no one who is not a knight should carry, were not given to them without reason: rather, there was reason enough, and they have great significance.

'The shield which hangs around his neck,* and by which he is protected in front, signifies that, as it stands between him and blows, in the same way the knight should stand in front of the Holy Church against all evildoers, whether robbers or pagans. And if the Holy Church is attacked, or in danger of receiving a blow, the knight should stand forward, as her son, and receive the blow, for she should be protected and defended by her son; for if a mother is beaten or abused in front of her son, and he does not avenge her, then her bread should be denied him and her door closed to him.

'The hauberk which the knight wears, and which protects him all over, signifies that in the same way the Holy Church should be enclosed and surrounded by the knight's defence, for his defence should be so resolute and his precaution so prudent that, whenever the evildoer comes to the door into or out of the Holy Church, he will find the knight alert and ready to defend her.

'The helm which the knight has on his head, and which can be seen above all the other armour, signifies that in the same way the knight should be seen before all others to oppose those who wish to harm or do evil to the Holy Church, and should be like a watchtower, the residence of the watchman, which can be seen from all around, above the other houses, to frighten evildoers and thieves.

'The lance which the knight carries, which is so long that it stabs before he can be reached, signifies that, as fear of the lance, with its strong shaft and sharp head, makes unarmed men draw back for fear of death, in the same way the knight should be so fierce and brave and vigorous that the fear of him spreads so far that no thief or evildoer is so daring as to go near the Holy Church, but instead flees far away, for fear of the knight, against [144] whom he should be powerless, just as the unarmed man is powerless against the lance with its sharp head.

'The sword which the knight has belted on has two sharp edges, and not without reason. Of all the arms, the sword is the most honourable and the most noble; the one which has the most dignity, for you can do harm with it in three ways. You can thrust and kill by stabbing with the point, and you can cut right and left with the two edges. The two edges signify that the knight should be a servant to Our Lord and to His people; and one edge of the sword should strike those who are enemies of Our Lord and despisers of His faith; and the other should take vengeance on those who are destroyers of the human company, that is, those who take from one another, who kill one another. Such should be the strength of the two edges, but the point is different. The point signifies obedience, for all men should obey the knight. The point rightly signifies obedience, for it stabs, and nothing so stabs the heart, not loss of land nor of wealth, as being forced to obey.

'That is the significance of the sword, but the horse on which the knight sits, and which carries him in every need, signifies the people, for in the same way they should carry the knight in every need, and he should sit above them. The people should carry the knight in this way, in that they should find and obtain for him everything he needs to live honourably, because he guards and protects them, night and day. And the knight should sit above the people, in that as the man who sits on a horse spurs it, and directs it where he pleases, in the same way the knight should direct the people as he pleases, by rightful authority, because they are under him, as they should be. Thus you understand that the knight should be lord over the people and a servant to the Lord God. He should be lord over the people in all things, and he should be a servant to the Lord God, in that he should protect and defend and maintain the Holy Church, that is, the clergy who serve the Holy Church, and the widows and orphans, and the tithes and alms which are assigned to the Holy Church. And as the people maintain him materially and obtain for him whatever he needs, so the Holy Church should maintain him spiritually, and obtain for him the life which will have no end, that is, by prayers and orisons and alms, so that God will be his eternal saviour, as he is the earthly protector and defender of the Holy Church. [145] Thus all the knight's material needs should fall to the people, and all the needs pertaining to his soul should be the concern of the Holy Church.

'A knight should have two hearts, one as hard and impenetrable as diamond, and the other as soft and pliable as hot wax. The one which is as hard as diamond should oppose those who are treacherous and cruel, for as diamond cannot be polished, in the same way the knight should be fierce and cruel towards the cruel men who do their best to damage and destroy justice. And as soft, hot wax can be shaped and made to do whatever you wish, in the same way good and compassionate people should be able to lead the knight to everything which pertains to graciousness and gentleness. But he should take good care that the heart of wax is not accessible to those who are cruel and treacherous, for any good he did them would be utterly wasted; and the Scriptures tell us that the judge damns himself when he delivers a guilty man from death and lets him go. And if he savagely attacks, with a heart as hard as diamond, the good people who need only compassion and mercy, then he has lost his soul, for the Scriptures say that a man who loves treachery and cruelty hates his own soul, and God Himself says in the Gospels that whatever you do to those in need, you do to Him.

'A man who dares to receive knighthood should have all these things. And anyone who does not wish to act in the way I have described to you here should take good care not to be a knight; for when he strays from the right path, he will be disgraced, firstly in the world, and then before the Lord God. The day he receives the order of knighthood, he promises the Lord God that he will behave in the way described to him by whoever makes him a knight—who knows better than I', the lady said, 'how to describe it. And once he has broken his word to the Lord God and to Our Lord,* then he has rightly forfeited the honour he expected to have in the eternal bliss, and he is quite rightly disgraced in the world, for the men of valour in the world should not tolerate among themselves a man who has broken his word to his Maker. But a man who wishes to be a knight must have the finest and purest of hearts; and anyone who does not wish to be like that should take care not to undertake so noble an enterprise, for it would be better for a youth to live all his life without knighthood than to be disgraced on earth and lost to the Lord God, for knighthood is a terrible burden.

'Now,' she said, 'King's Son, I have described to you some of the points pertaining to true knighthood, but I have not told you all of them, [146] for I am not able to. Now tell me, do you wish to accept knighthood, or forgo it?'

'My lady,' the boy said, 'since knighthood first began, was there ever a knight who had all these qualities?'

'Yes,' she said, 'a good many, as the Holy Scriptures bear witness—before Jesus Christ suffered death, at the time when the people of Israel served Our Lord, faithfully and loyally, and fought against the Philistines and the other heathen peoples, who were their near neighbours, to glorify and promote His religion. Among them were John the Hyrcanian,* and Judas Maccabaeus,* the excellent knight, who chose to be killed and cut to pieces rather than abandon the religion of God Our Lord, for no heathen ever made him shamefully turn tail in battle. So, too, were his brother Simon, and King David, and many others, of whom I shall not speak now, who were before the coming of Our Lord. And since His passion there have been some who were endowed with all the true qualities. Among them were Joseph of Arimathaea, the noble knight, who took Jesus Christ down from the Holy Cross with his own hands and laid Him in the sepulchre; so, too, were his son Galahad, the noble king of Hoselice, which was later called Wales in his honour,* and all the kings descended from him, whose names I do not know. So were King Pelles of Listenois, who was the noblest of that same lineage when he was alive, and his brother Alain the Thickset.* All these were among the true, courteous knights, and true men of worth, who maintained knighthood with honour both in the world and before the Lord God.'

'My lady,' the youth said, 'since there have been so many knights who were full of all the prowess which you have described to me, then anyone who refused knighthood, and feared to accept it, for fear he could not achieve such virtue, would be full of great cowardice. Even so, I do not blame some for cowardice, if they dare not be knights, nor others, if they are knights, for everyone should act, it seems to me, according to what he finds in his heart, whether cowardice or prowess. But for my own part, I am certain that, if ever I can find someone who will make me a knight, I shall not hold back for fear that I should be a bad candidate for knighthood; for God may well have put more good in me than I realize, and He certainly still has the power to give me plenty of sense and valour, if they are lacking. Whatever comes of it, I shall not, for fear of anything, forgo receiving the noble order of knighthood, if I can find [147] someone who will give me that honour. And if God will supply the good qualities, I shall be pleased, but I shall certainly dare to put in heart and body and trouble and effort.'

'What, King's Son?' the lady said; 'does your heart then favour your becoming a knight?'

'My lady,' he said, 'there is nothing I want more, if I can find someone who will fulfil my wish.'

'In God's name,' she said, 'your wish will be wholly fulfilled, for you will be a knight, and soon. And you should know that that is why I was weeping earlier, when you came to me, and I told you to go away, or my heart would break in my breast; for I have given you all the love a mother could give her child, and I do not know how I can possibly do without you, for my heart will be terribly grieved. However, I had rather endure great unhappiness, than that you should lose the noble order of knighthood on my account: and I do not think knighthood will be wasted on you. And if you knew who your father was, and from what people your lineage comes on your mother's side, I do not think you would have any fears about being a man of valour, for no one who comes from such a lineage should have any inclination towards cowardice. But you will not learn any more about that for the moment, not until I wish it, so I do not want you to ask me any more. You will shortly be made a knight by the hand of the most worthy man in the world at the moment, that is, by the hand of King Arthur. We shall set out this week which has just begun, so that we reach him, at the latest, on the Friday before the feast of Saint John; the feast will be the following Sunday, and that is only a week from next Sunday. And I want you to be made a knight on the day of the feast of Saint John, so you will not wait any longer. And as my lord Saint John was the most praiseworthy and meritorious man ever conceived of a woman by fleshly union, in the same way may God, who was born of the Virgin to redeem His people, give you the gift of surpassing in virtue and knightly deeds all the knights now living. And I know a great part of what will happen to you.'

Thus the Lady of the Lake promised the boy that he would shortly be a knight; and he could not have been more pleased.

'Now, take care', she said, 'that no one knows anything about it, and I shall get ready the things you need, without anyone paying any attention to it.'

The lady certainly provided everything the boy needed, for [148] she had procured for him, some time before, all that a knight needs: a white hauberk, light and strong, and a silvered helm, very fine and beautiful, and a shield, all snow-white with a beautiful silver boss,* because she did not wish there to be anything which was not white. And she had ready for him a sword which was well tried on many occasions, both before and after he had it; it was reasonably big, not very heavy, and extremely sharp. And a lance was prepared for him, with a white shaft, which was short and thick and strong, and a white head, sharp and pointed. Besides all this, the lady had ready for him a big horse, strong and swift, of well-proven speed and courage: it was all white, like driven snow. And for his knighting, she had ready a robe of white samite, a tunic and a cloak; the cloak was lined with ermine, so that there would be nothing which was not white, and the tunic was lined with white sendal.

In this way, the lady provided the youth with everything he needed to be a knight, and set off three days later, early in the morning. It was a Tuesday, and there was a week from the next Sunday until the feast of Saint John. The lady started on her way, and made for King Arthur's court in great style, for there were forty horses in her company, and every one of them was white; and those who rode them were also dressed in white. In the party there were five knights, and the damsel's lover,* who was very handsome and valorous. There were also three damsels with the lady: the one who had been wounded protecting the boys,* and two others; and there were the three it was right to take, that is, Lionel and Bors, and with them Lambegue, and there were many other youths.

They rode until they reached the sea, and then they took ship, and landed in Britain on a Sunday evening, at the port of Floudehueg.* From there they rode according to reliable news of King Arthur; and they were told that the king would be in Camelot for the feast. They set out and travelled until they came, on the Thursday evening, to a castle called Lawenor, which is twenty-two English leagues from Camelot. In the morning, the lady set off very early, to travel through the morning, for it was very hot, and she rode through the forest to within two English leagues of Camelot; she was extremely pensive and downcast, for her heart was greatly pained because the youth was going to leave her, and she gave heartfelt sighs and wept bitterly. With that, though, the story now stops speaking of her for a while, and returns to King Arthur.

[149] [M. XXIIa] On that day, the story says, King Arthur was in Camelot, for he was in residence there; he had many knights with him, and intended to hold court there on the day of the feast of Saint John. On that Friday morning the king rose as soon as he could see daylight, for he wished to go into the woods to shoot, and he heard mass as early as he could. As soon as he had done so, he mounted and left the town by the Welsh Gate, and a number of his companions went with him. His nephew, Sir Gawain, was there, his face still bandaged from a wound given him by Gasoain of Estrangot just three weeks earlier, when the two fought in the king's presence, because Gasoain had accused Gawain of treachery before the whole court. Also with them were Sir Yvain the Tall, the son of King Urien; Kay, the seneschal; Tor, the son of King Ares of Autice; Lucan, the butler;[1] Bedivere, the constable; and many other knights of the king's own household.

When the king was within three bowshots of the forest, he

---

[1] i.e. the king's cup-bearer.

saw emerging from it a litter, carried swiftly and gently between two palfreys. Looking, he saw that the litter was coming straight towards him. When it drew near, he saw in it a knight, in full armour except that he had no shield or helm. The knight had been wounded in the body by two lances, and both the broken shafts, with their heads, were still in the wounds, and showing right through both sides of the hauberk. A sword was embedded in his head, so that barely half the blade showed above his coif,* and what did show was blood-stained and very rusty. The knight was a big man, comely and well-built, but the story does not reveal his name at this point. Later on, however, you will find out his name,* how he was wounded, and why he carried the broken shafts and heads in his wounds for so long.

When he met the group of riders, he asked which was the king, and several people pointed him out. He halted the litter, and greeted the king, who willingly stopped to listen to him and to look at him in amazement.

'King Arthur,' he said, 'God save you, the best king living, as all bear witness, the truest and the most powerful, he who helps the helpless, who counsels and supports them.'

'Sir,' said the king, 'God bless you and give you health, for I think you have great need of it.'

[150] 'My lord,' said the knight, 'I have come to you for aid and assistance, for it is said that you never fail a person in need. I beg you to help me, for the Lord's sake.'

'In what do you want my help?' asked the king.

'I wish you', the knight replied, 'to have this sword and these broken shafts removed, which are killing me.'

'Of course,' said the king, 'gladly.'

He reached forward to pull the shafts out himself, but the knight cried:

'Ah! my lord! do not be so hasty. They cannot be withdrawn like that.'

'How, then?' asked the king.

'My lord,' he replied, 'whoever withdraws them will have to swear, on holy relics, that he will do his best to avenge me on all those who say they love the man who gave me these wounds more than they do me.'

At this, the king drew back, and said to the knight:

'Sir knight, it is a very difficult thing that you ask, for the man who wounded you like this may have so many friends* that there is no knight in the world, nor any two or three, who could accomplish it. If you wish, though, I shall avenge you on whoever did this, if he is a man I may kill without dishonouring myself; and if he is my vassal,* there are plenty of knights here who would gladly take this burden upon themselves, in order to win honour and renown.'

'Neither you nor anyone else,' the knight said, 'will ever avenge me on the man who did this to me. I myself took revenge on him, for I cut off his head, after he wounded me like this.'

'Then, in God's name's,' said the king, 'I should say that you are well avenged, and I should not dare promise you more, for fear of breaking my word. Nor shall I advise anyone else to make you such a promise.'

'My lord,' the knight said, 'I was told that everyone can find help at your court, but now it seems that I have quite failed to do so. None the less, I shall certainly not move from here until I see whether God will heed me, for if there is as much prowess at your court as I have been told, then I shall be healed before I leave.'

'I should be delighted', the king said, 'to have you under my roof for as long as you please.'

Thereupon the knight went off to Camelot, and came to the king's residence. He had his squires carry him up into the hall, and lay him in the most beautiful and richly made of the many beds he could see there. [151] At that time, no serving-man of King Arthur's household was so bold as to deny entry to a knight, or refuse him a bed, however sumptuous.

Thus the wounded knight was lodged. Meanwhile, the king went into the forest; he and his companions talked a good deal about the knight, and everyone said that they had never heard a knight make such an outrageous request. All the same, Gawain said that, God willing, the knight would not go unsatisfied from the king's dwelling.

'I do not know about that,' the king said, 'but let all my companions understand this: if any of them were to undertake such a piece of foolishness, he would never again enjoy my friendship; for this task may well prove to be one which no one knight, or two or three, or even twenty or thirty, could accomplish. Besides, we do not yet know why this knight has made such an outrageous request, whether it is to bring good, or harm, to my household.'

Thus the king and his companions spoke of the knight.

The king spent the whole day shooting in the forest, until it was almost vespers, and then turned for home. As he came out of the forest, along a path which joined the main highway, he looked to his right and saw the Lady of the Lake's party approaching. At the very front he saw two servants on foot, driving two white pack-horses. Loaded on one of the horses was a small, lightweight pavilion, one of the finest and most beautiful ever seen; on the other, the robe in which the youth was to be made a knight, another robe for ceremonies, and a third for riding. These robes were in two chests, on top of which were tied a hauberk and mail leggings. Behind the two pack-horses came two squires on white hacks, one carrying a snow-white shield, and the other the helm, very fine and elegant. After these came two others, one carrying the lance, whose shaft and head were all white, and with a sword slung around his neck, in a white scabbard with a white baldric. The other was leading a splendid horse, white as snow. Following these came squires and serving-men in great numbers, and then the three damsels and the knights, all mounted on white horses.

The whole party were riding in twos along the road. Last of all came the lady, with the youth, instructing him and teaching him how to conduct himself at the court of King Arthur, and at any other he might visit. She also stressed that, if he held honour dear, [152] he should be made a knight that Sunday without fail, for she wished it so, and if he were not, it would be a great misfortune for him. He replied that he would seek no delay, for he wished he were a knight already.

They rode along talking until their party neared that of the king. The king and his party had been looking at them in amazement, because they were all dressed in white and riding white horses. The king pointed them out to Sir Gawain and Sir Yvain, and said that he had never seen such a large party ride so elegantly. Word of King Arthur's presence reached the Lady of the Lake. She quickened her pace and, with the youth, overtook the whole group, and came before the king, who had been waiting for her since he had observed her elegant company and seen her hasten towards him, for he supposed she wished to speak to him.

She was richly turned out, for she was dressed in a tunic and cloak of white samite, trimmed with ermine, and she rode a little white palfrey, as beautiful and well formed as anyone could describe. It was very fine, and its bridle was of pure white silver, as were the breast-strap and the stirrups, while the saddle was of ivory, most skilfully carved with small figures of knights and ladies. The saddle-housing was of the same white samite as the lady's clothes, and reached down to the ground. Thus attired and mounted, the lady came before the king. Beside her was the youth, dressed in an excellent white woollen cloth. He was wonderfully handsome and well formed, and mounted on a strong and swift hunter, which carried him rapidly along. The lady moved her wimple from in front of her mouth, and greeted the king, who was still prompt enough to greet her first.

'My lord,' she said, 'God bless you, best of all earthly kings. Arthur,' she went on, 'I have come a very long way to see you. I come to ask you for a boon, which you should not refuse me, for it can bring you neither shame nor harm, and it will cost you nothing.'

'Damsel,' said the king, 'even if it were to cost me a great deal, you should have it, as long as it brought no shame to me, nor harm to my friends. Name your boon without hesitation, for it would need to be great indeed before I should refuse you.'

'My lord, many thanks,' she said, 'I ask you, then, to knight this youth here with me, with the arms and equipment he has, when he requests it.'

[153] 'Damsel,' said the king, 'I am pleased that you have come here, and I thank you for bringing him to me, for he is a very handsome youth. I shall gladly knight him whenever he wishes. However, you assured me that you would not ask a boon whereby I had harm or shame, yet if I did as you have asked I should incur shame: I am not accustomed to make anyone a knight unless I provide the robes and the arms. Leave the youth with me, though, and I shall willingly make him a knight, for I shall supply what pertains to me, that is, the arms and equipment and the accolade, and may God supply the rest, that is, prowess and the other qualities which a knight should have.'

'My lord,' she said, 'perhaps you do not usually make anyone a knight except at your own expense; it may be that you have never been asked to do so. If you are asked, though, and you do so, it seems to me that you will have no shame from it. And understand this: this youth should not, must not be knighted with other arms and in other robes than those which he has here. If you wish, make him a knight, and if you do not wish to do so, I shall take him somewhere else; and I,

I myself, should knight him, rather than let him remain unknighted.'

'Sire,' said Sir Yvain, 'do not refuse to make him a knight as the lady asks, since she wishes it. Even if you were to incur some slight dishonour, you should not let such a comely young man as this leave, for I cannot recall ever seeing so fair a youth.'

Then the king agreed to carry out the lady's wishes, and she thanked him warmly. She gave the youth the two pack-horses and two of the most beautiful palfreys in the world, all of them white, and four squires to serve him.

Then the lady took leave of the king, who begged her to stay, but she said that she could not do so under any circumstances.

'Lady,' said the king, 'since you will not stay, which distresses me greatly, tell me your name and who you are, for I should very much like to know.'

'My lord,' she said, 'I should not conceal my name from such a noble man as yourself, so I shall tell you. They call me the Lady of the Lake.'

The king was very surprised by this name, for he had never heard of her. Then the lady left him, and the youth accompanied her for almost a bowshot. She said to him:

'Dear King's Son, you are leaving me, and I want you to know that you are not my son, but the son of one of the noblest men, [154] and the best knights, in the world, and of one of the best and fairest women who ever lived. You will not learn the truth about either your father or your mother at present, but you will do so shortly. Be sure that your thoughts and feelings are as fine as your body is fair, for you are as comely as God can make a child, and it would be a great pity if your prowess did not match your looks. Be sure, too, that you ask the king tomorrow evening to make you a knight. Once you are knighted, do not stay another night under his roof, but go through all the land seeking adventures and wonders, for that will enable you to win honour and renown. Do not stop in one place any longer than you need. Take care to be so enterprising that no one ever undertakes to perform a knightly deed which you have neglected. If the king asks you your name, or who you are, or who I am, tell him frankly that you do not know, except that I am a lady who brought you up; I have also told your squires not to say more than that. I would say in parting that I want you to know I did not make you behave unworthily when I caused you to be served by those two king's sons, who were with you, for you are no less noble than they. They are both your first cousins, and because I have given you all the love which comes from nurturing a child, I shall keep them with me as long as I can, to remind me of you. Even when the time comes for Lionel to become a knight, I shall still have Bors.'

When he heard that the two boys were his cousins, he was quite delighted, and said to the lady:

'What a good thing you have told me this, for I am greatly cheered, both by the pleasure it gives me, and by the comfort it will be to you.'

Then the lady took off a small ring, and put it on the boy's finger, telling him it had the power to reveal all enchantments. Thereupon she commended him to God, and kissed him tenderly. As they parted, she said:

'Dear King's Son, I shall give you this advice, in parting: the more terrible and dangerous adventures you accomplish, the more confidently you should undertake them, for if you are unable to accomplish an adventure, through such prowess as God has given any knight, the man is not yet born who can succeed where you have failed. There is much I would say to you, but I cannot, for my heart is wrung, and I cannot speak. Go now, good and fair, [155] gracious and sought-after by all, loved by all women more than any other knight—I know you will be all these things.'

With that she kissed him warmly on the mouth, the cheeks,

and the eyes, and rode off, so grief-stricken that no one could make her speak. The boy was greatly moved, so that, despite himself, tears came to his eyes. He ran to his two cousins, embraced first Lionel and then Bors, and said to Lionel:

'Lionel, Lionel, do not be downcast or in despair because King Claudas has your land in his power, for you will find you have more friends than you think, when the time comes to get it back.'

After that, he embraced all the others one by one, and then rode off at a gallop, and caught up with the king and his company, who were waiting to see him. The king took him by the chin, and saw that he was so handsome and well made in every way that he could find no fault in him. Sir Yvain said to him:

'Sire, take a good look, for I do not think you have ever seen a youth with so fair a face. God did not stint him, if he gave him qualities in proportion to his beauty.'

Sir Yvain and the others talked about the youth so much that he was quite disconcerted; the king saw as much, and so did not ask him anything about himself, but left it for another time. Then he said to Sir Yvain:

'I am putting the youth in your care, for no one could teach him better than you how to conduct himself.'

He gave the youth by the hand to Sir Yvain, who thanked him. They arrived at Camelot, where the throng was so thick around the youth, with people trying to see him, that it was hard to turn round. He dismounted at Sir Yvain's lodging, and Sir Yvain and all his household, and everyone who saw him, said that they had never seen such a handsome young man. The next day, Saturday, the youth went to Sir Yvain, and said:

'My lord, please ask my lord the king to make me a knight, as he promised my lady, for I wish to be knighted tomorrow, without further delay.'

'What?' said Sir Yvain, 'my friend, do you wish to be

knighted so soon?' When he replied that he did, Sir Yvain said, 'My friend, would you not do better to wait a while and perfect your knowledge of arms?'

'My lord,' said the youth, 'I do not wish to remain a squire any longer, [156] and I beg you to ask my lord the king to make me a knight tomorrow, without further delay.'

'Of course,' he said, 'with pleasure.'

Sir Yvain went to the king, and said:

'Sire, your youth sends me to ask you to make him a knight.'

'Which youth?' asked the king.

'Sire,' he replied, 'the youth who was brought to you yesterday evening, whom you put in my care.'

At that moment the queen walked through the hall; at her side was Sir Gawain, the king's nephew. The king looked at Sir Yvain, and said:

'Do you mean the youth the lady brought to me, dressed in a white robe?'

'Indeed,' said Sir Yvain,' 'I mean him.'

'What?' said the king, 'does he want to be a knight already?'

'Yes, indeed,' he said, 'tomorrow!'

'Gawain,' said the king, 'come and hear about the youth who arrived yesterday, and who already wishes to be a knight.'

'Indeed,' Sir Gawain said, 'he is quite right, and I think he will make a good knight, for he is very handsome,* and certainly seems as though he comes from a noble family.'

'Who is this youth?' asked the queen.

'Who, my lady?' said Sir Yvain. 'The fairest youth you ever set eyes on.' Then he told her how the young man had been brought to the king the day before, and about the elegant arrival of the lady who brought him.

'What?' said the queen: 'he came to court yesterday evening, and wishes to be knighted tomorrow?'

'Indeed, my lady,' said Sir Yvain, 'for he is very keen to be a knight.'

'I should very much like to see him,' said the queen; and the king said:

'In God's name, I think you will find him the most comely and well-made youth you have ever seen.'

Then he asked Sir Yvain to go and fetch him. 'And see that he is as richly dressed', he said, 'as you know he should be—I do not think he is short of finery.'

Then the king himself told the queen how the Lady had asked him to knight the youth, but only with his own arms and robes, and that she was called the Lady of the Lake. The queen was greatly surprised, and was very impatient to see the youth.

[157] Sir Yvain went to the youth, and made him dress and adorn himself as richly as possible. When he could see no room for improvement, he led the young man to court, on his own splendid horse. However, he did not lead him there in secret, for there were so many people around him that they filled the street. The news spread through the town that the handsome youth who had arrived the previous evening was to be made a knight the next day, and that he was coming to court, wearing a knight's robe. Then the townspeople, men and women, rushed to their windows, saying, as they saw him pass, that they had never seen such a handsome young knight-to-be. He arrived at court, and dismounted. The word spread through the hall and the chambers, and knights, ladies, and damsels rushed out, while even the king and queen went to the windows.

When the youth had dismounted, Sir Yvain took him by the left hand and led him up into the hall. The king and queen came to meet them, took the youth by the hands, and went to sit on a couch, while he sat down on the floor in front of them, on the greenery with which the hall was strewn. The king took great pleasure in looking at him. If he had thought him handsome when he arrived, it was as nothing compared with his beauty now, and it seemed to the king that he was now much bigger and stronger. The queen said that she hoped God would make him a man of valour, for He had given him beauty in abundance.

The queen looked at the youth a great deal, and he at her, whenever he was able to do so discreetly. He wondered where such great beauty as that which he saw in her could come from. The beauty of the Lady of the Lake, he thought, or of any other woman he had ever seen, could not compare with this. He was certainly not wrong to esteem the queen above all other women, for she was the lady of ladies and the fount of beauty; yet if he had known her merits, he would have been even more eager to look at her, for no woman, rich or poor, could match her worth.

She asked Sir Yvain the youth's name, and he replied that he did not know.

'Do you know whose son he is,' she said, 'or where he is from?'

'No, my lady,' he said, 'I only know that he is from Gaul, for he has that manner of speech.'

Then the queen took the youth by the hand, and asked him where he was from. When he felt her touch, he started as though from sleep, for he was so engrossed in thinking about her that he did not hear what she said. She saw that he was overwhelmed, and asked him again, 'Tell me [158] where you are from.' He looked at her ingenuously and said, with a sigh, that he did not know. She asked him his name again, and he said that he did not know what it was. The queen saw that he was troubled and thoughtful, but she did not dare think it was because of her; none the less she rather suspected it, and said no more for the moment. And since she did not want to encourage his foolishness, she got up from the couch, and to prevent anyone from thinking ignoble thoughts or noticing that which she suspected, she said that this young man seemed to her to be a little simple, and, whether or not that was the case, he had been badly brought up.

'My lady,' said Sir Yvain, 'we do not know the truth of the matter, you and I. Perhaps he has been forbidden to tell us his name, or who he is.'

She said that that was quite possible. However, they said all this out of earshot of the youth.

The queen went to her chambers, and when the time came to go to vespers, Sir Yvain led the youth there by the hand. When they returned from vespers, the king and queen and the knights went into a beautiful garden beside the river, behind the hall, and adjoining the king's residence. Sir Yvain took the youth there also, and behind them came a great crowd of other youths who were to be knighted the next day. When they left the garden, they went up into the hall by some steps which led down to the river, and they had to pass through the chamber where the knight was lying, who had the lance-shafts and the sword still in him. The stench from his wounds was so strong that the knights covered their noses with their cloaks, and hurried past.

The youth asked Sir Yvain why the knights were covering their noses in this way.

'My friend,' Sir Yvain said, 'it is because of a wounded knight who is lying in here.'

'My lord,' said the youth, 'then why is he lying here? Would he not be better in lodgings down in the town?'

'Yes, indeed,' said Sir Yvain, 'but he has stayed here to get help, if God will send it to him.' Then he told him of how whoever drew the weapons from the knight's wounds would have to swear to avenge him, and of what that vengeance entailed.

'My lord,' the youth said, 'I should like to see him, if you please.'

'And so you shall,' said Sir Yvain; 'come with me.'

[159] Sir Yvain led him to the knight, and the youth asked him:

'Sir knight, who gave you these terrible wounds?'

'My friend,' he said, 'it was a knight that I killed.'

'And why do you not have the weapons removed?' asked the youth.

'Because', he replied, 'I can find no knight bold enough to remove them.'

'Why, by the Lord's mercy?' said the youth. 'In God's name, I will do it this instant, if you wish, if it does not require great strength to pull out those broken shafts.'

'I should like you to do it,' said the knight, 'provided that you accept the conditions which go with it.'

'What are they?' asked the youth.*

'They are such', said Sir Yvain, 'that there are perhaps no two or three knights in the world, no, nor even twenty, who could fulfil them.'

Then he described the conditions fully, at which the youth became thoughtful. And Sir Yvain, who was very shrewd, took him by the hand.

'Come along,' he said, 'you should not yet be thinking of such great deeds.'

'And why not?' asked the youth.

'Because', he replied, 'there are here some of the most valorous men in the world, and they are not prepared to undertake this; much less should you, who are not even a knight yet.'

'What?' said the wounded knight, 'is he not yet a knight, then?'

'No,' said Sir Yvain, 'but he will be knighted tomorrow, and he already wears a knight's robe, as you can see.'

When the youth heard Sir Yvain say that he was not yet a knight, he did not dare utter another word, except to commend the wounded knight to God. He replied that he hoped God would make him a man of valour. Then Sir Yvain led him to the hall, where the tables were set up,* and the cloths on them, and they sat down to eat. After the meal, Sir Yvain took the youth to his lodgings, and when night fell, he took him to church, and stayed with him all night long while he kept vigil until daybreak. In the morning, he took him back to his lodgings, and made him sleep until it was time for high mass, when he led him to church with the king, for on important feast-days the king always heard mass—and always high mass—in the largest and finest church in the town where he was staying. As they were about to go to church, arms were brought for all those who were to be knighted, [160] and they armed themselves after the fashion of the time. Then the king gave them the accolade, but he would not belt on their swords until they came back from church. When they had received the accolade, they went to church and heard mass, all armed after the fashion of the time, for that was the practice. As soon as mass was over and they came out of the church, the youth left Sir Yvain and went up to the hall. He went to the wounded knight, and said that he would remove the weapons now, if he wished.

'I should certainly be very pleased,' said the knight, 'if you accept the conditions,' and he repeated them.

The youth said that he was quite ready to swear to it. Then he went over to a window and stretched out his hand towards a church which he could see, and swore, in front of the knight's squires,* that he would do his best to avenge him on all those who said that they loved the man who had given him these wounds more than the knight himself. Then the delighted knight said to the youth:

'Sir, now you can remove these weapons. How pleased I am to see you!'

The youth took hold of the sword which was embedded in the knight's head, and drew it out, so gently that the knight scarcely felt it. Then he pulled out the lance-shafts. While he was doing this, a squire chanced to see him and, running down into the courtyard in front of the hall, where the king was belting on the swords of the new knights, he told Sir Yvain how the youth had removed the weapons from the knight's wounds. Sir Yvain went running into the knight's chamber like a madman, and saw the knight, free of the weapons, who was saying to the youth:

'Ah! noble knight, may God make you a man of valour: you certainly will be if you live long enough. Now I should be quite well if I had a doctor to tend me.'

The youth saw Sir Yvain, and said:

'Ha! my lord, for heaven's sake, get him a doctor.'

'What?' said Sir Yvain, 'have you removed the weapons, then?'

'Yes, my lord,' he replied, 'as you can see, for I felt such compassion that I could no longer endure his great suffering.'

'You have not acted wisely,' Sir Yvain said, 'and it will be considered very foolish of you, for there are here some of the best knights in the world, who did not wish to undertake this task, because no one could perform it; yet you, who do not appreciate what it means, have taken it on. What you have done distresses me greatly, and as God is my witness, I should have preferred [161] that the knight leave here disappointed, however much harm that caused him, and however much shame it brought on the king and his household, for if you lived long enough, you might have achieved great things.'

'Ah! my lord,' he said, 'it is far better that I should die in this undertaking, if I should do so, than that this knight should die, for he may well be of great prowess, while no one yet knows my worth. Besides, I have done nothing which can bring reproach on the king and his household. But, for heaven's sake, my lord, since things have gone this far, send for a doctor to heal the knight.'

Greatly upset, Sir Yvain replied that he would not suffer for want of a doctor. He sent for one, and led the youth into the hall. The king was up there, having already heard the news that the youth had removed the weapons.

'What, Yvain,' said the king, 'has your youth truly removed the weapons from the wounded knight?'

'Yes, sire,' Sir Yvain said.

'Indeed,' said the king, 'you must be sorry about that, and it is a wonder that you allowed it. I am very displeased with you for letting the fairest youth in the world undertake a task in which he will surely die.'

'Sire,' said Sir Yvain, 'by the loyalty I owe you as my lord, I was not present at the time, and I have greatly rebuked and reproached him for it. I would rather have had one of my arms broken than that he should have done it.'

'Indeed,' said the king, 'you would have been quite right, for I have never seen a man who would be such a loss as he seemingly will be, since he has taken on a task which no one could perform.'

'Ah! my lord,' said the youth, 'by the Lord's mercy, it is far better that I should die, than one of the renowned knights of your household, for I cannot amount to much yet.'

The king bowed his head, so upset that tears came to his eyes.

The news spread all through the court, so that the queen heard what had occurred. She was very upset, for she was afraid that the youth loved her so much that he had undertaken the task for her sake, and she said that it was a great sadness, and a great misfortune. Everyone greatly pitied the youth, and because of the great sorrow [162] that they all felt, no one remembered about the youth's sword, which the king had forgotten to belt on. Then the tablecloths were spread, and all the new knights disarmed and sat down to eat.

When the king had been sitting at table for some time, a knight came into the hall, fully armed except for his helm and his ventail, which he had let down. He approached the king, and greeted him.

'King Arthur,' he said, 'God save you and all your company: I speak on behalf of the Lady of Nohaut, whom I serve.

My lady has sent me to you to say that the King of Northumberland is waging war upon her, and is laying siege to one of her castles. He has done her great harm, killing many of her men and laying waste her land, and he is demanding the fulfilment of an agreement which my lady in no way recognizes. The two sides have had discussions, both between knights and between churchmen, and the king has said that he is ready to prove, in accordance with a judgement, that my lady made the agreement whose fulfilment he is demanding. The terms of the judgement are that, if the king wishes to prove her in the wrong, my lady must defend herself as well as she can,[1] by means of one knight against another, two against two, three against three, or as many as she can find, if she so wishes. For this reason my lady sends to ask you, since you are her liege lord, and she your liege woman, to assist her in this time of need, and to send her a knight who is capable of defending her honour against another, for she intends to choose combat between two single knights to prove her case.'

'My friend,' the king said to the knight, 'I shall gladly help her. I fully recognize that I should do so, for she is my liege woman, and holds all her land from me. Besides, even if she held nothing from me, she is such a worthy and gracious lady, so noble and beautiful, that I ought to help her anyway.'

Those who were serving led the knight who had brought the message to a table, and there the question of help rested. As soon as they began to remove the tablecloths, Sir Yvain's youth sprang up, went to the king and, kneeling down before him, said humbly:

'My lord, you have made me a knight, for which I thank you, and now I ask as a boon that you allow me to provide the assistance which this knight has requested.'

'My friend,' the king said, 'you do not know what you are

---

[1] i.e. by combat of champions.

asking, for you are too young to know what a difficult knightly
task involves; [163] the King of Northumberland has a great
many good knights, and I know he will entrust the combat to
the one he considers best. And you are at an age when you
are not yet ready to take on such a heavy burden, and it would
be a great pity if by some misfortune you were defeated and
killed, for you might yet achieve great things. You are so fair
and nobly made, and your courage is so great, that I feel you
must come from a family of very high estate. Moreover, you
came to me out of noble sentiments, for you aspire to win
honour and renown, and it would upset me greatly if you
came to your death as a result of a boon I had granted you.
Besides, you have already undertaken such a task that you
should stop at that: and may God grant that you carry it out
successfully, for it involves great danger.'

'My lord,' said the youth, 'this is the first request I have
made of you, since you made me a knight, and take care, for
the sake of your honour, that you do not refuse me a thing
which it is reasonable to ask.* I ask you again, as a boon, to
send me to help the lady in this matter; and if you refuse me,
you will do me a great disservice, for everyone will esteem
me the less. I myself shall have a lower opinion of my worth,
as God is my witness, if you are not prepared to entrust me
with a mission of assistance which can be carried out by a
single knight.'

Then Sir Gawain and his cousin, Sir Yvain* sprang
forward, and said to the king:

'Ah! sire, for the Lord's sake, grant him this boon, for we
are sure he will perform the task very well. Moreover, you
cannot, with good grace, refuse him.'

'Indeed,' said the king, 'I too think he will perform it
well—and may God grant it be so—and I shall gladly entrust
him with it. Here, my friend,' he went on, 'I grant you the
task of aiding the Lady of Nohaut, and may God grant that

you carry it out in such a way as to bring honour and renown to yourself, and honour to me.'

'My lord, many thanks,' said the youth.

With that he took leave of the king, and of Sir Gawain and the other companions,[1] and Sir Yvain took him to his lodgings, to arm himself. The knight who had come to seek help went to the king, and said:

'My lord, I shall leave now, for I gather you have entrusted the combat to this new knight; take care that he is up to such a task.'

'Indeed,' said the king, 'he asked me for it as a boon, for I should otherwise have sent one of the best knights of my household; none the less, I think the affair is in excellent hands.'

[164] 'My lord,' said the other, 'by your leave.'

'Go with God,' said the king, 'and greet your lady on my behalf, and tell her that if she is afraid to entrust the combat to a single knight, I will send her two, three, or as many as she wishes.'

'Many thanks, my lord,' he said.

Then he left, and went to find the youth, who was arming himself in Sir Yvain's lodgings. When he was fully armed except for his head and hands, he said to Sir Yvain:

'Ha! my lord, I have been very forgetful!'

'In what way?' asked Sir Yvain.

'My lord,' he said, 'I did not take leave of my lady the queen.'

'You are quite right to say so,' said Sir Yvain; 'let us go to her.'

'Sir,' the youth said to the knight who was waiting for him, 'you go on out of town, and I shall spur after you as soon as I have spoken to my lady the queen. And you,' he said to his squires, 'go with him, and take all my equipment.'

_____
[1] i.e. of the Round Table.

Then he quietly told one of the squires to take his sword as well, for he aspired to be knighted by another hand than that of the king.*

'Sir,' said the knight who was waiting for him, 'I shall go on as far as the edge of the forest, and shall wait for you there.'

Then the knight and the youth's squires rode off, and Sir Yvain and the youth went to court. They passed through the hall where the king and many good knights were still sitting, the youth with his ventail lowered, and came to the queen's chambers. When the youth saw her, he did not fail to recognize her.* He knelt down before her, and looked at her very demurely for as long as he dared, until embarrassment overcame him, and he looked down at the floor. Sir Yvain said to the queen:

'My lady, here is the youth you saw yesterday evening, whom the king has made a knight, and who has come to take leave of you.'

'What?' said the queen; 'is he leaving already?'

'Yes, my lady,' said Sir Yvain, 'he is to help the Lady of Nohaut on the king's behalf.'

'Ha! by the Lord, why does my husband allow him to go? He already had enough to do because he removed the weapons from the knight's wounds.'

'Indeed, my lady,' said Sir Yvain, 'it distresses my lord the king, but the youth asked for the task as a boon.'

[165] Then everyone said:

'It is the youth who removed the weapons from the knight's wounds. Lord, what a courageous act!'

'Lord,' said the ladies and damsels who were present, 'how handsome and elegant and altogether well made he is, and how he seems sure to be very valiant!'

Then the queen took him by the hand, and said:

'Stand up, dear sir, for I do not know who you are. It may

be that you are of nobler birth than I realize, and it is not courteous of me to allow you to kneel before me.'

'Ah, my lady,' he said, with a sigh, 'first you must forgive me the foolish thing I have done.'

'What foolish thing is that?' she asked.

'My lady,' he said, 'I left here without taking leave of you.'

'My dear friend,' said the queen, 'you are so young that you should certainly be forgiven such a misdemeanour, and I forgive you gladly.'

'My lady,' he said, 'I thank you. My lady,' he went on, 'if you please, I should like to consider myself your knight, wherever I may be.'

'Certainly,' she said, 'I should like that very much.'

'Then, my lady,' he said, 'I shall go, by your leave.'

'Go with God,' she said, 'dear friend.'*

He replied under his breath:

'I thank you, my lady, since you are pleased to call me that.'

Then the queen raised him by the hand, and he was delighted to feel her bare hand touching his. He took leave of the ladies and damsels, and Sir Yvain led him back through the hall. When they reached his lodgings, he helped the youth to arm his head and hands, but when he came to belt on his sword for him, he remembered that the king had never done so, and he said:

'By my head, sir, you are not yet a knight.'

'Why not?' asked the youth.

'Because', Sir Yvain replied, 'the king did not belt on your sword. Let us go to him now, and he will do so.'

'In that case, my lord,' he said, 'wait for me, and I shall hurry after my squires, who have taken my sword, for I should not wish the king to make me a knight with any other.'

'I shall come with you,' said Sir Yvain.

[166] 'My lord,' he said, 'do not do so; I shall ride after

them with all the speed I can get from my horse, and come straight back to you here.'

He rode away, and Sir Yvain waited for him. However, he did not intend to return, for he did not reckon to be made a knight by the king, but by the hand of another, from which he thought he would gain more. Sir Yvain waited for him a long time, and when he saw that he was not coming back, he went straight to the king, and said:

'Sire, we are badly let down regarding the youth who is going to give assistance at Nohaut.'

'What?' said the king.

'Indeed,' he said, 'you did not belt on his sword.'

Then he told the king how the youth was supposed to come back when he went to fetch his sword. The king very much wondered why he had not returned, since Sir Yvain had told him that he was not yet a knight.

'Indeed,' said Sir Gawain, 'I think he must be a man of very high rank, and perhaps he took offence that my lord the king did not belt on his sword before those of the others, and that is why he has gone away.'

The queen agreed that that was quite possible, and many of the knights said the same. Now, though, the story falls silent about the king and queen and their company, and returns to the youth who was going to the rescue of the Lady of Nohaut.

[M. XXIIIa] The youth rode after the knight who had come to seek help, and after his equipment, which had gone on ahead, and caught up with them at the edge of the forest. They rode together through the forest until none.* It was very hot, and the youth took off his helm, and gave it to one of his squires; then he fell into a profound reverie. Meanwhile the knight, who was riding in front, turned off the main highway and on to a little path. When they had gone some way along the path, a branch struck the youth in the face, and scratched him; he stopped dreaming and looked around, and saw that they were off the main road.

'What is this?' he said to the knight; 'was the way not straight, and the going easier on the main road than on this little path?'

'Yes, indeed,' said the knight, 'but it was by no means as safe.'

'And why is that?' asked the youth.

'I will not tell you that, if I choose not to,' said the knight.

'In God's name,' he said, 'you shall tell me, for in taking this way you have caused me more hardship than you realize.'

'And what hardship is that, my friend?' asked the knight.

[167] 'Something you could not make up to me,'* said the youth. 'But now tell me why the other way was not safe.'

'I will not,' said the knight.

'No?' said the youth.

Then he took his sword from the squire who was carrying it, and came swiftly back to the knight.

'Now, you will tell me,' he said, 'quickly, or you are a dead man.'

'Dead?' the knight said, and began to laugh. 'Do you think you could kill me so quickly?'

'Certainly,' said the youth, 'you are a dead man, if you do not tell me this instant.'

'I am not as easy to kill as you think,' said the knight, 'but I shall tell you before you attack me, for I should serve my lady very badly if I were to let you fight me. Now, come back with me, and I shall show you why I led you off the main road.'

He led the way back along the path, the youth following with his equipment. They arrived back on the road, and they had not gone far along it when they saw, a little to the right, a block of stone beside a beautiful spring. The youth came to the spring and, looking a little way off, he saw a very fine pavilion pitched right in the middle of a wide open space.

'Sir,' the knight said to the youth,' 'I shall now tell you, if you wish, why I left the main road.'

'Tell me,' he said.

'In that pavilion over there,' said the knight, 'is a very beautiful maiden, and she is guarded by a knight who is at least six inches taller than other knights, and stronger and more robust. He is very fierce and cruel towards all those whom he defeats, which means all those who fight with him, for he is so strong that no one can withstand him. That is why I led you off the road.'

'I wish to go and see him,' said the youth.

'You will not do so,' he said, 'if you take my advice.'

'I will go,' he replied.

'By my faith,' said the knight, 'I am sorry to hear it, and you will be acting unwisely. And I shall not accompany you any further, let me tell you.'

'Accompany me or not, as you wish,' said the youth, 'for it is all one to me.'

[168] Then the youth dismounted and, taking his sword in one hand and his helm in the other, he left the knight and his squires by the block of stone and went over to the pavilion, his drawn sword in his hand. He was going to open the entrance-flap, but the big knight was sitting in front of it, in a very fine chair. He said to the youth:

'Do it at your peril. You have no business to go in there.'

'Oh, yes I have,' said the youth, 'for I wish to see a damsel who is inside.'

'She cannot be seen', said the knight, 'by all those who wish to see her.'

'I do not know', said the youth, 'by whom she can be seen, but I will see her.'

Then he was about to force his way into the pavilion.

'Stop, sir,' said the knight, 'do not go in there, for my damsel is sleeping, and I should certainly not wish her to wake up until she is ready. However, since you are so keen to see her,' he said, 'I shall not fight with you about it, for I should gain no honour by killing you, but I shall show her to you as soon as she wakes up.'

'Why would you gain no honour by killing me?' asked the youth.

'Because', he said, 'you are so young, and I am much bigger and stronger than you are.'

'I do not care', said the youth, 'why you will not fight me, if you give me your word that you will show me the maiden when she is awake.'

'I give you my word,' the knight said.

The youth left the pavilion and went towards a leafy shelter which was less than a bowshot away. Sitting in front of it he saw two damsels, elegantly dressed. He went towards them, his sword in his right hand and his helm in his left. When he drew near them, they did not move, but one said:

'Lord, what a handsome knight this man is, who is coming here!'

'Yes, indeed,' said the other, 'he is the most handsome knight in the world. What a shame that he is such a coward.'

'As God is my witness,' said the first, 'you speak the truth. He is no knight, since he did not dare to see my lady, who is the most beautiful creature in the world, for fear of the big knight who was guarding her.'

He clearly heard what they said, and he stopped and said to them:

'As God is my true witness, you are absolutely right.'

[169] Then he turned back towards the pavilion at the edge of the forest,* but when he came to the entrance, he found no sign of the big knight. He opened the entrance-flap, but he saw no lady or damsel inside. He was astonished, and wondered where the pavilion's occupants could have gone. He looked around him, but saw nothing. Then he went back to the two maidens he had seen in front of the shelter, but he could not find either of them. He was now so upset

that he was almost beside himself. He returned to the block of stone where he had left the knight and his equipment, and the knight asked him what he had done.

'I have not done anything,' he said. 'The maiden has eluded me, which distresses me greatly.' Then he told him what had occurred. 'However,' he said, 'I shall certainly not rest until I have seen the damsel.'

Then he mounted his horse and gave his sword and helm back to his squires.

'What is this, sir?' said the knight, 'do you mean to go after the damsel?'

'Yes,' said the youth, 'and I shall search until I find her.'

'What?' said the knight; 'you are supposed to go to my lady's assistance.'

'So I shall,' said the youth; 'I shall easily be there before the day of the combat.'

'What do you know of when it will be?' asked the knight.

'I know very well,' said the youth, 'that you told my lord the king that it had not yet been decided when the combat should take place, nor how many knights should be involved. But go on to your lady and greet her on my behalf, and tell her I am coming to deal with her affair, and I shall be there soon.'

'Then I commend you to God,' said the knight, 'for I am going; as soon as you have seen the damsel, though, come on to Nohaut.'

'I shall,' he said.

Then the knight rode off one way, and the youth the other, with his squires. A little after vespers, he met a knight in full armour, who asked him where he was going.

'I am going', said the youth, 'about some business.'

'Tell me what it is,' said the knight.

'I will not,' said the youth.

[170] 'I know very well where you are going,' said the knight.

'Where, then?' he asked.

'You are looking for a damsel,' said the knight, 'who is guarded by a big knight.'

'You are right,' said the youth, 'who told you?'

'I knew it,' the knight said

'I know very well who told you,' said the youth.

'Who, then?'

'A knight told you,' said the youth, 'who parted from me earlier, and who is going to the Lady of Nohaut.'

'Whoever told me,' said the knight, 'the fact is that I know, and I shall take you to her, if you wish.'

'Take me, then,' said the youth.

'I shall not do so this evening,' said the knight, 'for we should not be there in daylight, but we shall go there in the morning. And if you dared, I should take you to see one of the most beautiful damsels you have ever seen: it is not far from here, and on the way to the damsel that you are seeking.'

'I should like that very much,' said the youth; 'take me there, then.'

'By my faith,' said the other, 'I will not take you there except on one condition.'

'What is that?' asked the youth.

'I shall tell you,' he said. 'The maiden is held captive in a small meadow in the middle of a lake, under a magnificent sycamore, which grows in the middle of the meadow. She sits there all day long on a cushion, all alone. In the evening, two fully armed knights come there, their helms laced on, and remove her from there and take her away with them; and every morning they bring her back to the lake. If she had two knights who would fight against those two, however, the maiden would be free, if her two knights could defeat the other two in battle. I would be one knight, if you would be the other.'

The youth replied that he would do so willingly, 'on condition that you give me your word that, in the morning, you will take me to where I can find the big knight who guards the damsel of the pavilion.'

'Since you are making a condition,' said the knight, 'I shall make one also: if we win the maiden who is in the lake, I wish her to be mine.'

'I agree,' said the youth.

'And I agree to your request also,' said the knight.

Then they rode together straight towards the lake. [171] Night was falling when they reached it. On the far side they saw two knights, who had already arrived, and the knight said to the youth:

'There they are, the two knights who mean to take away the damsel. Now take your shield and lance, lace on your helm and belt on your sword.'

The youth was so eager for the joust that he quite forgot about his shield, but one of his squires laced on his helm, and he took a lance. The two of them went to meet the two knights. They all rode fast on good horses, and struck one another great blows on the shields, those that had them. One of the knights who guarded the damsel struck the youth on the hauberk, so that he pierced it on the left shoulder, and thrust the whole lance-head into his shoulder. The youth also struck him, and knocked him to the ground, and the lance broke as he fell. Meanwhile the other two knights had knocked one another down. Then the youth dismounted, and when the knight who had brought him there saw that he had neither lance, sword, nor shield, he watched to see what he would do; and the youth went to him, and said:

'Give me your sword, for my squires are too far away.'

'Gladly,' said the knight.

He gave it to him, and the youth said:

'Now move back and leave them both to me.'

When the knight who had wounded him heard him say that they should both be left to him, he began to laugh. Then he went up to him, and said:

'Sir, I will certainly give you my sword as well, if you wish, and I will not fight with you any more today.'

'Nor will I, in truth,' said the other knight.

'By the Holy Cross,' said the youth, 'then you will give up the maiden.'

'We will give her up to you,' they both said, 'and do you know why? We can plainly see that you are extremely courageous, and may yet achieve great things, and you are so badly wounded that you may well die if you are hurt any more. That is why we have done you this kindness.'

'I do not care,' said the youth, 'why you have done it, as long as the maiden is released. Now give her to me, for I want her.'

'Gladly,' said the knights.

One of them drew out a key, threw it into the meadow, and said:

[172] 'Damsel, unlock that boat and come here, for this knight has won you.'

She unlocked the boat, which was chained at the edge of the meadow, and came over. The two knights who had been guarding her left and went about their business. Immediately, four squires arrived, with a pavilion loaded on a pack-horse, and pitched it nearby in a shady place. Then they prepared a copious meal. They were in the service of the knight who had brought the youth there. When the food was ready, they ate, and after the meal the maiden ordered the squires to make up three beds. The youth who had won her looked at her, and asked why she had ordered three beds to be made up.

'For you,' she said, 'and for this knight and for me.'

'For me?' he said; 'I shall sleep with you.'

'You will not.'

'Yes, I will.'

'Very well,' she said, 'if you wish.'

'Then I release you from that obligation,' he said.

Then they went to bed and slept until morning. In the morning, when they were up, the youth said to the knight:

'Sir, take me where you are supposed to take me.'

'Gladly,' said the knight, 'on condition that, if you win the damsel, she shall be mine.'

'Agreed,' the youth said.

They both mounted, and the maiden with them, and rode until they reached the block of stone.

'There is the pavilion,' the knight said to the youth, 'but you must do something which this damsel begs of you, as do I.'

'What is that?' he asked.

'Belt on your sword,' said the knight, 'and hang your shield around your neck; and you have a good lance which this damsel has given to one of your squires for you.'

'I will gladly take the shield', said the youth, 'and the lance, but I cannot, and should not, belt on the sword, until I am commanded otherwise.'[1]

'Then allow me', said the knight, 'to hang it from your saddle-bow, so that you may draw it, if need be, for you are dealing with a very fierce man.'

The knight and the maiden begged him until he agreed, and they hung [173] the sword from his saddle-bow. Then he took his shield and lance and went over to the pavilion, where he found the big knight, just as he had done the first time.

'I have come', he said, 'to ask you to show me the damsel, as you promised me yesterday.'

The other said that he would not see her without a fight.

'If I must fight,' said the youth, 'I shall do so, rather than not see her. Arm yourself quickly, for I have business elsewhere.'

Then the big knight stood up, and began to laugh at the youth saying that he should arm himself.

---

[1] i.e. by the queen.

'Fie!' he said, 'as if I should arm myself on your account!'

He leapt upon a horse which was nearby and took up a shield and a lance, and the youth did likewise. Then they rode together as fast as their horses would carry them, and struck one another great heavy blows on the shields. The big knight broke his lance, so that the splinters flew, and the youth struck him with such force that the leather of his shield tore and the planks were forced apart; the lance-head passed through, and struck the knight in the left side, breaking one of his ribs. And the blow was so violent that the reins snapped off in his hand, and the back of the saddle broke, and he was knocked to the ground with such force that he was quite stunned; as he fell, the lance broke. The knight passed out, for he was severely wounded, and the youth thought he was dead, which distressed him, because the knight was not armoured. He dismounted and watched to see what the knight would do. When he came round, he saw the blood which streamed from his body, and feared he was dying. He sat up, and the youth said to him:

'Now I will see the damsel.'

'Indeed, sir,' he said, 'I give her up to you. Cursed be the hour I ever saw her, for she has caused my death.'

So he gave the damsel up to him. Before the youth would let him go, however, he made him swear that he would never again fight with any knight, except in self-defence. Then the knight who had brought the youth there came up, and the damsel also, and they were quite taken aback at the remarkable things he had done. He went into the pavilion and took the damsel, who had just then risen, by the hand, and gave her to the knight.

'Here, sir knight,' he said, 'now you have two.'

'Sir,' the knight said, 'they cannot be mine, for they are too beautiful, and you have won them, not I, so they should be yours.'

'They certainly cannot be mine,' said the youth, 'for it was agreed that you should have them both.'

[174] 'Sir,' said the knight, 'since you do not want them, tell me what to do with them, for I will do as you wish.'

'Will you, now?' said the youth.

'Yes,' he said, 'I give you my word, faithfully.'

'Then take them', the youth said, 'to the court of my lord King Arthur, and tell my lady the queen that the youth who has gone to the aid of the Lady of Nohaut sends them to her. Tell her also that I send her word that, to win me to her for ever, she should make me a knight, and send me a sword so that I may be her knight, for my lord the king did not belt on my sword yesterday, when he made me a knight.'

When the knight heard that he was newly knighted, he was taken aback.

'Sir,' he said, 'where shall I find you on my return?'

'Come directly to Nohaut,' said the youth.

The knight then went off to court and delivered his message, and related to the queen the remarkable deeds he had seen the youth do. She was delighted, and sent him a very fine sword, with a rich scabbard and baldric. The knight took the sword, and rode until he came to Nohaut, for he knew the way well. When he drew near the town, he found the youth, who had not yet arrived, and gave him the sword on behalf of the queen.

'And she sends you word', he said, 'that you should belt it on.'

He did so willingly, and gave the knight the one which was hung from his saddle-bow, saying that now he was a knight, by the grace of God and of his lady. And it is for this reason that the story has called him 'the youth' until now.[1] The knight who had sought help at court for the Lady of Nohaut had already arrived, three days earlier, and he had sung the

---

[1] i.e. he was still a squire, his knighting incomplete.

new knight's praises to his lady to such an extent that she was awaiting him with great impatience, and did not wish anyone else to undertake her combat. When he arrived, he was welcomed by many people, for the knight who came with him went ahead to spread the word. The lady mounted, along with many of her followers, and went to meet him, and welcomed him as warmly as one can a stranger knight.

When he saw the lady, he was not at all disconcerted by her beauty, and did not pay much attention to it; yet she was extremely beautiful. However, not all beauty touched his heart,[1] and he only said:

'Madam, my lord King Arthur sends me to you to fight your battle, and I am ready to do so now, or whenever you please.'

'Sir,' she said, 'blessings on my lord the king, and welcome to you; I am very glad to receive you.'

Then she looked, and saw that his hauberk was damaged on the shoulder, where he [175] was wounded when he won the damsel at the lake. The wound had worsened considerably, for he had neglected it.

'Sir,' she said, 'you are wounded.'

'Madam,' he said, 'I have no wound bad enough to prevent me from doing you this service when you please, and I am quite prepared to do it now, or tomorrow.'

The lady had him disarmed and found the wound was very large and deep, and said:

'You are in no condition to fight, until you are healed, and I can certainly still have the combat postponed.'

'Madam,' he said, 'I have much more to do elsewhere than here, so haste is necessary, both for me and for you.'

However, she said that under no circumstances would she allow him to fight in that state, and sent for doctors for him and put him to bed in her chambers. There she kept him for a fortnight, until he was fully recovered.

---

[1] i.e. only that of the queen.

Within that fortnight, word reached King Arthur's court that the Lady of Nohaut was not yet free, and Kay the seneschal said to the king:

'Sire, did you think such a young man as that could perform such a task? Send me there, for one should send a man of valour on such business.'

And the king allowed him to go.

Sir Kay travelled until he reached Nohaut, and he sent a squire on ahead. The lady and her followers mounted, and went to meet him and received him warmly. The new knight was with them, now fully recovered.

'Madam,' Kay said, 'my lord the king sends me to you to fight your battle; and he would have sent me, or another man of valour, long since, but a newly made knight asked him for the task as a boon, and he granted it to him. When he heard that your affair had not been settled, though, he sent me to deal with it.'

'My lord,' said the lady, 'my thanks to my lord the king, to the knight he sent, and to you. My affair has not been neglected by the knight, though, for he wished to deal with it on the first day he was here, but I did not wish him to, because he was wounded; now he is recovered, and he will do it.'

'Madam,' said Kay, 'that is impossible. Since I have come here, I shall do it; otherwise I should be disgraced, and it would not be to the honour of my lord the king.'

When the lady heard this, she was very worried, and did not know what to do, for she dearly wanted the new knight to undertake the combat, [176] but she did not know what to do about the seneschal, because he had great influence over the king, whose vassal she was, and so could be of service or disservice to her. Then the new knight stepped forward and said to the seneschal:

'Indeed, Sir Kay, I would have done it the first day, had my lady wished it, and I am still ready, and I ask her not to allow someone else to do it, for I should, since I was here first.'

'My friend,' said Kay, 'that is impossible, now that I have come.'

'Truly,' the new knight said, 'it would be a great pity if my lady were to suffer because the better man did not do it.'

'That is true,' said Kay.

'Then we two shall fight one another,' said the new knight, 'and whoever wins will fight the battle.'

Kay said that he agreed.

'In God's name,' said the lady, 'that will never happen, please God, but I shall settle the matter in a way which is honourable for my lord the king, who sent you here, and for the two of you, for I can entrust my combat to a single knight, to two, or to as many as I wish. So, I shall send word to the King of Northumberland that two knights will fight for me.'

In this way the lady shrewdly appeased them.

In the morning, on one side the king and his followers came from the castle where they were lodged to an open space outside Nohaut, where the combat was to take place. On the other side the lady came with her two knights and her other followers. When the conditions had been repeated before her followers, everyone drew back. The four knights moved some distance apart, then each pair went towards the other. Sir Kay and his opponent struck one another on the shields, so that their lances flew in pieces, but neither of them fell, and they drew their swords and attacked each other. The new knight and his opponent met, and the Northumbrian knight struck him and made his shield hit him on the temple, and the lance flew in pieces. The new knight struck him below the shield-boss, so that he forced the shield against his arm and his arm against his body, and he hit him so violently that the reins snapped off in his hand and his spine struck the back of the saddle, and he knocked him over his horse's crupper to the ground. As he fell, the lance broke. However, he did not lie on the ground for long, but leapt quickly to his feet. The new knight called to Sir Kay:

'Sir Kay, come and take this one and leave that one to me.'

Kay did not answer him, but went on fighting fiercely with his opponent. Then the new knight drew back, [177] dismounted and went towards his opponent, sword in hand, and thrust his shield in front of his face. The other knight did the same, and they gave one another great blows, on shields and helms, arms and shoulders, wherever they could reach. They fought for a long time, until the other knight could no longer endure it, and gave ground more and more, and the new knight drove him backwards. The knight dodged as much as he could, but it did not help him at all, for the new knight pressed him hard. It was clear that he had much the worse of it and was greatly at a disadvantage. Meanwhile, Kay and his opponent had killed one another's horses, and were on foot. Again the new knight called:

'Come here, Sir Kay, for you can see how it is; and leave that one to me, for I have better things to do than to stay here all day.'

Kay was very ashamed, and said angrily:

'Sir, you take care of yours, and leave mine to me.'

Then the new knight again attacked his opponent, who would gladly have defended himself if he could, but his defence was of little use. When the new knight saw that he had so much the better of him, he pressed him less hard, for he did not want to shame Sir Kay, and he wished the fight to end peacefully.* Sir Kay, for his part, fought with his opponent until he got the better of him. The King of Northumberland saw that his men could no longer resist them, and he sent word to the lady to propose peace. He offered to go away, along with his men, and to leave her her land, free from obligation, and said that he would never again trouble her or her land. He guaranteed all this with an oath and with hostages, and that is how they made peace. The lady went to the two knights who were fighting for her, and said that peace had been made to her satisfaction, and she stopped the fighting. The King of Northumberland went away and took his men with him, and the lady was left in genuine peace.

In the morning, Sir Kay went back to court, and told the king how the affair had gone, and thanked him warmly on behalf of the Lady of Nohaut. The new knight remained at Nohaut, for the lady kept him there as long as she could. When she could not keep him any longer, she was very upset. He left on a Monday morning, and the lady herself accompanied him, with a large number of knights, and she insisted that she and her land were at his disposal. When she had accompanied him some way, the knight obliged her to return. When the others all returned, the knight who had brought him the sword from the queen did not go with them, [178] but accompanied him willingly, for he held him in great affection and esteem, and he said to him:

'Sir, I am entirely at your disposal, and I beg you, for the Lord's sake, not to be displeased by any wrong I may have done you.'

'By what wrong?' asked the knight.

'By the fact,' he said, 'that I took you to fight the two knights for the maiden at the lake, for I only did it to bring you honour, and I shall tell you how it was. My lady said that she would test the knight that the king sent to fight her battle, before she committed him to it. So she sent me out, and also, to fight with you, the two knights with whom we jousted. That is why they did not dare fight any more, when I gave you my sword, and you told me to leave them both to you, for they thought you were more badly hurt than you were.'

'And the big knight,' said the other, 'who was he?'

'Sir,' he said, 'he is a very valiant knight named Antoagais, and he offered to fight my lady's battle, provided that she grant him her love. She said that, if he were a better knight than the one sent by the king, she would grant him her love and entrust her battle to him. He desired my lady's love more than anything, and that is why he would not deign to fight you except without armour. Had he defeated you, he would have fought the battle. Now I have told you why these encounters were secretly arranged, and I beg you, for the Lord's sake, to forgive me this wrong.'

'Indeed,' he said, 'I see no wrong in that, and if there was any, I forgive you for it.'

'Thank you, sir,' he said. 'Rest assured that I am your knight at all times.'

He thanked him, and then they commended one another to God, and parted.

The new knight rode away with his squires, and decided that he would like to travel in complete secrecy, so that no one should recognize him, as he wished to win honour and renown. He entered a great forest, and rode all day without meeting any adventure worth mentioning. That night he slept in the forest in a religious house, where he was greatly honoured. In the morning he left his squires, ordering them to wait for him, and not to leave for a month if they did not see him. Then he left the house, which was at least thirty English leagues from Nohaut.

[179] In that house there was a tomb called Leucan's tomb. This Leucan was the nephew of Joseph of Arimathaea, from whom was descended the great lineage by which Britain was later enlightened, for they brought the Grail there and conquered the heathen land, and his body lay in the house of religion, as you have heard.

When the new knight had left the house, he rode as chance directed him, now this way, now that, until he was right out of the land of Nohaut. One day it happened that, having ridden until midday, he felt a great desire to drink. He rode towards a river, and when he reached it, he dismounted and drank, and then sat down beside the river and fell into a profound reverie. Then a fully armed knight came up on the other side of the water and rode headlong into the ford, so that he splashed water over the knight who was thinking, and made him all wet. He stopped thinking, and stood up and said to the knight:

'Sir knight, now you have made me wet, and you have caused me annoyance in another way, for you have interrupted my thoughts.'

'At the moment I am not in the least concerned', said the other, 'with you or your thoughts.'

Then the new knight mounted, for he wished to leave without a fight, to see if he could recapture his earlier sweet thoughts. He rode into the ford to cross over, and the knight said to him:

'You cross at your peril, sir knight, for my lady the queen has ordered me to guard this ford, and to prevent anyone from crossing it.'

The new knight asked which queen.

'The wife of King Arthur,' said the other.

When he heard that, he turned aside and began to ride upstream, but the knight went after him, and took hold of his bridle.

'Stop,' he said; 'you must give up this horse.'

'Why?' asked the new knight.

'Because,' he said, 'you started to cross the ford.'

The new knight took one foot out of the stirrup, but when the knight said nothing more, he looked at him and said:

'Tell me, who commands it?'

The other said that it was the queen. 'Do you say so honestly,' the new knight asked, 'as a true knight?' He replied that there was no command but his own. 'Yours!' the new knight said; 'by my head, you will not take away my horse today on your say-so.'

Yet still the other held his bridle.

[180] 'Let go of my bridle,' said the new knight.

'I will not,' said the other.

The new knight reached for his sword and drew it half-way out of the scabbard. The other let go and said:

'Truly, you will regret drawing your sword.'

Then he rode some distance away and took his shield by the straps,* tucked his lance under his arm, and galloped towards the new knight, who also covered himself with his shield, and rode to meet him. The knight who guarded the ford struck him, so that his lance flew into pieces, while the new knight struck him, and knocked him to the ground. He went over to the horse, caught it and brought it to him:

'Here is your horse,' he said, 'I am making amends for knocking you down, but I did it to defend myself.'

The other knight was very angry that he had knocked him down, for he did not know who he was. He mounted, and said to him:

'Knight, tell me who you are.'

'I will tell you no such thing,' he said, and went on upstream regardless. The other again took hold of his bridle, and said:

'Now I will learn who you are, before you escape me.'

'Not today, certainly,' he said.

'Then you must fight me,' said the other.

'I shall not fight with you any more today,' said the new knight, 'for you are very well protected, since my lady is your safeguard. A man of valour does not win renown in that way, though, bringing trouble and dishonour on knights errant while secure in the protection of noble ladies.'

He replied that it was not the queen's protection which made him want to fight, 'for,' he said, 'I am not really in her service. So you must fight me, or tell me your name.'

'If you give me your word,' said the new knight, 'that you are not in her service, I shall do one of those two things.'

He gave his word.

'Then you shall have your fight,' said the new knight, 'if you wish, for you will not learn who I am.'

He said that he wished for nothing better. Then, still on horseback, they attacked one another very fiercely with their swords. The other knight was very valorous, and his name was Alybon, son of the vavasour of the Queen's Ford. The ford took its name from the fact that the queen found it before anyone else, in the first two years after King Arthur married her. When the seven kings attacked Arthur in camp at dawn, by the Humber where he was encamped, when all [181] were routed and each man fled where he could, that is where the king rallied, with Sir Gawain, King Urien and his brother King Lot, and Sir Yvain, who was still a young knight of little renown, and also Sir Kay, who that day performed the great act of valour because of which he was held in high esteem, and called seneschal before he actually was. They had the good fortune to come there to the ford, and the queen, who was fleeing, had crossed over, when Kay said that he would run no further until he saw what he was running from. Then they saw the seven kings come galloping, two bowshots ahead of all their men, who were intent on the great booty in the tents. King Urien said that they should cross over the ford, for once on the other side they would have nothing to fear. Then Kay said, a curse on anyone who crossed the water, whoever he might be, before he had jousted with a king. 'They are only', he said, 'as many as we.' King Urien said: 'But Kay, they are seven and we are six.' 'I do not care,' Kay replied, 'for I shall kill two myself. Let each of you take heed what he will do.' He spoke the truth, for he killed one with his lance and another with his sword, and each of the others killed one. That was the most glorious adventure which ever befell King Arthur.

That was the adventure of the ford, but now we shall tell you about the two knights who were fighting. The combat had lasted so long that they had given one another many wounds, but in the end Alybon could stand no more. When he saw that there was no help for it, he said that he would not fight any longer. His opponent said that he would not get away so easily.

'Why not?' he asked; 'we are not fighting over any quarrel; and if we have a quarrel, I give you best.'

'We have a quarrel,' said the new knight, 'because you made me wet, and caused me dishonour.'

'I will make amends,' said the other, 'according to your wishes.'

'Then I forgive you,' he said.

'Thank you,' said Alybon; 'but now, please tell me your name.' However, the other knight said that he would not tell him. 'Then I would ask you', Alybon said, 'not to be upset if I go somewhere where someone will tell me.'

He replied that he was happy for him to go wherever he pleased, and with that they parted. The knight who had kept the ford went directly to King Arthur's court, where he was well known. There he went straight to the queen, and said:

'My lady, I have come a long way to ask you to tell me, if you [182] know, the name of the knight who has white armour and rides a white horse.'

'Why do you ask,' said the queen, 'as God is your witness, and by the person you most love?'

'My lady,' he replied, 'because I wish to thank you on account of him.'

'And why is that?' asked the queen.

He told her what had happened, and all that was said. 'And I think, my lady,' he said, 'that if I had told him that you ordered it, he would have given me his horse.'

'He would have been very foolish', she said, 'to have given you his horse because of a lie, for I never told you to guard the ford.'

'My lady,' he said, 'that is not all he did, for he returned my horse to me when he had knocked me down, and I had you to thank for that, and then afterwards we fought together for a long time.'

'Which of you had the worst of it?' asked the queen.

'Indeed, my lady,' he replied, 'I did: I have no wish to lie about it. But now tell me who he is.'

'As God is my witness,' she said, 'I do not know his name or where he is from, but my lord the king made him a knight at the feast of Saint John, and he has since done numerous deeds of arms in many places, seen by people from this court and by others. But, for the Lord's sake, tell me if he is fit and well.'

'Yes, my lady,' he said, 'perfectly.'

The news spread until it was all over the court, and the king was delighted, as were most of those who heard it. The story says no more about the king or the queen at this point, returning instead to the knight in the white armour, who was riding on his way.

[M. XXVIa] When the White Knight parted from Alybon, the vavasour's son, he rode all day without meeting any adventure worth mentioning. He slept the night in the house of a forester, who gave him good lodging. In the morning he rose early and rode through the morning until about terce. Then he met a damsel on a palfrey, lamenting dreadfully. He asked her what was the matter, and she said that she was more sorrowful than she had ever been. He asked her why.

'They have just killed my lover,' she said, 'one of the fairest knights in the world, in a castle back there.'

'Damsel,' he said, 'why?'

'Sir,' she replied, 'because of the evil customs of the place. Cursed be the soul of the man who established them, for no knight errant ever entered the castle who did not die there.'

[183] 'Will any knight ever enter there,' he asked, 'and survive?'

'Yes,' she replied, 'if he can meet the demands of the adventure, but he would have to be a better knight than any yet living.'

'Damsel,' he said, 'what are the demands of the adventure? Tell me.'

'If you with to know,' she said, 'then go there, for this is the way.'

With that she rode swiftly away, sorrowing as before. The knight rode, following the tracks, until he saw the castle. Then he rode straight there; and when he was opposite the gate, he looked at the castle, and saw that it was proudly and splendidly situated, for the whole fortress sat high on natural rock. It was by no means small, for it stretched more than a crossbowshot in every direction. At the foot of the rock, on one side, ran the Humber; and on the other side ran a great stream which came from more than forty springs, which all welled up within a bowshot of the foot of the rock. The knight rode up the slope, straight to the castle gate, and when he came near he saw it was closed and fastened securely; and indeed, that gate was never left open. The castle was called the Dolorous Guard, because every knight errant who ever went there was either killed, or at the very least was impris-oned there as soon as he was defeated; and all who went there were defeated, for no one could endure the necessary amount of fighting: there were two walls, with a gate in each wall, and at each gate the knight errant would have to fight ten knights. However, the fight was strangely organized, for as soon as one knight was tired, and did not wish to fight any longer, then another would be ready to take his place and fight instead of him. Then, when that one was tired, another would come. Thus a single knight could not defeat them all, unless he was so valiant and so fortunate that he was able to kill them all, one after the other. High on the second wall, right above the gate, there was a mounted knight made of copper, big and sturdy, in full armour and holding a great axe in his hands. He had been set up there by enchantment, and as long as he remained standing, the castle was in no danger of being conquered by any man. As soon as the man who was to conquer the castle entered the first gate, however, and could see him, the copper knight would immediately crash to the ground. Then all the enchantments of the castle, which was full of them, would come to an end, so that they would be clearly visible. Yet they would not be entirely ended until the man who conquered the castle [184] stayed there for forty days, without spending a single night outside. Such was the strength of the enchantments of the castle. Below the castle was a very pleasant town, where a knight errant could find everything he might need. The town was called Chaneviere, and was situated right on the river Humber.

When the knight in white armour came to the gate and saw it was closed, he was very upset. Then a very beautiful damsel came towards him; she greeted him, and he her.

'Damsel,' he said, 'can you tell me anything about the conditions* of the castle?'

The damsel was well veiled, for if her face had been visible, he would certainly have recognized her. She told him all about the conditions, and how he would have to fight, and against what odds, if he wished to enter the castle. 'But if you take my advice,' she said, 'you will not even think of going in there.'

'Damsel,' he said, 'I will not let the matter rest there; either I shall find out what goes on inside, or I shall be put with the other men of worth who have been killed there, for I could well have a less glorious life.'

Thereupon the damsel left. It was already late, going on towards evening. At that moment the knight heard a man up above the gate, who asked him:

'Sir knight, what do you want?'

'I should like', he replied, 'to come inside.'

'Indeed,' said the man on guard, 'you will surely regret it if you enter.'

'I would not know,' he said, 'but for the Lord's sake, good friend, hurry the business up, for it will soon be night.'

Then the other sounded a hunting-horn, and shortly afterwards a knight came out through the wicket in the gate; he was fully armoured, and his horse was led after him. He said to the new knight:

'Sir knight, you must go down there, for there is not enough room here for us to fight freely.'

He replied that that suited him well.

Then they went down to the foot of the hill, and rode some distance apart, then tucked their lances under their arms, thrust their elbows against their shields,[1] and rode together as fast as their horses could go, and struck one another on the shields, the hardest blows they could manage. The knight from the castle broke his lance, and the knight with the white shield struck him high on the shield-boss, so that he cut through the leather and split the planks apart. The lance-head was sharp, and the blow heavy, so that [185] the hauberk could not withstand it, as it was struck with great force, and the links gave. The point passed through the knight's body, and he flew out of the saddle and fell to the ground; he did not get up, for he was dead. When the White Knight saw him on the ground, he dismounted, for he did not realize he was dead, and he went with drawn sword to attack him. When he saw the knight was not getting up again, he wrenched the helm from his head. And he was extremely put out when he saw that he was dead.

Then the horn sounded, and another knight came rushing out. When the other saw him come, he remounted and took up his lance again, pulling it from the dead knight's body. Then they galloped towards one another as fast as their

---

[1] i.e. took a firm grip.

horses could go. The knight from the castle missed, while
the White Knight struck him a blow his shield could not
withstand, though his hauberk remained intact. The White
Knight, who had great strength and greater courage, struck
him well and hurled him out of the saddle and over his
horse's crupper to the ground. He broke his right arm in the
fall, and passed out. The knight who had knocked him down
dismounted again, and immediately wrenched the helm from
his head. When the other knight came to, he threatened to
cut his head off unless he swore to be his prisoner.* Then
the horn was sounded again, and another fully armed knight
came down the hill. The White Knight hurried to make his
opponent yield, pressing him so closely that, afraid he would
be killed, he swore to be his prisoner. Then he leapt back on
to his horse and took up his lance again, which was still stuck
in the knight's shield, and rode to meet the newcomer. He
knocked him violently to the ground also, and his lance broke.
The knight did not stay on the ground for long, but sprang
up. The White Knight dismounted again and put his shield
in front of him, and attacked the other boldly, sword in hand,
and they gave one another great blows wherever they thought
it would cause injury. The knight from the castle could not
endure it for long, though, and began to give ground. And
when he saw that he was having the worst of it, he signalled
with his sword to the watchman, who blew the horn again.

Then another knight came rushing out; he looked big and
robust, and a capable fighter. However, the White Knight did
not leave his opponent because of this, but attacked him and
gave him many wounds. His opponent defended himself as
well as he could, but made no effort to do more than that.
The knight who was coming to the rescue called:

'Leave him, sir knight, for I am coming in his place.'

'I do not care,' he said, 'how many of you there are, as long
as I can defeat you all.'

'You have no right to go on attacking him,' said the other knight, 'for I have come to protect him.'

[186] 'And how will you protect him,' said the White Knight, 'when you cannot even protect yourself?'

Then he took the lance of the knight with whom he had just fought, and leapt on to his horse. He charged towards the newcomer, and struck him with all his might, so hard that he knocked him and his horse into the middle of the stream from a spring. Then he went back to the first knight, whom that one was rescuing, and who was already trying to remount his horse. He went over to him, and struck him with his horse's chest, so that he knocked him back down to the ground, then rode over him until he was quite battered, and unable to get up. Then he looked, and saw the knight lying in the stream, who was already getting up again. He went towards him, sword in hand, and struck him without slowing down, so that he completely stunned him and knocked him down again in a daze, and rode his horse over him also, as much as he had the other, so that he badly injured him and he passed out from the pain. Then he went back to the first knight, dismounted, and unlaced the other's headgear and removed both his helm and coif, so that he swore to be his prisoner.* At once the horn was sounded, and out came a fifth knight. When the White Knight saw him, he again attacked the knight lying in the stream, wrenched the helm from his head also, and gave him a great blow with the flat of his sword, so that, before the other knight arrived, he had sworn to be his prisoner.

When he saw that he had already defeated four, he cared little for the rest. He went to his horse, remounted, and attacked the knight with drawn sword, for he had no lance. The other splintered his lance against him, without slowing down. The White Knight rode up to him, and gave him such a blow with his sword, with all his anger and strength behind it, that he sheared through the helm and the coif beside the left temple, so that the steel struck above the knight's ear and cut right through it and his cheek, down to his neck. The blow cut into his neck, so that he had great difficulty in holding up his helm, and so stunned him that he could not stay in the saddle, and fell to the ground in a daze. As he fell, the point of his helm embedded itself in the ground, so that his neck was nearly broken. The force of the fall brought blood bursting from his mouth, nose, and ears, and he passed out. Then it began to grow very dark, so that the people on the walls could see little of how they were faring down below. At that point they shut the wicket-gate, and the townspeople who were on the walls said that they had never seen such a nimble and confident knight. Meanwhile, he had managed to defeat the fifth knight, who swore to go as his prisoner wherever he wished. Then the damsel who had spoken to him in front of the gate arrived, and said to him:

[187] 'Come with me, sir knight, for you will do no more fighting tonight.'

'Damsel,' he said, 'there are still many to defeat.'

'That is true,' she said, 'but no more will come out today, for the wicket-gate is closed. However, you can be here in good time in the morning.'

'I am sorry, damsel,' he said, 'that no more will come out, for whatever happens, I should have less left to do if I had dealt with more. You certainly know whether they are treating me correctly, so tell me.'

'Yes, rest assured that they are,' she said, 'for the fighting must not continue once night falls. In the morning, though, you will be able to begin again;* and were it not for the fact that a knight who comes here to fight must not be kept waiting, there would have been no blow struck this evening, for it was very late. You should welcome this break, for you are very tired.'

'Tired!' he said. 'Damsel, you would see if I am tired, if it were daylight.'

He was very ashamed and upset, for he was afraid she had seen him acquit himself badly in some way.

'Come with me,' she said.

'Damsel,' he said, 'where to?'

'To a place where I shall give you good lodging,' she said.

Then he told the knights that he had defeated to follow him, which they did, for they all had the horses from which they had fallen.

The damsel led the knight down into the town, to a very fine lodging; and he had great need of it. When they were in the lodging, the damsel, who was still veiled, took him into a chamber to disarm. He looked, and saw three shields hanging up in the chamber, all with their covers still on them. He asked the damsel to whom the shields belonged, and she said that they belonged to a knight of hers.

'Damsel,' he said, 'I should very much like to see them uncovered, if you would not mind.'

She had them uncovered, and he saw that they were all three white, and on the first there was one diagonal red band,* on the second, there were two, and on the third, three. He looked at the shields for a long time. While he was looking at them, the damsel came out of another chamber, richly attired. Her face was uncovered, and there were a great many lights in the room.

'Sir knight,' she said, 'what do you think of the shields?'

'Damsel,' he replied, 'they are very fine.'

Then he looked at her; and when he saw her unveiled, he recognized her at once. He went to her with open arms, and said:

'Ah! dear damsel, I am pleased to see you, more than [188] any other damsel; but, for the Lord's sake, tell me, how is my good lady?'

'Very well,' she said. Then she drew him to one side, and told him that her mistress, the Lady of the Lake, had sent her to him. 'And tomorrow', she said, 'you will learn your name and the name of your father. That will happen up there in the castle, of which you will be lord before vespers are rung: I have it for a fact from the mouth of my lady herself. And the three shields you have seen are yours, and you should know that they are quite extraordinary, for as soon as you hang the shield with a single band around your neck, you will acquire the strength and prowess of another knight, in addition to your own. If you put on the shield with two bands, you will have the prowess of two knights; and from the one with three bands you will acquire the prowess of three knights. I shall have them brought to the battleground tomorrow. Now, take care that you do not rely too much on your youth, but as soon as you feel your strength waning, take the shield with the single band, and then, if you feel the need, the one with two bands. But when you wish to make havoc of all things, and to astonish the whole world, then take the one with three bands, for then you will see the most manifest wonders that you ever heard of, wonders beyond your imagination. But take good care that you do not remain in the service of King Arthur, or of anyone else, until you are known for your prowess in many lands: that is what my lady wishes you to do, so that you improve yourself and rise to greater heights.'

The damsel spoke with him for a long time, and they sat down to a meal when it was ready. That night, those up in the castle and those down in the town were anxious to see the knight, and they all prayed to Our Lord to give him strength and might to defeat all the knights as he had defeated those five, for they all fervently wished the enchantments and the evil customs of the castle to cease for ever. They spent the night in that way, and in the morning the damsel told the knight to hear mass, and then he armed himself. When he was armed, the damsel led him up to the outer gate, and said to him:

'Do you know what you have to do, if you wish to win the

lordship of this castle, and to put an end to the enchantments? Before nightfall, you must defeat ten knights at this first gate, and ten at the second.'

'What?' he said: 'have I not already defeated five knights at the first gate?'

'No,' she replied, 'for nothing which you have done there will help you, any more than if you had never struck a blow. Even if you had defeated [189] nine of the knights at one of the gates, and the time was up, you would have to begin all over again, for you must defeat them all before nightfall. And you can be sure that you will defeat them all. I can assure you of another thing, besides, which is that you will never die in battle while you have a helm on your head and a hauberk on your back. That is something which should reassure you greatly.'

'Indeed,' he said, 'then I am sure that I shall not die shamefully.'

While they were talking like this, the horn sounded, and a knight came out, in full armour except for his helm, and said to the White Knight:

'Sir knight, what do you want?'

He replied that he wanted to attempt the adventure of the castle.

'You will find no one', said the knight, 'to respond to that request, as long as you hold our knights captive, but as soon as you return them, you can attempt the adventure at once.'

'The knights', he said, 'will not prevent me from trying the adventure again,* but take care that you do not wrongfully make me return them, for that would be underhand.'

The other said:

'Sir knight, rest assured that you are obliged to return them, but they must not bear arms against you. If you wish, you may make them swear it, and I advise you to do so. Let me say, too, that I hope you are valorous enough to conquer the castle, for this misery has lasted long enough. However, I must keep faith and do what is required by my fief.'

Then the White Knight released the four knights, and they went into the castle. Then straightaway out came a fully armed knight, and once he was outside the wicket-gate, he leapt on to his horse, which had been led out. Then the two knights went down to the foot of the hill and began to joust, as near the gate as they could. The knight from the castle struck the other on the shield with all his might, so that it banged against his temple; but the lance did not break, for it was very strong. The White Knight also struck him, and wounded him in the arm, through his shield and the sleeve of his hauberk, and thrust his shield against his side so hard that his spine was bent against the saddle, and he knocked him over his horse's crupper to the ground; he was badly hurt by the force of the fall. The White Knight dismounted; but as he was about to attack the other, he saw as many as nine knights come out of the first gate and down the slope. One knight [190] left the others and rode down to the battle-ground, where he stopped a little way off. When the White Knight saw him, he feared some treachery. He leapt back on to his horse and took his lance, then rode towards the knight he saw coming, and struck him very violently, and the knight him, so that their lances flew into pieces, but neither of them fell. When the White Knight saw the other had not fallen, and that both lances were shattered, he was furious, and cursed all lance-makers, for not making lances so that they could not be broken. Then he reached for his sword. Meanwhile the first knight was on his feet again, but had lost his horse, and he had thrown down his shield because his arm could not hold it up, and was making for the rock as quickly as he could. The White Knight rode after him as fast as his horse could go. When the knight heard him coming, he looked round and tried to draw his sword, but he did not have time, for the White Knight went over to him, and gave

him such a blow on top of the helm that he sent him
staggering, and he nearly fell. The White Knight rushed on
past, then came back towards him, just as he had drawn his
sword, and gave him such a blow on the right arm, before he
could defend himself, that he crippled him, and his sword
dropped in the middle of the field.

'What, sir knight,' said the other knight, who came galloping up, 'do you mean to fight us both?'

'Yes,' he said, 'and a third, if he comes, as willingly as two.'

'By my faith,' said the other, 'we should not dare to strike
you both at once except with your permission.'

'Since you are here', he said, 'to help one another, go on
and help each other as best you can. It does not worry me if
there are two of you, any more than one, nor would three
worry me any more than two, since I shall defeat the larger
number just as I should the smaller.'

When the knight heard that, he was greatly dismayed, and
he realized that the other was extremely courageous. Then
they came together, with drawn swords, and gave one another
great blows on the helm. When the White Knight saw the
knight he had wounded in both arms going away again, he
charged over to him once more, and wrenched his helm from
his head. The other tried to flee up the hill, and the White
Knight went back to him, and struck him furiously on the
coif, so that he clove him to the shoulders, and he fell. The
second knight came up with him, and gave him a great blow
on the helm, which bent him forwards; as he rode past, the
White Knight struck backhand with his sword, and chanced
to hit the nosepiece of his helm, cutting right through it to
his cheeks. The force of the blow bent him backward over
the back of the saddle, and he passed out. The White Knight
went back to him, and [191] wrenched the helm from his
head also, and cried to him to swear to be his prisoner, but
he could not answer. The White Knight struck him again

with his sword, in the mouth, which was quite unprotected and covered in blood, and clove him right back to the ears, and said, might God never be his witness if he went on feeling sorry about killing them, since he could not defeat them in any other way. The knight fell to the ground. Then the other knights saw clearly that he was dead, and one of them left the others, who had already reached the bottom of the hill. He shattered his lance on the White Knight, and when that failed him, he drew his sword and gave him great blows wherever he could. The White Knight in turn attacked him so fiercely that everyone was taken aback, and in a short time he reduced him to such a state that he could no longer endure it and called another knight. Another came, and the knight who could no longer endure the fighting fled into the castle, while the other, quite fresh, took his place.

They pressed the White Knight in this way until prime was long past, and it might have been after terce. Then a squire arrived, carrying around his neck a white shield with a diagonal red band. The White Knight's shield was already in such a state that there was very little of it left, and he himself was short of breath, and weakening, and he had lost a good deal of blood, for he was wounded in several places. He had inflicted many wounds and injuries on his opponents, too, but each one would flee into the castle and a fresh knight would come in his place.

When the White Knight saw that he could not make an end of the matter in this way, he was very annoyed that it was taking so long to win the great honour he expected. Then he threw down what little was left of his shield, and seized the one which the squire had brought. Then he felt his strength doubled, and was so sprightly and nimble that he felt no ill-effect from any blow or wound that he had received. At once he charged them all, and struck out to right and left, and did such remarkable deeds that everyone who saw it was taken aback. He split their helms, he laid open their shields, he broke their hauberks on the arms and shoulders. And they often wounded him, for as soon as one could no longer stand the fray, another came in his place, which caused him great distress. He kept up the fight in this way until after terce, and they gave him many wounds, great and small. Then the damsel who had brought him to the gate came, and with her the squire who had brought the shield, and he was carrying the one with two bands. The knight had already pressed his opponents so hard that they had started up the hill and were going towards the gate, so as to have their help nearer at hand. The people of the castle watched from the walls as the knight [192] drove them all back by himself, and they were all dumbfounded, and prayed that God would sustain him in what he had begun.

The defenders avoided his blows until they came to the gate, and then they all attacked him again. And their help came quickly and often, so that he could not make an end of the matter. Then the damsel took hold of his bridle and took the shield from around his neck herself, and put the one with two bands there. The knights wondered why she did it, and they would have been pleased if he had not come back, for they were very ashamed to be fighting a single knight, who had pressed them so hard. Then he returned to the fray, and reduced them in a short time to such a state that none of them dared meet a blow from him, even the freshest of them avoiding his blows. And there was not a knight from the castle who had been in the fight who had not felt his blows, and they all said that they had never seen a knight of his strength. More than all the others, though, the lord of the castle* was taken aback by it; he was watching them from his position up on the wall, and was so grieved that he was nearly distracted at not being in the fray. He could not be there, though, and was not supposed to, according to the customs of the castle, until all the others were defeated. And he was very much afraid that he would see his great sorrow,* which he had never thought any single knight could achieve.

The White Knight drove them back ignominiously, and they saw clearly that they could not resist him, whatever changes they made, for he pressed them so closely that those who were tired were not able to go in at the wicket-gate, nor those inside to come out. In a short time he had so exerted himself* that he had reduced five of them to such a state that none of them was able to get up, for two were dead, and three lay mortally wounded, besides the two he had killed at the outset. When he saw that there were only three left, they did not worry him at all. Then he attacked them very fiercely, and they gave ground to him, and fled as best they could, avoiding his blows. Then the biggest and most robust of the three came forward, and said that he would not get himself killed, for much more valorous men than he had lost their lives there, and he gave him his sword, and swore to be his prisoner. And when the other two saw that, they did the same.

Then the White Knight listened, and heard a great crash. He looked up, and saw that it was the gate opening. He was delighted, for he had never thought to see it. By now it was nearly none. When he went up the hill, he saw, through the gate, the ten knights of the second gate all bunched in front of the wicket-gate. Then [193] the damsel who had brought the shields stopped him, and unlaced his helm herself, for it was no longer of any use. She gave it to her squire and took another which she was holding, very fine and good, and laced it on for him. Then she took the shield from around his neck and put the one with the three bands there. And he said:

'Ha! damsel, you have disgraced me, for you would have me defeat them without any of my own prowess. There was plenty left of the one which you have taken.'

'Do not worry,' she said, 'for I wish the second gate to be conquered more gloriously than this one.'

Then the squire gave him a lance with a remarkably strong shaft and a head as sharp as a scythe. And the damsel told him she wanted to see how he could joust again, for she knew well enough how he could use his sword. The knight took the lance and went in through the gate. The damsel told him to look up above the second gate; and he looked, and saw the copper knight, big and strange. And as soon as he saw him, the copper knight fell from his high position, and landed on one of the knights who were below the gate, breaking his neck and knocking him from his horse, dead. The White Knight, however, was not at all disconcerted, but charged the whole band; and he hit one man, striking him so hard that he hurled him down dead. When the others saw those two dead, and that the copper knight had collapsed, they did not see what they could rely on, and they leapt off their horses and went in through the wicket-gate as quickly as they could. The White Knight sprang down, and drew his sword, with which he gave them great blows wherever he could reach; and he managed to make the last three, who could not go through in time, swear to be his prisoners. He went through the wicket-gate after the other five, but he did not catch any of them. Then he met a number of ladies and damsels and townspeople, who greeted him very warmly and said:

'Sir, you need do no more than you have done, since they have given up the gate to you.'

Then a damsel brought the keys, and they opened the gate for him at once. And it let out such a shriek that the knight was quite astonished. He asked those around him whether he had to do anything else which was part of the adventure. The townspeople, who were impatient to be free, replied that he had still to fight with the lord of the castle, before he took off his helm or any of his armour.

'I am quite ready to do that,' he said. 'Where can I find him?'

[194] 'My lord,' said a youth who was there, 'you have

missed the lord, for he is going away as fast as his horse will carry him, grieving so bitterly that he is nearly overcome.'

Everyone in the castle was very distressed by this news. They led the knight to a very strange cemetery, which was between the two walls. He was amazed when he saw it, for it was enclosed on all sides by closely crenellated walls, and on many of the battlements there were knights' heads in their helms, and next to each battlement was a tomb, on which there was writing which said: 'Here lies such-and-such a man, and there is his head.' However, it did not say that next to the battlements where there were no heads; instead the writing said: 'Here will lie such-and-such a man.' The names of many good knights from King Arthur's land were there, and from other places, some of the best knights known. In the middle of the cemetery there was a great slab of metal, wonderfully worked with gold and precious stones and enamel. There was writing on it, which said: 'This slab will never be raised by the hand or efforts of any man, except the man who will capture this dolorous castle, and the name of that man is written underneath here.'

Many people had tried, both by force and by craft, to raise that tombstone, to find out the name of the good knight. The lord of the castle had often made great efforts to find out who the knight was, for he would have had him killed, if he could. Then they led the knight to the slab, just as he was, in full armour, and showed him the writing, which he was well able to read, as he had spent much time learning. When he had read it, he looked the slab up and down, and saw that if it had been in the middle of a road, completely unencumbered, four of the strongest knights in the world would still have had difficulty in lifting the smaller of the two ends. Then he took hold of it with both hands by the larger end, and raised it until it was at least a foot higher than his head. Then he saw the writing which said: 'Here will lie Lancelot of the Lake, the son of King Ban of Benwick.' Then he lowered the slab

again, and he knew that it was his name which he had seen.
Then he looked, and saw the damsel who served his lady,
who had seen the name as well as he had.

'What did you see?' she asked.

'Nothing.'

'Yes, you did,' she said; 'tell me.'

'Ha!' he said, 'by the Lord's mercy.'[1]

'For the Lord's sake,' she said, 'I saw it as well as you did.'

[195] Then she whispered it in his ear. And he was very
upset, and begged and adjured her by everything he could
not to speak of it to anyone.

'I shall not,' she said; 'do not worry.'

Then the people of the castle led him to one of the most
beautiful halls* in the world, though it was small; and they
disarmed him and treated him with great honour. The hall
belonged to the lord of the castle, and was rich in all the
things which the court of a noble man should have.

Thus the White Knight conquered the Dolorous Guard.
And the damsel was with him, and made him stay there to
recover from his wounds and injuries, which were numerous.
The people of the castle, though, were very unhappy that
their lord had escaped, for if he had been captured, he would
have revealed all the conditions of the castle. Now, they
feared these would never be known, for they were afraid that
they would not be able to keep this knight there for forty
days; for if he stayed there, then all the enchantments and
marvels, which occurred day and night, would come to an
end, for as it was no one there could eat or drink in safety,
nor go to bed or get up. So they were happy and unhappy in
the town, and they gave their new lord as warm a welcome as
they ought. The story says no more about him at this point,
though, but takes another direction, as you will hear.

[M. XXVa] When the White Knight conquered the Dolo-

---

[1] i.e. do not ask me to tell you.

rous Guard and raised the slab, there was a youth in the place, of noble birth, very valorous and sprightly, who was a brother of a knight of King Arthur's household, whose name was Aiglin of the Valleys. The youth was sure that if the news were known at court, it would be keenly received, for no one thought that any knight could do it.[1] He mounted a huge hunter, and left the castle between none and vespers to take the news to court, for he had seen what the knight had done, that day and the previous evening, and what arms he bore.* He spent that night as far on his way as he could. The next day he set off very early, and journeyed until he arrived, on the third day, at Caerleon. That day, before he reached there, he met Alybon, the son of the vavasour of the Queen's Ford. Alybon asked him:

'Young man, where are you going so fast? Do you have some urgent business?'

'Yes,' he said; 'I am going to King Arthur's court, with extraordinary news.'

'What news?' asked the knight.

'The Dolorous Guard has been conquered.'

[196] 'That is a lie,' Alybon said; 'it is impossible.'

'No, it is true,' the youth said, 'for I saw him with my own eyes go through the two gates and defeat all the knights.'

'What arms did he have?' the knight asked.

'He bears white arms,' the youth said, 'and he had a white horse.'

'Oho!' said Alybon; 'young man, take this news to court, for you will find many who will rejoice over it.'

The youth arrived at court, and when he saw the king, he said:

'King Arthur, God save you. I bring the most extraordinary news ever to come under your roof.'

'Tell me the news, then,' said the king, 'for it should certainly be heard, if it is so extraordinary.'

[1] i.e. capture the Dolorous Guard.

'I tell you', the youth said, 'that the Dolorous Guard has been conquered, and a knight has gone in through the two gates by force of arms.'

'That is impossible,' everyone said.

'It is true,' the youth said, 'for I saw him with my own eyes go in there and defeat the knights.'

'Young man,' the king said, 'do not say it if it is not true.'

'My lord,' he said, 'if I am lying to you about it, then hang me.'

Then his brother Aiglin came in, having come from his lodgings; and when he saw him kneeling before the king, he said:

'Dear brother, welcome. What business brings you to court?'

And he sprang up, and told him the news.

'What?' said the king; 'Aiglin, is he your brother, then?'*

'Yes, indeed, sire,' he said.

'Then he is certainly to be believed,' said the king, 'for he would not lie.'

'By my faith,' said Aiglin, 'he would not dare lie. But it is such a remarkable thing that I myself should hesitate to believe it unless I had seen it.'

Then he asked the youth what arms the knight had; and he said, white arms, and a white horse. Then Sir Gawain said that it was the new knight. Then a great many of the knights said that they would go and see if it was true, and they prepared to arm. Sir Gawain, though, said that it was not a good idea for so many to go, and only ten should go. The king himself and all the others agreed with this, and the king selected the ten who [197] were to go. Sir Gawain was the first of these ten, and Sir Yvain the second, and Galegantin the Welshman the third, and Galescondet the fourth, and Tor, the son of Ares, the fifth, and Caradoc Shortarm the sixth, Yvain the Bastard* the seventh, Gasoain of Estrangot the eighth, the Gay Galantin the ninth, and Aiglin of the

Valleys the tenth. With that company, Sir Gawain left Caerleon, and they spent that night with a hermit who had been
in King Arthur's household when he was newly crowned, and
he gave them good lodging because they were part of the
king's household. After they had eaten, the hermit said to Sir
Gawain:

'Sir, where are you going?'

And he said: 'To the Dolorous Guard.'

'Sir,' he said, 'what for?'

'We have been told', Sir Gawain said, 'that a knight has
gone in there by force of arms.'

'That is impossible,' the hermit said.

'It is true,' said the youth, 'for I saw him go in there with
my own eyes.'

'Let me tell you', said the hermit, 'that if all the world were
to go there, no one could go in there until one man has been
in, and that man will be the son of the king who died of grief:
that is what the old men say.'

They spent the night there, and in the morning they left
after mass and travelled for three days. On the fourth day, at
about terce, they met a man on the road, riding a little mule,
and wearing a blue cape. Sir Gawain greeted him, and said:

'Sir, what kind of man are you?'

'Sir,' he said, 'I am a monk.'

'Can you read?' Sir Gawain asked.

'Yes, sir,' he said, 'by the grace of God.'

'And do you know the way to the Dolorous Guard?'

'Yes, sir, very well. Why do you ask?'

'Because', he said, 'you must accompany us there.'

'Accompany you, sir?' he said; 'and who are you?'

'I am a knight,' he said.

'And what is your name, sir?' he asked.

'My name is Gawain.'

'Ha! sir, is that who you are? I shall gladly go with you, but
I do not know why you are going there.'

'We have been told', Sir Gawain said, 'that a knight has conquered it.'

[198] 'Indeed, sir,' the clerk* said, 'I know nothing of that, but it is hard to believe.'

They travelled until they reached the castle hill. When they went up it, they found the first gate open; and Aiglin's brother said to Sir Gawain:

'See, my lord. You never saw the gate open before.'

They went in and found the second gate closed. They saw a man above the gate, and Sir Gawain said to him:

'Sir, can we come in?'

And he replied that they could not. 'But tell me who you are.'

'I am Gawain,' he said, 'the nephew of King Arthur, and these others are companions of the Round Table.'

'My lord,' the man said, 'go now and find lodging down there in the town for tonight; and in the morning, come back here.'

They went and lodged down in the town. The news reached the White Knight that Sir Gawain had been at the gate, with nine companions; and he ordered that the gate should not be opened to anyone, that night or the next day. And the people of the castle, who would have liked King Arthur to come with all his power to put an end to the evil customs, went to the cemetery and put writing on some of the tombs where there had never been any before, and on the battlement opposite each tomb they put a helm.

In the morning Sir Gawain came back with his company. When he reached the gate, he found it still closed, as he had when he arrived in the evening. He asked the man up above the gate whether they could go in.

'No, my lord,' he said, 'but if you have anyone in your company who can read, tell me.' And they said that they had. 'Wait there for me, then,' he said.

The watchman came down from the walls and went into

the cemetery by the postern, and opened a little gate to Sir Gawain; and they all went in. The clerk began to read the writing on the tombs, and on one of them he found written: 'Here lies such-and-such a man, and there is his head.' It said the same on many of the tombs, and named many knights of King Arthur's household and from his land. When Sir Gawain heard that they were dead, he wept bitterly, for he and all the others thought that it was true. And so it was in some cases, but it was a lie in all the cases where the writing had been done the previous night.

When they had all wept for a long time, the clerk came to another [199] tomb, at one end of the cemetery, and found writing on it; and then, as soon as he had read it, he began to weep bitterly. Sir Gawain asked him what he had seen.

'What?' he said; 'bitter sorrow.'

'What sorrow?' he asked; 'tell us.'

'Here', he said, 'lies the prodigy.'

'Who?' they asked.

'The best of the good,' he said, 'who conquered this Guard.'

When the knights heard that, they beat their palms together and grieved bitterly, and they said to one another: 'Dear Lord God, who can it be?' And each man said that he did not know, unless it was the new knight, whom the king knighted on the day of the feast of Saint John. 'For this youth', they said, 'saw him come in here. Now you can see that they have killed him.' They grieved terribly, but Sir Gawain and Sir Yvain grieved more than all the others, and lamented his loss very tenderly, and said that they had never seen a man make such a good beginning as he did, and if he had lived, his prowess would have been remarkable.

When they had been there a long while, they left the cemetery and went back in front of the gate that was closed, and found the door of a garden open. They went in and came to the galleries* of a magnificent hall, where they saw a beautiful damsel, who was weeping bitterly. They thought she was very beautiful. Sir Gawain asked her very courteously what was the matter, that she wept so bitterly.

'What is the matter!' she said. 'I have every reason, for they have killed here the fairest knight in the world and the most valorous there ever was, and he was a young, beardless boy.'

'Damsel,' said Sir Gawain, 'what arms did he have?'

'White arms', she said, 'and a white horse.'

Then they all began to grieve again, and said that they would not leave until they knew something of the conditions of the castle. So they stayed there and waited to see how things would turn out. Now, though, the story leaves them all, and says no more about them, or about the castle and those inside it, until it is time to speak of them again.

[M. XXVIa] At the time that Sir Gawain had the writing read, which said that the knight in white armour was dead, Aiglin of the Valleys sent his brother back to King Arthur to tell him the news. He journeyed until he found the king, and said to him:

'King Arthur, I led your nephew and your companions to the Dolorous Guard, where they found a cemetery in which many of the good [200] knights of your land lie dead. That was inside the first gate. And the new knight himself, who went to provide assistance at Nohaut, and who had conquered the castle hill,* he lies dead there.'

When the king heard that, he was very upset, and wept bitterly, both for the new knight and for the others, and the whole court was troubled. The king said that he would go there, and he said to the queen:

'My lady, choose from among your ladies and damsels those you would most like, for you will come with me.'

They set off in the morning and travelled for two days. On the third day, the king stopped for the night by a river, in tents and pavilions. It was extremely hot, and in the evening he had sat down at the edge of the water, and put his legs in, and four knights were holding a silk cloth above his head. And he fell into a reverie. Straightaway, a fully armed knight came up on the other side of the river, and rode into the water. When he was near the king, he asked the others:

'Who is that knight?'

And the king himself replied:

'Sir knight, I am the king.'

'Indeed,' he said, 'I was looking for you.'

He set spurs to his horse and couched his lance to strike the king. The water was deep, so that the horse had to swim; and when he drew near the king, the knights reached out towards him, and grasped the lance and took it from him. And the man who held it struck the knight with it so hard that the water almost closed over his head, and another sprang into the water and grasped his bridle.

'Ha!' said the king, 'do not do that, for he will drown.'

And he let go of the bridle. When the knight heard the king say that, he turned away and said: 'Indeed, it is really true!' With that he rode out of the water, and went away as he had come. That knight was the lord of the Dolorous Guard, and he was so grieved at having lost his castle that he did not care what became of him; and he had decided to kill King Arthur, because he thought it was through him that he had lost his castle, which used to dominate and oppress his whole land. Now he would have to fall back on the power of the others.* When he had boasted the day before that he would kill him, a knight had replied that King Arthur would never be dispossessed by any man, or die a coward's death, because he had performed so many good and honourable actions in his life. That was why he said: 'Indeed, it is really true!' And he considered himself a fool, for having set out to kill him.

[201] The king spent that night by the river, and in the morning he set off early, and travelled far enough that, the

next day, he reached the Dolorous Guard. They went up as far as the first gate, which they found firmly closed. The king was very upset and said to the queen and his men that he had expected to find the gate open.

'Now I do not know', he said, 'what has become of my nephew and my companions.'

Then he asked the youth who had brought him the news:

'Friend, did you not tell me that this gate was open?'

'Yes, my lord,' he said; 'and so it was, when I left here: ask that man up there.'

The king looked up above the gate and saw a man who seemed to be a watchman; and he asked him:

'Sir, has this gate been opened?'

'Yes, my lord,' the man said.

'And, sir, can you help us to come inside?'

'Who are you?' asked the other.

'I am King Arthur.'

'My lord,' he said, 'to you, as the most worthy man in the world, I shall give all the help I can. And who is that lady?'

'That', he said, 'is the queen.'

'My lord,' he said, 'I shall do whatever I can, both for you and for her.'

Then he went away. And before long he brought back an old, white-haired man. When the king saw him, he said:

'Good sir, do let us come inside.'

'My lord,' he said, 'I shall not do so for the moment. But go now and find lodging for the night, and tomorrow, at about prime, send a knight to me. If I can open the gate to him, I shall; and if I cannot, then send me another at about terce; and if the gate is not opened then, send me another at about vespers, and so on until one comes to whom I can open it.'

'Willingly,' the king said, 'but, for the Lord's sake, at least tell me if you have any news of my nephew, Gawain.'

'My lord,' he said. 'you will certainly hear word of him, and soon.'

Then the king went down and lodged on the plain below, in the open, because of the springs there. In the morning, at the hour of prime, he sent a knight to the gate. And they sent him back when the [202] worthy old man had asked him whom he served and what his name was. He went back to the king, and said:

'Sir, I cannot get you in there, for they will not open the gate to me.'

At the hour of terce the king sent another knight, and they sent him back. At the hour of midday he again sent one, and they sent him back, and the same at the hour of none, and at the hour of vespers. He did the same for three days, sending one at each hour, and they always sent them back. Now though, the story falls silent about the king and queen and their company at this point, and returns to speak of Sir Gawain and his companions, and of the adventures which befell them after they arrived at the castle.

[M. XXVIIa] The story says that when Sir Gawain and his companions learned of the death of the White Knight and of the king's other companions, both from the writing and from the damsel to whom they spoke in the gallery, they were very upset, as the story has described. They stayed there until nightfall; and then they went down from the castle to lodge, and met a grey-haired vavasour, who seemed to be a very worthy man. He asked Sir Gawain who he was.

'Why do you ask?' said Sir Gawain.

'Sir,' he said, 'rest assured that I only ask for your good.'

'And I shall tell you,' he said, 'for you seem a worthy man. I am Gawain.'

When the vavasour saw the tears which were still falling from his eyes, he asked him why he was weeping. And he said that he was weeping over the death of the king's companions that he had seen up there in the castle.

'My lord,' he said, 'now do not grieve so, until you know why, for you are such a valorous man that you should not be so readily dismayed. But you should know that I came here from my residence to fetch you, for this land is not safe outside a fortress at the moment, while the lord of this castle is furious. For that reason, I advise you to come and lodge with me for tonight, and for as long as you stay in this country. And shall I tell you where? In a fine, strong castle, where you will have everything a knight needs. And each morning, as long as you wish to stay here, you can come here after mass, before or after eating. And you should know that most of what you saw up there is just lies and enchantments. But I shall show you truth, for I [203] shall take you to see, alive and well, some of those of the king's companions who the writing up there says are dead.'

When Sir Gawain heard that, he was delighted; and he said that in that case he would go, for there was nowhere he would not go, to see so many men of valour. The vavasour went in front, and the ten companions followed. When he was a long crossbowshot away from the Dolorous Guard, he said something in the ear of his son, who was with him, and he[1] went swiftly on ahead. They rode sedately after him until they drew near a small castle, which stood on an island in the Humber, on a high rock, the most unassailable for its size that anyone knew of. When they reached the river, a boat was brought for them, and they got in and crossed over to the island. Then the ten companions were taken to a chamber to disarm. When they were disarmed, they went to look over the fortress, which was magnificent. And when they came to the middle storey, they met well over forty armed knights and men-at-arms, who attacked them. They tried to go back out, but the doors were firmly closed behind them. They saw that resistance was useless, and Sir Gawain ordered that no one

---

[1] i.e. the son.

was to resist. And they did not, apart from Galegantin the Welshman, who threw himself at one of them, knocked him to the floor under him and wrenched the sword from his hands, and resisted until he was wounded, and might well have been killed. Then Sir Gawain himself ran to seize him. They tied his hands behind his back, and the same for all the others. Gasoain of Estrangot, who was very valorous and a good speaker, said that, as God was his witness, Galegantin was quite right if he would rather die than be taken prisoner. 'For I have never seen', he said, 'such outrageous treachery, for we were offered hospitality, and now we are taken prisoner and tied up before we have eaten or drunk.'

Then they were taken downstairs. And Yvain the Bastard saw the vavasour who had brought them there, who was in the kitchen, seeing that they prepared the meal quickly. And he said:

'Hey! Whore's son, traitor, you had given us lodging in good faith!'*

'Sir knight,' he replied, 'I made you no promise which has not been kept in full, for you will be lodged in one of the most secure buildings in the whole of Britain, and you will be put with your companions, whom I promised to show you.'

'A curse', said Gasoain, 'on anyone who wishes for any other lodging, for they¹ are as good as returned from the dead.'

[204] With that they went on. Galegantin, however, was still angry that they had wounded him, and he cared little now what they might do to him, for he was afraid he would die in the prison; but he was keen to avenge himself while he was alive. Then he took aim at the vavasour whom Yvain had reproached for his treachery, and threw himself at him, as he stood in front of the fire, and kicked him so hard that he knocked him full length on to the hot coals; and if his² hands

---

¹ i.e. the companions.   ² i.e. Galegantin's.

had not been tied, he[1] would have been completely burned before he could get up. Then the uproar began again, and they rushed at Galegantin with axes and swords, and but for their lord they would have killed him. Then they took them all down into a very strong dungeon, which had iron doors, and thick walls of stone blocks joined with iron and lead. Imprisoned there were King Yder and Guivret of Lambale and Yvain of Leonel and Cadoain of Caermurzin, and Kehedin the Small and Kay of Estraus and Girflet, the son of Do, and Dodinel the Wild and Duke Taulas and Mador of the Gate, and Lohot, the son of King Arthur* (who fathered him by the beautiful damsel called Lisanor, before he married the queen); and he contracted a fatal illness in that prison. Also with them was Gaheris of Caraheu. All those men were imprisoned there. When Sir Gawain and his companions saw them, they were overjoyed, for they had been missing for a long time. And the others were happy and unhappy when they saw them brought in there: happy because they had never expected to see them again, and unhappy because they were entering a wretched captivity. At this point, though, the story stops speaking of them for the moment, and returns to the knight who had conquered the castle.

[M. XXVIIIa] After Sir Gawain and his companions were captured, it was a long while before the knight who had conquered the Dolorous Guard heard anything about it; and when he did, he was as upset as he could be. One day it happened that he was sitting at table in a high turret at the end of the great hall, and he was eating in such splendour that anyone who saw the servers and the plate would have been astonished. As he was eating in this way, a squire came in, weeping bitterly. The damsel from the lake, who was eating with the White Knight, asked him what was the matter. 'Indeed, damsel,' he said, 'I was as moved as I have ever

---

[1] i.e. the vavasour.

been, by a damsel passing below this rock, grieving as bitterly as she could.'

'And did she say why?' asked the knight.

'She is lamenting', he said, 'the loss of Sir Gawain and Sir Yvain, and of some other knights.'

[205] 'And which way is she going?' asked the knight.

'My lord,' he said, 'she is following the road to Wales.'

'Ah! Sir Yvain,' the White Knight said, 'you were such a good mentor and companion to me, and you did whatever I wished. And Sir Gawain, for his part, caused me to be granted the first boon I asked of my lord the king, and said that he thought I should perform the task very well. That was a great recommendation, and may God never be my witness if I ever rest until I know where you are.'

Then he sprang up from the table and ordered his arms to be brought. They were brought to him, and he had himself armed from head to foot. The damsel asked him where he meant to go.

'I shall go', he said, 'after the damsel, to find out where Sir Gawain and his company are.'

'I shall come', she said, 'to see what happens.'

'No, you will not,' he said; 'you will not come, but will wait for me here until I come back. And I charge you, by the loyalty you owe my lady,[1] not to leave here before you see me again, which will be very soon.'

She bowed to his wishes. He left and rode after the damsel who was weeping over Sir Gawain, until he caught up with her at the edge of the forest. Then he asked her, for the Lord's sake, to give him news of Sir Gawain.

'I shall give you the news,' she said, 'which could not be worse, for he and nine companions are prisoners of the man who was lord of the Dolorous Guard.'

'Ah! damsel,' he said, 'since you have told me that much, tell me where they are prisoners.'

---

[1] i.e. the Lady of the Lake.

She looked at him, and said:

'Take off your helm, so that I can see you.'

He took it off; and she ran to him with open arms. Then he recognized her, and saw that she was a damsel in the service of his lady, the Lady of the Lake, and he greeted her very warmly. She told him that her lady had sent her to him because of something which she had forgotten to say to the other maiden, who came before.

'But I was told,' she said, 'in the place where Sir Gawain is imprisoned, that you lay dead in the Dolorous Guard, and so I did not wish to go in there, for I could not even bear the sight of it.'[1]

'What was the message,' he said, 'that my lady forgot to send me?'

'It was', she said, 'that you should not devote your heart to a love which makes you grow indolent, but to one which makes you improve, for a heart which becomes indolent through love cannot achieve noble things, for it does not dare. But a man who [206] always aims to improve can achieve noble things, just as he dares to undertake them.'

And he again said to her:

'Sir Gawain, dear friend—where is he is prison?'

'I shall take you there,' she said.

Then they returned together, and came to a small thicket, which overlooked the island where Sir Gawain was, and the damsel said:

'Hide here, for no one can come out without us seeing him, and we shall not be seen.'

He did that; and when they had waited for a long while, they saw as many as fifteen fully armed knights come out, and cross the river in a large boat, and set off towards the Dolorous Guard. The knight let them come near; and when he saw that they were armed, he charged them as fast as his

---

[1]. i.e. the Dolorous Guard.

horse could go, and put the white shield with three bands in front of his chest, for the damsel that he had left in the castle made him carry it. As soon as they saw him, though, there was not one of them so bold he did not turn tail, and the lord of the Dolorous Guard first of all, for all the others were his men. When they reached the river again, they could not get into the boat in time, because he was close behind them. He killed the first one he reached with his lance, then put his hand to his sword and attacked the others, and kept back four of them, killed or crippled. The others reached safety across the water on the island.

Thus the lord of the Dolorous Guard, Brandin of the Isles (for that was his name), escaped. And the knight went back to the Dolorous Guard, very distressed, and went in through a false postern.*

The next day was the fourth since the king had come to the Dolorous Guard. When prime came, he sent a knight to the gate as arranged, but no one dared open the gate before the White Knight ordered it. The knight went back to the king and told him what he had found, and the king was very upset. Then he sat down by the stream from a spring and fell into a profound reverie until it was nearly past terce. And the knights said to the queen:

'My lady, terce is passing, and the king has not sent anyone to the gate. What shall we do?'

'Indeed,' she said, 'I do not know. I should not dare send someone there unless he ordered it, and he is deep in thought.'

The knight who had conquered the castle had come back out by the false postern to see the king's party, and he had [207] told the gatekeeper that if the king sent someone there at terce, the gate should be opened to him, but that no one from inside was to go out. However, there were many of the people of the castle on the walls, who would dearly have liked the dolorous customs to cease. The gatekeeper, who did not dare say a word or let anyone out, signed to an old man to call King Arthur. And he shouted: 'King Arthur, the hour is passing, the hour is passing.' And all the others began to shout the same thing, so that the whole valley echoed.

When the queen and the knights heard the voices, they went up to the gate, and they were very anxious because the king was still lost in thought. Then the knight who had conquered the castle came forward: he had round his neck the white shield with one red band, and he rode at great speed up to the gate. When he saw the queen, he said:

'The Lord God bless you.'

And she replied, very sombrely, God bless him.

'My lady,' he said, 'would you like to go in there?'

'Indeed, yes,' she said, 'very much.'

'In God's name,' he said, 'for you, the gate will be opened.'

'Many thanks, sir,' she said.

The knight immediately called the watchman and said: 'Open the gate.' 'Certainly, my lord,' he said. He opened the gate, and the knight went in. However, he was so overwhelmed by the queen that he quite forgot himself, and thought about nothing but looking at her. He went up above the gate, and watched her from there. The gate was closed again as soon as he was inside; and it let out such a shriek that the king was roused from his thoughts, and asked what it was; and there were many who told him. And he told Kay the seneschal to go and find out whether he could go inside. He went there, and met the queen, who was just about to go back, for she thought that the knight had mocked her, and she told him about it. Then Kay looked up, and saw the knight above the gate, and said:

'Ha! sir knight, you have behaved ignobly, in mocking my lady.'

However, he did not hear him. Then the damsel who had led him to the Dolorous Prison—that was the name of the small castle where Sir Gawain was imprisoned—came to him. And when she heard Kay's reproaches, she nudged him and said:

'Do you not hear what that knight is reproaching you for, then?'

'Which knight?' he said.

She showed him.

'Sir,' he said, 'what did you say?'

[208] 'I said', Kay replied, 'that you must consider my lady and me fools, since you will not deign to open the gate to her, although you promised to do so; and you will not deign to speak to me.'

'Who are you?' the knight asked.

'I am Kay the seneschal.'

Then the knight looked, and saw the queen, who by now was going away in vexation, and he was so upset that he was nearly distracted, because he could see that she was angry. He went to the watchman, and said:

'Did I not tell you to let my lady the queen come in here?'

'You never mentioned it,' said the other.

He put his hand on his sword and swore terribly.

'Let me tell you', he said, 'that if you were not so old, I should kill you here and now for your stupidity, and myself for my deafness, if I did not have such a good warrant for it. Now, open the gate quickly and see that it is not closed again.'

Then his horse was brought to him, and he mounted, pensive and sorrowful. Then he went back to the false postern, and went out. And no matter how the maiden asked him where he was going, he would only tell her that he would come back soon. 'And see', he said, 'that you do not follow me at all.' Thereupon she left him. The watchman opened the gate; and the news reached the king, and he went there at once, and he and the queen went in, and all the others after them. They did not stand on ceremony at all, but whoever could go in first, went in. And when they were inside, they found the second gate closed. Then they went to the cemetery, and the king ordered his clerks to read the writing. They began to read out the names of many knights of his household and from other lands, until they came to a tomb on which Sir Gawain's name was written, and it said: 'Here lies Sir Gawain, and there is his head.' After that they saw on another tomb: 'Here lies Sir Yvain, the son of King Urien, and there lies his head.' Then on another they found 'Here lies Yvain the Bastard, and there is his head.' It said the same of all the companions Sir Gawain had taken with him. When the king heard it, he was nearly distracted with grief, and so were the queen and all the others. When they had grieved for a long while, the king asked the watchman, whom he saw on the second wall, whether the first gate would ever be closed to them; and he said that it would not.

'And how', the king asked, 'can we get in at that second one?'

'My lord,' he said, 'send someone here, as you have done these last four days.'

[209] In the evening the king and his company withdrew to their camp. That night there was such great distress among his party that no one ate or drank at all. Now, though, the story again speaks of the White Knight for a while, how he left the castle when the queen was refused entry at the gate.

[M. XXIXa] The story says that the White Knight rode, downcast and pensive, because he had angered his lady the queen, for he loved her with such a great love, from the first day he was thought to be a knight,* that he did not love himself or anyone else as much. And because he was afraid that his lady would hate him for ever, he inwardly resolved to do such deeds of arms that he would get back Sir Gawain, or die. By doing that, if he could, he hoped to regain his lady's love. Thus he rode, downcast and pensive, straight towards the Dolorous Prison, and again went into the thicket. It might have been after midday when he arrived there. He was there for a long time, until the evening was drawing well in. Then he looked, and saw, coming on a large donkey, a hermit, who entered the wood very near him: he went, chanting his liturgical hours, to his hermitage in the forest nearby. The hermit was very old, and had been a knight, one of the fairest under the sun, and he had become a hermit in his prime because of a great loss he suffered, seeing all his twelve sons die within a year. When he entered the wood, the White Knight went to meet him and asked where he had come from. He stopped what he was saying, and replied very gently that he had come from the small castle.

'Sir,' the knight said, 'what were you doing there?'

The good man began to weep.

'Indeed, sir,' the hermit said, 'I went there in haste to two knights who are very sick.'

Then he showed him the chalice* which he was carrying under his cape. The knight asked him who the two men were, who were so sick. And he said that they belonged to King Arthur's household: one was called Galegantin the Welshman, and he was sick from wounds; and the other was Lohot, the king's son, who was sick with an illness he had caught in the prison; and they were both in grave danger. Then the White Knight began to sigh very heavily, and asked him about Sir Gawain and his cousin, Sir Yvain. And the hermit said that he saw them quite fit and well.

'And you, sir, who are you?'

'Sir,' he said, 'I am a knight errant.'

'Ah!' the hermit said; 'I know something of who you are. You captured the Dolorous Guard. But what are you waiting for here?'

[210] The knight said that he would very much like to make an effort to free the king's knights, if it were possible.

'And I shall certainly help you,' the hermit said, 'if you will listen to my advice.' The knight said that he would. 'I tell you', said the hermit, 'that when I was about to mount, just now, I heard two squires talking about their equipment, for they did not notice me. And one said to the other that they would mount early in the night to attack King Arthur in the dark. I know that the man to whom the Dolorous Guard belonged hates the king more than anyone except you, for he is afraid he will apply his force and effort to putting an end to the perilous customs of the castle. He thinks that is what has brought him here. For that reason, I should advise you to warn my lord the king of this matter, and then they[1] can all be captured. And if you do not warn him, I shall do so.'

The knight said that he would warn him.

'But first,' he said, 'I wish to see your hermitage.'

'I should be pleased,' said the good man.

Then he went in front, and the knight followed, until they reached the hermitage; and the knight saw that it was very pleasant, and it was built on a high knoll and completely surrounded with great oaks, tall and thick, and then with big Welsh ditches,* and outside there was a big, thick hedge. Then the knight took leave of the hermit and said that he would go to warn the king about his enemies.

'Sir,' said the hermit, 'if you need us,*do not hesitate to come to us.'

He said that he would not. Then he left, and went back to where he had met the hermit, and waited there for a long time. Night came on; and he thought that he would not under any circumstances warn the king, for he meant to deal with the matter alone. Then the moon began to rise, and throughout the castle they rose and made ready. Very soon, they came out and crossed the water, and he let them ride until they were all past him, and followed them at a distance. When they were near the Dolorous Guard, they moved into the cover of the hill, and rode quietly, so as not to be noticed;

---

[1] i.e. Brandin's men.

and those in the camp[1] would never have been aware of them until they rushed in among them.

When they were so close that all that remained was to charge, they dismounted and tightened their horses' girths. Then they remounted and went to rush into the camp. However, the knight was following close behind them. He had a strong, swift horse, and was carrying a lance with a short, thick shaft and sharp head. [211] And he had plenty of courage, for he aimed to put the men he was following to flight, although they numbered 150. He charged them, and shouted at them very loudly. They thought they had been betrayed, and were so taken aback that not one of them made any attempt to defend himself. He struck the first one he reached so hard that he hurled him down dead. He left the lance in his body, and drew his sword and dealt great blows to left and right to those who dared face him. They did not linger long, however, for the camp was roused by the uproar. The watchmen, who had seen the armed men, began to shout: 'To arms! To arms!' Then the attackers began to withdraw below the castle; and he pursued them, giving them tremendous blows, and he cut their shields and helms to pieces, and hacked mail off their hauberks, on the arms and shoulders. He crashed into them with horse and body together; he threw them to the ground, grasping the rims of their shields and their necks and their helms.

Thus the White Knight pressed them; and they were so disconcerted by the remarkable deeds he was doing that they really thought it was the whole of King Arthur's army. Then they passed near the gate of the castle; and the watchman on the wall began to shout: 'To arms! To arms!' And the knight who was pursuing them saw the king's men, who by now were galloping after them. Then he caught sight of one who seemed to be the richest and the most elegantly armed of

[1] i.e. King Arthur's men.

them all, and he thought he must be the lord of all the others; and so he was. He went towards him, and gave him such a blow on the helm with his sword that he quite stunned him, and made him hang on to his horse's neck with both arms. Then King Arthur's troops arrived at the gallop; and the others heard them coming, and plied their spurs and fled with all the speed they could get from their horses. However, the one whom the White Knight had struck was still dazed, and his horse headed for the Humber, which ran the other side of the castle, and it carried him swiftly away. The White Knight, who did not wish to let him go, followed close behind him, and went up to him. And he was so dazed that he could not see anything. The White Knight grasped him by the neck, and pulled him to the ground, and rode over his body until he was quite battered. Then he dismounted, and wrenched the helm from his head, which he threatened to cut off. However, the other could not reply, for he was lying unconscious. Then the knight thought he must be dead, and was greatly distressed on account of Sir Gawain and the others, for he was sure that that meant he had lost them.*

The other was unconscious for a long while; and the White Knight was very grieved, and wept, and said that he would never again ride [212] over a knight, unless he wished to kill him, for he was sure it had burst the heart of this one. After a long while the knight came to, and moaned dreadfully. The White Knight gave no sign that it worried him, but said that he would cut off his head, and let down his ventail and raised his sword. The other begged for mercy, for he was badly hurt. And he recognized the knight by the shield he was carrying, which was the one with a single band.

'Ah!' he said, 'noble knight, do not kill me, if you love King Arthur at all, for you would be acting very foolishly.'

'Then you must promise to go as my prisoner wherever I wish.'

'Willingly,' he said; 'anywhere except inside that castle there, but I will not go there under any circumstances.'

'Yes, you will,' he said, 'for I shall take you there by force.'

'If you manage to take me there,' said the other, 'you will take me there dead, for I will never go in there alive. And you should know that you would then lose Sir Gawain and twenty-two other companions of the king. If you send me somewhere else as a prisoner, I shall give them up to you tomorrow before nightfall, for I can see that you are the best knight in the world, and the most fortunate.'

When he heard that, he was overjoyed, more than he had ever been before, and said that, if he would do that, he would not take him into the castle. The other promised it, and gave him his sword.

'Sir,' he said, 'where do you wish to take me as a prisoner?'

'To a hermit,' the other said, 'who is nearby in the forest. And you will lead me there yourself.'

The other said, indeed he would, straight there. The White Knight made him mount behind him, and he did so with great difficulty, for he was badly hurt. In that way they made straight for the hermitage. King Arthur's men were by now coming back from the pursuit, in which they had achieved nothing, for those whom they were pursuing had all rushed into the forest. The king had gone to meet them, and was coming back with them. And the White Knight had come back over the ground where the fight had been, and had picked up a lance, which one of the fugitives had dropped. He saw the king and his men, and the king likewise saw the two of them.[1]

'Ha! sir,' the captured knight said, 'there are the king's men. I should not like to fall into his power under any circumstances; so take care that I do not fall into the hands of anyone other than yourself, for I have trusted you.'

[1] i.e. the White Knight and Brandin.

[213] 'Do not worry,' he said, 'for if he takes you away, he will have to kill me first, or reduce me to such a state that I cannot help you.'

Then he rode on at his own pace. And Kay the seneschal went after him, and called to him:

'Stop, sir knight, for my lord the king wishes to know who you are.'

He did not reply, but rode on, regardless; and Kay went up to him, and said:

'Sir knight, you are very haughty, since you will not deign to speak to me.'

'What do you want?' he asked.

'I want to know', Kay said, 'who you are.'

'I am a knight.'

'And that man behind you,' said Kay, 'is he a prisoner?'

'Yes,' he said; 'what of it?'

Then Kay recognized him as the man who had had the gate opened.

'Oho!' he said, 'you are the one who made my lady the queen wait around outside the gate yesterday. And that knight you are taking away recently tried to kill my lord the king; I recognize him by his arms.'

The knight did not reply to anything Kay said, but kept riding. Kay took offence, and said:

'Sir knight, this man is the king's enemy, and I am his[1] sworn man, and I should break my oath if I allowed you to take him back like this. Give him to me, and I shall hand him over to my lord the king.'

'The man has not yet come', he said, 'who can take him away by force.'

'I shall be that man,' said Kay.

Then he was about to seize the defeated knight, but the other told him that, if he laid a hand on him, he would cut it off at once.

---

[1] i.e. King Arthur's.

'Indeed?' said Kay; 'set him down, then; and whoever can take him away by force, let him do so.'

'As God is my witness,' the other said, 'he will not dismount on your account.'

Kay rode some distance away, then came swiftly back. And the White Knight took aim by the light of the moon. Kay broke his lance; and the other struck him low down beside the saddle-bow, and put the lance-head and shaft through his left thigh, so that he pinned him to the cantle of the saddle. He struck him well, and knocked him to the ground; and as he fell, the lance broke. And the White Knight said:

'Sir Kay, now you can see whether the Lady of Nohaut would have been badly served.'*

[214] With that he left. The king and his men came to where Kay was lying, and found him unconscious, and they carried him to the tents on his shield.*

The White Knight had gone into the forest, and he rode until he reached the hermit's dwelling. The defeated knight called at the gate, and the hermit-knight* opened it to him. When they had dismounted, the White Knight had the door of the chapel opened.* He told the hermit what they had agreed, and made the defeated knight swear to keep to it faithfully. 'And I swear to you', he said afterwards, 'that, if I see that you are trying to cheat me, I shall cut off your head.'

When they returned,* the defeated knight immediately sent the hermit to the Dolorous Prison to fetch his seneschal. First, however, the White Knight made him swear on the Holy Gospel that he would discharge the task in good faith. The hermit mounted his donkey and went to the little castle, and with the tokens* which the prisoner had given him, brought back the seneschal alone. He arrived, and his lord told him, in front of the White Knight, to fetch Sir Gawain and all the other companions of the king, and that they should come fully armed. Afterwards he made the seneschal swear that he would do that. The seneschal left, then—and by now it was broad daylight—and he did as his lord had ordered. When they arrived, it was well after prime. The lord asked the seneschal:

'On what terms did you bring these knights?'

'They promised me', he said, 'that they would not leave here except with your permission.'

'Gentlemen,' the lord said to them, 'I order you, on your oath, to do as this knight orders you, as his prisoners, and for my part I release you.'

The White Knight stood with bowed head, so that they should not recognize him, and he was fully armed, including his helm. Then all the knights agreed to be his prisoners. The lord released them from their oaths, and then left the hermitage. And the hermit said to the White Knight:

'What, sir? Are you letting Brandin go? Then you have lost everything, for the enchantments of the Dolorous Guard will never cease except through him.'

'I cannot do any more,' he said, 'for I have given him my word.'

The hermit wept bitterly at that. Then the knight called all the king's companions, and said:

'Gentlemen, I ask you, both for your good and for my honour, not to [215] move from here until you see me again; and that will be tonight or in the morning.'

They all gave their word. Then he left and went to the Dolorous Guard. It was nearly terce, and the king had sent a knight to the gate at prime, and they had sent him back.

The White Knight went into the castle by the false postern and went to the great hall where the two maidens were waiting for him. The one who had brought him the shields said:

'Sir, have I been a prisoner* long enough, now?'

'Not yet, dear friend, not until I have made an end of the business of Sir Gawain, and the king has come in here. Then you and I shall go away together.'

Then he took the shield from around his neck, and picked up the one with two bands. Then he went to the gatekeeper, and asked whether the king had sent anyone to the gate that day.

'Yes,' he said, 'at prime.'

'Now, be sure', he said, 'that when next he sends someone, you say that you will only open the gate to Kay the seneschal.'

With that he went out of the castle and went around the hill until he arrived at the king's camp. Terce was already passing, and the people of the castle began to shout: 'The hour is passing, the hour is passing.' The king was reclining by the stream from a spring, deep in thought. When he heard the clamour, he sent a knight; and the watchman told him he would only open the gate to Kay the seneschal. The knight went and told the king; and the king said that he would have him[1] carried there, rather than miss going in, for he was lying sick from the wound he had received the previous night. The king had him carried to the gate; and the queen and many of the knights went towards the castle. The knight who was carrying the white shield with two red bands went up to the queen and greeted her, and she greeted him.

'My lady,' he said, 'where are you going?'

'Sir knight,' she said, 'I am going to that gate, to see whether my lord the king will be able to go in there.'

'And you, my lady,' he said, 'would you like to go in there?'

'Indeed, yes,' she said, 'very much.'

'Then you shall,' he said.

Then he went to the gate, and called the gatekeeper, who came to open the gate. And the knight did nothing but look at the queen on horseback as she came up the hill, and he was thinking so much about her that he quite forgot himself. The gatekeeper called to him to go in. And the knight continued to look back, until the gatekeeper closed the gate

[1] i.e. Kay.

again. It let out [216] a great shriek, and the king, who was
thinking by the spring, asked what it was he had heard. Then
Kay, whom four squires were carrying on a cloth, came to
the gate, and found the watchman up above. He asked Kay
who he was, and he gave his name. 'Then you shall come in,'
the watchman said. With that he opened the gate, and the
king and his company went forward, and those on the walls
said to him:

'My lord, do you wish to come inside?' And he said that he
did. 'Then,' they said, 'you must give your word faithfully as
a king that you and your company will not force any man or
woman here to speak.' And he gave his word.

Then the gates were opened, and they all went in; and
inside they saw a magnificent castle. All the houses in the
town had galleries in front, either upstairs or downstairs, and
they were all filled with ladies or damsels and knights and
other people. They were all weeping, and no one said a word
in the whole castle. They did this because they wished to
dismay the king, so that he would be pleased when they
deigned to speak to him, for they did not expect anyone other
than the king to help them in their distress; and for that
reason they made him give his word that they would not be
forced to speak by him or his company. The king dismounted
in a very large and beautiful hall, but he did not find anyone
there, man or woman, and that had been done deliberately by
the people of the castle. The king was quite disconcerted by
this, and said to the queen and his knights:

'Now I am inside, and I know no more about the conditions
than I knew when I was outside.'

'My lord,' the queen said, 'we shall have to put up with it
for now: perhaps the man who has shown us this much will
show us more.'

'Sire,' the others said, 'the queen speaks well and truly.'

Thus they spoke together.

The White Knight had gone into the great hall, and he

took the shield from around his neck and picked up the one with three bands, leaving the one with two. Then he left the hall to go to Sir Gawain. He went through the streets, and a clamour went up throughout the castle, with people shouting: 'Capture him, capture him.' Then the king and queen and all the others rushed out, and saw the gates firmly closed. When the White Knight saw the gates being closed, he looked towards where he saw the king was lodged, and saw the queen outside the door of the hall. And he resolved not to leave without seeing her. Then he went in that direction, and when he was near her, he dismounted and greeted her. And all the people began to shout: 'Capture him, king; capture him, king; capture him, king.'

The king went towards the knight, and greeted him; and the knight greeted him.

[217] 'Those people', the king said, 'are shouting to me that I should capture you.'

'My lord,' he said, 'you certainly have the power, if you think it would be right.'

'Why', said the king, 'are they shouting that I should capture you?'

'My lord, have someone ask them, for I do not think I have done anything wrong.'

The king sent someone to find out. And the people had gone into the other bailey. The king said to the queen and his knights:

'I am very confused, for I know nothing of the conditions here.'

'My lord,' said the knight, 'would you like to know about them?'

'Indeed, yes,' he said, 'very much.'

And the queen said:

'Sir knight, he would very much like to know about them.'

The knight was very distressed, as he did not have the time

and opportunity to tell him about them, and it brought tears to his eyes. He said to the king:

'My lord, please let me go.'

The king was courteous, and let him go. And when he was mounted, he said to the queen:

'And you, my lady, would you care to know about the conditions here?'

'Indeed, yes,' she said, 'very much.'

Having mounted, he began to leave.

'Sir knight,' she said, 'I should very much like to know about them.'

And he replied, weeping:

'Truly, my lady, I am very sorry, for I am doing great wrong in concealing them, but this is not the time to reveal them.'

With that he went back out by the false postern and spurred away with all the speed he could get from his horse; and he came to the forest, and rushed into it. The king's messengers came back from asking the people why they had shouted that he should capture the knight, and they said to him:

'Sire, those people send you word that you can learn all about the conditions here from that knight.'

'Ha!' said the king, 'we are badly served, for I let him go.'

As they were talking like this, the castle gate opened, and in came knights and ladies and damsels, bringing the king's food, all prepared. These were the townspeople, and they had shouted so that his men would capture the knight, for they[1] were not to lay a hand on him; and they still assumed that the king would have kept him there. When they learned that he had let him go, they grieved terribly. And the king said that he was just as upset as they were.

'I did not realize,' he said.

---

[1] i.e. the townspeople.

That night the king and all his party had good lodging. [218] Behind the hall where he slept there was a tall turret, but the castle wall was between the two. That turret adjoined the great hall which had belonged to the lord of the castle. In the turret was a watchman who sounded in the new day* very early. Then the king and queen and all the others rose, and went out into the courtyard. Now, though, the story again tells of the White Knight for a while, when he left the castle by permission of the king, who had stopped him.

[M. XXXa] When the White Knight left the king and queen, he went straight to Sir Gawain and the other companions, and said:

'Gentlemen, I release you from the obligation which keeps you in my charge, on condition that you stay here tonight. And in the morning you must go to the Dolorous Guard, where you will find the king and my lady; greet them both on my behalf, and thank them for the fact that you are out of prison, for you should know that it is because of her.'

'Ah! sir,' said Sir Gawain, 'tell us who you are.'

'Sir,' he said, 'I am a knight, and that is all you may know for now, and I beg you not to be upset about it.'

With that he commended them to God, and rode as far as he could that evening, straight for the religious house where he had left his squires.* He spent that night with a vavasour, and in the morning he began riding very early, in the direction the vavasour himself showed him. And no more will be said of him for the moment: instead the story returns to speak of Sir Gawain and of his uncle, the king.

[M. XXXIa] When the king had risen in the morning and gone into the courtyard in front of his lodging, he did not know what to do. And in the turret where the watchman had sounded in the new day, in a chamber below the watchman's storey, there were two maidens, the ones that the Lady of the Lake had sent to the knight. The one who had brought the

shields had gone to the windows; and when she saw the
queen, she called to her and said:

'My lady, you had good lodging last night, while mine was
very bad.'

The queen looked up at her.

'Indeed, damsel,' she said, 'I did not know you were there.
Could I have helped you?'

'Yes, my lady, easily.'

'How is that?' the queen asked.

'I shall not tell you at the moment,' said the maiden.

She said that because she suspected that the White Knight
loved the queen—and she thought she loved him, too—
because he did not wish to leave the castle until he had [219]
seen her, and the other maiden had told her how she had
seen him overwhelmed by her, the day the king went in at the
first gate.

While the queen and the damsel were talking like this, a
large party of knights arrived, and came in through the gate:
it was Sir Gawain and his company. Then the king was
overjoyed, and he kissed his nephew and all the others, and
asked them where they had been.

'By my faith,' said Sir Gawain, 'we do not know, except
that we were taken to a small castle, and when we expected
to be given lodging, we were taken prisoner. However, a
knight has freed us and told us to thank you and my lady for
it.'

'And do you know who he is?' said the king.

He said that they did not, but he carried a white shield
with three red bands.

'Oh!' the queen said, 'it is your knight, the one who left
you yesterday evening, after the people shouted.'

'Did you see him disarmed?' the king asked Sir Gawain.

'No,' he said, 'for he would never take off his helm. And
that makes me suspect that someone here would recognize
him if he were disarmed.'

'By my faith,' said the king, 'now I can leave.'

The maiden who was up in the turret heard him and cried to him:

'What, King Arthur?' she said; 'you are going away, leaving me in captivity, and knowing nothing about the conditions here?'

'Damsel,' said the king, 'it distresses me that I do not know about them.'

Sir Gawain asked what they meant; and the king told him, and he was very surprised.

'Damsel,' said the king, 'could I free you?'

'Yes, my lord,' she said, 'but it would mean considerable effort.'

'Effort?' he said; 'I should be glad to make it, if I knew how.'

'Damsel,' said Sir Gawain, 'since my lord the king has said that he will make the effort, he will do so. Tell us, though, how and by what you can be freed.'

'I can only be freed by the knight that the king allowed to go.'

'And how shall we recognize him?' asked Sir Gawain.

'At the first encounter* which takes place in the kingdom of Logres,' she said, 'you will have news of him, and at the second, and at the third.'

[220] 'Damsel,' said Sir Gawain, 'if he sent you word to leave, would you come out of there?'

'Indeed, no,' she said, 'not unless I saw him in person.'

'Sire,' he said, 'rest assured that I shall not stay more than one night in any town, unless I am a prisoner or sick, until I know who this knight is.'

When the king heard that, he was very upset; and Sir Gawain said:

'Sire, the King from Over the Borders has attacked you, and is making war on you. Send him word that you will be in his land a month from today—that will be the third day after the feast of Our Lady,* in September—and he should take steps to defend himself, for he will need to. At that encounter, if God wills and it pleases Him, you will hear news of this matter.'

And the king said:

'Let it be as you wish; but you will stay here until then.'

'That is impossible,'* Sir Gawain said.

Then the king sent his messenger to the King from Over the Borders of Galone, to tell him the day they had decided on for the encounter. Then he left the town, and Sir Gawain took leave of him, and embarked on his quest. With that, though, the story falls silent about him and King Arthur, and returns to speak of the knight who conquered the Dolorous Guard.

[M. XXXIIa] When the knight who conquered the Dolorous Guard left the house of the vavasour who gave him lodging, the night he left Sir Gawain and his companions with the hermit in the forest, he journeyed until he reached the house of religion where his squires were. However, he only stayed there one night. They had heard a good deal there about the knight who conquered the Dolorous Guard, but no one knew it was him. In the morning he left there and rode all day without meeting any adventure worth mentioning. The next day, he rose early and rode until about terce; and then he met a damsel on a sweat-soaked palfrey. The knight had let down his ventail and taken off his gauntlets,* and his squires were carrying his lance and his helm, and his shield in a shield-cover. He greeted the damsel, and she him.

'Damsel,' he said, 'what urgent business drives you so fast?'

'Sir,' she said, 'I bear news which should please every knight who wishes to win honour and renown.'

[221] 'What news?' he asked.

'My lady the queen sends word to all knights that on the third day after the feast of Our Lady, in September, a great encounter will take place between King Arthur and the King from Over the Borders of Galone, at the edge of their two lands, on the open ground between Godoarre* and the Maine.'

'Which queen', he said, 'says this?'

'The wife of King Arthur,' she said; 'and, for the Lord's sake, if you have any news of the knight who conquered the Dolorous Guard, tell me, for my lady sends him word that, if he hopes ever to enjoy her friendship and company, he should be there, for she would very much like to see him.'

Then the knight was quite overwhelmed, and said nothing for a long while. And the damsel continued to beg him, if he knew anything of the knight, to tell her. He was very much afraid she would recognize him, and he kept his head bowed, and said:

'Damsel, by the person you most love, do you know the knight?'

She said that she did not.

'I will tell you', he said, 'that last night I slept where he slept. And let my lady know that he will be at the encounter, unless he dies in the meantime, for no other obstacle will keep him away.'

'Lord,' she said, 'how relieved I am now!'

With that she left, and the knight started on his way and travelled all week until after the hour of prime on Saturday. Then he met a large party of people, in a great, dense forest. There were many people in the party, on foot and on horseback. In between all the others was a big knight on horseback, and he had a man attached by the neck with a fine rope to the tail of his palfrey. The man was barefoot, dressed in shirt and breeches; he was blindfolded, and his hands were tied behind his back; and he was one of the most handsome men you could find. Thus the big knight led him along, and he had a woman's head hung around his neck by the hair.

The White Knight saw this man, who was very handsome, and he stopped and asked him who he was.

'Sir,' he said, 'I am a knight of my lady the queen, and these people hate me, and are taking me to my death in the shameful way that you see, for they dare not kill me except in secret.'

The White Knight asked him which queen's name he was invoking; and he said, that of the queen of Britain.[1]

[222] Then the White Knight said:

'Truly, one should not treat a knight as shamefully as you are treating him.'

'Yes, one should,' said the big knight who was pulling him along, 'when he is treacherous and disloyal, for then he has renounced knighthood.'

'And this man,' said the White Knight, 'why are you pulling him along like this? What wrong has he done you?'

'He has done me wrong in that I have found him guilty of treachery, and I shall give him justice in accordance with the wrong he has done.'

The White Knight said to him:

'Sir, it is not right for a knight to put another knight to death himself in this way, but if he has betrayed you, then try him for it in a court. Then you can take your revenge with honour.'

'I shall not try him for it', he said, 'in any court but my own, for I have already found him guilty.'

'Of what?' asked the White Knight.

'Of dishonouring me with my wife,' he said; 'and he still has her head hanging around his neck by the hair.'

The knight who was tied answered and swore forcefully that he never once thought of bringing him dishonour.

'Ah! sir,' said the White Knight, 'since he denies the offence so forcefully, you have no right to put him to death. I

---

[1] i.e. Guinevere.

suggest you let him go now, for the sake of the Lord and of your honour, and for my sake—I, who never before asked you for anything. And if he has done you some wrong, seek justice for it in the way I have told you.'

The other said and swore that he would not seek justice any further afield, since he held him prisoner.

'By my faith,' said the White Knight, 'you will be a doing a great wrong if you kill him, since he is a knight of my lady the queen.'

And he said that he would certainly not spare him for the queen's sake.

'No?' said the White Knight, 'then let me tell you that he will not die today at your hands, for I am giving him safe conduct and protection against all those I see here.'

Then he cut through the blindfold over his eyes and the rope which was tied around his neck. The knight's men rushed to get bows and arrows and made as though they meant to kill him. And he said to the big knight:

'Sir, move your men back, for if they hit me or my horse, I shall kill you first, and them afterwards.'

And most of them had no armour. Then the knight[1] laced on [223] his helm and armed his hands and took his lance and shield. And there were some who shot at him, not to kill him, but because their lord ordered it; and they missed him quite deliberately, because they were sorry about the knight's death.* He realized that they did not mean to kill him, and so he did not wish to do them any harm. He charged at their lord, who was ordering them to shoot, and struck him in the stomach with the butt of his lance so hard that he knocked him flat on the ground, and almost broke all his bones. Then all the others fled; and he took the horse from which he had knocked the other, and led it to the knight he had untied and said:

[1] i.e. the White Knight.

'Now mount, sir knight, and come with me.'

The knight mounted and went to the other knight, and said:

'Sir, I am very near to safety, for near here there is a stronghold where I should have nothing to fear, if I were there, and I shall go there, if you agree.'

'I should be glad,' the knight said.

And the other said:

'Sir, in whose name shall I thank my lady the queen for the fact that you have saved me, for I do not know what you are called?'

'Describe my shield to her,' he said, 'for you may not know my name, and be sure to tell her that you are free because of her.'

The knight went to the queen and thanked her for the knight's intervention, and described his shield; and she knew at once that it was the knight who had conquered the Dolorous Guard, and she was overjoyed.

The knight[1] travelled on his way, until it grew very dark. It was Saturday, the story says, and he passed by a brattice,* and heard a damsel singing, very loudly and clearly. When he was past, he fell into a profound reverie, and his horse carried him wherever it wished. The ground was marshy, and it had dried out, for the summer had been very long and hot—and it still was, for it was the week of the Assumption—and the cracks were large and deep. The horse was by no means fresh, for it had done a long day's journey, and it caught its forelegs and fell into a very big crevasse. The knight lay under it for a long time, until his squires lifted him up. Then he felt that he was badly hurt and he was in great pain and had great difficulty in remounting, while the back of his saddle was broken, and his shield was split in three pieces. Then he rode until he came to a cemetery, and saw a monk

---

[1] i.e. the White Knight.

kneeling in front of a cross. He greeted him, and the man greeted him.

'Sir,' one of the squires said to the good man, 'this knight [224] is badly hurt. For the sake of holy charity, tell me where he can find lodging for tonight, for riding causes him great pain.'

'In God's name,' said the good man, 'I shall tell you. Now, follow me.'

Then he led the way, and they followed him. Then he asked the knight how he had been hurt, and he told him.

'My lord,' said the good man. 'I shall give you some very good advice, if you will listen to it.'

He said that he would gladly listen to it.

'I advise you,' he said, 'and warn you never to ride on a Saturday after none except on very serious business.* And let me tell you that it will bring you more good and less harm.'

He promised him that it would never happen to him again, if he could help it.

'And you, sir, why had you gone to the place where we found you, at such an hour?'

'My lord,' he said, 'my father and mother are buried there, for it is a cemetery, and I go there every day to say my Paternoster, and whatever prayers God has taught me, and to pray for their souls.'

Thereupon they arrived at a house of religion, from which the worthy man came, and they were warmly received. The knight stayed there ten whole days, at the request of the brothers, and was bathed and treated, for he was very badly hurt.

On the eleventh day he left, leaving there the shield with three bands, for he did not wish to be recognized, and taking one which his squires had had made in a city near the hermitage where he had been ill. This shield was red with a diagonal white band. Thus the knight travelled for a long while, until one day he happened to meet an armed knight, who asked him who he was.

'I am a knight', he said, 'of King Arthur.'

'Of King Arthur?' he said; 'then you can certainly say that you serve the most foolish king in the world.'

'Why?' asked the knight who had been ill.

'Because', he said, 'his household is full of foolish pride.'

'Why do you say that?' he asked.

'It happened', said the other, 'that a wounded knight went there this year, and a knight swore to him that he would avenge him on all those who said that they loved the man who gave him the wounds better than the knight himself.* And if he had the prowess of Sir Gawain and four like him,* he would still fail.'

[225] 'Why?' said the other; 'surely you are not one of those who love the dead man better than the wounded man?'

'Certainly I am,' he said.

'Indeed?' said the other; 'you should be sorry about that.'

'Why?' he said; 'are you the knight who undertook the task?'

'I shall do my best in the matter,' he said. 'Nevertheless, before I have to fight with you, I beg you to say that you love the wounded man better than the man who wounded him.'

'Then I should be lying,' the other said, 'and may God never be my witness if I lie about it.'

'By my faith,' he said, 'then I shall have to fight you.'

'I ask for nothing better,' said the other.

Then they both moved some distance apart, and rode as fast as their horses could go, and struck one another on the shields so hard that, strong as they were, each had his spine bent over the back of his saddle. The knight who had been ill struck the other so hard that shield and hauberk did not save him, and he put lance-head and shaft through his body. The other, for his part, struck him so hard that he put his lance clean through his trunk. They were strong and valorous, and their blows were so violent that they knocked each other to the ground. And as they fell, both the lances broke. The knight who was ill was not fatally wounded, and he sprang up, for he considered the other very valorous, as he had given him the best blow he had ever received. He made a big effort to show great prowess, and went towards the other with drawn sword; however, it was to no purpose, for he was dead, struck through the innards. When he saw that he was dead, he wept with grief, for he considered him a very valorous knight.

Then he tried to ride, but he could not stand it. None the less, he mounted, and rode in great pain as far as a nearby forest. Then his squires made him a litter, and equipped it very richly with everything necessary and covered it with a very rich silk cloth, for the Lady of the Lake had given him many rich and beautiful silks, and the richest bed that you could want for a knight. When they had prepared the litter, they laid their lord in it and rode slowly on their way. The litter went along very smoothly, for he was carried by two of the most beautiful palfreys you could wish for, which his lady had also given him. Thus the knight went off in the litter. [226] At this point, though, the story stops speaking of him for a while, and returns to Sir Gawain, who was looking for him.

[M. XXXIIIa] Sir Gawain, the story says, when he had embarked on his quest for the knight who conquered the Dolorous Guard, travelled for two whole weeks, without hearing any news of him, until one day he happened to meet a damsel on a palfrey. He greeted her, and she him.

'Damsel,' he said, 'do you have any news of the knight who conquered the Dolorous Guard?'

'Oho!' she said, 'I am sure you are Gawain, the nephew of King Arthur, who left the damsel in captivity.'

'Truly, damsel,' he said, 'I was sorry about it. But, damsel, for the Lord's sake, tell me if you know anything about the man I am looking for.'

'No,' she said, 'but they would certainly tell you at the Dolorous Guard.'

'Will you tell me any more?' he asked.

'No.'

He went on, and so did she; and he travelled until he reached the far edge of a forest. The maiden who had spoken to him was the one who had recently been sent to the knight that Sir Gawain was looking for, by the Lady of the Lake. And she was looking for him herself, for the other maiden[1] had sent her. When he was out of the forest, he saw before him some very beautiful pavilions, pitched in a large meadow, and there were easily enough there to shelter 200 knights. He looked to his right, and saw, coming out of the forest, the two palfreys which were carrying the White Knight in the litter, and the road they were following met his. Sir Gawain waited for the litter, which pleased him greatly, for he had never seen one so fine. Then he asked the squires to whom it belonged.

'My lord,' they said, 'to a wounded knight.'

The wounded knight had the cloth raised and asked Sir Gawain who he was; and he said that he was a knight of King Arthur's household. When he heard that, he was afraid that he would recognize him, and he covered himself up again. Sir Gawain asked him who he was, and he said that he was a knight going about some business. The knight went on, while Sir Gawain continued to wait at the edge of the forest to find out to whom the pavilions belonged. Two knights came out of one and went, on foot, to disport themselves in the forest. Sir Gawain greeted them, and asked them to whom the pavilions belonged. And they said:

'To the King of a Hundred Knights, who is going to the encounter.'

---

[1] i.e. the maiden waiting in the Dolorous Guard.

'Which side', said Sir Gawain, 'will he be on?'

'With the King from Over the Borders,' they said; 'and you, who are you?'

[227]'I am a knight,' he said, 'going about my business.'

The King of a Hundred Knights was so called because he never rode out of his land without taking a hundred knights. And when he wished, he had many more than that, for he was rich and powerful, cousin to Galehot, the son of the Beautiful Giantess, and lord of the land of Estregor, which bordered with the kingdom of North Wales and the duchy of Cambenic.

Sir Gawain left the two knights and commended them to God. Then he looked, and saw squires bringing a dead knight out of the forest. He turned and went over there, and asked them who killed him. They told him that a knight killed him that day, who carried a red shield with a white band; and they told him that it was because he would not say that he loved a wounded man better than the man who wounded him. 'And he himself', they said, 'is badly wounded.' Then it occurred to Sir Gawain that it was the knight in the litter, and he thought he must be the one who removed the weapons from the knight's wounds at Camelot. Then he turned and went after him, past the pavilions of the King of a Hundred Knights.

The men in the pavilions thought he had come to seek a knightly encounter, and they sent him an armed knight. And he said that he had not come for that, for he had something else to do. With that he went on, and when he had gone some way, he saw a very fine pavilion, on its own, and he saw a number of lances leant against it. He went to the pavilion, and found a number of squires outside it, and as many as five shields leant against the pavilion, upside-down. Then he asked the squires to whom the pavilion belonged.

'My lord,' they said, 'to a knight who is lying down inside.'

He dismounted and went into the pavilion, and saw four

knights lying on two beds, and on a third, which was larger, lay another by himself, on a quilt made of gold-worked cloth, and he was covered with an ermine bedspread. He asked:

'Who are you, sir knight, lying there?'

The other sat up.

'And you, who are you,' he said, 'who ask?'

Then Sir Gawain realized that it was Helys the Blond, and he told him who he was. And Helys sprang up and said:

'You are welcome.'

Then they made much of one another, being companions who loved one another.

'And where are you going in this way?' asked Helys.

[228] 'I was following a litter,' he said, 'which passed by here just now.'

'It is too late to go on today,' said Helys; 'you must stop for the night.'

And he agreed.

As they were talking like this, Helys's squires came in from outside.

'My lord,' they said, 'you are missing wonderful things. The whole world is going along this road. You never saw such a crowd.'

Then they disarmed Sir Gawain.

'Sir,' Helys said, 'do let us go and see these knights who are passing, in such a way that they do not see us.'

'How shall we do that?' asked Sir Gawain.

'Our squires', Helys replied, 'will make us a shelter of branches, and we shall be inside it.'

Sir Gawain said that that was fine.

The squires made the shelter, and they went inside and saw all those who arrived and passed by on the road. As they were watching in this way, they saw two groups of fully armed knights coming. There were ten knights in each, and in between rode four squires who were holding a cloth on four poles. Under the cloth rode a lady, whose palfrey and other trappings were very rich and elegant. She was dressed in a tunic and cloak of crimson samite, trimmed with ermine, and her hair was loose. And she was remarkably beautiful. Then Helys said to Sir Gawain:

'There is one of the most beautiful women I have ever seen. I do not know if she is a lady or a maiden, but truly,' he went on,* 'she is very beautiful.'

After that they saw twenty knights of the King of a Hundred Knights coming after them.[1] And they[2] said to those escorting her:

'Gentlemen, the king sends you word that you are to take this lady to see him.'

They said that they would not.

'Yes, you will,' said the others, 'or we shall fight you.'

The lady's knights saw that there was no alternative. They turned to meet them, twenty against twenty. There were some who knocked one another down, and some who broke their lances without falling. They drew their swords, and began to fight, on foot and on horseback. Sir Gawain and Helys had gone out of the shelter to watch them; and Sir Gawain said to Helys:

'Let us separate them, for the king has some of his best knights there, and those of the lady may not be such experienced warriors.'

Then they went to them and separated them, and told them to stop the fighting, and they would take the lady to the king. They stopped; and Sir Gawain and Helys mounted two horses, and took the lady to the [229] king. He came out of the pavilion to meet them, and saw that she was very beautiful, and thought she seemed a very noble lady.

'My lord,' said Sir Gawain, 'we have brought this lady to see you, and we shall take her back.'

'Madam,' said the king, 'first tell me who you are.'

---

[1] i.e. the lady's party.   [2] i.e. the knights.

She said that she was the Lady of Nohaut.

'Indeed,' he said, 'I can well believe it,* and if I had known, I should have come after you myself.'

Then Helys and Sir Gawain took the lady back to beyond their pavilion. There she left them, and the two of them stayed behind. She went on her way towards the encounter, for at that time the ladies of quality went to them. At this point, though, the story stops speaking of her and Sir Gawain for a while, and returns to speak of the White Knight, who was going along in the litter.

[M. XXXIVa] When the knight in the litter left Sir Gawain, he travelled as far as a beautiful stretch of open country, which was no more than three leagues from there. In that open country rose a very beautiful spring, under one of the biggest sycamores he had ever seen. Then the knight got out to rest, and slept a little. And he sent two of his squires on from there to a city, to prepare his lodging. When he had slept, it was drawing towards evening. Then he got in again, and at once a squire passed him, on a hack, at full gallop. The knight heard the noise, and lifted up the cloth and asked the squire where he was going in such haste.

'I am seeking help,' he said, 'for the King of a Hundred Knights has detained the Lady of Nohaut.'

At once the knight had the litter turned around, and said that he wished to help. When he had gone some way, he met the lady; and she asked his squires:

'Who is in that litter?'

'My lady,' they said, 'it is a wounded knight who had heard that you were detained, and was coming to help you.'

Then she herself raised the cover of the litter, and the knight wrapped himself up well, so that she should not recognize him.

'Sir,' she said, 'were you coming to help me?'

'Yes, madam,' he said.

'Thank you,' she said; 'as you were coming to help me, you shall stay with me.'

'Madam,' he said, 'I shall not, for you will go faster than I shall, for I am unwell.'

[230] Thereupon the lady left, without recognizing the knight. And the litter went at a more gentle pace, until in the late evening he came to the city called Orkenise.* In that city the knight took a red shield, leaving his there, for he did not wish to be recognized at the encounter. And it was only a short day's journey from there to the encounter. That night his wounds were well looked after, for an old knight, who knew a good deal about wounds, looked at them for him. The day of the encounter was not for another five days, and so he stayed on in the town, on the knight's advice, and his wound was much improved. On the fifth day, the knight set off, still travelling in the litter, and reached Godoarre while it was still evening. The area was already so crowded that one could not find lodging there, but nearby there was a monastery where they gave him hospitality, because he was ill, and he was lodged in a beautiful and comfortable chamber. In the morning the knight heard mass, and then promptly had himself armed. And King Arthur had come with a great force; and he was not able to lodge in the castle, but camped outside instead. In the morning he had it announced that no one from his household or among those who had come with him should bear arms that day. Many good knights of his household were very unhappy about that. However, there were others there who had not come for his sake, or in his army, but some to win renown, and others for gain.* These armed themselves as soon as it was morning, and went on to the battleground.

The King from Over the Borders had come out of the line to join battle; but when he saw that King Arthur was not bearing arms in person, he withdrew again. And many of the lively knights bachelor* of his army went to joust with those who were waiting for them on the battleground. The tourney started, well contested, for on King Arthur's side there were many men of valour who had not shown themselves,* so as to have the opportunity to tourney. Sir Gawain was there, and Helys the Blond, and the Good and Handsome, his brother, Gales the Gay, and Tor, the son of Ares, and many other good knights. On the other side were Malaguin, the King of a Hundred Knights, and Helain the Dragon, and Duke Galot of Yberge, and many others who were very valorous. The jousting began on the two sides; and the queen went into the castle and went up on to the walls to see the tournament, and with her went many ladies, damsels, and knights, and they watched many knights who were fighting well.

Then the knight of the litter came, and around his neck he had the red shield. He passed in front of the queen, then entered the lists* and went to joust with a knight. They struck one another, so that their lances flew into pieces. They crashed into one another with bodies and faces.* The [231] knight of the litter remained in the saddle, and the other flew over his horse's crupper to the ground.

'Now,' most people said, 'I have seen a new knight* perform a very fine joust.'

The knight went back and took a lance from one of his squires, and re-entered the lists, and struck a knight, so that he knocked him to the ground. Then he began to knock knights down, and to carry shields away from necks, and to break lances; and he fought so well that all the knights were astonished, and said to Sir Gawain:

'Do you know that knight?'

'No,' he said, 'but he is fighting so well that I am lingering to watch him, for his knightly deeds are greatly to my liking.'

Those on the walls said that the knight with the red arms was surpassing everyone. The King of a Hundred Knights asked who he was; and he was told he was a knight who was surpassing everyone and who had red arms. The king took his shield and asked for a lance, and charged along the lists, and the knight with the red shield charged to meet him, and they struck one another so hard that their lances flew into pieces, but they did not knock each other down. The king was very upset that he had not knocked him down, and the other was even more upset that he had not knocked the king down. They took new lances and charged towards one another again. The horses went very fast, and they struck one another very hard. The knight with the red shield struck the king through the shield and through both sides of the hauberk* and through the side, but he did not wound him very badly. And the king struck him on the exposed hauberk,* between the breast and the shoulder, and put the lance-head through him. The lances broke, and they crashed together with bodies and horses, and knocked one another to the ground. The king leapt to his feet again, and put his shield in front of him, and pulled out his sword. And when the knight fell, face down, the lance-head passed right out through his shoulder, and that wound burst open and bled, and the old wound also bled profusely. When he saw the king, who had his shield on his arm and his sword drawn, he sprang up, very upset, and put his shield in front of him, and pulled out his sword and went towards the king; and they struck one another great blows. The knight with the red arms was bleeding freely. The king's men galloped up to remount him; and Sir Gawain and those who were on the side of the knight galloped after the king and pursued him a long way. Then they brought the knight his horse, and as he was going to mount, he fell down unconscious. They saw the blood around him, and everyone said: 'He is a dead man.' They dismounted, and pulled out the lance, and saw that he had two great wounds.

[232] Word reached the King of a Hundred Knights that he had killed the good knight. He was very distressed, and threw down his shield and lance, saying that he would not

bear arms again that day, and perhaps never again, for things had turned out very badly for him, when he had killed such a knight. The knight lay unconscious, and they disarmed him and bandaged his wounds. The queen and those who were with her saw that everything had stopped because the knight was wounded.

'Let us go', she said, 'and see him.'

She mounted and went out through the gate. And the clamour began, with everyone saying 'Turn aside, here is the queen.' There were many who helped her dismount, and everyone again cried: 'Make way, here is the queen.'

The knight had come to, and heard what they were saying. He opened his eyes and saw the queen, and struggled into a sitting position.

'Sir,' the queen said, 'how are you?'

'Very well, my lady,' he said; 'I am in no pain.'*

As he said that, the bandages broke and his wounds burst open and bled, and he passed out again. 'He is a dead man,' everyone said. And the queen went away at once. The knights asked where the wounded knight was lodged, and his squires said, in a house of religion. They found him a very good doctor and had him carried to his lodging. The doctor examined the wounds and said that he would not die of them, but he ordered that no one was to go near him for the rest of the day, for he did not need excitement. All the knights went away, but it occurred to Sir Gawain that he had heard no news of the man he was looking for, and he was supposed to hear word at the encounter.*

'And I have not heard or seen anything, except that this knight has surpassed everyone. I ought to go and talk to him, to enquire and discover whether he knows anything of the man I am looking for.'

He went to his[1] lodging and asked the doctor what he thought.

---

[1] i.e. the wounded knight's.

'I think,' the doctor said, 'that he will recover, although his wounds have bled a great deal.'

'His wounds?' said Sir Gawain; 'how many does he have, then?'

'He has two very large ones,' the doctor said, 'one from today and an old one.'

When Sir Gawain heard about the old wound, he thought for a moment and then said to the doctor:

'Do you truly say there are two wounds?'

'Yes,' he said, 'assuredly.'

'Ha! master,'* he said, 'now, enquire how he came here.'

The doctor asked the squires, and they dared not keep it from him, and said that he [233] came in a litter. He told Sir Gawain, who begged him to let him speak to the knight, and he took him to him.

'My lord,' he said, 'here is Sir Gawain, who has come to see you.'

Sir Gawain sat down beside him and enquired whether he had any news of the knight who let King Arthur into the Dolorous Guard. He said very little in reply, but he did say:

'Sir, I am ill, and I am not interested in what you are asking me.'

When Sir Gawain saw that he would not learn any more for the moment, he stood up and left, and thought that he was so ill that he could not talk to him, but he would come and see him tomorrow, and ask him more. He went away to his lodging; and when it was dark, the wounded knight called his doctor and said:

'Ah! master, I cannot stay here, for it would be bad for me if I were recognized. I beg you, for the Lord's sake, to come with me; and if you are not prepared to come, then tell me what to do, for I shall leave tonight.'

'Will anything make you stay?' the doctor asked.

'No.'

'And how will you go?'

'In a litter,' he said; 'I have an excellent one.'

'I will go with you,' the doctor said, 'for, if I did not, you might soon die, and that would be a great pity.'

He was overjoyed. Then they started on their journey, and left secretly. Now, though, the story falls silent about him and his company for a while, and speaks of King Arthur and Sir Gawain.

[M. XXXVa] In the morning Sir Gawain went to talk to the knight, and was told that he had left around midnight. He was very upset, and went back and found the king and his companions armed. And he went to arm, without making himself known. When they were out of the castle, they jousted with those from the other side. However, the battle did not last long, for the others could not withstand the king's forces. And once he* arrived, then no one resisted except in retreat. The king chased them as far as their castle and drove them headlong in there. And as he was returning to the camp, he met Sir Gawain, his drawn sword in his hand. He recognized his sword, and asked:

'Gawain, dear nephew, what success have you had in your quest?'

'Sire,' he said, 'none as yet.'

[234] While they were talking like this, a very elegantly turned-out knight said to the king:

'My lord, the King from Over the Borders and the King of a Hundred Knights send you word: they are well aware that no one could withstand your force; however, if you would accept an encounter with them on another day, and come with such numbers that the knights who came could bear arms,* they would undertake it seven weeks from today.'

'I will not concern myself with it,' said the king.

'Sir,' said Sir Gawain, 'my lord's household will accept it against the two of them, if they wish, at a later date, the Monday before Advent.'*

The other said that they would be willing; and Sir Gawain

sent Lucan the butler to the two kings to see if they were willing to do that, and they agreed.

King Arthur went back to his country with the queen, and the armies dispersed. And the knights looked forward to the appointed day. Sir Gawain embarked on his quest; and as soon as he left the king, he met a damsel, riding very swiftly on a fast mule. He greeted her, and she him, and he asked her if she had some urgent business.

'Yes,' she said, 'and very dolorous. And you, where are you going in this way?'

'Damsel,' he said, 'I am going about some business in which I have not yet fared as well as I should wish. Dear friend,' he said, 'can you give me news of the knight who let the king into the Dolorous Guard?'

'I shall certainly give you news of him,' she said, 'if you will tell me what I wish to know.'

'Ask me,' he said, 'and if I know, I shall tell you.'

'Is it true that the knight with the red arms is dead, the one who was the victor at the encounter?'

'Not at all,' he said; 'in fact, his doctor told me he would recover all right.'

When she heard that, she lost consciousness, and fell fainting on to the neck of the mule. He ran to hold her up, and when she came to, he asked her why she had fainted.

'Sir, from joy,' she said.

'Damsel,' he said, 'do you know him, the knight?'

'Yes, sir,' she said.

'Now, tell me in return about the man I asked about.'

'It is him,'* she said, 'understand that. And what is your name?'

'[235] 'My name is Gawain.'

'Ah! sir,' she said, 'I am pleased to see you. And, for the Lord's sake, would you like me to come with you?'

'I should be delighted,' he said.

They rode together, and he said:

'Damsel, do you love the knight?'

'Yes, sir,' she said, 'more than any other man, but not in the way you are thinking. I should not want him to marry me. And the man who has me will not make a bad match, for I am quite a rich woman; but, please God, he will make a better. Sir,' she went on, 'do you remember meeting a damsel the other day?'

'Yes,' he said, 'was that you? You reproached me for having left the damsel in the Dolorous Guard, and then I saw the knight we are looking for.'

'That is the truth,' she said. 'And I nearly died because of him, for I was told he was mortally wounded, and I fell ill. Then I was told he would be at this encounter; and today a squire again told me he had been killed.'

'Damsel,' he said, 'since you know him, you can tell me his name, and you will have freed me from this quest.'*

'As God is my true witness,' she said, 'I do not know it. However, I shall know it as soon as I find him, and then I shall tell you.'

He thanked her.

'Now, tell me,' he said, 'did you hear any word of him, where you have come from?'

'No.'

'Nor I,' he said, 'where I have come from. So, I suggest that we look for a road which leads elsewhere.'

'All right,' she said.

Before long, they found an old road through the forest, and beside it, a ruined minster and a cemetery. They took that road, and when they came to the minster, they dismounted and went in to pray. Beside the minster was an anchoress, at a window near the altar, where she was reading her psalter. When they saw her, they asked her if she had any news.

'I have none', she said to Sir Gawain, 'which can be of

much use to you, except that, if you are taking that maiden, do not go that way.'

'Why not?' he asked.

[236] 'Because near here there is a knight who will take her from you, and he will quickly kill you.'

'Who is he?' asked Sir Gawain.

'Brehu the Pitiless.'

'Sir,' the maiden said, 'let us go another way.'

'Indeed,' he said, 'I should have a pretty task, if I left my road for everything I heard!'

They left the minster and went on their way. Now, though, the story falls silent about them for a while, and returns to the wounded knight in the litter.

[M. XXXIVa] When the knight in the litter left the encounter in the night, he and his doctor and his company travelled through the most remote regions they could find and which they knew of, for they thought they might be recognized. The next day was fiercely hot, and when it was past terce, he got out at a crossroads, in the shadow of a great elm, to sleep. Then a damsel came by with a great troop of knights. And when she came up to them, she asked the doctor:

'Who is that knight?'

'My lady,' he said, 'he is a knight who is ill.'

The lady dismounted, and uncovered his face, and immediately began to weep bitterly.

'My friend,' she said to the doctor, 'for the Lord's sake, will he recover?'

'Yes, my lady,' he said, 'rest assured.'

Then the knight woke up, and she began to kiss him on the eyes and the mouth. He looked, and realized that it was the Lady of Nohaut, and tried to cover his face.

'It is no use,' she said. 'You will come with me, and you will be taken care of more richly than anywhere else in the world. And you, sir,' she said to the doctor, 'for the Lord's sake advise him to do that.'

The knight saw that there was no escape, and so he agreed, and she was delighted. Then they helped him back into the litter and they rode on together. The lady told him how she was looking for him, and would never have stopped searching through lands until she found him. Thus they rode in easy stages and slept most nights in pavilions, for the lady had two very fine ones. They came to the Dolorous Guard, and the lady expected to sleep down in the town,* but the knight said that he would not go in there for anything.

'Why not?' she asked.

He did not reply, but looked at the gate, and began to weep bitterly, and said:

[237] 'Ah! gate, gate, why were you not opened in time?'

He was talking about the gate where he made the queen wait around, when he was overwhelmed on the walls. And he thought the queen knew it as well as he did,* and that she would hate him for ever because of it.

'Were you ever here before?' asked the lady.

He was so troubled that he could not reply. And she at once thought that it was he who had conquered the castle, and she did not dare say any more about it, because she saw he was upset. They travelled until they reached the lady's castle, which was ten leagues from Nohaut. In that castle the lady kept the knight company as long as he was ill, and he had whatever he needed. And the story stops speaking of him for a while and returns to Sir Gawain and the maiden.

[M. XXXVIIa] Sir Gawain and the maiden left the anchoress and rode until they emerged from the forest and found a magnificent pavilion in a large stretch of open country. They did not stop there, but went on past. And before long a squire came very swiftly after them, on a hunter, and caught up with them and said to Sir Gawain:

'Sir knight, my lord sends you word that you are to send or bring this lady to him.'

'Who is your lord?' he asked.

'Brehu the Pitiless,' said the squire.

'I will neither bring her,' said Sir Gawain, 'nor send her to him, unless she goes of her own free will.'

'I shall go,' she said, 'rather than let you fight with him.'

'You are not going there today,' he said.

The squire turned back; and when Sir Gawain and the maiden had gone some way, Brehu came after them, fully armed, and cried very loudly:

'Leave me the maiden, or you will pay dearly.'

'I will not leave her,' Sir Gawain said.

They turned aside on to the open ground. Brehu struck Sir Gawain, so that his lance flew into pieces; and Sir Gawain struck him, so that he knocked him to the ground, and then caught his horse, and brought it back to him.

'Here is your horse,' he said, 'for I have better things to do, and I am going on.'

'Who are you,' he said, 'that you give me back my horse when you have knocked me down?'

'I am Gawain.'

'Where are you going?' asked Brehu.

[238] 'We are looking', he said, 'for the knight with red arms, who was victorious at the encounter.'

'I shall not tell you what I know about him at the moment,' said Brehu, 'for I am going about some business, but if you were to be in this spot two weeks from today, I should give you reliable news of him.'

'We shall be here,' he said, 'if we hear no word before then.'

With that they parted, and Sir Gawain travelled for the whole fortnight, without hearing any word; so he went back to that spot, and the maiden with him, and they met Brehu.

'What can you tell me?' asked Sir Gawain.

'I shall give you news of him,' said Brehu, 'provided that you will give me what I ask.'

'Agreed,' said Sir Gawain; 'if it is something I can and should give you.'

'Then let me tell you', he said, 'that he is in a castle which the Lady of Nohaut holds from two brothers, to whom it belongs, and they are her nephews. I have been there three times since I saw you. The first time, I saw him fencing, and his doctor said to him, when he had fenced for a while: "That is enough, my lord." The next day, I saw that he allowed him to exert himself more. Three days ago I was there again, and I saw him outside the castle on horseback, a shield around his neck and a lance in his hand, and he was seeing whether he could bear arms yet. Now it only remains', he went on, 'to go there; and if it is him,[1] then give me my recompense, and if not, then you are under no obligation.'

Then they all went away, and journeyed until they reached the castle. Brehu remained outside, and they went into the castle, as far as the lady's residence. The knight who was ill heard that Sir Gawain was coming, and he said to his doctor:

'Master, Sir Gawain is coming here, and you are to tell him that I am very ill.'

'Gladly, my lord,' he said.

Then he put him to bed in a dark chamber, and then went back out. Sir Gawain and the maiden arrived, and the lady of the castle received Sir Gawain very warmly. Then he asked the doctor privately if he would please let him see the knight.

'My lord,' he said, 'that is impossible, for he is too ill.'

'If I cannot see him,' Sir Gawain said, 'let this damsel see him.'

'Willingly,' said the other, who did not realize.

He led her to the chamber, and she opened a window.* When the knight saw her, he covered his face. She ran to

---

[1] i.e. the knight Gawain is seeking.

uncover it, [239] but he reached out towards her, and took her by the arm. She saw his hand, and recognized it, and kissed it until she fainted over it. And when she came to, she said: 'It is no use hiding.'

Then she drew out a letter, and broke the seal, and read that the maiden who was left in the Dolorous Guard greeted Lancelot of the Lake, the son of King Ban of Benwick, and sent him word that she would remain a prisoner as long as he pleased, but he should know that he had behaved despicably towards her, and she loyally towards him. When he heard that, he was very grieved, and began to weep bitterly. Then he called the maiden, and said:

'Dear friend, go quickly, and tell her that I beg her forgiveness, for I have wronged her badly. And she is to leave there now, for I wish it.'

'That is impossible,' she said; 'she will not leave unless she sees you or that ring on your finger.'*

'She is right,' he said, 'for where the ring is, there am I. Now here it is: take it to her.'

The damsel went gaily back out of the chamber; and he begged her not to tell anyone his name. She went outside, and Sir Gawain said to her:

'My friend, what can you tell me?'

'Good news,' she said.

'Will you tell me the knight's name?'

'I shall take you somewhere where you will discover it; and he is the knight who was victorious at the encounter.'

Then they left, and found Brehu waiting for them at the gate.

'Sir Gawain,' he said, 'do you owe me any recompense?'

'Yes.'

'Then I shall follow you until you have something I would like.'

Thus the three of them went along, until on the third day

they reached the Dolorous Guard; and Sir Gawain recognized the castle.

'I know very well,' he said to the damsel, 'where you are taking me.'

'I shall bring you only good,' she said.

They reached the castle, and found it closed. Then they went to the gate near the tower, and the damsel called. And the gatekeeper said that she could not go in.

'Here,' she said, 'take this token to the damsel in that tower.'

He opened the wicket-gate, and she gave him the ring from the knight of the litter. He closed it again, and then went to the damsel in the tower, and said:

'My lady, there are a damsel and a knight outside, and they send you this token to be allowed in.'

She looked at the ring, and said:

[240] 'Go quickly. Let them come in.'

He went to the gate, and opened it, and they went in. The damsel from the tower went to meet them, and said:

'Welcome. Now I shall come away with you whenever you wish.'

Meanwhile, Brehu had remained outside at the gate.

'Damsel,' said Sir Gawain, 'I do not yet know the name of the knight who let my lord King Arthur in here.'

The maiden who had brought him there spoke privately with the other, who said to Sir Gawain:

'I shall tell you the knight's name, but first you must come where I take you.'

Then she led him to the cemetery and showed him the tombs.

'You have been here before,' she said.

'Yes, indeed,' he said.

Then she led him to a tomb.

'On this tomb,' she said, 'was written, recently: "Here lies Gawain, the nephew of King Arthur, and there is his head."'

And the same for all your companions. You did not find any of that when you came here.'

'How did it happen, then?' he asked.

'Those are the enchantments of this place,' she replied.

'Now, tell me the knight's name,' he said.

'You will find it,' she said, 'under that slab of metal.'

He went to the slab and tried it, but he could not lift it at all; and he was very upset.

'Damsel,' he said, 'could I find out the knight's name another way?'

'Yes,' she said, 'if you take me to find him, I shall let you know it.'

'How can I be sure of that?' he said.

'I give you my word,' she said, 'faithfully.'

'Then I shall take you,' he said.

Then they went out of the cemetery; and the damsel mounted a palfrey which was brought for her. When they went out through the gate, they met Brehu.

'Sir Gawain,' he said, 'I now ask you for my boon.'

'What?'

'That maiden you have found in there.'

'Brehu,' he said, 'I cannot give her away, for she is not mine; and I only promised you something which I could and should give you.'

[241] 'There was no proviso,' Brehu said.

'Yes, there was,' said Sir Gawain, 'that one, and if you wish, I am ready to submit that to the judgement of my uncle's companions, and let it be as they decide, combat or otherwise.'

Brehu said that he would do no such thing, but would fight there and then. None the less, the maidens entreated him until he agreed to put it off until the day of the encounter, when they would ask the knights what should be done, provided that, if the knights' decision did not suit Brehu, he could still have his combat. Sir Gawain agreed to that.

Thereupon they set out. The story says no more about them at this point, though, until it has spoken of the knight of the litter.

[M. XXXVIIIa] The knight was in the care of the Lady of Nohaut until he was somewhat recovered, and he greatly desired to bear arms, from which he had had a long rest. He went to the lady, and took leave of her. Then he left, with his doctor, whom the lady had paid handsomely for his service. And the knight asked him:

'Master, am I not well enough to bear arms, then?'

'No,' he said; 'you might take on such a great task that you would be back to square one.'

'A great task, master! No one can refrain from that, when the need arises.'

'Then take care', the doctor said, 'to begin with.'

'Truly,' he said, 'if I can use all my limbs, it seems to me that I am well.'

'Do you not intend to go to the encounter, then?' asked the doctor.

'Yes,' he said.

'And which would you prefer, to be fit at the encounter and ill in the meantime, or to be ill then and well beforehand?'

'I should not want', the knight said, 'to miss bearing arms at the encounter for anything.'

'Then I suggest', said the doctor, 'that you rest until then, and then you will be fit and well and in full vigour.'

'Since you suggest it,' said the knight, 'I shall do that. However, I shall not return where I have just come from, but shall go to a hermit, a very holy man, that I know.'

They set out together, for the doctor did not wish to leave him before the encounter, and they went along until they reached the dwelling of the Hermit of the Thicket—that was his name; and he was the one with whom he had [242] left Brandin of the Isles a prisoner, the man who was lord of the Dolorous Guard. The hermit was overjoyed and received them with great honour, but he was very much dismayed by the knight's wounds. The knight stayed there until his doctor told him he was fitter and sounder in body and limbs than he had ever been; and there were still two weeks until the encounter. Now the story again stops speaking of him and his company for a time and returns to speak of Sir Gawain.

[M. XXXIXa] Sir Gawain, when he left the Dolorous Guard, travelled with his two maidens and Brehu the Pitiless until they came to the castle where the wounded knight had stayed. When they did not find him, they were very upset; and Sir Gawain said that he did not expect to hear any news of him before the encounter.

'What?' said the maiden who had been a prisoner, 'will there be an encounter soon?'

'Yes,' he said, 'less than a month from now.'

'He will be there,' she said, 'unless he meets with some obstacle.'

Thereupon they left and rode where they were led by Brehu, who said that he knew the roads better than anyone.

'I want you to know one thing,' he said to Sir Gawain; 'it would be very difficult to take these two maidens away from us, if I were to help you.'

'That is true,' said Sir Gawain, 'and if you did not help me, you would be perfidious.'

Thus they travelled until evening, when they saw a pavilion, and near the pavilion there was a river. By the river there was a hunted stag, and the dogs had caught it on the bank. After it came a knight, a horn around his neck and a huntsman with him, and they were sounding the kill. Sir Gawain and his company went there, and when the knight saw them, he greeted them.

'Gentlemen,' he said, 'if you would care for some of this stag, I shall give you some. And if you would care to stop for the night, this pavilion is mine, and I shall give you lodging, if you wish.'

'Sir,' said Sir Gawain, 'many thanks, and we will stop.'

He dismounted, and squires took their arms. When they were disarmed, Brehu spoke privately with the knight, who then went to Sir Gawain.

'Sir,' he said, 'I have given you lodging, and for tonight you have nothing to fear. [243] But tomorrow, once you have left, I give you no such guarantee.'

'Sir,' said Sir Gawain, 'I should be sorry if you were to do me harm.'

The knight gave them excellent hospitality. In the morning, Sir Gawain and Brehu and the two maidens left, and travelled for much of the day, until they met two fully armed knights. The knights never spoke to them, but took their shields by the straps and charged towards Sir Gawain, and he towards them, and he thought Brehu would do the same, but he did not move. One of the knights struck Sir Gawain on the shield, so that his lance flew into pieces; and Sir Gawain struck him, so that he knocked him to the ground. The other struck Sir Gawain's horse in the flank, and killed it, and he was left on foot. And when the one who had killed the horse saw that he was on foot, he dismounted. Now all three were on foot. The two attacked Sir Gawain, and he defended himself against them very well and did them more harm than they did him. They fought in this way for a long while, and the two could never make Sir Gawain give ground, while he often made them retreat.

When the maiden who led Sir Gawain to the Dolorous Guard saw that the fight was in earnest, she was afraid for him and began to cry out very energetically. Then she flung herself down from her palfrey and rushed between them, crying like a madwoman:

'Whore's sons! coward knights, do you wish to kill the most valorous man in the world so treacherously?'*

'Damsel, who is he?' asked one of them.

'Who?' she said, 'he is Sir Gawain, the nephew of King Arthur.'

He looked at his companion.

'In God's name,' he said, 'I shall not fight with him any more, and a curse on the man who made us come here.'

'Sir,' said the other, 'by the person you most love, are you Sir Gawain?'

And he told him he was.

'Ah! sir,' they said, 'for the Lord's sake, forgive us the wrong we have done you, for just as we now consider you the most valorous man in the world, so we did consider you the most perfidious man in the world. And we shall leave you, now.'

'You are leaving me in a strange fashion,' said Sir Gawain, 'having killed my horse.'

'Sir,' said the one who had killed it, 'I shall give you mine in place of yours.'

[244] And he took it. And that was the knight who had given Sir Gawain and his maidens lodging, but Brehu had given him to understand that Sir Gawain was guilty of all the treachery in the world. The two knights mounted one horse, and Brehu accompanied them some way. Then he went back to Sir Gawain and made as if to ride with him again. Sir Gawain looked at him.

'Brehu,' he said, 'you are not coming with me, for you have behaved treacherously towards me, and I do not care for your company. And I am ready to prove you guilty of that treachery here and now, and you will have the combat you have so desired.'

'I will not fight at the moment,' Brehu said, 'but you had a fright, all the same.'

With that he went away. Sir Gawain and his two maidens travelled until they came to a river. There was a fairly narrow bridge across the river, and at the end of the bridge, on the other side, there was a brattice and a closed gate. In front of the gate stood two men-at-arms with Danish axes.* Sir Gawain sent the two maidens across first, and he went on to the bridge after them. The men-at-arms said to him:

'There is no point in coming. You cannot pass here.'

'I cannot, then,' he said.

Then he dismounted, and drove his horse in front of him, and followed it on foot. He listened, and heard a noise; and he looked, and saw twenty knights following him, and he thought they were coming to do him harm. He went to the end of the bridge, and waited for them, and put his shield in front of him and held out his lance. They were coming very swiftly; and those who came first struck him on the shield, so that their lances flew into pieces. They attacked him on foot and on horseback, and he defended himself so well that he wounded many of them and killed many of their horses with his lance. And as long as it lasted, no one went near him, and when it failed him, he reached for his sword and attacked them and often drove them headlong off the bridge. When they saw that he was defending himself so well and that he was doing them more harm than they were doing him, they drew back. And the gate of the castle* behind him opened, and knights came out and took the two maidens, and led them away. When Sir Gawain saw that, he was very upset.

'Gentlemen,' he said, 'what you are doing is the most vile cowardice, for on the one hand twenty of you are fighting with me, and on the other, my maidens are being taken from me.'

'It is quite justified,' said one of the knights, 'for you behaved treacherously towards me, concerning our agreement.'

[245] 'Ha! Brehu, you are lying like a traitor; and I shall prove it, if you wish, in front of all those you have brought here.'

'Indeed,' said the damsel who had led him to the Dolorous Guard, 'he is truly a traitor; and if you were not the most valorous man in the world, he would have had you killed twice today.'

Then the men who were taking the maidens away asked who the knight was.

'It is Sir Gawain,' said one.

Then one of them[1] went back and said:

'Now, Sir Gawain, go wherever you please over there, but not over here. And I guarantee your safety for tonight, as far as I and all those here are concerned; and do not worry about the maidens, for I give you my word on peril of my soul that they will be taken care of with as much honour as if they were my sisters. And if I could give them back to you without breaking my oath, I should take them no further.'

Sir Gawain thanked him; and he had him given a lance, and ordered all the knights to go away. He went after the maidens that he was having taken away; and Sir Gawain left the bridge and went upstream on his horse. When he found a ford, he crossed over and went very fast, following the tracks he found, until he came to the edge of a forest. Then he met a damsel who was holding a wounded knight in her lap. Sir Gawain greeted her, and asked if she had seen some knights taking away two maidens.

'Yes,' she said, 'it was my misfortune that I saw them, for they have killed my lover.'

'Damsel, which way are they going?'

'Sir,' she said, 'wait a little while and I shall take you to where they are.'

Thereupon a squire came up on a hunter, an axe in his hand.

'What is it, my lady?' he said.

'I am afraid', she said, 'that your lord is dying. See to him, and I shall take this knight after the man who has killed him.'

She mounted her palfrey, and went with Sir Gawain. They

---

[1] i.e. the knights.

travelled until they came to a great river; there was no bridge, but they found a boat there, and an oar. They put their horses in the boat and got in after them; and Sir Gawain rowed them across. When he reached the other side, he found a fully-armed knight, who said to him:

'Do not get out, for you would have to fight me, as I guard this crossing.'

[246] 'I should be sorry to have to fight,' he said, 'for I have much else to do.'

'Who are you?' asked the knight.

'I am a knight', he said, 'of King Arthur's household.'

'What is your name?' said the other.

'My name is Gawain.'

'Then I shall let you pass,' said the other:* 'where do you wish to go?'

'I am following some other knights,' he said, 'who are taking away two damsels.'

'By my faith,' said the knight of the crossing, 'they are making straight for that castle over there.'

And he showed him, far away on top of a hill, a very strong castle. Then he told him that there were very wicked people in the castle.

'But if you wish to go there,' he said, 'I shall come with you and help you as much as I can.'

Sir Gawain thanked him.

'Sir Gawain,' the knight said, 'I shall tell you the custom of that castle. We shall have to fight an equal number of knights; and even if we defeat them, we shall not be safe from the others.'

'That is an evil custom,' said Sir Gawain.

Thus they rode together, and the damsel with them. And for now the story falls silent about the three of them for a while and returns to speak for a time of the knight of the litter.

[M. XLa] The knight of the litter lay up at the hermit's

dwelling until he was fully recovered and fit and very keen to bear arms. And there were now only two weeks until the encounter. Then he took leave of the hermit. He left with his doctor, who had looked after him very well, and his four squires. And when he was some six leagues from the hermitage, he called his doctor.

'Master,' he said, 'I must go about some business where you cannot come, for it would be too far for you to go, and I wish to go alone. I beg you not to be upset about it, and I thank you very much for the great attention you have devoted to me. And let me say that I shall always be at your service.'

Thereupon the doctor left him. And the knight travelled all day in the manner of someone who did not wish to be recognized. That was why he had separated from the doctor, so that he should not reveal anything about him in some place where he wished to conceal his identity. And he had his shield covered, so that no one should see it; and it was still the red shield. Thus he rode, in a different direction from the place where the encounter [247] was to be, to mislead the doctor. When he had travelled until about none, a squire caught up with him on a great, sweat-soaked hunter, and he appeared to be very distressed. And the knight asked him:

'Young man, where are you going so fast?'

'I have some desperately urgent business,' he said.

'What business?' asked the knight.

'My lady the queen is a prisoner in the Dolorous Guard.'

'Which queen?' asked the knight.

'The wife of King Arthur,' the squire said.

'Why is she there?' asked the knight.

'Because', he said, 'King Arthur let the knight who had conquered the castle go; and my lady had been brought to this encounter, and she lodged yesterday evening in the castle. Now they have made her a prisoner and they say that, for all King Arthur's might, she will never get out until she makes the knight come back, just as the king let him go. My lady is sending her messengers in every direction to ask the knight to help her; otherwise she will be dishonoured, for they will give her to the man who was lord of the castle, if he comes and destroys the enchantments; and he will be glad to do so, to dishonour King Arthur.'

'My friend,' said the knight, 'would the queen be freed if that knight came to the Dolorous Guard?'

'Yes, assuredly,' said the squire.

'That will be no obstacle,' he said. 'Now, go back at once and tell her that she shall have the knight in the morning, or even tonight, she may count on it.'

'My lord,' the squire said, 'I should not dare return unless I spoke to him.'

'Go on,' he said, 'and tell her confidently that you have spoken to him.'

'Are you he?' asked the squire; 'for I should not dare tell her that unless I knew it for certain.'

'Go on,' he said, 'for I am he—and you have made me say something unworthy.'

Thereupon the squire left, as fast as his horse could go. And the knight quickened his pace and went after him. It was night when he arrived, and as soon as he was inside the gate, he saw all the streets lit with large candles and torches. And the gate was closed again at once. Then the squire who had gone to look for him came to meet him. When the knight saw him, he asked:

'Where is my lady, the queen?'

'My lord, I shall take you there.'

He went in front and the knight followed, until they reached the great hall. Underneath the great hall the rock was chiselled out, and there was only [248] one entrance, and the door was of iron, so thick that nothing could break through it. The knight had taken off his helm, but he had not let down his ventail. And the squire gave him a handful of candles, and said:

'Light the way in front of you, and I shall close these doors again.'

He thought the squire was telling him the truth, but he was not: in fact he had betrayed him, for the queen had not set foot there. He closed the door again, as quickly as he could. When the knight saw he was trapped, he was distressed, for he was well aware he could not get out of there when he wished. The knight was in there all night, and in the morning a fairly elderly damsel came to him, and spoke to him through a window, and said:

'Sir knight, you see how it is. You cannot get out of here without coming to terms.'

'What terms, madam?' he asked.

'You are the man', she said, 'who conquered the fief* of this castle, and you should have brought peace to the castle, but you left it secretly.'

'Madam,' he said, 'is my lady the queen free yet?'

'Yes,' she said, 'and you are here instead of her, and the enchantments of this place must be ended by you.'

'How', he said, 'can I end them?'

'If you swear to do your best in whatever the adventure brings, you will be released from here.'

And he agreed. Then holy relics were brought to the window, and the knight swore as she had specified. They opened the iron door, and he went out. And they brought him very good food, for he had not eaten at all since the morning of the previous day. When he had eaten, they described the adventure to him and told him that he would have to stay in the castle for forty days, or go and fetch the keys of the enchantments. He said that he would go and fetch the keys, if he knew where they were. 'But hurry the business up,' he said, 'for I have a good deal to do elsewhere.'

They brought him his arms, and when he was armed, they took him to the cemetery where the tombs were. From the cemetery they went into a chapel which was at the end near

the tower; and when they were inside, they showed him the
entrance to an underground vault, and said that the key of
the enchantments was inside. He crossed himself and went
in, holding his shield in front of his face, and his sword
drawn. He could not see anything, except the opening of a
door, and beyond it he could see a great light. He went to
that door. When he was through the door, he heard a great
noise around him. He went on all the same; and then it
seemed to him that the whole vault was about to [249] collapse
and that the ground was spinning. He held on to the wall and
went along it until he came to a door further on, the entrance
to another chamber. When he reached the door, he saw two
knights cast in copper; and each of them held a steel sword,
so big and heavy that two men would have had difficulty in
lifting one, and they guarded the way in through the door,
and they struck out with the swords so often that nothing
could pass without receiving a blow. The knight was not
afraid of them, but thrust his shield over his head, and leapt
through. And one of them gave him such a blow that it cut
clean through his shield; and the blow landed on his right
shoulder, and sliced through the links of the hauberk so
cruelly that the red blood ran down his body. He fell on all
fours on the ground, but quickly sprang up again and picked
up his sword, which he had dropped, and put his shield in
front of his face, and he never looked back. He came to
another door, and saw on the threshold a well, the smell from
which was horrible; and all the noise which was heard in
there came from that well, which was at least six feet across.
The knight saw the well, black and terrible; and on the other
side was a man whose head was as black as ink, and blue
flame leapt from his mouth, and his eyes glowed like two
burning coals, and his teeth the same. The man held an axe
in his hand, and as the knight approached, he took it in both
hands and lifted it up to bar the way. The knight did not see
how he could go in there, for if there had only been the well,

it would have been a terrible place for an armed knight to cross.* Then he put his sword back in the scabbard and pulled the shield from around his neck, and took it in his right hand by the straps. Then he went some way back into the chamber, and charged as fast as he could go up to the edge of the well; and he threw the shield in front of him and struck the man who held the axe with it, so hard that the shield shattered completely, while the man never moved. And he immediately threw himself after it with all the force of his approach, and crashed into the other so hard that he would have fallen into the well if he had not held on to him.* Then the man dropped the axe, for the knight had taken him firmly by the throat with his strong hands, and so squeezed him that he could not stay on his feet, but fell to the ground, and could not get up. The knight dragged him to the well by the throat, and threw him in.

Then he drew his sword from the scabbard again, and saw in front of him a copper damsel, very finely cast, and she held the keys of the enchantments in her right hand. He took them, and then went to a copper pillar [250] which was in the middle of the chamber, and read the writing which he saw on it, which said: 'The large key is for here, and the small one unlocks the perilous chest.' The knight unlocked the pillar with the large key; and when he came to the chest, he listened and heard inside it such a great clamour and outcry that it made the whole pillar shake. He crossed himself, then made to unlock the chest. And he saw that thirty copper tubes came out of it, and from each tube came a hideous voice, and each one louder than the last.* From those voices came the enchantments and wonders of the place. He put the key in the chest. And when he had opened it, out sprang a great whirlwind and such a great clamour that he thought all the devils of hell must be there; and so they were, for these were devils. And he fell unconscious; and when he came to, he took the key from the chest, and carried it back with him, and the one from the pillar likewise. Then he left. And when he came to the well, he found the place as level as the middle of the chamber.* He looked back, and saw the pillar collapse to the ground, and the copper damsel likewise, and saw the two knights who guarded the door completely shattered. He went out with the keys, and saw all the people of the castle coming to meet him. He went into the cemetery, and could not see any of the tombs, or the helms and heads which had been on the battlements.

Then they all made much of him, and he offered the keys on the altar of the chapel. And they took him to the great hall. It would be hard to describe the fuss they made of him, and they admitted how they had had the squire follow him and tell him that the queen was imprisoned there: 'For we thought that your great prowess would make you become a prisoner instead of her.' When he heard that the queen had not been there, he felt cheated; even so, he would not have wished to have it[1] still to do.

He stayed that night in the Dolorous Guard, and in the morning he left, for they could not keep him there any longer. From then on, the castle was called the Joyous Guard. Thus the knight went away, and travelled in easy stages until he reached the encounter. And the story does not speak here of anything which befell him in the meantime, except that in the city where he had had the red shield made,* he had made a white shield with a black band, and he carried that one at the encounter. Now the story returns to Sir Gawain.

[M. XLIa] Now Sir Gawain went along, with the knight of the crossing and the damsel who had left her lover wounded, and they travelled [251] as far as the castle which the knight had shown him. At the castle entrance there was a very narrow and evil bridge over deep, black water. The knight who was with Sir Gawain dismounted and said:

_____
[1] i.e. the disenchanting of the castle.

'Sir, I shall go first, and you will remain this side. And if I call you, then come and help me, for there are the two knights who are waiting for us.'

He said that he would do that. The knight crossed the bridge, fully armed, on foot. When he was across, two unarmed knights came up to him and told him he must fight. The gate was opened, and a fully armed knight came out, and charged the knight, and he him. And they fought together for a long while. The knight from the castle could not withstand the other, and said:

'I will not fight with you any more.'

'Very well,' said the other.

And he[1] had a horse brought to him.[2]

'Mount,' he said.

Then he mounted, and another knight came out, on horseback, and charged towards him. They struck one another so hard that they knocked one another to the ground, and sprang back to their feet, with drawn swords, and attacked each other. Then a fully armed knight came out, on foot, and helped the knight from the castle. And the other defended himself against them very vigorously. When he had fought with them for a while, he looked towards Sir Gawain, and said:

'Brother, come and help me.'

Sir Gawain crossed the bridge on foot, and went to help him. And once he arrived, the others could not withstand them, and they drove them in through the gate, which closed behind them. The knight who was helping Sir Gawain was hot, and took off his helm; and Sir Gawain realized that it was his brother, Keheriet, and he was overjoyed. The knight who had said to Keheriet: 'I will not fight with you any more' was there; and Sir Gawain said:

'What shall we do about bringing across our horses, and that maiden there?'

---

[1] i.e. the castle knight.   [2] i.e. the crossing knight.

'Have the maiden's palfrey come first,' the knight said, 'and the horses will come after it.'

Thus they brought them across, and the maiden came after them. Sir Gawain asked the knight if he had any news of the maidens who were taken from him.

'They are up there,' he said, 'in that hall.'

Then Keheriet gave him the horse that he[1] had given him, and he mounted it, and the maiden mounted her palfrey. And in that way the four of them went [252] up to the hall. As they went in, they saw an elderly knight, sitting in a chair covered with a very rich quilt, and in front of him sat the damsels. When they saw Sir Gawain, they were overjoyed. And he said to the knight sitting in the chair:

'Sir, these maidens were wrongfully taken from me, and so I shall take them away.'

'Sir, you would be behaving outrageously,' said the knight.

'Sir,' said Sir Gawain, 'we are three knights,* and there are three maidens here. So, fight us, with two companions; and if you can defeat us, then you are free to have them.'

'I will do no such thing,' said the knight; 'now, though, stop here with me for tonight, and I shall give you proper hospitality.'

'We shall gladly accept your hospitality,' said Sir Gawain.

The knight gave them excellent lodging, and in the morning they left, taking the three maidens with them.

'Sir,' the lord of the house said to Sir Gawain, 'you are taking my maidens away by force; and when I can, I shall avenge it.'

'Indeed,' said Sir Gawain, 'I think I have the right to take them, as they are mine, and I made you a fair offer.'*

They went away and rode until they came to the edge of a forest, and they saw ten armed knights crossing a stretch of open country and coming towards them. The damsel whose

---

[1] i.e. the castle knight.

lover had been wounded recognized them and said to Sir
Gawain:

'There are the scoundrels who killed my lover and took
your maidens from you.'

The others were approaching all the while; and one of
them said:

'Gawain, Gawain, leave the maidens, for you are taking
them away in a shameful manner. Now I have found you
guilty of shameful conduct twice, in this case and when you
broke our agreement.'

Then Sir Gawain realized that it was Brehu the Pitiless.

'Brehu,' he said, 'I am not like you, who tried to have me
treacherously killed. And if you dared to defend yourself
against that charge, I should prove it in combat against you,
here and now.'

Then he told Keheriet how the two knights attacked him,
and Brehu failed to help him.

'What?' said Keheriet, 'Brehu, you would not be so bold as
to defend yourself against a charge of treachery?'

'I should certainly defend myself', he said, 'against a better
man than you.'

[253] 'As God is my witness,' said Keheriet, 'you will need
to.'

Brehu began to go away, with his men.

'Understand this,' said Keheriet, 'that I defy you.* And if
you do not turn around, I shall strike you from behind, and
you will be disgraced.'

Then he charged him. Brehu heard him coming, and
turned to meet him, and they gave one another great blows
on the shields. Brehu broke his lance; and Keheriet struck
him right through his shield and hauberk, and stabbed him
in the breast. He struck him violently, and knocked him to
the ground. And all the other nine struck Keheriet's shield
and his horse, which they killed, knocking them both[1] to the

---

[1] i.e. Keheriet and his horse.

ground. Then Sir Gawain and the knight went towards them, and struck two of them. However,* Sir Gawain killed his man, and the other knight killed another. And Keheriet leapt on to one of the horses, and all the others[1] turned and fled. Keheriet went back to Brehu, and attacked him, but first he dismounted. And Brehu said that he would not fight the three of them.

'But I will fight you, if you dare,' he said to Keheriet, 'at King Arthur's court. Then we shall see who is the better man.' Keheriet agreed. 'Swear', he said,* 'to do that.' And he swore.

Then they gave him back his horse, and he left. And they had caught the horse which belonged to the knight whom Sir Gawain had knocked down,* and they made him mount it. And the maiden whose lover was wounded took her leave, and commended them to God. Sir Gawain gave her the captured knight, and made him swear to conduct himself as her prisoner.

'Sir,' she said, 'many thanks, for you have now avenged me to my satisfaction, for the man you killed gave my lover the fatal blow.'

With that she left; and Sir Gawain and his company travelled until they reached the encounter, the very day it was to take place, and there were already many knights assembled there. The two maidens went into the castle; and Sir Gawain and Keheriet and the other knight did not bear arms that day. The tournament was very well contested, for there were many knights on both sides.

Then the White Knight came to do battle, carrying the white shield with the black band, and he began to joust so vigorously that all those who were not armed watched him in amazement, and so did a great many of those who were armed; and he had plenty of strong lances; and he fought so well in every knightly action that he surpassed everyone.

---

[1] i.e. Brehu's men.

[254] Keheriet went to Sir Gawain and said:

'Sir, here is a knight who is jousting very vigorously, and on the other side are two of our brothers. And if they meet each other often, one of them is sure to pay dearly. Ask the knight, for our sake, to avoid meeting our brothers, and I shall go and say the same to them.'

Sir Gawain's two brothers were not on the other side because they wished to be against King Arthur's companions, but when an encounter was to take place, it often happened that the lively knights bachelor and the poor men* tourneyed first, and the next day or the day after everyone tourneyed, both barons and knights bachelor.

Sir Gawain went to the knight, and said:

'Sir, I beg and request you not to meet with those two knights on the other side.'

Then he pointed them out to him; and the knight said that he would not do so, unless it was in self-defence.

Keheriet went to his brothers, and said the same to them.

'Why should we not meet him, then?' they asked.

'Because', Keheriet said, 'he is our equal.'*

'As God is my witness,' said Agravain, 'are we to avoid him, because he is fighting so well?'

They would not listen to Keheriet; instead Agravain went at once to joust with the knight, and struck him, so that his lance flew into pieces. And the knight struck him, so that he knocked him to the ground. He took the horse, and gave it to Sir Gawain, and said:

'Here, sir, I cannot help it.'

'So I see,' said Sir Gawain.

When Guerrehet saw his brother fall, he went to joust with the knight, and spurred his horse along the lists, and the other spurred to meet him. The horses went very fast, and the lances were short and thick, and the knights strong and sturdy. And they struck one another on the shields so hard that their lances flew into pieces, but neither of them fell.

Both were angry and unhappy about that, for each would dearly have liked to knock down his opponent. Then they moved some distance apart and took thick lances, and came together very fast, and gave one another great blows on the shields. Guerrehet broke his lance, and the knight struck him so hard that he knocked him and his horse to the ground all in a heap.

Keheriet saw it, and pointed it out to Sir Gawain.

'Look, sir,' he said, 'now it is worse.'

That day the knight surpassed everyone in every knightly action. [255] When Sir Gawain saw that he was surpassing everyone in this way, and that he had knocked down his two brothers, he thought he was the knight that he was looking for. Then he went to the castle and called the damsel who was supposed to tell him the knight's name. And she mounted a palfrey and came to him outside the walls.

'Damsel,' he said, 'what about the name of the knight that you were supposed to tell me?'

'Indeed,' she said, 'I think he is the one who has surpassed everyone.'

'Now, let us take note, then,' he said, 'of which way he goes at the end of the tournament.'

'That is a good idea,' she said.

Not long after that the tournament ended, and it was late evening. The knight who had been the victor left and went into the forest; he thought he could go away without being noticed, and he was staying in the forest with an old knight, well out of the way. Sir Gawain and the maiden went after him, and caught up with him in the forest.

'God be with you, sir,' said Sir Gawain.

The other looked, and recognized him at once, and said, God bless him. However, he was very upset that he had caught up with him.

'Sir,' said Sir Gawain, 'have the kindness to tell me who you are.'

'Sir,' he said, 'I am a knight, as you can see.'

'A knight', said Sir Gawain, 'you certainly are, one of the best in the world. But have the kindness to tell me your name.'

'I will not tell you,' he said.

'Ha! dear friend,' the maiden said, 'tell him. And if you do not tell him, I shall do so, for he has endured so much trouble that he ought to know.'

He did not answer, but remained silent.

'Sir,' the maiden said to Sir Gawain, 'I can see that he will not tell you. But I shall, for I will not break my oath.* Let me tell you that he is Lancelot of the Lake, the son of King Ban of Benwick, the one who was the victor at the encounter today; and he was the victor at the other, also, with red arms, and he let the king into the Dolorous Guard.'

'I am overjoyed to hear that,' said Sir Gawain.

'And you should love him dearly,' she said, 'as he is the one who freed you from prison. And it is because of him that I was in the Dolorous Guard for so long.'

Then Sir Gawain showed him great respect, and said:

'Sir, for the Lord's sake, tell me if what she has told me is true.'

[256] The other blushed, so that his whole face grew hot, and looked very angrily at the maiden, and said to Sir Gawain:

'Sir, she has told you what she pleased, but she could as well have remained silent. And for my part I will tell you nothing, for I do not wish to say that it is true, nor do I say that she is lying.'

'Truly, sir,' said Sir Gawain, 'if you do not say so, then I believe it is true. So I shall leave now, for I have found all that I was looking for, by the grace of God.'

With that Sir Gawain went away, and returned to the castle, and made many people happy with the accomplishment of his quest. And the knight went away in the other direction, and the damsel followed him, and he looked very displeased. And two of his squires, who had been with him all day at the tournament, had gone ahead to his lodging.

Thus the knight became known to Sir Gawain, and for that reason he did not dare go to the encounter the next day, for he was afraid of being delayed. And the story falls silent about him and his company just now, and returns to Sir Gawain, who was delighted that he had brought his quest to an end.

[M. XLIIa] The next day Sir Gawain bore arms, and fought very well. And this story relates no more about it, except that King Arthur's companions had the best of it; and the King from Over the Borders suffered heavy losses, and he himself was severely wounded. And because of that distress the encounter came to an end, nothing further being done, and Keheriet was held to be the best knight of both sides.

After the encounter Sir Gawain went away to the court of his uncle, the king, taking with him the other maiden, who had stayed,* and he found the king in Carlisle.* When the king saw him, he made much of him, and so did the queen and all the court. And the king asked him:

'Dear nephew, have you accomplished your quest, yet?'

'Yes, sire,' he said.

'Who', said the king, 'was the knight who let us into the Dolorous Guard?'

'It was Lancelot of the Lake,' he said, 'the son of King Ban of Benwick. And he was the one who was victorious at the encounter between you and the King from Over the Borders, when he carried red arms, and he was also victorious at the one that we have just come from. I spoke to him; and let me tell you that he is one of the most handsome knights in the world, and one of the most well formed in every way; and he is also one of the best knights now living, and if he lives long, he will be quite the best.'

[257] The news spread until everyone there heard it,

knights and ladies. And then for the first time the name of Lancelot of the Lake, the son of King Ban of Benwick, was known at court, and that he was alive and well, at which many people were overjoyed, who had thought for a long time that he had died in infancy. And that is how Sir Gawain brought his name to court. At this point, though, the story says no more about Sir Gawain or the king, but returns to the knight whose name was brought to court.

[M. XLIIIa] When the knight became known to Sir Gawain, he spent the night with the vavasour in the forest. The next day he and the damsel and his squires rose early, and rode in a different direction from the encounter, for he did not dare go there, for fear of being recognized. He rode fully armed except for his helm and his shield, which he had carried in its cover all the time. And the damsel told him about Sir Gawain's deeds of prowess, as she had seen them.

Thus they rode for a long time, until one day they happened to approach a broad and shallow stream. And when they came to the stream, they could not see any bridge; there was a ford, however, and overlooking the ford on the other side there was a tall brattice, and the stream was enclosed by a high palisade for a good bowshot on either side of the the brattice. They reached the ford, and the squires crossed first, and then the damsel, and the knight went behind, and crossed over. When they reached the brattice, the man who was guarding it let the squires and the damsel pass. And when they were inside, he closed the gate. The knight asked if he could pass, like the others; and he said:

'Who are you?'

'I am a knight', he said, 'of King Arthur.'

'Then you cannot pass here,' said the gatekeeper; 'neither you nor anyone in the service of Arthur.'

'I cannot help that,' he said; 'in that case, let my squires and my maiden come back to me.'

The other said that he would not. When the knight saw

that he could do no more there, he turned away. And there was a lady at a window in the brattice, and she called the squire who was carrying the knight's shield, and uncovered it herself. And when she had seen it, she called the gatekeeper.

'Quickly, now,' she said, 'go after the knight, for he is the best in the world.'

He leapt on a hack and galloped across the stream, and brought the knight back. The lady went to meet him and said, before he reached the brattice:

[258] 'Sir knight, by the person you most love, tell me that you will stop here for tonight, unless you have some business which means you would be disgraced if you stopped so early.'

'Madam,' he said, 'you have so adjured me that I shall stop.'

He went into the brattice, and she took him to some magnificent chambers upstairs, and his arms were removed. He was left in just his tunic, and he was remarkably handsome and pleasing; and the lady was very pleased to look at him. Many people prepared the meal. And when they were about to eat, a fully armed knight came in, and he was the lord of the house. The lady sprang up to meet him, and said:

'My lord, you have a guest.'

'Who is it?' he asked.

'It is the good knight', she said, 'who was victorious at the encounter the other day.'

'I shall not believe you', he said, 'unless I see his shield.'

The lady rushed to a hook where it was hanging, and showed it to him without its cover. And the knight, whose shield it was, was very upset, and said:

'Look here! madam, you have given me lodging, and now you are causing me shame and vexation.'

'Indeed, sir,' she said, 'I thought I was doing you great honour.'

'Sir,' said the lord of the house, 'do not be upset, for in all the world, you are the knight I most desire to get to know.'

Then he had himself disarmed, and then sat down beside him, and told him that he had knocked him down so hard, at the encounter, him and his horse, that it had nearly burst his heart. They talked until the meal was ready, and then ate. After the meal the stranger knight asked the lord of the house where he had come from, armed like that.

'Sir,' he said, 'from a bridge below here, which I guard every day against King Arthur's knights.'

'Why?' asked the other.

'Sir, to see if a knight will pass there, who swore to a wounded knight that he would avenge him on all those who said that they loved the man who wounded him better than the knight himself. And the wounded man was my mortal enemy, and the man who wounded him was the man I most loved, for he was my mother's brother. And I should dearly like him[1] to come by here, for I should be glad to die, provided that I had killed him.'

When the knight heard that, he was very upset by what the other had said, and he said no more about it. The beds were made ready, and [259] they went to bed. However, the knight was ill at ease, and wept and grieved terribly, for the next day he would have to fight with the man who had shown him more honour and friendship than anyone else ever had. And he could not refrain from it, for then he would break his oath; and he was so worried that he did not know what to do, whether to fight with his host or break his oath. He suffered that anguish more than half the night, and in the morning he rose early and armed fully except for his head and hands. Then he went to his host, who was just about to arm.

'Dear host,' he said, 'you have done me great honour and service; and in leaving your dwelling I beg you to grant me a boon, for your own great advantage and to win my friendship for ever.'

---

[1] i.e. the knight who swore the oath.

Then he fell at his feet. And the other ran to lift him up, very put out, and said that whatever boon he asked for, he should have it, unless it disgraced him.[1] And he said that it meant great advantage for him,[1] if he would grant it. The lord said he would agree to it, to win his friendship for ever.

'Many thanks,' he said, 'and I ask you to say, as long as I am here, that you love the wounded man better than the man who wounded him.'

'Ha! Holy Mary!' said the other, 'you are the knight who is supposed to avenge the wounded man.'

'Indeed,' he said, weeping, 'it is true.'

The other fainted; and when he came to, he said to the knight:

'Sir, go now; and I will tell you that I love the wounded man better than the dead man.'

And at once he fainted again. The knight left, with his squires and his maiden. When he had gone some way, he looked round and saw his host spurring after him, in full armour. And when he caught up with him, he said:

'Sir knight, do not think me treacherous, for I promised you nothing except for as long as you were in my house. Now, though, let me tell you that I love the dead man more; and you cannot leave without fighting me.'

When the knight saw that there was no alternative, he turned towards him, and the other did the same. They struck one another at the horses' full gallop, so hard that they knocked one another to the ground, the horses on top of them. They quickly sprang up again, and took the shields from around their necks and pulled out their swords, and gave one another great blows high and low until each of them, strong and valorous as he was, had lost blood in many places. In the [260] end, though, the host could not withstand him whom no one could withstand, and he began to give

---

[1] i.e. the host.

ground in spite of himself. And the good knight pressed him very closely, and often begged him to say that he loved the wounded man better than the dead man. Then the other threatened him more than he had done at the outset, and swore that he would never say that. Then the good knight attacked him again, and drove him to the edge of a river which ran beside them. And then he again begged him to say that he loved the wounded man better than the dead man. And he would not do so. Then the good knight grew angry and attacked him, and pressed him so hard, and so loaded him down with blows, that he knocked him to the ground on all fours. He leapt upon him, and wrenched the helm from his head, and still he begged him to say that by which he could save himself. And he would not. Then the good knight was very angry and said that he would not die, please God, by any weapon of his, and he dragged him to the water and threw him in. And when he saw him drowned, he began to weep very bitterly. Now, though, the story stops talking at this point about him and the adventures which befell him, and returns to speak of King Arthur, where it left him.

[M. XLIVa] King Arthur, the story says, had been in residence in Carlisle for a long time in this period, and not much was happening there in the way of adventures. It annoyed the king's companions that they had resided there so long and were seeing nothing of what they were used to seeing.* It annoyed Kay the seneschal very much, and he often spoke of it and said, in the king's presence, that this stay was very annoying and had lasted too long. And the king asked him:

'Kay, what do you wish us to do?'

'Indeed,' he said, 'I should advise that we go to Camelot, for the city is more beautiful, and the most agreeable and eventful that you have, and we shall often hear and see things which we do not hear or see here; for you have been in residence here more than two months, and we have not seen anything happen of any consequence.'

'Then let us go to Camelot,' said the king, 'since you advise it.'

The king was going to set off the next day. However, a great wonder befell him in the night, for he dreamed that all the hair on his head fell out, and all the hairs in his beard; and he was very frightened by this, and so he stayed on in the town. The third night after that it again befell him that he dreamed that all the fingers fell off his hands, except the thumbs. Then he was much more troubled than before. And the third night from then, he dreamed that all the toes fell off his feet, except the big toes. Then he was more troubled than before, and told his chaplain.

[261] 'Sire,' he said, 'do not worry, for dreams are meaningless.'

Then the king told the queen, and she said the same.

'In God's name,' he said, 'I shall not leave the matter there.'

He sent word to his bishops and his archbishops, to be with him in twenty days' time in Camelot, and to bring with them all the wisest clerks they could find. Thereupon he left Carlisle, and went via his castles and strongholds, until on the fifteenth day he reached Camelot. On the twentieth day his clerks arrived, and he asked them for advice about his dreams. They chose ten of the very wisest among them, and said that they would advise him, if anyone were to do so. The king had them locked up securely and said that they would never leave his prison until they told him the meaning of his dreams. They tested the power of their wisdom for nine days, and then they went to the king and said that they had found nothing.

'It is no use,' the king said, 'you will not escape me in that way.'

They asked him to give them three days' respite, and he

gave it to them. Then they went before him again and said that they could not find anything. They asked him for a further respite; and he gave it to them. Then they again told him that they still knew nothing, 'but', they said, 'give us a further respite of three days, just as you dreamed it every third night.'

'Now, you shall have it,' said the king, 'but understand that you will not have any longer.'

When the third day came, they said that they had found nothing.

'It is no use,' the king said, 'I shall have you all put to death unless you tell me the truth.'

'You must do as you please with us,' they said, 'for we shall not tell you any more.'

Then the king decided to put the fear of death into them, so he had a great fire made and ordered that five of them should be put in it, and the other five hanged. That is what the king ordered, in their presence, but privately he ordered his bailiffs to do no more than put the fear of death into them. Five were taken to the gallows; and when they had the ropes around their necks, they were afraid of dying, and said that, if the other five would speak, they would. The news reached those who were to be burned, and they said that, since the others had offered, then they would speak. Then they were brought into the hall before the king; and the wisest of them said:

[262] 'Sire, we shall tell you what we have found, but we do not want you to consider us liars if it does not happen, for we should be pleased. And, whatever happens, we want you to give us your word that no harm will come to us.'

The king gave them his word; and the other said:

'Sire, understand that you must lose all earthly honour, and those you most rely on will fail you in spite of themselves, for that is how it must be.'

The king was greatly troubled at this; and then he asked him:

'Now, tell me if anything can save me from it.'

'Indeed, sire,' said the learned man, 'we have seen something, but it is such great foolishness even to think it that we dare not tell you.'

'Tell me without hesitation,' the king said, 'for you cannot tell me worse than you have told me.'

'Then I will tell you,' said the other; 'nothing can save you from losing all earthly honour, unless you are saved by the Lion in Water and the Doctor without Medicine, through the counsel* of the Flower. And that seemed to us such great foolishness that we did not dare speak of it.'

The king was very worried by this thing. And one day he said that he would go into the woods to shoot, and set off very early and told Sir Gawain that he would go with him, and Kay the seneschal and those he wanted. And with that the story falls silent about him and his party for the moment, and returns to the knight whose name Sir Gawain had brought to court, when he left the place where he fought with his host.

[M. XLVa] When the knight who had been victorious at the encounter left the spot where he fought with his host, he travelled all day without meeting any further adventures. He spent the night with a widowed lady at the edge of the forest, and from there it was no more than five English leagues to Camelot. The knight rose early and left his lodging, and he travelled with his maiden and his squires until he met a squire.

'Young man,' he said, 'do you have any news?'

'Yes,' said the other; 'my lady the queen is here in Camelot.'

'Which queen?' asked the knight.

'The wife of King Arthur,' said the squire.

The knight left him and rode until he was in front of a

fortified house, and he saw at a window a lady in surcoat*
and shift, and she was looking at the meadows and the nearby
forest. The lady was veiled, and with her was a damsel, her
hair down around her shoulders. [263] The knight began to
look at the lady, so that he quite forgot himself. And just then
a knight in full armour came by there.

'Sir knight,' he said, 'what are you looking at?'

The other did not say a word in reply, for he had not heard
him. The knight nudged him, and again asked him what he
was looking at.

'I am looking', he said, 'at what I please, and you are not
courteous, to shake me out of my thoughts.'

'By the person you most love,' said the stranger knight, 'do
you know who the lady is, that you are looking at?'

'I believe I know very well who she is,' the knight said.

'And who is she?' said the other.

'It is my lady the queen,' he said.

'As God is my witness,' said the other, 'you know her
peculiarly well. The devils of hell make you look at ladies.'*

'Why?' said the other.

'Because', he said, 'you would not dare follow me in front
of the queen, where I should go.'

'Indeed,' said the good knight, 'if you go somewhere where
I dare not follow you, you will have surpassed all the most
daring men who ever lived.'

'We shall see,' said the other.

With that he turned away, and the knight went after him.
When they had gone some way, the other said to the good
knight:

'Sir, you will stop with me for tonight, and in the morning
I shall take you where I have promised.'*

The other asked if it must be like that; and he said that it
must. And the other replied that in that case he would stop.
He spent that night with the knight, and it was on the
Camelot river, and they stopped there before noon. That

night the knight and his maiden and his squires were given excellent lodging. And the story will say no more about him for the moment, until it has spoken of King Arthur.

[M. XLVIa] The story says that the king came back from the hunt before none. And in the evening, when he was sitting at supper, in came an elderly knight, who seemed to be a man of worth. The knight was armed except for his head and hands, and he went right to the king, with his sword belted on, and he did not greet the king, but said to him, right in front of his table:

'King, I am sent to you by the most valorous man for his age now living—that is, Galehot, the son of the Giantess. He sends you word that you are to give up your land to him, for he has conquered thirty kingdoms, [264] but he does not wish to be crowned until he has the kingdom of Logres. For that reason he sends you word that you are to give up your land to him, or to hold it from him. And if you will be his man, he will cherish you more than all the kings he has conquered.'

'Sir,' the king said, 'I have never held my land from anyone except God, and I will never hold it from this man.'

'Indeed,' the knight said, 'I am sorry about that, for you will lose honour and land.'

'I do not care what you say,' the king said, 'for he will never be able to do all that, please God.'

'King Arthur,' the knight said, 'now, understand then that my lord defies you, and I tell you on his behalf that he will be in your land within a month. And once he enters it, he will not leave until he has conquered it all, and he will take from you your wife, Guinevere, whom he has heard so esteemed for beauty and merit above all earthly ladies.'

The king replied:

'Sir knight, I heard what you have said, and your great threats will not make me any more afraid. But let each man do the best he can. And if your lord takes my land from me, I shall be sorry, but he will never be able to.'

Thereupon the knight left. And when he reached the door of the hall, he turned towards the king and said:

'Ah! Lord, what sorrow and what misfortune!'

Then he mounted a horse and went away with two other knights who were waiting for him outside the gate. The king asked his nephew, Sir Gawain, if he had ever seen Galehot. He said that he had not, and most of the knights there said the same; however, Galegantin the Welshman, who had travelled through many lands, came forward and said to the king:

'Sire, I have seen Galehot. He is at least six inches taller than any knight known, and of all the men in the world, he is the most loved by his people, and the one who has conquered most, for his age, for he is a young knight. And those who know him say that he is the most noble and gracious knight in the world, and the most generous. However,' he said, 'I do not say that because I think that he or anyone else could ever have power over you, for if I thought that, may God never be my witness if I should not rather be dead than alive.'

The king left it at that, and said that in the morning he wished to go hunting again, and he called on those he pleased to go, and said that he would set off as early as he could after hearing mass. In the morning the king set off, [265] when he had heard mass, and went into the forest. And the story says no more about him at this point, but returns to speak of the knight who had been victorious at the encounter, when he stopped for the night with the knight he was supposed to follow.

[M. XLVIIa] When the knight who was victorious at the encounter had spent the night with the knight who disturbed him from his thoughts, he rose very early and followed his host where he wished to lead him; however, he left the maiden and his squires at the house, for he expected to go back by there. The host went ahead, and the other followed him, and they went along until they were approaching Camelot. The good knight looked at the town, and he thought that he had seen it before. Then he looked at the town's situation and the tower and the minsters, until he remembered that this was Camelot, where he was made a knight. And he fell into a profound reverie, and so rode more slowly, and his host went swiftly ahead, to see if he would lag behind from cowardice or in thought. The knight who was going ahead rode until he arrived near the king's residence. The king's custom was always to have his residence on a river, for the most part, and the river was between the knight and the king's residence. When he arrived near the residence he looked in that direction and saw a lady in the galleries. It was the queen, who had accompanied the king, who was going hunting, just as far as the galleries, and she was leaning there because she had no desire to sleep, and she had on a surcoat and a short cloak, and had veiled herself because of the cold weather, which had just begun. When she saw the knight, she unveiled herself. He stopped on the other side of the river and said:

'Madam, who are you? If you are the queen, tell me.'

'Yes, sir, I am. But why do you ask?'

'Indeed, my lady, because you should be the queen, and if you were not, you certainly look like a queen. And I am very pleased to look at you because of the most foolish knight I ever saw.'

'Who is that, sir knight?' said the queen; 'is it you?'

'No, indeed, my lady,' he said, 'it is someone else.'

Then he started away towards the forest. The queen called him back, and asked him to tell her who the knight was, because of whom he was looking at her. He would not tell her, because he was afraid he would have shame and harm from it and that the queen would know the knight who was following him. And he went away, not in the direction the king had taken, but another way. Before long the other knight came after him down along the river, and he stopped right at the edge of the water in the meadows beside the river and saw women washing clothes, and asked them:

[266] 'Have you seen a knight pass by here?'

They replied that they had not; and they spoke the truth, for they had only just then arrived, and had not seen the knight who had passed.

When the queen saw that he could find no one to give him news of him, she shouted:

'Sir knight, I saw the knight you are asking for. He is going away towards that forest.'

He looked up, and saw the queen in the galleries, and he recognized her at once by her voice.

'Did you, now, my lady?' he said; 'and which way is he going?'

'He is going into that forest.' And she pointed out which way. 'And go quickly, for he reached there some while ago.'

The knight set spurs to his horse as soon as she said: 'Go quickly.' However, he let it go where it wished, for he had eyes only for the queen. The horse wanted to drink, and headed for the water, and jumped in. The bank was high and the water deep, for where the queen was was not near the ford, and the water lapped at the walls of the residence where the queen was. When the horse reached there,* it could not get out, and so it turned back again, and began swimming, until it was thoroughly tired. The water was so deep that the horse became short of breath, and the water came up to the knight's shoulders; and he made no effort to get out, and let the horse go where it wished. When the queen saw him in such danger, she began to cry out: 'Holy Mary!'

Then Yvain, the son of King Urien, arrived, all dressed to go hunting, for he thought he had risen early enough, but he had delayed too long.* Sir Yvain came on a hunter, and he had his bow and quiver, and had on thick winter hose, for the

cold weather had begun. The sun was already high and very
hot, as hot as it can be between the feast of All Saints and
Christmas. When he reached the hall, he asked where the
king was. And when he heard that he had left, he asked
where the queen was, and was told that she was in the
galleries. Then Sir Yvain went there; and when the queen
saw him, she began to cry out:

'Ah! Sir Yvain,' she said, 'there is a knight in the water
here who is about to be drowned.'

'By the Lord's mercy, my lady,' he said, 'how?'

'Sir,' she said, 'his horse jumped in with him, and he will
soon drown.'

When Sir Yvain saw him in such danger, he was very
moved. [267] Then he went down and ran to the water, and
went in, the story says, up to his neck. By now the horse was
so weary and bemused that it had no strength left, and the
water had closed over the knight's helm once. Sir Yvain
caught the horse by the bridle, and led it to the bank. He
pulled it out of the water; and the knight was all wet, body
and armour. Sir Yvain asked him:

'Sir, who are you? How did you get into the water here?'

'Sir, I am a knight, and was watering my horse.'

'You were not watering it very well,' said Sir Yvain, 'for
you were nearly drowned. And where are you going?'

'Sir,' he said, 'I was following a knight.'

Sir Yvain would have recognized him at once, if he had
had the shield that he carried at the encounter, but he had
left it at the house of the knight he was following, and taken
one which was old and blackened. Because of that his host
thought that he would be recognized in the king's household.
And Sir Yvain thought less of him because of it, for he
thought he was of low standing. He asked him if he was going
to follow the knight; and he said that he was.

He took him to the ford and he went across. Then he[1]

---

[1] i.e. the White Knight.

began to look at the queen, and his horse carried him down along the river. He had not gone far when he met Daguenet the Fool, who asked him where he was going. He was lost in thought, and said nothing. And Daguenet said: 'You are my prisoner.' And he took him back, without the knight offering any resistance. Sir Yvain had gone back to the queen, and she said:

'Truly, the knight would have been drowned, but for you.'

'My lady,' he said, 'that would have been a pity, for he is very handsome.'

'He has again behaved in an extraordinary fashion,' she said, 'for he is going away down there, and he was supposed to follow a knight.'

Before long they saw the knight and Daguenet coming.

'Look,' said the queen, 'someone has captured our knight.'

Then Sir Yvain went to the ford, to meet them. When he saw that it was Daguenet, he was quite astonished. He took them to the queen.

'My lady,' he said, 'Daguenet has captured this knight. Daguenet,' he went on, 'by the loyalty you owe my lord the king, how did you capture him?'

'I met him along by the river,' he said, 'and he would not say a word to me. And I took hold of his bridle, and he never resisted, so I brought him away a prisoner.'

'That may well be,' said Sir Yvain, 'and I shall stand surety for his release, if you agree.'

'I should be pleased,' said Daguenet.

[268] The queen laughed a good deal over this, as did all those who heard it, for by now many knights and ladies and damsels had arrived. This Daguenet was a knight, certainly, but he was a simple fool and the most cowardly specimen of humanity that anyone knew of. And everyone made fun of him because of the very foolish things he said and did, for he would go in search of adventures and say on his return that he had killed a knight, or two or three.* And that is why he

so gloried in this one. The queen looked at the knight, and saw that his body and limbs were well formed, so that no one could have been better formed.

'Daguenet,' said the queen, 'by the loyalty you owe my lord the king and me, do you know who he is?'

'My lady,' he said to the queen, 'as God is my witness, I do not, and he never spoke to me, not even a single word.'

The knight was holding his lance by the middle, and when he heard the queen speak, he looked up, and his hand relaxed and the lance fell, so that its head passed through the samite of the queen's cloak. She looked at him, and then said to Sir Yvain, in a low voice:

'This knight does not seem very sensible.'

'No, indeed. It was not from good sense that he let himself be taken away like that by Daguenet, when with a little resistance he could have prevented it. And he has not spoken to us yet. I shall ask him who he is. Sir knight, who are you?' he said.

The other looked around and saw that he was in the hall.

'Sir,' he said, 'I am a knight, as you can see.'

'And what are you doing here?'

'Sir, I do not know,' he said.

'You are the prisoner', said Sir Yvain, 'of a knight, and I have stood surety for your release.'

'I well believe it,'* he said.

'Sir knight, will you tell me any more?' said Sir Yvain.

'Sir, I do not know what to tell you.'

'My lady,' Sir Yvain said to the queen, 'I have stood surety for his release. If you would be my guarantee, I should let him go.'

'Against Daguenet?'* she said.

'Yes, indeed,' he said.

And she laughed.

'I shall certainly be your guarantee', she said, 'against him.'

'Then I shall let him go,' he said.

Sir Yvain gave him his lance, and took him down by the steps, and showed him the ford.

[269] 'Sir, there is the ford, and there is the way the knight you are following went.'

The other crossed the ford, and started towards the forest after the knight. And Sir Yvain went quickly to his lodging and mounted a horse, without any spurs, and went after the knight into the forest, some distance behind, as he did not wish him to notice him. The knight went into the forest, and looked for the knight he was following, and saw on a hill the pennon of a lance. He went in that direction; and when he arrived there, the knight came down to meet him.

'Sir knight,' said the one who was following him, 'I have followed you until now I have caught up with you. And what do you want?'*

'I want you to give me your horse and arms.'

'I will not do that,' said the knight.

'Yes, you will,' he said, 'whether you like it or not, or else I shall take them from you by force.'

'I will not do it, if I can help it,' said the knight.

The knight who had come down the hill rode away on to open ground and took his shield and lance, and went towards him. The other could see that he meant to strike him, and so he did the same. They spurred the horses towards one another. The knight who had come down the hill struck the other on the shield, so that his lance flew into pieces. And the other struck him so hard that he knocked him to the ground over his horse's crupper. He caught the horse by the bridle, and brought it back to him.

'Here is your horse,' he said. 'And I am leaving, for I have better things to do than to linger here.'

The knight leapt to his feet again and said:

'You are not leaving like that. You must fight with me.'

'With you?'

'Yes, indeed.'

The knight drew back and dismounted from his horse and pulled out his sword, and put his shield in front of him and attacked the knight. The other also drew his sword, and they attacked one another very nimbly and struck one another on the helms and shields. The knight that Daguenet had captured pressed him hard and attacked him very fiercely, and the other constantly gave ground, for he could see that he would not be able to withstand him, and he said:

'Stop, I will not fight with you any longer, but come where I shall take you, and I shall show you remarkable things.'

'And where is that?' asked the knight that Daguenet captured.

[270] 'It is not far,' he said.

'Then I shall go,' said the other.

They mounted their horses. Daguenet's knight had not broken his lance, and the knight went in front and he followed. Sir Yvain had heard everything that they had said and decided that he would go on after them. When the knight who was in front had gone some way, leading the other, he said:

'Over there are two giants who have laid waste part of this country, and no one who loves King Arthur and the queen and those of his household dares pass near here where they live. Now, go up to them,' he said, 'if you wish. Here is one and there is the other.'

The knight wasted no more words, but took his shield by the straps and tucked his lance under his arm and set spurs to his horse, directing its head towards the giant, who saw him coming, and called to him from a long way off, very loudly:

'Knight, if you hate King Arthur and the queen and the people of his household, then come forward confidently, for you have nothing to fear from us. And if you love them, you are a dead man.'

'By my faith, I love them,' he said.

The giant raised a great club, thinking to strike the knight. However, he was so tall, and had such long arms, that he overreached the knight and his horse and struck the club on the ground. And the knight struck him through the body with his lance, and hurled him down dead as he passed by. The other giant raised his own club and struck the horse on the crupper, so that he broke both its thighs. The knight leapt to his feet, and pulled out his sword, upset by the death of his horse, and put his shield in front of him and went towards the giant. The giant raised the club to strike and struck the shield, and what he hit, he knocked to the ground.* And the knight struck the giant on the arm with his sword, so that he sent his hand flying off, with the club in it. The giant raised his foot, thinking to kick him. And the knight struck him on the leg, and sent his foot flying off; and the giant fell. A maiden passed by where Sir Yvain was watching this. She was very beautiful and well dressed.

'Sir knight,' she said, 'that is the third.'

Sir Yvain did not understand why she said that, but went towards the knight. And when the knight saw him, he said:

'Have you seen, sir knight, how these churls have killed my horse? Now I shall have to go on foot.'

[271] 'Sir, you will not, please God,' said Sir Yvain, 'for I shall give you mine. But tell this knight here to take me up behind him as far as Camelot.'

'Sir,' he said, 'many thanks for your horse, for you could not give it to me at a better moment.'

Then he said to the knight who had led him there: 'Dismount.' And the knight dismounted. Then he said to Sir Yvain:

'Sir, mount in the saddle, and he will mount behind you.'

Sir Yvain promptly mounted in the saddle, and the knight mounted behind him, armed as he was. Thus the knight who had defeated the giants went about his business; and Sir Yvain and the other knight went to Camelot. When they arrived there, the queen was dressed and ready and had heard mass, and Sir Gawain was bringing her back from the minster. The hall was filled with knights, and those who were at the windows of the galleries said:

'There is a remarkable thing. Sir Yvain is coming here, and bringing an armed knight.'

And Sir Yvain was at the foot of the steps, and he dismounted.

'Sir,' said the knight, 'I am going.'

'Go with God,' said Sir Yvain, 'and may He give you good fortune.'

The knight went away; and Sir Yvain went up into the hall and met the queen and Sir Gawain, who had just come from the minster.

'Sir Gawain,' said Sir Yvain, 'there is talk of the wonders of Camelot, for many occur here, so they say. Indeed, they are right, but I do not think there is a knight in this place who ever saw as many here as I have seen today.'

'Tell us about them, then,' said Sir Gawain.

He began to relate, in the presence of the queen and Sir Gawain and all the others, everything he had seen the knight do; and he told them how he fought with the knight, and how he would have defeated him in combat, had he wished, and how he killed one of the giants, and how he cut off the hand and foot of the other. And Daguenet sprang forward, and cried:

'It is the knight I captured, who has done all this.'

'Yes, indeed,' said Sir Yvain, 'it certainly is.'

'In God's name,' he said, 'that is the sort of knight I can capture! I am very cowardly, now! Sir Gawain, in God's name, if you had captured him, you would be very pleased with yourself.'

And Sir Yvain said to Sir Gawain:

[272] 'I shall tell you more still. When the knight had killed

the giants, a maiden came up to me and said: "Sir knight, that is the third."'

Sir Gawain heard that, and bowed his head and smiled. The queen noticed, and took Sir Gawain by the hand, and they went and sat by a window. And she said to him:

'By the loyalty you owe the king and me, tell me why you laughed just now.'

'I shall tell you,' he said; 'because the maiden said to him: "That is the third", so Sir Yvain said. Do you remember', he said, 'what the maiden said to you in the Dolorous Guard, the one who was a prisoner in the turret? You heard it as well as I.'

'I do not remember,' the queen said.

'She told us,' Sir Gawain said, 'that we should hear word of the knight who let us into the Dolorous Guard at the first encounter which took place in the kingdom of Logres, and at the second, and at the third. And this is the third, and so the knight who killed the giants is Lancelot of the Lake, you may know that for a fact.'

'I can well believe you,' the queen said.

However, Daguenet made such a fuss that nothing could compete with him, and he told everyone that he had captured the good knight who killed the giants. 'You do not capture such knights.'

Thus they waited until vespers, when the king came back. They told him the news that a knight had killed the giants. The king was overjoyed, as were his companions and all the people of the country. And Daguenet went to him and said:

'Sire, by the loyalty I owe you, I captured that good knight.'

The king laughed heartily at that, as did all the others. With that, though, the story leaves them, and it says no more about the king and his company at this point, but returns to the knight who killed the giants.

[M. XLVIIIa] At this point the story says that when the knight had killed the giants, he rode through the forest until he was right out of it. Then the evening began to draw in, and he met a vavasour coming from the forest. The vavasour had no company except for a single squire who was carrying, loaded on his horse,* a roe-deer which they had caught in the forest. When the vavasour saw the knight coming, he greeted him and said:

'Sir, it is right* to stop for tonight, and I have excellent lodging for you, if you wish, and you would have some of this deer.'

[273] The knight could see that it was time to stop, and he accepted the lodging and went after the vavasour. Then the damsel who had said to Sir Yvain: 'That is the third' came up; and the four of them went to the vavasour's house. That night they were given good lodging; and in the morning, when they had heard mass, the knight went on his way again, as he was going in search of adventure.

One day it happened that he and the maiden were riding along, and they came at the hour of terce to a causeway, which stretched for at least a league; and there was a wide, deep marsh on both sides. At the head of the causeway was a knight in full armour. When the knight approached—the one Daguenet captured—the other moved forward and asked him who he was. He replied that he was a knight of King Arthur.

'In God's name,' said the other, 'you will not pass by here, then—nor will any knight in the service of King Arthur, for I hate him more than any other man, and I shall never cherish any man who loves him.'

'Why?' asked the other.

'Because those of his household have done my family very great harm.'

'What harm?' he asked.

'It happened that an armed, wounded knight went to him, a long time ago,* who had two broken lance-shafts through his body. He begged him to have the weapons removed, and he had them removed by a knight who swore on holy relics that he would avenge him on all those who said that they loved the man who wounded him better than the knight himself. Recently he killed my cousin, a very valorous knight. But he has more to do than he realizes, the man who has undertaken this, for there are still many of the dead man's relatives* to be killed.'

'What?' said the knight Daguenet captured, 'are you one of those who love the dead man better than the wounded man?'

'I ought to love him better,' he said, 'as he was my uncle.'

'Indeed,' said the other, 'I am sorry about that, for I shall have to fight you, and I thought to go on my way unhindered.'

'Are you then the knight', said the other, 'who is supposed to avenge the wounded knight?'

And he said that he would do his best.

'Then I tell you that you must kill me, or I shall avenge my cousin.'

They turned towards one another as swiftly as their [274] horses could gallop. The knight of the causeway broke his lance, and the other struck him so hard with his lance that he knocked him to the ground. However, he was young and nimble, and quickly leapt to his feet again, and put his shield in front of him, and drew his sword, and they attacked one another very fiercely. They gave each other great blows on top of the helms, and dented them on their heads, and they split one another's hauberks in many places. However, the outcome of the battle was that the knight of the causeway began to tire and gave ground before him more and more. He pressed him very hard, for he still had plenty of wind and strength, and he sent a large piece of his shield flying in pieces. And the other had lost a great deal of blood, and one of the laces of his helm was broken. And he[1] flung himself at him, and wrenched it from his head and threw it as far away as he could, and said:

[1] i.e. Daguenet's knight.

'Now you will have to agree that you love the wounded man more than the dead man.'

'I see no reason yet', the other said, 'why I should say it.'

'You must say it,' he said, 'or you will die.'

Then he attacked him, and the other thrust what was left of his shield above his head, and defended himself very vigorously for a long while. In the end, though, he could not withstand him, and he began to give ground once more. The other entreated him to say that he loved the wounded man better than the dead man, but he would not. Then the knight[1] launched a blow at him, and hit him on the left arm, and gave him a bad wound. The other dropped his shield, and attacked him, with his head unprotected, as he had no helm and no shield, and gave him the hardest blow he could. And as he recovered, the other launched a blow at his head, and struck him so hard that he clove him to the teeth, and he fell dead. And he was greatly upset,* if he could have put it right. Then he went to his horse, which the maiden was holding, and mounted, and the two of them went away along the causeway.

They rode in this way until they approached a city, which was called the Hill of Malohaut. Then two squires caught up with them, one of whom brought the knight's[2] shield and the other his helm, and they passed him[1] by without a word, and went on at full gallop. The knight and his maiden travelled towards the city, and he drew near the gate; and then a great uproar began. And more than forty men, knights and men-at-arms, came to meet him, and they shouted at him very energetically and charged at him all together, and so covered him with blows from their lances, him and his horse, that they knocked [275] them both to the ground, and killed the horse. And he was left on foot, and defended himself very vigorously with his sword, and cut their lances to pieces and killed the horses of those he could reach. However, when he

---

[1] i.e. Daguenet's knight.   [2] i.e. the knight of the causeway.

saw that he could not withstand them, he flung himself on to the steps of a fortified house which was there. There he defended himself as long as he could, until the lady of the town arrived. And they had pressed him so closely that they had already forced him to his knees two or three times. And she told him to surrender to her.

'Madam,' he said, 'what have I done wrong?'

'You have killed the son of my seneschal here,' she said.

'Madam,' he said, 'I am sorry, but I had to do it.'

'Surrender to me,' she said, 'for I wish it and advise you to do it.'

He offered her his sword; and she took him to her residence, and no one touched him after that. The lady took him away to prison, and put him in a gaol which stood at the end of the hall. This gaol was of stone, and it was broad at the bottom and narrow at the top, and it measured two toises* in every direction, and was as high as the roof of the hall. In each side of the gaol there were two windows of glass, so clear that the man inside could see everyone who entered the hall. The gaol was very fine, and it was closed with iron grilles, high and strong. The knight could move about inside, as far as the length of a chain which was attached to his shackles allowed. However, his maiden knew nothing of this, for she had gone away from the gate, where she had been shut out; and she assumed that the knight was dead, and was so distressed that she did not dare return to her lady, the Lady of the Lake, but became a nun at the first religious house she found. Here the story falls silent about her and the knight and the lady who had him in prison, and returns to King Arthur.

[M. XLIXa] One day it happened, the story says, when King Arthur was staying in Camelot, that the damsel of the borders of Selice sent a messenger to him; and she sent him word that Galehot, the son of the Giantess, had entered her land and had taken it all from her, apart from two castles which she had at the near edge of her land.

'King Arthur,' the messenger said, 'for that reason she sends to ask you to come and defend your land,* for she cannot hold out for long, if you do not come.'

'I shall come speedily,' the king said. 'Has he many troops?'

'My lord, he has at least one hundred thousand mounted men.'

[276] 'Now, my friend, tell your lady that I shall set off this very night or tomorrow to go to meet Galehot.'

'Sire,' said his men, 'you must not do so, but wait for your followers, for he has brought a great many troops, and you are here with just your household, and you should not put yourself at risk.'

'May God never be my witness,' the king said, 'if ever a man enters my land to do harm, and I spend more than one night in any town until I reach there.'

In the morning the king set off and travelled until he reached the maiden's¹ castle, and at least seven thousand knights camped in his pavilions, for he had no more than that as yet. However, he had sent summons everywhere, near and far, and sent word for everyone to come there, both on horseback and on foot, and for each man to bring what followers he could.

Galehot was camped at the castle he had besieged; and he had brought great numbers of footsoldiers who shot and carried poisoned arrows, and they were well armed in the manner of footsoldiers, and had brought iron nets which came on wagons and carts; and there were so many of these nets that they had enclosed Galehot's whole army with them, so that the army had nothing to fear from the rear. Galehot heard that King Arthur had come, but did not yet have many troops. He sent, from amongst his men, for the thirty kings he had conquered, and as many of the others as he pleased.

¹ i.e. the maiden of the borders of Selice.

'Gentlemen,' he said, 'King Arthur has come, but he does not have many troops, I am told; and it would not be to my honour if I engaged him while he has so few troops. However, I do want some of my men to engage his.'

'Sire,' said the King of a Hundred Knights, 'send me, in the morning.'

'All right,' said Galehot.

In the morning, at daybreak, the King of a Hundred Knights went to look over King Arthur's army. Near the castle where the king[1] was, there was a city called the Hill of Malohaut, but, while it was near, it was still seven English leagues away. Between the city and the king, and nearer the army than the city, there was a high hill. The King of a Hundred Knights went up there to look over King Arthur's army, and it seemed to him that there were more than seven thousand knights there; and he returned to Galehot and said:

'Sire, I have estimated their numbers, and they have no more than ten thousand knights.'

[277] He exaggerated deliberately, because he did not wish to be reproached by Galehot's men. And Galehot replied:

'Take ten thousand knights, those you please, and go and engage them.'

'Gladly, sire,' said the King of a Hundred Knights.

He chose ten thousand knights, those he wanted, and those kings and barons.* They armed fully and went off in irregular order towards the king's army, with never a battalion ordered or a company formed.* Word reached the army that Galehot's knights were coming, all in irregular order. Those in the army armed very quickly, and Sir Gawain went to his uncle, the king:

'Sire, Galehot's knights are coming to engage us, but he himself is not coming. And since he is not coming, you will not go, either.'

---

[1] i.e. King Arthur.

'No,' the king said. 'But you go,' he said to Sir Gawain, 'and take what men we have, and organize your companies and order your battalions, and see that you are prudent, for they have greater numbers than we have at the moment.'

'Sire,' said Sir Gawain, 'we shall do the best we can.'

Sir Gawain and the other knights crossed the water at the fords, for the army was camped by a river. They crossed the water, and organized their companies and battalions. Galehot's men came, all in irregular order, and Sir Gawain sent one battalion forward to engage them. They came fresh and eager and keen to do battle, and the others* received them well. The battle began. Galehot's men came in such numbers that the others could not withstand them. When Sir Gawain saw that it was time, he sent them another battalion, and then a third, and then a fourth. And when he saw that all ten thousand had come, he himself rode to engage them. All the seven thousand fought very well, but Sir Gawain himself fought best of all. There were many of the renowned knights of the king's household there, who did many knightly deeds. On Galehot's side, too, there were many who fought well.

The battle lasted a long while. Many knightly deeds were done on both sides. Galehot's troops could not withstand King Arthur's troops, despite their greater numbers, and the seven thousand routed them and drove them from the field. When the King of a Hundred Knights saw that [278] his men had been put to rout and were fleeing, he was very distressed in his heart, for he for his part was a very good knight. He took a messenger and sent him to ask Galehot to send them reinforcements, for they could not withstand King Arthur's household. And Galehot sent thirty thousand.

They came very swiftly at full gallop, and clouds of dust rose a long way off, as from such great numbers. Sir Gawain saw them a long way off, he and King Arthur's men; small wonder if they were alarmed. The King of a Hundred Knights and his men saw them coming, and they were overjoyed, and turned their horses' heads back and went to strike King Arthur's men very hard, and they struck them, as well or better. Sir Gawain drew back, and his men closed ranks, fearing the force coming after them. And the others came at full speed, keen to do battle.

'Now, gentlemen, knights,' said Sir Gawain, 'we shall see who fights well, for there is no hope for us otherwise. Now it will be apparent who loves the king's honour, and his own.'

Sir Gawain and his men turned very fiercely to meet them head on and went to strike them, and the others struck them, so hard that their lances flew into pieces, and there were some who knocked one another down. There was a prodigious battle there with swords and lances, and King Arthur's troops endured a great deal and fought very well. However, the force was so great on the other side that, but for Sir Gawain's prowess, they would all have been captured: no one would have escaped. He fought so well, though, that no knight ever fought better. Fighting well was no use, those on the other side were too many. By their weight of numbers they drove them as far as a ford. There Sir Gawain and the good knights of the king's household endured the most of all. They forced them* across the ford. Outside the gate the battle was prodigious. There Sir Gawain resisted strongly, until King Arthur's troops were inside; and even so, they suffered heavy losses there, for Galehot's household captured many of their knights. They withdrew, for it was late evening.

Sir Gawain was not forced into the castle, but he was so maltreated outside it, and took so many knocks and blows there, that he was in great pain. As Galehot's men made their withdrawal, he fell from his horse unconscious, without anyone touching him: but he had [279] endured great strain all day, and had made such strenuous efforts in fighting well that he was reduced to such a state that they carried him to his lodging. The king and queen and all the others were very much afraid for him and feared that he was injured internally from the effort of the remarkable deeds he had done.

Near there was the city of Malohaut. The city was held by a lady who had been married, and had children, but her husband was dead. However, she was a very good and wise lady, and was much loved and esteemed by all who knew her. And the people of her land so loved and esteemed her that when other people asked them: 'What is your lady like?', they replied that she was the queen among ladies.

This lady had a knight in prison,* and she was holding him in a gaol which was made of stone, and the stone was so clear that he could see all those outside, and all those outside could see him. The gaol was narrow and tall, so that he could easily stand up in it, and it was quite long, at least a large stone's throw.* There the lady held the knight in prison. In the evening after the encounter had taken place, the knights of the country came to the lady's city, and told the lady the news of the encounter. The lady asked who had fought the best; and they said, Sir Gawain, for they thought no knight ever fought better. The knight who was in the gaol heard the news, and when the men-at-arms who were guarding him brought him food, he asked which knight of the lady's household was on the best terms with her, and they named a knight, a very worthy man, who was on very good terms with her.

'Gentlemen, do get him to speak to me.'

'We shall gladly tell him,' said the men-at-arms.

They went to the knight, and said:

'The prisoner knight wishes to speak to you.'

He went to the gaol. When the other saw him, he stood up to meet him.

'Sir,' he said, 'I have sent you word, and I wish to ask you to ask my lady[1] to allow me to speak to her.'

---

[1] i.e. the lady whose prisoner he is.

'Gladly, sir,' said the knight.

He left the gaol and went to his lady, and said:

'My lady, grant me a boon.'

'What boon?' she said.

'Grant it to me,' he said; 'I shall tell you what it is.'

'Tell me', she said, 'without hesitation. If you need any-thing, it is yours.'

'Thank you, my lady,' he said; 'you have granted me that you will speak to the knight that you have in prison.'

[280] 'Gladly,' she said; 'bring him here.'

The knight went to fetch him, and took him to his lady, and then he went away again, and left him with her.

'What did you want, sir?' said the lady. 'Did you want to speak to me? So I was told.'

'Yes, indeed, madam,' he said; 'I am your prisoner, and I wanted to ask you to ransom me, for I have heard that King Arthur is in this country. I am a poor knight bachelor, and some of his men know me. They would give me my ransom soon enough.'

'Sir,' she said, 'I am not holding you out of greed for your ransom, but for justice. You know very well that you commit-ted a great outrage, and that is why I took you prisoner.'

'Madam,' he said, 'I cannot deny the fact, but I had to do it, for I could not honourably let the matter drop. But if you were pleased to ransom me, you would be doing a good deed, for I have heard that there was an encounter today in this country. And in three days' time there is to be another, so the knights were saying just now in the hall here. If you agree, I should like to ask you to let me go there; and I should guarantee you that I would return to your prison in the evening, if I was not physically prevented.'

'I will do that,' she said, 'on condition that you tell me your name.'

'That', he said, 'I cannot do.'

'Then you will not go,' she said.

'Let me go,' he said, 'and I give you my word that I shall tell you it as soon as it is time to do so.'

'You give me your word?' she said.

'Yes.'

'Then you shall go,' she said, 'but you must swear to place yourself in my prison in the evening, if you are not physically prevented.'

He swore, and she took his oath. He went back to his gaol, and was there that evening and all the next day and the next night. And King Arthur's forces continued to grow, coming from all parts. Galehot's men went to him, and said:

'Sire, will your troops engage King Arthur's troops tomorrow?'

'Yes,' said Galehot, 'I shall choose those I wish to go.'

'You will choose!' they said. 'That is out of the question. If you wish to send those who went the last time, all the others will go, whether you like it or not, for they are so keen to engage their knights [281] that you could not restrain them. But send all those who did not go, and all those who went will remain with you.'

'All right,' Galehot said. 'Now, the sixty thousand who did not go will go, and three days from tomorrow,* I shall go myself.'

The night passed. In the morning the king ordered that none of his knights was to cross the water, but those in the army should arm themselves and organize their companies. And when they saw Galehot's troops, then they should cross the water. The knights from all over the country had all joined the army, those from the city of the Hill of Malohaut and those from the other lands round about.

The lady of the city had given the knight that she had in prison a horse and a red shield and his own arms which he had when she took him prisoner, for he would have no others. The next day at daybreak he went out of the city and travelled towards King Arthur's army, and he saw the knights on both sides, fully armed. He stopped by the ford, and did not cross over. Near this ford was a shelter where King Arthur was standing, to watch the battle, with the queen and ladies and damsels, filling the shelter. And Sir Gawain had had himself carried there, ill as he was.* The knight with the red shield stopped by the ford and leant on his lance.

And Galehot's troops were coming in full battle array. In the first battalion came the king he had first conquered; and as they approached, he left his men, his shield on his arm, and went ahead on his own. The idle fellows and the braggarts* who were with King Arthur's army began to shout loudly: 'Their knights are coming, there they are.' And the First Conquered King was getting very near. The idle fellows began to say to the knight with the red shield:

'Sir knight, there is one of their knights coming. What are you waiting for? He is coming all alone.'

They said it many times, and he did not reply. And the First Conquered King was coming very fast. The knaves had said it to him so much that they were all tired of it. One fine idle fellow went up to him and took the shield from around his neck, and hung it around his own; and he did not move. Another knave who was on foot thought that the knight was stupid, and bent down towards the water and picked up a clod, and struck him on the nasal of the helm with it.

'Cowardly good-for-nothing,' said the knave, 'what are you dreaming about?'

The clod was wet, and the water went in his eyes. He blinked his eyes because he felt the water, and heard the clamour, and looked around and saw the First Conquered King, who by now was very near. He set [282] spurs to his horse and lowered his lance, and went swiftly to meet him. And the king struck him in the chest.* The hauberk was strong, and did not break, and the lance flew into pieces. The knight struck him on the shield so hard that he knocked him and his horse down in a heap. As the horse got up again, the

knave who had taken the shield, and had it around his neck,
grasped it by the bridle. The knight never looked at it, for, if
he had wished, he could have caught it before the knave did,
but he was not thinking about that.[1] And the idle fellow who
had taken his shield went up to him and put it around his
neck.

'Here, sir,' he said, 'it is in better hands than I thought.'

The knight looked up and saw that he was hanging his
shield around his neck, and he did not react, but took it. The
companions of the king he had knocked down galloped
forward, when they saw their lord fall; and King Arthur's
battalions made ready. And when they were ready, they went
to the ford and crossed the water. The knights engaged one
another, and the knight with the red shield charged forward
to joust with one of the knights of the king he had knocked
down, and struck him, so that he knocked him to the ground,
and his lance flew into pieces. And a knave went after him,
and took the horse. The battle began, well contested, between
King Arthur's and Galehot's troops. King Arthur's battalions
crossed the water in great numbers, one after the other, and
on the other side came Galehot's troops, very keen to engage
King Arthur's troops. And they[2] drove them back at lance
point, so that they left dead and wounded that day. None the
less, Galehot's troops fought very well, and King Arthur's
better; and they needed to, for they were many fewer, being
only twenty thousand, while the others were sixty thousand.
The fighting lasted a long time, and it was a good battle;
many knightly deeds were done, and King Arthur's companions and the renowned knights of his household fought very
well. King Arthur's and Galehot's troops did great deeds of
arms that day, but the knight with the red arms surpassed
everyone; and in the evening he left, and they did not know
what became of him.

---

[1] i.e. booty.   [2] i.e. King Arthur's men.

The king was very much afraid he would lose his land and his honour, and his men had failed him badly,* as the wise clerks had told him, and he was very frightened. On the other side, Galehot also spoke to his followers and said that he had no great honour in making war on King Arthur in this manner, for the king had too few men.

'And if I conquered his land at this point,' he said, 'I should have not honour, but shame.'

'Sire,' said his men, 'what do you mean to do?'

[283] 'I shall tell you,' he said. 'At the moment it no longer pleases me to make war on him in this manner; instead I shall give him a truce for a year, on condition that he brings all his forces at the end of the year. Then I shall have greater honour in conquering him than I should have now.'

So that night passed, and the next day came. Then a worthy man, full of great wisdom, came to King Arthur's camp. When the king heard that he was coming, he was greatly comforted, and he thought that God was sending him help. Then the king mounted and went to meet him with a great company of men, and greeted him humbly; however, the worthy man did not return his greeting, but said in angry fashion:

'I do not care for you or for your greeting, nor do I like it, for you are the vilest of all sinners. And you will see that, for you are near to losing all earthly honour.'

Then everyone drew back, and the king and the worthy man rode together. And the king said:

'Good master, tell me why you do not care for my greeting and why I am such a vile sinner.'

'I shall tell you,' said the worthy man, 'for I know what you are better than you yourself. Even so, you know very well that you were not engendered in a union of lawful marriage, but in the great sin of adultery.* And you should know that no mortal man gave you the dominion you hold to take care of, but God alone gave it to you so that you should take good care of it, and you have taken such bad care of it for Him that you, who should take care of it, are destroying it. For the right of the poor and the powerless cannot reach you: instead the faithless rich man is heard and honoured before you because of his wealth, while the righteous poor man has no justice because of his poverty. The right of widows and orphans has perished under your dominion. And God will call you most cruelly to account for this, for He Himself said through the mouth of His prophet David that He is the guardian of the poor and sustains the orphans and will destroy the ways of the sinners. That is how you take care of God's people, over whom He has given you earthly dominion. And that will bring you to destruction, for God will destroy the sinners. Therefore He will destroy you, for you are the vilest of sinners.'

'Ha! dear master,' he said, 'for the Lord's sake, advise me, for I am very frightened.'

And the worthy man said:

[284] 'It is extraordinary behaviour, to ask for advice if you will not listen to it.'

'Truly, good master,' the king said, 'I shall obey you in everything you tell me.'

Thus the two of them went, talking alone together, to the king's tent; and the king spoke again, and said:

'Good master, advise me, for the Lord's sake, for I have great need of it.'

And the worthy man said:

'The advice will still come in time, if you will listen to it, and I shall teach you the beginning of the way to Our Lord. Now go to your chapel and send for the men of highest rank and the best clerks you know of in the army, and confess, to all of them together, all the sins of which the tongue can unburden itself and that the heart can recall. And take care that your heart is in your words, for confession has no value if the heart does not repent what the tongue confesses. You are far removed from Our Lord's love through your sin, and you cannot be reconciled except first by spoken confession, then by true repentance of the heart, then by physical suffering and works of alms and charity. Such is the right way to the Lord God. Now go, and confess in this manner, and you must be scourged by your confessors, for that is a sign of humility. If I were authorized to hear confession, I should hear yours; but no one who is not ordained should do that, unless some urgent need impels him to it. For that reason I should not hear your confession, for you will have plenty of the shepherds of the Holy Church.[1] After your confession, though, you will come to me, and God will send you advice if lack of faith does not hinder you. Now go, and do as I have told you, and do not omit to confess anything which your conscience can reproach you.'

Then the king assembled his bishops and his archbishops, of whom there were many with the army. When they were together in the chapel, the king went before them, in only his breeches, weeping and groaning, and with his two hands full of thin twigs. He threw these down in front of them and, weeping, told them to take vengeance on him for God: 'for I am the vilest and most faithless sinner in the world'.

When they heard that, they were very much taken aback, and said:

'Sire, what is it? What is the matter?'

'I come to you,' he said, 'to you as my fathers, and I wish [285] to confess my great folly* to God in your presence, for I am the vilest sinner who ever lived.'

Then they were very much moved and began to weep. He was on his knees before them, undressed and barefoot, until he had confessed, to the best of his belief, all the great sins with which he thought he was afflicted. After that they scourged him, and he accepted it very humbly. Then he went

---

[1] i.e. priests.

back to his master, who at once asked him what he had done.
He said that he had confessed all the great sins that he could
remember having committed. And the worthy man said:

'Did you confess your great sin concerning King Ban of
Benwick, who died in your service, and his wife, who has
been dispossessed since the death of her husband? I say
nothing for the moment of her son, whom she also lost, but
the one loss is much less serious than the other.'

Then the king was very much taken aback and said:

'Indeed, master, I did not confess to that, and the sin is
very great, but truly, I had forgotten it.'

Then the king went to his chapel and found his clerks still
in the chapel, talking about his confession, and he confessed
his sin to them. However, they did not impose penance on
him for that sin or the others, for they could not all agree on
one thing, and so they gave themselves a respite until after
the battle, so that they could deliberate further.

Thereupon the king returned to his master and told him
what he had done. And then he said:

'Now, dear master, for the Lord's sake, advise me, and I
shall obey you in everything you suggest, for I am very
frightened about my men failing me like this, for I have loved
them dearly.'

'Ha!' said the worthy man, 'small wonder if your men are
failing you, for when a man fails himself, others will certainly
fail him. And you failed when you erred against your Lord
regarding the dominion that you should have held from Him,
and from no one else. For that reason they must fail you, for
God has given you this first sign, so that you may realize that
He means to remove you from your dominion, because He is
taking from you those by whose aid you have long maintained
it. Even so, some of them are failing you of their own free
will, and the others in spite of themselves. Those are failing
you of their own free will to whom you should have done
great honour* and given noble treatment and good fellow-

ship: that is, the lesser gentry of your land, by whom you should be maintained, for the kingdom cannot be held without the consent of the common people. [286] They have failed you of their own free will. The others, who are failing you in spite of themselves, are the men of your household, to whom you have given great riches, whom you have made the lords of your household. They are failing you in spite of themselves because God wishes it. So, no defence can endure against God's will. Thus they are all failing you, but some come in your hour of need of necessity, because they must protect their fiefs and their lands, and the others come because of the good things you have given them, and still give them. Thus some come of necessity, and the others willingly. However, those who come of necessity are no more good to you than if they were dead, for you do not have their hearts; and a body without a heart is powerless. Now take note of the value of shield and hauberk and sword and the power of the horse; without a man's heart, none of them has any value. If at this moment you had all the kings who have lived since the world began, all equipped in full armour, they would be no help to you, if their hearts were not in it, any more than they are now. Those who come of necessity in your hour of need are just the same; you have only their bodies, for you have lost their hearts. Do you feel I am telling you the truth?'

'Indeed, master,' said the king, 'I fully accept that you are telling me the truth, but for the Lord's sake, advise me what I can do, for the men who interpreted my dreams told me that this would befall me. Since you have advised me this far, for the Lord's sake, give me advice that will help me, if it is possible.'

'I shall advise you,' said the worthy man, 'and shall I tell you how? To the honour of your body and the profit of your soul. I shall teach you one of the finest arts you ever heard of, for I shall teach you to heal a sick heart in a healthy body, and that is fine medicine. You have given me your word that you will do as I suggest.'

'Indeed, master,' said the king, 'I certainly shall.'

'Then I shall now tell you,' said the worthy man, 'what you must do. You will have advice and help, and soon. And you will see what God will do to set you right with Him and with the world. You must go to your country, and you must go and stay in all the good towns, longer in one, less time in another, according to their merits. And be sure that you stay there until you have heard the rights and wrongs,* both great and small, for the poor man will be much happier, if right wins him his case before you, than if he had more* before someone else, and he will tell everyone that you yourself upheld his cause. That is how a king should act if he wishes to have the love of God and of the world, the love of the [287] world through humility, and the love of God through righteousness. That is the start of gaining honour and love. I shall tell you what you must do after that. As you stay in your towns, you must send for the noblemen of your land, and all the rich and poor knights, and they will gladly come in great numbers. And you must go to meet them, and give them noble companionship and great honours and a warm welcome, and provide them with ample good company. And when you see a poor knight bachelor whom poverty has in thrall and who has not neglected physical prowess, and he is down there* among the other poor men,* do not neglect him because of his poverty or his lowly birth; for beneath physical poverty lies* great richness of heart, while poverty of heart is often wrapped in an abundance of gold and land. However, because by yourself you could not recognize the good and the bad men in each land, you will have to inquire in each region you come to for the most trustworthy knight in whom prowess at arms is lodged, and give benefits and honours to those of his country according to his testimony, for no one recognizes a man of worth so well as a man rooted in great prowess. And when he points out the good poor man sitting far away among the other poor men, be sure that the company of the noblemen is not so dear to you that you do not get up from among them and go and sit beside the poor man and inquire about his situation, and get to know him, and he you. Then everyone will say: "Did you see what the king did, leaving all the rich men for that one who is poor?" In that way you will gain the love of the lowly people; for that will show great humility, and humility is a virtue by which one can increase and promote one's honour and advantage. And you will never see a man in whom there is good sense and merit, who, whatever his high estate, if you get up from beside him to keep company with a poor man, does not consider it sensible and worthy conduct. And if foolish men hold it against you, do not worry, for the blame of the foolish dies away, and the praise of the wise grows greater and stronger. When you have stayed with and got to know the poor men, then you will keep company with your barons, who are part of your kingdom, for the good of one should not suffer because of the other.

'When you have stayed in a town for as long as you please, then you will leave with whatever company you have had. Then good horses and fine arms will be got ready, rich cloths, beautiful gold and silver plate, an abundance of money. And when you see the good poor man whom the true witness* has made known to you, then look out one of your horses suitable for him, and mount it. [288] Then go alongside him, and make much of him, and dismount from your horse, and give it to him and say that he should at least ride for your sake. Afterwards have him given as much of your money as you think his way of life requires. You will give him the horse for his prowess and the money for his largesse and expense.

'That is how you must give to the poor man of valour. But you must give to the vavasour in a different way, for if he is well off in his dwelling, you must give him robes and palfreys to carry him about his affairs. But be sure that you have first sat on the palfrey, and he will tell everyone that he has the palfrey that you were riding. That is how you must give to the vavasours. However, do not neglect because of this to increase the fiefs of the needy with fine rents and rich lands, to each according to his station; for you will not lose by it, if you give to them: rather, you will win their hearts. Better care will be taken of the lands by many men of valour, if they have them, than it would be by you alone, for you are only one man, and whatever you can do, you can only do it through them. You should prefer that your men of valour hold a part of your land with honour than that you shamefully lose both it and them. After that you must give to the men of high estate, to the kings, the dukes, the counts, the noble barons. And what?[1] Rich plate, elegant jewellery, fine silks, good horses; do not aim to give them rich gifts, so much as beautiful and attractive ones, for one should not give a rich man valuable things, but attractive, not very valuable things, for it is a tiresome thing to pile riches on riches. To the poor man, though, one should give things which have more value than beauty, which are more useful than attractive, for poverty needs only betterment, and riches need only pleasure. The same things should not be given to everyone, for one should not give a man something of which he has plenty. That is how you will have to give, if you wish to give properly. And if you act in that way, the queen must do the same with the ladies and damsels of each region she comes to, so that you and she give in the way that the wise man commands.

'The wise man says that the giver should be as happy with his gift as is the man he gives it to. One should not give with bad grace, but always with a cheerful appearance, for a gift which is given cheerfully has twice the merit, while one which is given reluctantly brings no return. There is also another reason why you should never [289] tire of giving; for you

---

[1] i.e. what will you give them?

know very well that you cannot be destroyed by giving, but you can go to ruin by too much holding on, for no one was ever destroyed by largesse, but many have been ruined by avarice. Always give plenty, and you will have plenty to give, for everything you give will remain in your land, and the wealth of many other lands will come to yours. Giving will never come to an end as long as you wish it to continue, for you will never wear out the gold and silver of your land: rather, they will wear you out as the water wears out the mill-wheel. For that reason, you should apply yourself to giving tirelessly, and if you were to do this, you would win both worldly honour and the hearts of your people and the love of Our Lord. Those are the noble rewards to which man was ordained, and no one should aspire to win anything else. Do you feel I am advising you loyally?'

'Indeed, good master,' the king said, 'you have advised me very well, and I shall do as you have bidden me, if God grants that I return to my land with honour. But, for the Lord's sake, advise me about the remarkable thing that the men who interpreted my dreams told me: that nothing can save me from losing my land except the Lion in Water and the Doctor without Medicine through the counsel of the Flower. Enlighten me about these three things, if it is possible, for I do not understand, and you could certainly explain them to me, if you so wished.'

'Listen, then,' said the worthy man; 'I have shown you why you have lost the hearts of your people, and how you can recover them. And I shall also explain to you the three things you are asking about, so that you will see and know them clearly. None the less, they[1] did not know what they were telling you, any more than the madman who speaks and does not know whether he is speaking the truth or lies. However, I shall tell you the truth of it. And you should know that they

---

[1] i.e. King Arthur's clerks.

did not tell you that without reason, for the lion is God. God is signified by the lion, because of the characteristics of the lion which are different from those of other beasts, but the fact that they saw it in water is most remarkable. They called it "in water", because they thought they saw it in water. The water in which they thought they saw it is this world, for as a fish cannot live without water, in the same way we cannot live without the world; that is to say, without the things of the world. Those who told you that they had seen the lion were wrapped in this world; and because they were wrapped in and afflicted with the sin of the world, it therefore seemed to them that they had seen the lion in the water which signifies the world, for, if they had been as they should, loyal, chaste, charitable, compassionate, devout, and full of the other [290] virtues, they would not have seen the lion in the water, but up there in heaven. For heaven is the everlasting world, made ready for a man if he will follow the commandments of his Creator. And the man who lives in that way is not earthly but heavenly, for if his body is on earth, his spirit is already in heaven through good thoughts. However, the earth is not like that, but is a grave and a burial for the man who lives in the world in pride, in cruelty, in wickedness, in avarice, in greed, and in lust and in the other sins of damnation. Such were the clerks who interpreted your dreams to you, and for that reason they thought they saw the lion in the water which signifies sin. None the less, it was not in the water, for God has never been in sin, but was on His heavenly seat. However, the thickness of the air was so great between Him and them that they could only see Him in a place such as they were in. That was in water, for the great clerkly learning which was in them made them see the figure of the lion, by dint of searching. But because of this clerkly learning which was only earthly, they had only the sight of the lion, for they did not recognize it, and did not know what it could be, for they were earthly creatures, and the lion heavenly. For that reason they did not see its significance, and they thought they saw it in the water, by which they were deceived. And for that reason they called it "in water".

'That lion is Jesus Christ, who was born of the Virgin, for as the lion is lord of all the beasts, in the same way God is lord of all things. The lion has many other characteristics by which it signifies God, of which I shall not speak now, but I will tell you this much: that this is the lion from which you will have help, if you are ever to have it. It is Jesus Christ, the true lion. Have you now fully understood who the Lion is, and why He was called "in water"?'

'Master,' he said, 'I have fully understood that, and you have shown it to me very clearly. But, for the Lord's sake, tell me what the Doctor without Medicine can be, for I should not have thought that any doctor could be without medicine, and I still cannot make anything of it.'

'The more I consider you,' said the worthy man, 'the more foolish I find you, for, if you had reasonable good sense, you could understand these two things quite clearly one by the other. However, since I have begun to explain to you about the royal crown* on behalf of Our Lord, I shall explain it all to you, not for your sake, but for the sake of the common people. And I shall tell you who the Doctor without Medicine is. He is God, and there is no other doctor without medicine except Him alone; for all the other [291] doctors, whatever ability they have to recognize illnesses in the body and to know the cure, they do it all by the sense they have which came down from God and which* put the force in the herbs by which they are able to cure the body. And they know only how to cure the body; and not every body, even then, for it often happens that when they have made every effort to cure somebody, then he dies. And if they* happen to be able to cure the illnesses of the body, yet they have no power to cure the illnesses of the soul. But God has the power to do so, for as soon as a man comes to true confession, he will never be so burdened with vile sin that God will not look kindly on him. And as soon as He has looked on him, no other doctor will be needed, no bandage will need to be tied on: instead the wound is clean and healthy as soon as He has looked at it. This is the Doctor without Medicine, who uses no medicine on wounds of the soul or the body; instead everything is made clean and healthy by His gentle look. That is not what mortal doctors do, though, for when they have seen the illnesses, then they have to look for the herbs and medicines which are needed for that illness, and sometimes it is all wasted when death shows its dominion. But He is a true doctor who by His look alone gives health to the sick in soul and in body, and makes death stay away from the body for as long as He pleases, and saves from death of the soul for ever. This is the Doctor without Medicine. And let me tell you truly, if you have today been wholeheartedly to His potion—that is, your true confession—your body is cured, for you need to be cured, or you are disgraced on earth, while your soul will not experience everlasting death. Is He rightly called "without medicine"?'

'Dear master,' said the king, 'you have certainly shown me the true significance of the Lion in Water and the Doctor without Medicine. But now I am even more in need of advice than before about the Flower, for I can see that a flower cannot give counsel unless it speaks, and I do not see how a flower could speak.'

'Indeed,' said the worthy man, 'you will clearly see that a flower can speak and give counsel. Moreover, you cannot reach the true Lion or the Doctor without Medicine without the counsel of this flower. And if you ever get over this trouble you are in, it will be through the counsel of this flower. So, I shall tell you who this flower is and how its counsel will save you. This flower is the flower among flowers. From this flower came the fruit by which all things are sustained; [292] that is, the fruit by which the body is

sustained and the soul nourished; that is, the fruit which
satisfied the five thousand in the meadows when twelve
baskets were filled with the left-over scraps; that is, the fruit
by which the people of Israel were sustained for fifteen years*
in the desert, when man, so the Scriptures say, ate the bread
of angels; that is, the fruit by which Joseph of Arimathaea
and his companions were sustained when they were coming
from the promised land to this remote country, at the
command of Jesus Christ, and with His guidance; that is, the
fruit by which the Holy Church is also nourished every day;
that is, Jesus Christ, the Son of God. It is the flower from
which you must have help and counsel, if you are ever to
have it. It is His gentle Mother, the glorious Virgin, of whom
He was born contrary to nature's custom. That lady is rightly
called the Flower, for no woman before or after her ever bore
a child without first being deflowered by fleshly union. This
noble lady, though, was a virgin maiden, both before and
afterwards, for she never lost the flower of her maidenhead.
She should certainly be called the Flower among flowers,
then, since she kept her glorious flower sound and intact,
when all the other flowers perish, that is, in conceiving and
giving birth, and since from her came the Fruit which gives
life to all things. Through this Flower you will come to true
counsel, for she will reconcile you with her gentle son and
send you the help which will cause you to receive the honour
that you have begun to lose. If you do not come to salvation
of body and soul through this Flower, you cannot do so
through anyone else, for no one can intercede with the
Saviour as well as she can. She will never stop praying on
behalf of the wretched. And if you honour this Flower, her
counsel will release you from all dangers. This is the Flower
your clerks told you about, although they did not know it.
This is the Flower through which the true Lion and the
noble Doctor without Medicine will save you from losing
land and honour, if you do not prevent it. What do you think?

Do you still accept that I have been a true interpreter of your dreams?'

'Indeed, master,' the king said, 'you have explained it to me excellently, and you have so comforted me that I think I have escaped from all my fears, for my heart is very much more at ease than it was. And I give my word by God that I shall do as you have bidden me, if God grants that I return to my land with honour.'

While they were talking like this, two knights came there from Galehot's household. When the king saw them, he ordered that they should come before him. They came before him; and the king [293] who was called the King of a Hundred Knights spoke first; and the other was named the First Conquered King, because he was the first king that Galehot had placed under his dominion. King Arthur, who well knew how to honour a man of valour, did them great honour and stood up to meet them, without knowing that they were kings.

'My lord,' said the King of a Hundred Knights, 'we are sent here by Galehot, lord of the Foreign Isles, in whose service we are, and he says that he is very surprised that you have come with so poor a following to defend your land against him, you who are such a powerful man, for he had heard that you were the most powerful king in the whole world. For that reason my lord thinks that you do not have all your forces with you, and he would have no honour in conquerin you when you have so few men here, for you are in a very sorry state. So my lord is now giving you a truce for a year, on condition that you will have all your forces in this place, and he all of his, for he does not have them all at present. And you should know that he will not then leave until he has defeated you and conquered your land. And you should know that at the end of the year, whatever it costs, he will have in his household the good knight, the one with the red arms who was the victor at the encounter.'

'Gentlemen,' said the king, 'I hear what you are saying, but, please God, he will never have power or control over me or my land, and may God defend me from it.'

Thereupon the messengers left; and the king was left delighted and very worried, delighted about the truce he had been given, and worried about the good knight, who had fought to defend his land for him, whom Galehot meant to have in his household. Then the worthy man called him and said:

'Now you can see that the noble Flower has obtained for you from the noble Lion and the Doctor without Medicine that He will save you, if you do not forfeit it through indolence.'

'Master,' said the king, 'it is a good start; but I am very worried about the good knight who has defended my land for me, whom Galehot boasts he will have. Master, who can he be, for I do not know him?'

And the worthy man said:

'Let it be, for his actions will speak for themselves.'

'Ah! master,' he said, 'you can at least tell me if he will be on his[1] side at the end of the year.'

[294] And he replied that he would not. Then the king was very much comforted and greatly eased. Thereupon Galehot's troops began to disperse. King Arthur also dispersed his and took leave of his master, and returned to his country, and he had Sir Gawain, who was extremely ill, carried in a litter. Now, though, the story falls silent about King Arthur and Galehot and his household, and turns to the lady of the Hill of Malohaut, who was holding the good knight in prison.

[M. LIa] The story says that in the evening when the encounter broke up, as you have heard, he went straight back to Malohaut. However, it was dark when he arrived there; and he went as quietly as he could into the courtyard, where

---

[1] i.e. Galehot's.

the lady had people waiting for him, for she thought she could be sure of his coming. When he was disarmed, he immediately went into his gaol and lay down, for he was in such pain that he could not eat a thing. That evening the knights that the Lady of Malohaut had sent to the battle had arrived. The lady asked them for news of the encounter, how both sides had fought, and they said that a knight with red arms had surpassed everyone. When she heard that, she began to look at a maiden, who was her first cousin and had great influence in her household, and she was impatient for the knights to leave. As soon as she could, though, she got rid of them. Then she called her cousin:

'Tell me, dear cousin, could that be our knight?'

'My lady,' she said, 'I do not know.'

'Indeed,' she said, 'I should very much like to know, and if he was victorious there, it must show clearly on his body and armour.'

'My lady,' she said, 'we can soon see if it shows there.'

'And I wish to go and see,' said the lady, 'but take care that no living creature knows about it except the two of us, if you value your limbs.'

'Of course, my lady.'

Then the lady cleared the house so that only the two of them remained. The maiden carried a handful of candles, and they went first to the stable and saw the horse, which had wounds on the head and the neck and the chest and the legs, and the bones showed* in many places, and it was lying in front of the manger, looking very wretched, not eating or drinking. Then the lady said:

'As God is my witness, you certainly seem like the horse of a man of valour. And you, what do you say?' she asked her cousin.

'My lady,' she said, 'what can I say? I think the horse has had more hardship than rest. None the less, this is not the one he took with him.'

[295] 'Then rest assured', the lady said, 'that he has worn out more than one. Now, though, let us go and see his arms, and we shall see how they are feeling the effects of it.'

Then they went to a chamber where they[1] were and found the hauberk split and full of great holes on the shoulders and on the arms and in many other places. And his shield was split and shattered and hacked apart with sword-blows on the sides and the top right to the boss, so that there was very little of it left. And in what was left, there were great holes from lance-blows, so that in many places one could have put one's fists through it. And his helm was split and dented, with the nasal all hacked apart, and the circle hanging down, so that it would never again be of use to him or to anyone else. Then the lady said to her cousin:

'What do you think about these arms?'

'Truly, my lady,' she said, 'I think that the man who bore them has not been idle.'

'You might say', the lady said, 'that the most valorous man alive bore them.'

'My lady,' she said, 'that is quite possible, now that you say so.'

'Now come,' said the lady, 'and we shall go and see the knight, for I have not yet seen anything which I believe. His body will show the truth of the matter.'

Thereupon they went to the door of the gaol, and found it open. The lady took the candles in her hand and put her head in at the door, and saw the knight, who was lying naked in his bed. He had drawn the bedspread up over his chest, and had stuck his arms out because of the heat, and was sleeping very soundly. She looked, and saw that his face was swollen and battered and marked by the chain-mail, his neck and nose were grazed, and his forehead swollen, and his eyebrows grazed, and his shoulders terribly hacked and

[1] i.e. the arms.

wounded, and his arms all bruised from the blows he had
received, and his hands were big and swollen, full of blood.
Then she looked at the maiden, and began to smile.

'Truly,' the lady said, 'you are about to see something
remarkable.'

She moved into the gaol, and the maiden put her head in,
and took a good look all around. The lady gave her the
candles, and gathered up her skirts a little to go forward. The
maiden looked at her, and said:

'What is this, my lady? What do you mean to do?'

'I shall never have such a good opportunity to kiss him.'

'Oh, no, my lady,' she said, 'what are you saying? Do not
do anything so rash, for if he were to wake up, he would
think less of you and all ladies because of it. Do not be so
impulsive or so foolish that you forget about shame.'

[296] 'As God is my true witness,' the lady said, 'one could
not have shame from something one did for such a valorous
man.'

'No, one could not, my lady,' the maiden said, 'inasmuch
as it pleased him; but truly, if he refused it, the shame would
be doubled. And a man can have great physical valour and
not have the qualities of the heart. It might be that you could
never make so much of this one that he would not consider it
outrageous and unworthy, and you would have wasted your
love and your service.'

Following what the maiden said to her lady, she was able
to lead her away without her doing anything further. When
they reached their chambers, they began to talk about the
knight. And the maiden did her best to change the subject,
because she would have liked to stop her lady thinking about
him if it were possible, for she had a good idea of his love. In
the end she said:

'My lady, the knight's ideas are quite other than you
suppose, and supposition has let many people down.'

'As God is my witness,' said the lady, 'I suppose he has

such noble ideas that no man's were ever so noble. And may God, who has made him more handsome and better than all the others, grant that he carry out his ideas successfully, whatever they are.'

They talked about the knight a great deal that night, and the lady very much wondered why he did such deeds of arms. And she rather thought in her heart that he loved someone of very high rank, and she would dearly have liked to know who he was and on whom he had set his heart, and she would dearly have liked it to be on her. However, she sensed in him such great prowess and so proud a heart that she could not think he would love any but a very noble person. She decided, though, that she would find out, if it were possible; and she said no more about it. Now, though, the story falls silent about the lady and the maiden and the knight, and says no more about them at this point, but returns to King Arthur, who had repaired to his land.

[M. LIa] The story says that he went first of all to stay at Carlisle in Wales,* which was nearest and was a very comfortable castle in every way. The king stayed in the town twenty-three days and held court sumptuously every day, and closely followed his master's orders in everything. Within a fortnight Sir Gawain was fully recovered from his wounds, and the whole court was delighted. At the end of twenty-three days it happened that the king was sitting at dinner. When he had been eating for a while, he fell into a profound reverie; and it was apparent from his reverie that his heart was uneasy: in fact, anyone who saw him would have said that he was very much ill at ease. Then Sir Gawain, who was serving with the others,* went to him, and said:

[297] 'Sire, you are too deep in thought at this meal, and it will be held against you, for there are many knights here who are criticizing you for it.'

And the king answered, angrily:

'Gawain, Gawain, you have shaken me out of the most

courtly thoughts I ever had, and no one could rightly criticize me for it, for I was thinking about the best knight of all the men of valour. That is, the knight who was the victor at the encounter between Galehot and me, of whom Galehot has boasted that he will have him in his household. And I have known a time when, if the knights of my household and my companions knew of something that I desired, they would seek it for me, no matter how remote a land it was in. And it used to be said that all earthly prowess was in my household; but I say that now it is not, since the best knight in the world is not here.'

'Indeed, sire,' said Sir Gawain, 'you are quite right; and you will have the knight, please God, if he can be found anywhere in the world.'

With that Sir Gawain turned away; and when he reached the door of the hall, in which many good knights were sitting, he turned towards those at table and said, loud enough for all to hear:

'Gentlemen, knights, whoever would now embark on the most noble quest there has ever been, after that of the Grail, should follow me. Today all the renown and honour in the world await the man that God will give the good fortune to make the great find,* and there will be no point in anyone who neglects it[1] ever again engaging to win honour.'

Then Sir Gawain left, and knights sprang up after him, and tables began to empty. The king became upset because no one was left there, and he had Sir Gawain called back, and he came to him; and then he said:

'Dear nephew, you are making me angry. You are bringing great disgrace on me when you wish to take away all my company like this: and right now I am in a position where I need to hold court with more magnificence, wherever I am, than I used to; and no one ever saw such a great gathering to

---

[1] i.e. the quest.

find a single knight. Do you mean to take him by force with all the knights of my land? The less people bring him back, the greater will be the honour.'

Then Sir Gawain realized that the king was speaking the truth, and said:

'Sire, no more will come than you wish; and I did not say it out of desire for the company, for I shall only look for him [298] by myself; but if many knights were to look for him, each on his own, he would be found more quickly than if there were only one on the quest.'

'You are right,' said the king; 'now, let forty go, those you yourself choose, for I do not want the talk to have been started for nothing.'

Then Sir Gawain chose forty of those he most loved, for each man was delighted if he could go in his company. Then all forty went to arm, and then went before the king. Holy relics were brought, as was customary, for no knight would set off from the royal court in search of adventure without first swearing on holy relics that on his return he would tell the truth, to the best of his knowledge, about everything which befell him. Or, if he did not swear it when he set off, he would swear it on his return, before he was believed about anything. Then Sir Gawain knelt down to swear; and the king was present, and said:

'Gentlemen, knights, you are going away, and take care that it is not for nothing, for all of you go as knights of such valour that there is nothing so great that you should not be able to accomplish it.'

Then Sir Gawain thought and said to the armed knights, when he was on his knees:

'Gentlemen, if each man would include in his oath what I shall include in mine, I should swear.'

They all agreed to do so.

'Now,' he said, 'first swear to everything that I shall swear, and I shall swear last of all.'*

And they did so. After that Sir Gawain swore that he would tell the truth on his return, and that he would not come back without the knight he was going to look for, or reliable news of his whereabouts, and that he would not come back without every one of his companions, unless death took him.*

All the knights who were to go on the quest were worried by this oath. However, the king was the most worried of all, for he remembered about the day of the encounter which was to take place between him and Galehot.

'Dear nephew,' he said, 'you have done wrong not to make my encounter a reason for exemption from your oath.'*

'Sire,' he said, 'it is too late now.'

Thereupon he laced on his helm and mounted his horse and left the court with the company of knights that he had. There was Sir Yvain, the son of King Urien, and Kay the seneschal and Sagremor [299] the Impetuous and Lucan the butler and Yder, the son of Nut, and Girflet, the son of Do, and Yvain of the Little Lion* and Yvain of the White Hands and Yvain the Crooked and Yvain the Bastard and Galegantin the Welshman and Gasoain of Estrangot and the Gay Galantin and Caradigas and Agloas and Magloas and Duke Taulas and Quenut of Caerec and Guerrehet and his brother Agravain and Cadoain of Caermurzin and Kay of Estraus and Dodinel the Wild and Caradoc Shortarm and the King of Genes and the King of Marés and Helys the Blond and Sir Brandeliz* and Adayn the Fair and Osanain Braveheart* and Aiglin of the Valleys and Keheriet and Bliobleris and the Ugly Hero* and Gales the Bald and Aguissant of Scotland and Hervi of Rivel and Conan the Bold, and the fortieth was the Youth of Nort. These were the forty who went on the quest. However, there was not one of them so valorous or bold that he did not later consider himself a fool because of it, for later they were all called faithless and forsworn by the king himself, for they travelled the whole year, until the encounter, without ever finding the knight, or bringing back reliable news of his whereabouts. The story does not speak here of any adventure which befell them on the quest, because they all failed in their quest, but the encounter brought them all back again. And with that it falls silent about Sir Gawain and his company, and says no more about them, and returns to the Lady of Malohaut, who was very anxious to know the good knight's name and all about him, as she loved him as much as she could love.

[M. LIIa] Now the story says that one day she had him brought out of his gaol to speak to her. When he came before her, he was going to sit on the floor at her feet; and she, who wished to do him great honour, made him sit up beside her, and said:

'Sir knight, I have held you in my prison for a long while because of the great wrong you did. And I have treated you with great honour against the wishes of my seneschal and his family, for which you should be grateful to me. And you are, if there is as much good in you as I think.'

'Madam,' he said, 'I am so grateful to you that I am your knight whenever and wherever you need me.'

'Many thanks,' said the lady, 'and you will be able to prove it. I now ask you, then, to give me in return what I shall ask you for: that you tell me who you are and to what you aspire. If it is something that you wish to keep secret, rest assured that it will go no further.'

[300] 'Madam,' he said, 'by the Lord's mercy, as God is my witness, you cannot know that, for there is no one to whom I would tell it.'

'No?' she said; 'so you will not tell me under any circumstances?'

'Madam, you must do with me as you please, for if you were to cut off my head, I should not tell you.'

'Truly,' she said, 'you will regret concealing it from me, for by the loyalty I owe you, and by the person I most love, you will never get out of my house, until the encounter which is to take place between my lord King Arthur and Galehot. And let me tell you that you will have plenty of shame and discomfort from now on, for there is still nearly a year until the meeting. And if you had told me, you would have been freed from my prison today. And I shall find out in spite of you, for I shall go somewhere where someone will tell me.'

'Where, madam?'

'In God's name,' she said, 'to the court of King Arthur, where they know all the news.'

'Madam,' he said, 'I cannot help that.'

Thereupon she sent him back to the gaol and made a show of being very angry with him and of hating him very much, but she did not: in fact she loved him more than she had before, and her love grew greater and stronger every day. Then she called her cousin and said:

'Be sure to tell the knight that I hate him more than any other man and that I shall make him suffer all the hardships that a man can endure.'

That is what the lady said to her cousin to hide her feelings. And she continued to get ready to go to King Arthur's court to find out who the knight was, and she wished to go with great pomp. Four days later the lady set off, and left her cousin, the maiden, in her place, and said to her:

'Dear cousin, I am going to King Arthur, where I have much to do. And I have shown hate for the knight, because he would not tell me his name, but I would never hate him, for he is too valorous. And I ask and call on you, if my love and your honour are dear to you, to obtain for him everything you think his heart desires, provided that your honour is safe and that you can give him back to me.'*

She gave her her word. Thereupon the lady left and journeyed until she found the king in Logres, the city which was the capital of his kingdom. When he heard that she was coming, he and the queen went to meet her, and received her very warmly. Before they entered the [301] city, though, she did not have one knight who was not presented with a gift from the king, while the queen did the same for the ladies and maidens. This was in honour of the Lady of Malohaut, and he insisted that she lodge in his residence, for she had helped him greatly in his war.

The king and queen treated the lady with great honour. In the evening, after supper, they were sitting on a couch, and the king said to the lady:

'Truly, madam, you have made a great effort, coming so far from your land. Now, I can see that it is not without good reason, for you do not normally go so far from your country.'

'Indeed, my lord,' she said, 'it is not without good reason: rather, the business is important, and I shall tell you about it. It is true that I have a cousin who is being dispossessed by her neighbour, and she can find no knight who will uphold her cause,* for he is a very good knight and from a powerful family. She has no help but me, and I have come to you, so that you will help me to get the good knight, the one with the red arms who was the victor at the encounter the other day; for I have been told that if I had him, no one could undertake the combat better. That is why I have come to you. Now, help me, for I have great need of it.'

'Dear friend,' said the king, 'by the loyalty I owe my lady the queen here, whom I love more than anyone living, I never knew that knight, as far as I know, and I do not think he is from my household, or from my land; in fact, I am very keen to see him. And Sir Gawain is looking for him with thirty-nine knights, the best of my household; and they set off nearly a fortnight ago, and will not enter my house again until they have found him.'

The lady began to smile about the knights looking for him, because they were chasing shadows. The queen saw that, and thought to herself that she was not smiling for nothing, and she said:

'Truly, I believe you know where he is better than the king and I.'

And she replied:

'By the loyalty I owe my lord the king, whose liege woman I am, and you, who are my lady, I only came here to find out who he is, for I expected to hear news of him here.'

'Indeed,' said the queen, 'I thought that, because I saw you smile when my husband was talking about him.'

[302] 'My lady,' she said, 'that was because I felt let down, and because I had gone to such trouble for nothing. However, since I can hear no news of him, I ask your leave, and I shall leave in the morning, for I have much to do in my country.'

What?' said the king; 'do you think you are leaving already? You must not leave so soon, but must keep the queen company for a week or a fortnight, and you must take with you the knight you prefer, to undertake your combat, for you should understand that you are one of the ladies I should most like to honour in the world, for you helped me greatly in my hour of need.'

'My lord,' she said, 'many thanks for what you have said, but I could not in any way stay longer, not under any circumstances; and I shall not take any knight with me, since I cannot have the one I was seeking, for I have plenty of others.'

The king and queen entreated her so much that she stayed for three days. Then she left with the goodwill of them both, and went back to her country in hard stages, for she was very impatient to be back and to see the man over whom all those of great renown in the world were going to trouble; and she was very proud of herself for having in her power something that no one else could have. Thus she went back joyful and happy, and gave her cousin to understand that she had gone to the king's court because she thought that her prisoner was from the king's court, and that the king would hold it against her.*

'Now,' she said, 'I have learned that he is not from the
king's household or from his land. But how have you and he
been since?'

'Very well, madam,' she said. 'He has had whatever he
needed.'

Not long after that she had him brought out of his gaol
and spoke to him like an angry woman.

'Sir knight,' she said, 'you were reluctant the other day to
tell me who you are, and I have since learned enough about
you that I shall now ransom you, if you wish.'

'Madam,' he said, 'many thanks. I should gladly ransom
myself, if I could come up with your ransom.'

'Shall I tell you', she said, 'what your ransom will be? I
shall offer you three ransoms; and if you do not choose one
of them, then may God never be my witness if you ever get
out of my prison again, either for wealth or for entreaty. Now,
choose one of the three, if you wish to get out of my prison.'

'Now, madam, tell me your pleasure; and since I have
come to this, I shall have to choose one of them.'

[303] 'I tell you', she said, 'that if you tell me who you are
and what your name is, you will be released from my prison;
and if you will not tell me that, then tell us whom you love;
and if you will not do either of those, then tell me whether
you expect ever again to do such deeds of arms as you did
the other day at the encounter.'

When he heard that, he began to sigh very heavily, and
said:

'Madam, madam, you hate me very much, I can see, since
you will only ransom me shamefully. Madam, for the Lord's
sake, if you make me tell you what you want, which will
distress me greatly, what assurance do I have that you will let
me go freely?'

'I give you my word faithfully', she said, 'that as soon as
you have chosen one of the three ransoms, you can go freely.
Now it is up to you, whether you go or stay.'

Then the knight began to weep very bitterly, and said:

'Madam, I can see that I shall have to escape by paying a shameful ransom, if I wish to go. And since that is the case, it is better that I say something which disgraces me, rather than someone else, for you should understand that I shall not tell you who I am at any price, nor what my name is. And if I loved someone, as God is my true witness, you would never know whom, if I could help it. So I shall have to tell you the other thing, and I shall tell it, however much shame it causes me. Let me tell you this truly, that I expect to do still greater deeds of arms than I have ever done, if I am ordered to do so. Now it is the case that you have made me say something which shames me, and I shall now go, if you agree.'

'You have said enough,' she said. 'Now, go when you please, for I now understand more about you than I ever did before. However, because I have treated you with such honour, I ask you to give me in return something which will hardly put you out. And I say it more for your good than for mine.'

'Madam,' he said, 'tell me your wishes, and you shall have what you ask for, if it can be found.'

'Many thanks,' she said; 'and I ask you to stay here until the encounter. I shall have a good horse ready for you, and such arms as you wish to bear, and you will set off from here to go to the encounter, and I shall let you know the day it is to be.'

'Madam,' he said, 'I shall do as you wish.'

'Now I shall tell you', she said, 'what you will do. You will be in your gaol and will have whatever you ask for. And both my cousin and I will often keep you company. However, I do not want anyone to know that you have come to terms with me. And tell me what arms you wish to bear.'

[304] And he said, all black. With that he went away to his gaol. And the lady secretly had an all black shield made ready

for him, and a horse the same and a surcoat* and housings the same. Thus the knight stayed there.

Meanwhile the king was in his land and doing as his master had instructed him in honouring his people, until, before half the year was past, he had so recovered their hearts that they had built more than a thousand houses* at the battleground where the encounter was to take place; and they were all eager, for they would have preferred to die painfully in battle than that the king should lose his land while they were alive. Thus they all devoted themselves to the king because of the great graciousness he showed them, and went with him to the battleground in the greatest possible numbers a fortnight before the end of the truce. Then on the other hand Sir Gawain and his companions arrived from their quest, and they had had no success, and were all ashamed about it. However, the urgency of the king's need brought them back; and Sir Gawain said that it was better for them to be disgraced for the honour of their liege lord, than that he alone should be disgraced and dispossessed.

'And he cannot be disgraced', he said, 'without our being disgraced, but we can be without his being, for we can lose our land without any disgrace to him, but he cannot lose his without disgrace to us.'

Thus, because of Sir Gawain's words, the forty knights came to the encounter, and the king received them with great joy, for he was very much afraid that they would not come in time.

Thus the king came prepared to defend his land; and on the other side Galehot also came with great forces, as for one man he had brought the last time he brought two this time, so that the iron nets which had enclosed the first army could not enclose one-half of this one. When the end of the truce came, the poor men on the two sides were very keen to engage in battle. Then those in Galehot's confidence asked him whom he wished to send to engage in battle the first day, and how many troops. He said that he himself would not bear arms, then or at any other time, unless he needed to do so. 'And this time', he said, 'my troops will only engage to see the valour of King Arthur's knights; but next time they will engage so much in earnest that one of us will be left utterly defeated.' Then he ordered that the First Conquered King should engage on the first day, with thirty thousand men, to see how King Arthur's troops acquitted themselves, and if they needed more, he would send more. That is what Galehot said to his men.

[305] On the other side Sir Gawain also spoke to his uncle, the king, and said:

'Sire, if Galehot does not bear arms tomorrow, you will not bear them.'

'Dear nephew,' he said, 'that is true, but you will bear them, and will take some of my troops. And mind you fight well, as is needful.'

'Sire,' he said, 'as you please.'

In the morning they rose early on the two sides, and when they had heard mass, they went to arm, and little by little the king's troops passed the lists* and the two sides engaged one another. There were good jousts and hard fighting in many places. Then one of Galehot's companions went to engage in battle, who was very valorous and was later in King Arthur's household, and his name was Escarant the Poor, and he was a very renowned warrior and was the most loved of the poor knights among Galehot's companions. He engaged by himself a great company in which there were nearly a hundred knights, and he came so fiercely that the whole world watched him in wonder. There were many men of valour in the company, and they let him strike where he wished. He broke his lance where he thought it would do most good, and went straight through the company and struck a very valorous knight called Galeguinant, who was Sir Yvain's bastard brother, and was coming to the jousting, as fast as he could spur, to win honour and renown, of which he had a good deal already. As he came so quickly, Escarant met him, and they crashed into one another, after breaking their lances, with bodies and faces and horses, so hard that they knocked one another to the ground in a daze, the horses on top of them, and lay on the ground for a long while without getting up. Six of King Arthur's men charged forward to prevent Escarant's escape; and when his side saw that, they spurred over there. There were at least thirty knights, and they had already remounted Escarant and knocked down the six and captured Galeguinant, when Yvain the Bastard came galloping up, and some of the others after him. The fighting was very fierce there and those on Galehot's side defended themselves very well, but they could not withstand them for long, for they were outnumbered, and not such good knights as the others. So Galeguinant was vigorously rescued from them, and the other six likewise, and Escarant was knocked down again. The whole tournament gathered there to rescue Escarant and Galeguinant, and in a short time more than fifty thousand men were gathered, on the two sides.

[306] King Arthur's troops were fighting very well, for Galehot's were at least thirty thousand strong, and they were only twenty thousand and yet they had the better of the battle. Then the First Conquered King, who was a very valorous and confident knight, engaged in person and sustained them very well. However, once Sir Gawain arrived in person, then Galehot's troops only held out for a very short time, and began to retire in disarray. When Galehot saw them, he sent them so many knights that they covered all the fields. And when Sir Gawain saw them coming, he drew his troops close in around him and exhorted them to fight well.

Thereupon their enemies arrived at full speed and rushed among them as fiercely as they could. They received them with great vigour, for there were plenty of men of valour there. Sir Gawain did remarkable deeds there, and all his companions took heart and courage, and he sustained them all by himself.* However, fighting well was to no avail, as for one of his men there were three of Galehot's. They withstood them for a while, in dire straits, but in the end they left the field and were forced as far as their lists. There Sir Gawain displayed a great part of his prowess, for he endured so much that all those on his side were astonished, and all those on Galehot's side were quite taken aback.

When King Arthur saw that they could stand no more, he said that now he had waited too long, when he had let them be so battered. Then he sent what knights he had, and he gave them to Sir Yvain to command, and begged him to go prudently. When he arrived, all the enemy had already passed the lists. And Sir Gawain's horse had been killed, and he was on foot, and had great need of help. And as soon as they engaged, their enemies did not make a stand until they were passing the lists. There, however, they stood firm until the King from Over the Borders came galloping up at full speed, and with him a full twenty thousand. Then there was a great mêlée, and everyone fought very well. Sir Yvain, too, began to fight so well that he had never fought so well before, for he mounted Sir Gawain by force on a horse from which he had knocked the First Conquered King. And Sir Gawain had already been so beaten that there was never a day afterwards that he did not feel the worse for it. Then Sir Yvain's deeds of prowess began, while those of Sir Gawain did not cease.

[307] Thus the battle lasted all day, so that when one side had the worse of it, their men reinforced them little by little, until evening came and they began to withdraw on both sides. And there was not a man there so strong* that he was not thoroughly weary. As they were going away on the two sides, Sir Gawain did not go, having gone to the rescue of one of his companions, called Gaheris of Caraheu. Sir Yvain, who was already going away, knew nothing of this, and nor did the king's other companions, when a squire came galloping after

Sir Yvain and called to him that his kinsman* and companion would be captured, if he did not hurry. Then Sir Yvain returned as fast as his horse could go, and was so worried that he did not call a single man to him, but he had an ample following of men of valour. When he reached the fray, he found Sir Gawain in such a state that the blood was spurting from his mouth and nose, and he fully expected to die without confession, but he was still on his horse. Then the fighting became more intense, and there were greater losses than there had been all day, for many knights were captured and killed and wounded, as much on one side as on the other. All the same, though, King Arthur's troops had the best of it this time, and put the others to flight. Then they turned back, taking many prisoners with them, and things went very well for them.

The king was worried about his nephew, who was very badly wounded. And when the king spoke to him in front of his[1] tent, he[2] could not say a word to him, but fell to the ground unconscious without anyone touching him. Then the king and queen grieved terribly. All the doctors were sent for, and they put him to bed, and found that he had two ribs broken, and they assumed that he was injured internally. However, they did not dare say so, because the king would have been disheartened, and so they said that he should not be dismayed, for he would recover all right.

There was great grief in King Arthur's camp over Sir Gawain, and all the men of valour wept and said that no man of such valour could ever die.* However, there were many who rejoiced.* When Sir Gawain passed out in front of his tent, the knights of Malohaut saw it clearly, and they heard rumours that he was dying. When they reached Malohaut, the lady asked for news of the encounter; and they said that Sir Gawain had surpassed everyone, but that he was very

----

[1] i.e. Sir Gawain's.   [2] i.e. Sir Gawain.

severely wounded, even fatally. The lady was very distressed by this news, and said:

'Truly, it is a pity about Sir Gawain. No more noble knight will ever die.'

[308] The news about Sir Gawain spread until there was not a servant there who was not talking about it; and the knight of the gaol heard about it. If the others were distressed, he alone grieved over it more than all other men, and said:

'Truly, if he dies, the loss will never be made good.'

When the knights from there had left, the knight of the gaol arranged to speak to the lady, and said:

'Madam, is it true that Sir Gawain is dead?'

'Indeed,' she said, 'he is wounded beyond recovery, I have heard.'

'As God is my witness,' he said, 'that is a great sorrow for all the world, and on the day of his death all joy should come to an end. Madam, madam,' he went on, 'why have you betrayed me so wretchedly? You promised to let me know the day of the encounter.'

'If I promised it,' she said, 'I now keep my promise, for our side have already suffered quite heavy losses.'

'Madam,' he said, 'it is too late, now.'

'No, it is not,' she said, 'for you will still arrive in time, for the encounter will take place again three days from today.* And I have ready for you horse and arms, such as you told me. However, I suggest that you do not set off from here until the day of the encounter; then you will travel straight from here to the battleground, and you know the way.'

'Madam,' he said, 'as you wish.'

With that the knight went away again, to sleep, and the lady did the same. When the next day came, after breakfast, the lady went to the knight, and commended him to God, and said that she was going about some business. The knight thanked her warmly for the great honour she had done him, and said that he was her knight, and would be all his life.

Thereupon the lady left, and went to the army. The king and queen welcomed her as warmly as they could, in their distress, and took her to see Sir Gawain, whom she was very eager to see. However, she was delighted to find him looking better than she had been told. Thus they passed that night. And King Arthur awaited the next day with great trepidation, for he had lost many knights. And in the evening the Lady of Malohaut's cousin, who had remained in her house, made ready the knight's arms and put him to bed in her lady's bed and was at his bedside until he went to sleep, for the lady had asked her to do him every honour she could, provided her honour was safe.

In the morning the knight rose very early, and the maiden helped him to arm. When he had commended her to God, he left and travelled through the [309] morning until he reached the battleground at sunrise. He stopped by the river and leant on his lance in the same place where he had been at the first encounter, and began to look at the brattice where Sir Gawain was lying ill, because of the ladies and damsels who were going there. The queen had already gone there, and the Lady of Malohaut and many other ladies and damsels. King Arthur's troops had already armed, and those who desired to joust were crossing the water in great numbers, and Galehot's were doing the same. Before long the meadow was covered in many places with jousts and mêlées. And all the while the knight was thinking, leaning on his lance, and looking very tenderly towards the brattice where the ladies were. The Lady of Malohaut saw him, and recognized him at once, and began to speak, in the presence of the others:

'Lord,' she said, 'that knight I see by the river there—who can he be? He is neither harming our side, nor helping them.'

Then everyone began to look at him; and Sir Gawain said, could he see him. The Lady of Malohaut said that she would certainly arrange for him to see him clearly. Then she herself made a seat by a window, and they laid him on it, so that he could see clearly down along the river. He looked, and saw the knight with the black shield, who was thinking, leaning on his lance. And he said to the queen:

'My lady, my lady, now, do you remember that I was wounded once before and lying here, and a knight was thinking in the same way by the river there, either this one or another, but he bore red arms? And he was the one who was victorious at the encounter.'

'Dear nephew,' she said, 'that is quite possible, but why do you say it?'

'My lady,' he said, 'I say it because I should like it to be him, for I was never so glad to see the deeds of prowess of any knight as I was his. And we shall see plenty today.'

They talked of him for a long time; and he never moved from his position. King Arthur had already ordered his troops, and had formed four battalions, in each of which there were fifteen thousand men, and in the fifth there were more than twenty thousand. King Yder had command of the first battalion, who was a man of great valour and fought very well that day. The second was led by Hervi of Rivel: he was one of the knights in the world who knew most about war. The third was commanded by Aguissant, the King of Scotland, who was King Arthur's cousin; and he would have had the [310] first, if he had known as much about fighting as some. The fourth was commanded by King Yon. The fifth, in which there were more than twenty thousand men, was commanded by Sir Yvain, the son of King Urien, and was to engage last of all.

Thus King Arthur had formed five battalions. Galehot, for his part, formed the same number; and in each of four there were twenty thousand men, and in the fifth there were forty thousand.* Malaguin, his seneschal, had the first battalion: that is, the King of a Hundred Knights, who was very valorous and bold. The First Conquered King had the second. The King of Valdoan had the third; and King

Clamadeus of the Remote Isles led the fourth. King Bade-magu of Gorre, who was a man of great worth, both in knightly deeds and in council, led the fifth, in which were the forty thousand. Galehot did not bear a knight's arms that day, but wore a short habergeon* like that of a man-at-arms, an iron cap on his head like that of a man-at-arms, with his sword belted on and a short, thick staff in his hand; and he sat on a horse fitting for a man of valour, for he was the man who had the most excellent horses in the world.

Thus they were assembled on the two sides to engage in battle. And the Black Knight was still by the river, pensive. The Lady of Malohaut called the queen and said:

'My lady, do something good. Send to ask that knight to do deeds of arms for your sake and to show you which side he is on, ours or theirs. Then we shall find out what he means to do, and whether there is any merit in him.'

'Dear lady,' the queen said, 'I have enough to do, thinking about other things, for my lord the king is today in danger of losing all his land and all his honour; and my nephew is lying here reduced to the state that you see, and I see such difficulties that at the moment I have no desire or use for the great challenges and fun that I used to engage in, for I have plenty to think about. But you send word to him, and these other ladies, if they wish.'

'Indeed, my lady,' she said, 'I am quite ready to do so, if there is someone who will also send word to him. If you wish, send word to him, and I shall gladly be a part of it.'

'Madam,' said the queen, 'I will not concern myself with it. You and the others send word to him, if you wish.'

Then the Lady of Malohaut said that, if the other ladies for their part would send word to him, she would send it for her part. They all agreed to it; [311] and the queen lent them one of her damsels to carry the message. The Lady of Malohaut worded the message, and Sir Gawain added two of his own lances and a squire to carry them. Then the lady said to the maiden:

'Damsel, go to that knight who is thinking over there, and tell him that all the ladies and damsels of the king's household greet him, with the exception of my lady herself. And they send word to ask him, if he hopes ever to have benefit or honour in any place where one of them has power or authority, to do such deeds of arms today for their sake that they should be grateful to him. And present him with these two lances which Sir Gawain sends him.'

Thereupon the maiden mounted her palfrey, and the squire after her, who was carrying the lances, and they went to the knight; and the maiden stated her message. When he heard her mention Sir Gawain, he asked where he was; and the maiden said:

'He is in that brattice, and so are many ladies and damsels.'

He took leave of the maiden and told the squire to follow him. He looked at his feet and settled them firmly in the stirrups, and it seemed to Sir Gawain, who was watching him, that he grew a good six inches. Then he looked towards the brattice, and then turned away down across the meadows, plying his spurs. When Sir Gawain saw him going, he said to the queen:

'My lady, my lady, there is a knight, or there is none in all the world, for I never saw any knight bear arms so well or elegantly as that one bears them.'

Then they all ran, both ladies and damsels, to the windows and battlements to see him. And he went along as hard and as fast as his horse could go. And he saw to right and left very fine jousts and very fine mêlées; for a great part of the lively knights bachelor in the king's army had already passed the lists to do deeds of arms; and from Galehot's army, too, there came here ten, there thirty, here forty,* there a hundred, more in one place, less in another. He avoided all the mêlées and spurred towards a great company which he saw coming, in which there were perhaps a hundred knights. He plunged in among them and struck a knight, so that he knocked him to the ground all in a heap, both him and his horse. And when his lance was broken, he struck out with the broken shaft, as long as it lasted, down to his hand;* and then he rushed out to the squire who was carrying his two lances, and took one of them and dashed back among them.[1] And he jousted so skilfully that all the others stopped [312] jousting and fighting to watch him. He did such deeds of arms with the three lances, while they lasted, that Sir Gawain asserted that no man, to his knowledge, could have done as much. And as soon as he had broken all three, he went back by the river, in the same place where he had been before, and turned his face and looked very tenderly towards the brattice. And Sir Gawain spoke of him and said:

'My lady, do you see that knight? Let me tell you that he is the most valorous in the world. But you made a great mistake regarding the message which was sent to him, when you would not be named in it. And it may be that he considered that arrogant, for he can see that this affair concerns you more than the others. Perhaps he thinks that you thought little of him when you would not deign to send to ask him to do deeds of arms for your sake.'

'By my faith,' said the Lady of Malohaut, 'he is clearly showing the rest of us that he will do no more for us. Now, let anyone who has some word to send him, send it, for our challenge is ended for today.'

'My lady,' Sir Gawain said to the queen, 'do you think that what I have said to you is reasonable?'

'Dear nephew,' she said, 'what do you wish me to do?'

'My lady,' he said, 'I shall tell you. Anyone who has a man of valour has a great deal, for many things have been accomplished through one man of valour which otherwise

[1] i.e. the enemy.

would have come to nothing. I shall tell you what to do. Send greetings to this man, saying that you implore his help for the kingdom of Logres and for the honour of my lord the king, who today will go to ruin unless God and he[1] do something about it. And, if he ever hopes to have honour or joy in any place where you have authority, then let him do such deeds of arms today that you should be grateful to him, and let it show from his actions that he has devoted his prowess to the honour of my lord the king and to your own. And rest assured, if he wishes to prevent it, the king, my lord, will not have the worst of it today for all Galehot's power. And I shall send him ten lances, with sharp heads and short, thick, strong shafts, with which you will see many fine jousts done today. I shall also send three most excellent horses which I have, and they will all have trappings bearing my arms. And let me tell you that if he will do his best, he will use all three today.'

That is what Sir Gawain proposed; and the queen told him to say whatever he wished to the knight in her name, for she wholly agreed to it. The Lady of Malohaut was so happy about that that she was nearly flying, for it now seemed to her that she was achieving everything that she had always sought.* Then [313] Sir Gawain called the maiden who had taken the message, and sent her to the knight who was thinking, telling her exactly what he had said to the queen. Then he called four of his servants and ordered three of them to take the knight three of his horses, in full trappings, and the fourth to carry a bundle of ten lances, the strongest he had. Thereupon the maiden went away and told the knight what Sir Gawain and the queen were sending to ask him, and gave him the gifts. And the knight asked her:

'Damsel, where is she, my lady?'

'Sir,' she said, 'up there in that brattice, and ladies and damsels besides; and Sir Gawain is lying there ill. Rest assured, you will be well watched.'

---

[1] i.e. the pensive knight.

And the knight said:

'Damsel, tell my lady that it shall be as she pleases; and give Sir Gawain my thanks for the gift.'

Then he took the strongest of the lances that the squire was carrying, and told them[1] all to follow him. The damsel took her leave and went back, and told the queen and Sir Gawain what the knight had said to them. And the Lady of Malohaut began to smile very broadly. The knight charged down across the meadows, where many good knights were already engaged in battle on the two sides. King Yder's battalion had already passed the lists and was engaging the battalion of the King of a Hundred Knights; and both sides were fighting very well. He avoided all the mêlées and appeared not to see any of them and went straight past to the battalion led by the First Conquered King, in which there were at least twenty thousand knights. And he directed his horse's head towards them, and his heart and body with all his will, and rushed in among them as fast as his horse could go. He rushed in where he thought his blow would do most good, so that nothing he hit, knight or horse, stood before his lance, but he sent them flying all in a heap; and his lance shattered. This encounter was seen by several of King Arthur's knights: Sir Kay the seneschal and Sagremor the Impetuous and Girflet, the son of Do, and Yvain the Bastard and Sir Brandeliz and Keheriet, Sir Gawain's brother. These six were coming at full speed to do deeds of arms, for renown at arms* and high spirits inclined them to win honour, and even the fastest of them did not [314] think he would arrive in time.* Behind these six came at least a hundred, their helms laced on, gripping their lances, all ready to fight well. And Kay the seneschal, who had seen the knight engage in battle, called the five who were with him, and said:

'Gentlemen, you have just seen the finest encounter ever

[1] i.e. the squires.

performed by a single knight; and we are all here to win honour and renown, and we shall never in all our lives find such a good opportunity to exercise knightly valour, if we have any. And here and now I pledge myself to follow him, for he can only be a man of great valour. Whoever would now have honour should follow me, for I shall not leave him[1] today unless I leave him dead or crippled.'

With that he spurred forward, and all the others after him. The Black Knight, having broken his lance, had rushed out and taken another lance from his squires, and went swiftly back to the fray. The others went after him, and supported him, dashing after him into the battle. And he began to knock down knights and horses and to carry shields away from necks and to wrench helms from heads. He did such deeds of arms that all those who were with him were astonished; and those who were against him were taken aback. He did so much that all the lances that Sir Gawain had sent him were broken, and one of the horses dead, for it fell under him (and the squire brought him another and did up its girths very tight);* and as he was on foot in the press, the hundred companions came spurring up. One of his squires brought him a charger, and he leapt into the saddle and went among the others into the battle, sword in hand, as if he had not been in it all day.* When the companions saw under him the horse whose trappings bore Sir Gawain's arms, they were quite astonished and knew that he must be a man of great valour, and they followed him, all ready to do deeds of prowess or to die with honour in his company.

Then they began to do great deeds of arms. And at that time a knight would not take hold of another's bridle, and two or three would not strike one; but whoever could do the greatest deeds of arms, did so, and he could strike one knight, or two or three, or as many as he could. Thus the Black

---

[1] i.e. the knight.

Knight and his party did deeds of arms; but they were in dire straights, and they could not have stood it for long, but for a piece of good fortune which occurred, when the battalion of the King of a Hundred Knights was put to flight, for it could no longer withstand King Yder. So they[1] were retiring rapidly, and they[2] drove them[1] in on the First Conquered King. The King of a Hundred [315] Knights was very ashamed and distressed about it, for he for his part was a very good and confident knight. There the routed men rallied, finding great reinforcements. They far outnumbered the others, for they were more than forty thousand in two battalions, and on the side of Sir Gawain's companions there were only fifteen thousand, and yet they had broken them up when they engaged.

Then the Black Knight's great prowess showed, for he did not hit any knight without knocking him to the ground, willy-nilly. He knocked down knights and horses with lance-blows and with sword strokes, and by pulling on helms and the rims of shields, and by striking them violently with himself and his horse. He was certainly doing remarkable deeds, and as he came, with drawn sword, it often happened that he found nowhere to strike in his path, for they all fled from him, because where he struck squarely, iron and wood* could not withstand it, and no human being could endure his blows. And he was fighting so well that he was sustaining all those on his side by himself and resisting all those who were against him. And those on his side were fighting very well, partly because of his exploits and partly because of their great prowess. Thus they were all looking to him, and wondering who he was because of the great deeds of prowess he was doing.

The knight fought very well, and the news of it ran up and down so that throughout King Arthur's army they were

---

[1] i.e. the King of a Hundred Knights's men.   [2] i.e. Yder's men.

talking of nothing else, and the same in that of Galehot. And all those who had seen his deeds of prowess said that the earlier knight with red arms was as nothing compared to this one. He acquitted himself like this for a long while, and all the time the six companions that the story has named remained near him. Then his horse was killed under him, and he immediately leapt on to another which was brought to him. And then his party, which had stood firm and helped him all day, began to suffer badly. Then the seneschal called the squire who had brought the horse, and said:

'Friend, go quickly to Hervi of Rivel, there where you see that banner with equal bands of red and gold; and tell him that I send him word that now both I and all the world should complain about him, for he is allowing the best knight who ever carried a shield around his neck to die. And he should know for a fact that if that man dies here, the flower of the king's companions will die with him. And he, who should have helped him, will be considered a coward all the days of his life.'

Thereupon the squire left and went to Hervi, and stated his message to him [316] in full. When Hervi heard it, he was very taken aback and very ashamed, and said:

'So help me God, I have never acted disloyally, and I shall not start now, for I am too old.'*

Then he told his men to ride in close order.

'And you go ahead,' he said to the squire, 'and tell the seneschal from me that, if he can hold on until I reach the battleground, he will not consider me disloyal.'

The squire went back to Kay and told him what Hervi had said. Kay laughed, in difficulties as he was, and then asked the squire who the Black Knight was. And he said that he had no idea.

'Why, then,' he said, 'did Sir Gawain send him his horses?'

The squire replied that he knew no more than he had told him.

Then Kay put back on his helm, which he had taken off, and went furiously back to the fray.

Thereupon up came Hervi of Rivel with his force;* and as they engaged, they shouted so loudly that all over the meadows nothing was heard but 'Hervi'.* And Sir Gawain laughed at that, ill as he was. They dashed into the fray, their lances held firmly under their arms. Then the fighting was very fierce, and there were many horses riderless or killed, and many knights knocked down or killed or wounded, and you would have seen horses running away riderless in all directions, and others on top of knights' bodies, and much fine armour lying on the ground, for there was no one to pick it up. There Hervi of Rivel began to do deeds of arms in front of Kay the seneschal because of the message he had sent him, and that day he did more than was good for him at his age, for he was well past eighty.

King Arthur's troops fought very well, but the Black Knight was fighting exceptionally well. Once Hervi engaged, Gale-hot's troops only stood their ground for a short time, and yet they had a quarter more troops. However, as soon as the King of Valdoan saw that their troops had the worse of it, he reinforced them with his force, and they came at full gallop as fast as they could go. Then King Arthur's troops were in dire straits, as for one of them there were two of Galehot's men. And when they had been battered for a little while, then King Aguissant reinforced them. Then they were more or less equally matched, and more or less withstood each other. By now, the sun was very high. Then King Clamadeus engaged, and King Yon against him.

[317] Thus four battalions were engaged from one side, and four from the other; and there were at least twenty thousand more on Galehot's side than on that of the Black Knight. However, his side were holding out very well, and Galehot's had suffered heavy losses there, for King Arthur's troops had done great deeds of arms at the outset. And by

about midday, Galehot's troops were badly routed. They were at least twenty thousand more than the others, and yet they had the worst of it all the same. However, but for the Black Knight's exploits, those on his side would never have stood firm. He, though, disconcerted all his enemies by his exploits, so that it seemed to them that no amount of troops would help them. They were so daunted by the remarkable deeds he was doing that most of them turned tail and made straight for the tents, in disarray. When Galehot saw them, he wondered what could be happening, for he was well aware that his men had greater numbers; and he went to meet the fugitives and asked what was happening.

'What, sire?' said a knight who had no desire to tourney; 'whoever wishes to see remarkable things should go where we are coming from, and he will see the most remarkable which have ever been seen, or ever will be.'

'What?' said Galehot; 'which remarkable things are those, then?'

'Which, sire?' he said. 'Down there is a knight who is defeating everyone by himself; and no man can withstand him, and no one can endure his blows. And the earlier knight with red arms was not worth a farthing compared to this one. Nothing could weary him, for he has not stopped since this morning, and yet he is just as fierce and fresh as if he had not borne arms at all.'

'In God's name,' said Galehot, 'I shall soon see about that.'

Then he went to his great company, and separated ten thousand men from it, leaving thirty thousand. And he said to King Bademagu:

'Take care, if your honour and I are dear to you, that my company does not move, unless I myself come to fetch you in person. And you,' he said to the ten thousand, 'stay quietly on one side, far away from the others, until I come to you.'

With that he went into the battle, armed as he was,* and made all the fugitives return with him. By now his men were reduced to such a state that they were all being put to rout. However, when King Clamadeus saw them coming, he took heart once more, and shouted his battle-cry very loudly and rallied his troops there, and charged at his enemies very vigorously. And Galehot ordered those he was bringing to rush among them[1] at full gallop, as fast as they could spur. 'And do not [318] worry,' he said, 'for you will be well reinforced when you need it.' They charged forward at the worthy man's command, and rushed among them. Then all their men rallied, and Galehot's battle-cry was loudly shouted, for everyone thought that a large force had reinforced them; and they would have pushed the king's troops back very forcefully, but for the Black Knight. He, however, bore the brunt of it by himself, so that he rallied to wherever there was need or difficulty, ready to defend and to attack. There his horse was killed under him, and he was on foot; and that was the last of his horses. The press was thick around him, for they could not immediately reach him to remount him. While he was on foot, he fought so that no one could see him being cowardly or lax: rather, he was at the service of everyone, like a standard.* He struck out to right and left without pause; his sword was never seen idle; he hacked helms apart, he cut shields to pieces, he split hauberks on knights' shoulders or arms, he did remarkable deeds for all to see.

When Galehot saw these remarkable deeds that he was doing, he wondered how any knight could do it, and said to himself that he would not wish to have conquered all the lands under the heavens, if it meant that such a valorous man died through his fault. Then he set spurs to his horse and went into the press, staff in hand, to part the mêlée around the man who was on foot; and, with great difficulty, he made his troops draw back. Then he called the knight and said:

[1] i.e. the enemy.

'Now, sir knight, do not worry.'

He replied very boldly that he did not.

'Do you know', said Galehot, 'what I am going to tell you? I wish to explain to you a part of my customs. And let me tell you that I forbid any of my men to lay a hand on you while you are on foot, and no one is to pursue you beyond here. If you were idle, though, and stopped doing deeds of arms through cowardice, I should not guarantee you against being captured. But as long as you bear arms, you will not find anyone who will capture you. And if your horse is dead, do not be dismayed, for I shall give you as many horses as you can wear out today, and I shall be your squire all day. And if I cannot weary you, then no man alive can weary you.'*

Then he dismounted from his horse, and gave it to the knight, who mounted it without delay and went back to the fray, as sprightly as if [319] he had not struck a blow all day. Galehot mounted another horse which was brought to him and went up to his company, and called the ten thousand to him and told them to go and engage first.

'And you,' he said to King Bademagu, 'come afterwards; and do not engage as soon as these have engaged, but when the last of the enemy have come, then you engage. They will think that all my troops have come, when these ten thousand have engaged.* And I myself shall come to fetch you.'

With that he left with the ten thousand, and had them ride all spread out in open order, far apart, to make it seem as if there were more men. When they were near the battle, he had his horns and trumpets sounded, of which there were so many that they made the whole countryside tremble. When the knight heard them coming, it seemed to him that there was a large force there, and he drew near to his men and called them round him. And he said:

'Gentlemen, you are all friends of the king. I do not know your names, but you are considered men of great valour. Now we shall see who will be worthy of praise.'

Thereupon the others arrived, all in open order; and Sir
Yvain, who saw them coming, ordered his companies to go
slowly, and told his troops that they should all be confident
that 'we shall not lose anything today because of any force
that I have yet seen.' He said that, because he thought that
those were all of Galehot's troops. Sir Gawain was certain, as
soon as he saw them from where he was lying, that those
were not all of them.

When the ten thousand engaged, there was a great clamour. The others received them as vigorously as they could,
but Galehot's men came so fiercely that they knocked down
many of them when they arrived. When Sir Yvain came,
though, it comforted them greatly; and they had great need
of it, for by now they were giving ground everywhere; and
they rallied when Sir Yvain engaged. Galehot went back to
his company again and ordered them to ride so fiercely that
no troops ever went as fiercely before.

'And go and strike them at such a speed', he said, 'that not
one of them is left on horseback, for you are all fresh and
strong and rested, and you have not borne arms since you
came here. Now we shall see how hard you fight.'

[320] Thereupon the company rode down the slope. By
now their troops had much the worse of it, for Sir Yvain's
companions were fighting very fiercely, and he himself was
fighting better than all of them. However, no valour, his or
anyone else's, could compare with the exploits of the Black
Knight; but then he fought better than any man. When
Galehot's company arrived, though, the situation changed
dramatically, for they had a great weight of numbers. When
they arrived, the good knight was knocked to the ground,
along with the six companions who had been so close to him
all day. Then Galehot came galloping up and remounted him
on the horse on which he himself was sitting, for his own was
no good to him. As soon as he was remounted, he went back
to the fray, as sprightly as before, and began to do greater

deeds of arms, according to Galehot's own testimony, than any man could have done, so that everyone was dumbfounded. His exploits lasted like this until evening, and there was never a moment when he and his troops did not have the best of the battle.

When nightfall came, they began to disperse on the two sides; and he left as quietly as he could and went away up across the meadows between the hill and the river. Galehot, who was paying very close attention to him, saw him going, and spurred after him and followed him at a distance, by the path over the hill, until he came down and caught up with him. He rode up beside him as quietly as he could, and said:

'God bless you, sir.'

The other looked at him askance and returned his greeting with great reluctance.

'Sir,' said Galehot, 'who are you?'

'Sir, I am a knight, as you can see.'

'Indeed,' said Galehot, 'you are a knight, the best there is. And you are the man I should most like to honour in the world, and I have come to request you, as a favour, to come and lodge with me tonight.'

And the knight said to him, as though he had never seen him before:

'Who are you, sir, who ask me to lodge?'

'Sir,' he said, 'I am Galehot, the son of the Giantess, lord of all those troops there, against whom you have today defended King Arthur and his troops, whom I had completely in my power; and I should have conquered him, but for you.'

'What?' said the knight; 'you are an enemy of my lord [321] King Arthur and yet you ask me to lodge? You will never give me lodging, please God, in these circumstances.'

'Ah! sir,' said Galehot, 'I should do more for you than you suppose, and I have already started. And I ask you again, for the Lord's sake, to lodge with me tonight, on condition that I shall do absolutely whatever you dare request of me.'

Thereupon the knight stopped, and looked very hard at Galehot, and said:

'Truly, sir, you are very good at making promises. I do not know about how you keep them.'

And Galehot replied:

'Sir, let me tell you truly that of all the rich men in the world, I am the one who promises the least. And I tell you again that, if you come and lodge with me, I shall give you what you ask of me. And I shall give you whatever assurances you yourself propose.'

'Sir,' the knight said, 'you are considered a very worthy man, and it would not be honourable for you to promise something regarding which you would not in the end wish to keep your word.'

'Sir,' said Galehot, 'have no fear of that, for I should not lie to gain the whole kingdom of Logres. I shall swear to you as a faithful knight—for I am not yet a king—that I shall give you what you ask of me, in order to have your company for tonight. And if I can have it for longer, I shall do so. And if my oath is not enough for you, I shall give you whatever assurances you want.'

'Sir,' the knight said, 'it seems to me that you are very keen to have my company, if your intentions match your words. I shall lodge with you tonight, but you must swear that you will give me what I ask of you. And you must give me further guarantees, if I request it.'

Thus the two of them made their agreement, and Galehot swore that he would keep the agreement. Then they both went to the tents. The king's troops had already repaired to their tents; and Sir Gawain had clearly seen the knight going away, and was very anxious about it. If he had been well, he would have made a great effort to bring him back. And he had sent word to ask the king to come to him, for he wished to tell him to go after the knight and retain him in his service. As he was waiting for the king, he looked up across the meadows and saw Galehot coming, his right arm around the knight's shoulders, and he was bringing him between the hill and the river, so that King Arthur's troops should see him. When [322] Sir Gawain saw them, he was certain that Galehot had retained him, and he said to the queen, who was there:

'Ah! my lady, my lady, now you can say that our men are defeated and dead. See what Galehot has gained through his good sense.'

The queen looked, and saw the knight that Galehot was bringing, and she was so distracted that she could not utter a single word. Sir Gawain, too, grieved so much that he fainted three times in less time than it takes to go a small stone's throw.* The king was coming in, and he heard the clamour, with everyone saying: 'He is dead. He is dead.' He went to him and embraced him, weeping, and began to call him very tenderly, and Sir Gawain came to. When he saw the king, he began to reproach him very severely, and said:

'Sire, the time has now come that the clerks told you about. Look what a treasure you have lost. Your land will be taken from you by the man who all day today has protected it for you in battle. And if you were a man of worth, you would have retained him in your service, as the most worthy man living has done, who is taking him away in front of you, and yet he[1] never did him[2] anything but harm. And you have neglected him, who gave you back honour and land. Thus men of worth show themselves, wherever they are.'

Then the king saw the knight Galehot was leading away, and he was so grieved that he nearly fell down, and he could not help weeping. However, he looked as cheerful as he could, to comfort his nephew; and as soon as he could, he went to his tent and grieved excessively. All the men of valour were doing the same, each one individually. There was great

---

[1] i.e. the knight.   [2] i.e. Galehot.

grief in the king's army over the good knight that Galehot was taking away. They[1] continued to ride; and when they drew near the camp, the knight called Galehot and said:

'Sir, I am coming away with you. However, I ask you, before I enter your camp, to let me to speak with the two men in whom you have most faith in the world.'

And he agreed to that. Then Galehot left him and said to two of his men:

'Follow me, and you will see this very night the richest man in the world.'

And they said:

'What, sire? Are you not the richest man there is in the world, then?'

'No,' he said, 'but I shall be, before I sleep.'

These two were the King of a Hundred Knights and the First Conquered King: they were the two men in whom he had most faith. When they saw [323] the knight, they made much of him, for they recognized him at once by his arms. He asked them who they were, and they told him their names, as you have heard them. And he said:

'Gentlemen, your lord does you great honour, for he says that you are the two men he most trusts. He and I have an agreement that I wish you to hear, for he has sworn that in return for my lodging with him tonight he will give me what I ask of him. Ask him.'

And he said that it was true.

'Sir,' the knight said, 'I also wish to have the guarantee of these two men of worth.'

And Galehot agreed to that.

'Tell me how,' he said.

'They must swear to me that, if you fail to keep your promise to me, they will leave you and come away with me, wherever I wish; and they will be with me and against you,

---

[1] i.e. the knight and Galehot.

and will owe me what they owe you at the moment, and will owe you what they now owe me, as their mortal enemy.'

Galehot ordered them to swear, and the King of a Hundred Knights, who was his seneschal and his first cousin, said to him:

'Sire, you are such a worthy man and so wise that you certainly ought to know what you are ordering us to do, for it is a very great thing.'

'Do not concern yourself,' Galehot said, 'for it pleases me, and I know very well what I am doing. But swear to him what I have given him my word on.'

He told them what that was, and they both swore it to him. Then Galehot called the First Conquered King to one side and said:

'Go on ahead, and tell all my barons on my behalf to come to meet me right now, and to come with as much magnificence as they can. And tell them what I have gained this evening. And be sure that my tent contains all the comforts that can be found in the whole camp.'

Then the king went away, plying his spurs, and carried out his lord's orders; and Galehot kept the knight talking a long while, with his seneschal, until his orders could be carried out. Before long 200 knights came to meet them, who were all Galehot's men, and twenty-eight of them were kings, and the others were dukes and counts. Then the knight was honoured and made much of, so that no single unknown man was ever before welcomed as warmly as they welcomed him then. Everyone, great and small, said: 'Welcome to the flower of the knights of the world', so that the knight was very embarrassed. Thus they came to [324] Galehot's tent, and the comforts and amusements which were in there could not be told.

Such was the joy with which the knight was received and honoured. When he was disarmed, Galehot had a very rich and beautiful robe brought for him, and he put it on, very reluctantly. When it was time, they ate. Afterwards Galehot had four beds made up in his chamber, one very big and broad and high, and a second less big, and the other two, which were the same size, much smaller than the others. When the bed was ready, with all the finery which could be put in a bed (which was for the knight), and when it was time to go to bed, Galehot said to him:

'Sir, you will sleep in that bed up there.'

'Sir,' said the knight, 'who will sleep in those others, then?'

'Sir,' he said, 'my servants will sleep in them, and will keep you company. And I shall sleep in a chamber beyond, so that you will have more peace and be more at ease here.'

'Ah! sir, for the Lord's sake, do not make me sleep higher than the other knights, for you should not make me so unworthy.'*

'Do not worry,' Galehot said; 'you will never be considered unworthy because of anything you do for me.'

With that Galehot left; and the knight began to think about the great honour which Galehot had done him, and in his heart he esteemed him as highly as he possibly could. When he was in bed, he went to sleep very quickly, for he was extremely weary. When Galehot knew he was asleep, he lay down in the bed* next to his as quietly as he could, and two of his knights lay down in the other two; and there was no one else in there. That night the knight slept very soundly, and all night long he moaned in his sleep. Galehot heard him clearly, for he barely slept, but thought all night long about retaining the knight in his service. In the morning the knight rose and heard mass; and Galehot had already risen quietly, for he did not want the knight to notice. When they had heard mass, the knight asked for his arms; and Galehot asked him what for. He said that he was leaving; and Galehot said:

'Dear friend, do not go yet. And do not think that I wish to cheat you, for there is nothing you could ask for that you will not have in return for staying. And let me tell you that you could have the companionship of a richer man than I, but you will never have that of a man who loves you as much. And since I should do more than all the world to have your companionship, it is right that I should have it more than all the others.'

[325]'Sir,' the knight said, 'I shall stay, for I could not have better companionship than yours. And I shall tell you here and now the gift in return for which I shall stay. And if I do not get it, there is no point in talking about my staying.'

'Sir,' said Galehot, 'tell me without hesitation, and you will have it, if it is a gift which in my power.'

The knight called the two who were his surety, and said, in front of them:

'Sir, I ask that, as soon as you have the upper hand against King Arthur, so that his side has no hope of recovery, as soon as I call on you to do so, you go to him and ask his forgiveness and put yourself utterly at his mercy.'

When Galehot heard that, he was quite taken aback, and became thoughtful; and the two kings said to him:

'Sire, what are you thinking about? It is no use thinking at this point. You have gone so far that there is no question of turning back.'

'What?' he said; 'do you think I wish to change my mind? If the whole world was mine, I should dare give it all to him. I was thinking, though, of the noble thing he said, for no man every said anything so noble. Sir,' he said, 'may God never be my witness, if you do not have the gift, for I could not have shame from anything I did for you. But I beg you not to take your companionship from me to give it to someone else, since I should do more than anyone to have it.'

The knight gave him his word. That is how it stood. And the meal was all ready to eat. They were overjoyed in the army at the knight's staying; and those who did not know about the agreement, in King Arthur's army, grieved over it greatly.

Thus that day passed; and the next day Galehot and his companion rose, and went to hear mass. And Galehot said to him:

'Sir, today is a day of battle.* Do you wish to bear arms?'

He replied that he did.

'Then I beg you,' said Galehot, 'to wear my armour, as a beginning to our companionship.'

And he replied:

'Willingly, but you must not wear the armour of a man-at-arms.'

'No, if you wish it,' said Galehot.

Then they had the armour brought, and they armed the knight in all of it except the hauberk and the leggings, which were too big and [326] wide.* Then Galehot's troops armed, all together, and King Arthur's likewise. There were also some who passed the lists. The king had forbidden that any of them cross the water, for he was afraid of being defeated, and all because he had lost the good knight. However, no order could keep the lively knights bachelor from crossing the water, and in a short time there were good jousts and fierce fighting in many places. So in this way they began to engage on the two sides, for when Galehot's troops saw that their side were having the worst of it, they reinforced them; and King Arthur's troops did the same. So in this way all the troops now engaged in battle in front of the lists, and King Arthur's troops began to do great deeds of arms. The king was by his standard with four renowned knights, whom he had ordered to take the queen to safety, if they saw that things were turning to defeat.

When all King Arthur's troops had engaged, then the good knight went to engage, armed in Galehot's armour, and everyone who saw him thought that he was Galehot. They all said: 'There is Galehot, there is Galehot.' Sir Gawain, though, recognized him, and said:

'That is not Galehot, but the good knight who wore the

black armour the day before yesterday. I definitely recognize him.'

So said Sir Gawain. As soon as he engaged, then the king's troops only stood firm for a short time, for they were greatly disheartened because the good knight was against them; and in a short time they were driven as far as the lists, for there were great numbers of troops on Galehot's side. As they passed the lists, there were some who stood firm for a long while, and they endured a great deal. However, their endurance was to no avail, for they were in desperate straits. King Arthur's troops suffered greatly in sustaining the fight as they passed the lists. And the story says that the good knight had just as much trouble in keeping back Galehot's troops, to stop them going across, as he had had in pursuing King Arthur's troops, and even so the good knight had not pressed them too hard. When he had driven them across, he remained in the middle of the passage* to hold back the others, who were all mad keen to go across. Then he looked around him, and began to shout loudly for Galehot. And he came spurring up and said:

'Dear friend, what do you want?'

'What?' he said. 'I want something extraordinary.'

'Tell me,' said Galehot, 'without hesitation.'

'Sir,' said the knight, 'is it enough?'*

'Yes, indeed,' said Galehot. 'Tell me what you want.'

[327]'Sir,' the knight said, 'keep your promise to me, for now is the time.'

'In God's name,' said Galehot, 'it does not distress me at all, since you wish it.'

Then he spurred straight to the standard where the king was, who was nearly bursting with grief at seeing his troops defeated. The queen was already mounted, and the four knights were taking her away at a gallop, for they now had no hope of recovery, and they wished to take Sir Gawain away in a litter. He, though, said that he would rather die in that place than see all joy dead and all honour brought low in that way. And he was fainting so often that everyone who saw him assumed that he would die right then. When the good knight saw Galehot going away to make such a great sacrifice for him, he thought and said that no one ever had such a good friend and true companion. He was so moved that he sighed deeply and wept inside his helm, and said under his breath:

'Dear Lord God, who could deserve this?'

Galehot rode up to the standard and asked for King Arthur; and he came forward quite dismayed, as he expected to lose utterly all earthly honour. When Galehot saw him, he said:

'Come forward, and do not worry, for I wish to talk to you.'

Then everyone began to say: 'It is Galehot.' The king wondered what it could mean, and went forward. And as soon as Galehot saw him, he dismounted from his horse, and knelt down and put his hands together,* and said:

'My lord, I come to make amends to you for the wrong I have done you, and I regret it and put myself utterly in your power.'

When the king heard that, he was overjoyed, and raised his hands to the heavens, and was so delighted that he could not believe it; none the less, he looked cheerful and showed Galehot great respect. Galehot stood up again, for he was still on his knees; and then they kissed and made much of one another. And Galehot said:

'My lord, do as you please with me and have no fear, for I shall place myself in your power, wherever you wish. And if you agree, I shall go and withdraw my troops and then come back to you.'

'Go, then,' said the king, 'and come back soon, for I very much wish to talk to you.'

Thereupon Galehot went to his troops, and made them go back. And King Arthur at once sent after the queen, who was going away grieving bitterly, [328] and the messengers chased after her until they caught up with her and told her the great joy which had befallen her. She could not believe it until she heard the reliable word* that the king sent her, and then she returned very joyfully. The news of the peace spread until Sir Gawain heard it, for the king himself told him personally. He rejoiced more than anyone, and said:

'Sire, how did this come about?'

'Truly,' the king said, 'I do not know. It was Our Lord's pleasure.'

The king's joy was very great, and everyone wondered how this could happen. And Galehot had sent his troops away, and said to his companion:

'Dear companion, what do you wish me to do? I have followed your orders, and the king has told me to return to him. However, I shall come with you to our tents and keep you company for a while, for I have not done so very much, and I can easily make it up to the king.'

'Ah! sir,' the knight said, 'you must go to the king and give him all the companionship you can, for you have done me great service, and more than I could deserve. But I ask you this, for the Lord's sake: let no living creature know where I am.'

Galehot gave him his word. Thus they went, talking together, to their tents. It was proclaimed throughout the army that peace was made, and how, and most were upset, for they would have preferred war. Thereupon the two companions dismounted. When they were disarmed, Galehot put on his best robes to go to court, with his companion's permission, and he had it proclaimed throughout his army that whoever wished to leave should do so, apart from those who were in his household. After that he called the two kings in whom he had so much faith, and handed his companion over to them and asked them to treat him as they would himself. With that he went to court. The king was already disarmed, and went to meet him with the queen, who had arrived, and the Lady of Malohaut and many ladies and damsels. Afterwards they went to the brattice where Sir Gawain was ill. When he heard that Galehot was coming, he made a great effort to look cheerful, because he had never seen him close to. When they met, the two of them greeted each other; and Sir Gawain said:

'Sir, you are welcome, as the man in the world whose acquaintance I most wished to make in the way I now see.* [329] You should be very proud, for you are the man in the world who is most justly praised, and who is most loved by his people. And I believe that no one is as good as you at recognising a man of valour; and that has been apparent.'

That is what Sir Gawain said. Galehot asked him how he was; and he said:

'Sir, I have been very near to death, but my great joy at the friendship between you and my lord the king has completely cured me, for no one ought to have health or joy, when there is such enmity between the two most worthy men in the world.'

The king and the queen and Sir Gawain made much of Galehot, and they talked a good deal that day, of many things and of becoming acquainted. They did not talk about the Black Knight at all, though, because it would have been too soon, but spent the day in making much of one another until evening came. Then Galehot asked leave to go and see his followers; and the king gave it to him. 'But you must come back soon,' he said. He agreed, and went back to his companion and asked him how he had been since he left. And he replied: very well. And Galehot said:

'Sir, what shall I do? The king has entreated me to return to him, and it would distress me to leave you at this point.'

'Ah! sir,' the knight said, 'by the Lord's mercy, you must do as my lord the king wishes, for you should know that you never made the acquaintance of a worthier man than he. But

I wish to ask you to grant me a boon, for your good and for mine.'

Galehot said:

'Ask for whatever you want and whatever you please, for I shall never refuse you. I have preferred you to earthly honour.'

'Sir,' he said, 'many thanks. You have granted me that you will not ask me my name until I tell you it, or someone else tells you for me.'

'I shall be content with that,' said Galehot, 'since you wish it. It would have been the first thing I asked you, but I have no desire to know it until it is your wish.'

Then the knight asked him about the behaviour of King Arthur and his company, but he did not mention the queen. Galehot replied that the king was a very worthy man.

'And I am very sorry', he said, 'that I did not know him some time ago as I do now, for I should have benefited greatly from it. And my lady the queen [330] is so worthy that God never made a more worthy lady.'

When the knight heard him speak of the queen, he bowed his head and fell into such a profound reverie that he quite forgot himself. Galehot looked at him, and saw that the tears had come to his eyes and that he only refrained from weeping with great difficulty. He was very surprised and began to talk about something else. When he had talked for a long time, the knight said to him:

'Go, sir, and keep Sir Gawain and the king company, and see if you hear any news or talk of me. And tell me tomorrow what you have been told about me.'

'Gladly, sir,' said Galehot.

Then he embraced him and kissed him on the cheeks and commended him to God, and told the two kings that he was entrusting him to them like the heart in his breast.

Thus Galehot went away; and the knight remained in the care of the two worthy men, who did him as much honour as they could. That night Galehot slept in the king's tent, and the king himself slept there, with Sir Gawain, who had himself taken there, and Sir Yvain and many other knights. The queen slept in the brattice where Sir Gawain had lain ill, with the Lady of Malohaut, who constantly watched and listened to see how things would turn out; and there were many other ladies and damsels there.

As for the knight who had remained in the care of the two kings, there is no need to ask if he was honoured, for they made much more of him than he would have liked, and he was very embarrassed and upset. That night the two kings slept in Galehot's tent for the knight's sake, and gave him to understand that they would spend the night in the same way as Galehot had, the first night, so that he would not realize, for he would not have slept there for anything.* To begin with the knight slept very soundly; but when the early part of the night was past, he began to toss and turn, and before long he began to grieve so bitterly that all those who were sleeping beside him woke up. He wept as copiously as the tears could flood his eyes, but he did his best to keep from being heard. And as he wept he often said: 'Alas! unhappy wretch! What can I do?' However, he said it very quietly. His grieving and this anguish lasted all night long. In the morning, at daybreak, the two kings rose as quietly as they could; and they very much wondered what could be the matter with this knight, [331] who had grieved so bitterly. Galehot, for his part, had also risen very early, and had gone to his tent to see his companion, and he found the two kings up, and asked them how his companion was. They told him about the great grieving he had done all night long. When he heard that, he was extremely taken aback and very upset. Then he went into the chamber where he[1] was lying. He[1] heard him coming, and wiped his eyes, for he was weeping as bitterly as he ever

---

[1] i.e. the knight.

had in the night. When Galehot did not hear him saying a word, he went outside, for he thought he was asleep. Not long after that the knight got up. When he was up, Galehot went to him, and saw that his eyes were red and swollen, while he was so hoarse that he could barely say a word. And the sheets under him were as wet where his head had been as if they had just been taken out of water, for he had wept a great deal. None the less he made a great effort to look cheerful and stood up to meet Galehot, who took him by the hand, and drew him to one side alone and said:

'Dear companion, why are you overcome with grief like this? What is causing this grieving that you have done all night long?'

The other strenuously denied it and said that he often moaned in his sleep like that.

'Indeed,' said Galehot, 'it is quite apparent from your body and eyes that you have grieved terribly. But, for the Lord's sake, I beg you to tell me the reason. And rest assured that there is no trouble, however great, from which I should not help to extricate you, if anyone can do anything about it.'

When he heard that, he was so upset that he could not say a word, and began to weep as bitterly as if he had seen dead the person he most loved in the world, and he grieved so much that he nearly fainted. Galehot ran to take him in his arms, and kissed him on the mouth and eyes, and comforted him energetically, and said:

'Dear friend, tell me about your troubles, for there is no man in the world, however powerful, on whom you shall not have revenge as you wish, if he has caused you trouble.'

He said that no one had done him any wrong.

'Dear friend, then why are you sorrowing so? Are you sorry that I have made you my lord and companion?'

'Ah! sir, by the Lord's mercy, you have done more for me than I could deserve, and nothing is worrying me but my heart, [332] which has all the fears a mortal heart can have, and I am very much afraid that your graciousness will be the death of me.'

Galehot was very worried about this, and did his best to comfort his companion. Afterwards they went to hear mass. And when the priest had made the three parts of the Lord God's body, Galehot moved forward and took his companion by the hand and showed him the three parts that the priest was holding in his hands, and said:

'Sir, do you not believe that this is the body of Our Lord, then?'

'Sir,' the knight said, 'I do believe it, firmly.'

'My friend,' said Galehot, 'now do not fear me, then, for by those three parts of flesh that you see in the guise of bread, I shall never in my life do anything which grieves or vexes you. But I shall do my best to obtain all the things which I know will please you.'

'Sir,' he said, 'many thanks; you have done too much. It distresses me, for I do not see how I can possibly deserve it.'

Then they waited until after mass. And then Galehot again asked his companion what he was to do.

'Sir,' he said, 'you must not neglect my lord the king, but must go and keep him company. And if you hear anyone talk about me, conceal my whereabouts, as I have asked you.'

'Sir,' said Galehot, 'have no fear about that, for nothing you wish to conceal will ever be revealed by me.'

With that he left him, and again entrusted him to the two men of worth, who loved him dearly. And he went to King Arthur's court, and everyone made as much of him as they possibly could. After breakfast, Galehot and the king and the queen were reclining on the bed in which Sir Gawain was lying, and at length Sir Gawain said to Galehot:

'Sir, sir, now do not be upset by something that I am going to ask you.'

'Indeed,' said Galehot, 'I shall not.'

'Sir, this peace between you and my lord, by the person you most love, by whom was it brought about?'

'Indeed,' said Galèhot, 'you have so adjured me that I shall not lie to you. A knight brought it about.'

'And who is he?' asked Sir Gawain.

'As God is my true witness,' said Galehot, 'I do not know.'

[333] 'Was it the knight in black armour?' asked the queen.

'You can certainly tell us that much,' said Sir Gawain, 'if you wish to keep your word.'*

'Sir,' Galehot said, 'I kept my word regarding that which you adjured me about, when I told you that it was a knight, and I shall not tell you any more for the moment. And I should not have told you anything if you had not adjured me by the person I most love in the world. And let me tell you that the person I most love brought the peace about.'

'For the Lord's sake,' said the queen, 'it was the Black Knight, but let us see him.'

'Who, my lady? Truly, my lady, I can show him to you as much as one who knows nothing of him.'*

'Hush,' she said. 'He stayed with you, and yesterday he wore your armour.'

'My lady,' he said, 'that is true, but I have not seen him at all since the first time I left my lord.'*

'What?' said the king; 'do you not know him, the knight in black armour? And I thought he was from your land.'

'As God is my witness, my lord, he is not,' said Galehot.

'Sir,' said the king, 'nor is he from mine, for it is some time since I heard of any lost knight of whom there was no news.'

He and the queen pressed Galehot to tell them the Black Knight's name, but they could get no more out of him. Sir Gawain was afraid that it would annoy him, and said to the king:

'Sire, leave it at that now, for the knight is truly a man of valour, whoever he is. There is no knight in this world whom I should so much wish to resemble.'

Sir Gawain praised the knight greatly. And when everyone had stopped talking about him, Galehot started again, and said to the king:

'My lord, my lord, did you ever see a more valorous man than the knight with the black shield?'

'Indeed,' said the king, 'I never saw a man whom I should so much like to know because of his knightly valour.'

'No?' said Galehot; 'now, tell me, then, by the loyalty you owe my lady here and Sir Gawain, how much you would give to have his companionship for ever.'

'As God is my true witness,' he said, 'I should give him an equal share of everything I might have, with the exception of this lady herself, whom I should not share.'

'Indeed,' said Galehot, 'you would give a good deal. And you,' he said, 'Sir [334] Gawain, if God ever gives you the health you desire, what sacrifice would you make to have such a man of valour for ever?'

Sir Gawain thought for a while, as he never expected to be well again.

'If,' he said, 'God gives me the health I desire, I should wish there and then to be the most beautiful damsel in the world, fit and well, on condition that he loved me more than anything, as much as I loved him.'

'Indeed,' said Galehot, 'you have offered a good deal. And you, my lady,' he said, 'by the person you most love, what sacrifice would you make on condition that such a knight would always be in your service?'

'By the Lord,' she said, 'Sir Gawain has made every offer that a lady can make, and no lady can offer more.'

And they all began to laugh.

'And you, Galehot,' said Sir Gawain, 'who have challenged us all about it, what would you give, by the oath* that I made you swear today?'

'As God is my witness, I should change my great honour to shame, provided that I could always be as sure of him as I should wish him to be of me.'

'If God gives me joy,' said Sir Gawain, 'you have offered more than any of us.'

Then Sir Gawain thought that it was the Black Knight who had brought about the peace between the two of them, and that for his sake Galehot had changed his great honour to shame, when he saw that he was completely on top; and he said as much quietly to the queen (and that was the thing for which Galehot was held in highest esteem), and they could not see enough of him. They talked about the Black Knight for a long time; and after a while the queen stood up and said that she wished to go to Sir Gawain's brattice, where her chamber was. Galehot escorted her; and when they were up there, the queen took Galehot aside, and said:

'Galehot, I love you dearly, and it may be that I should do more for you than you suppose. And it is true that you have the good knight in your company and in your care, and he may be someone I know very well. And I beg you, if you value my love, to let me see him, on condition that whatever I can do for you I shall put at your disposal and in your power.'

'My lady,' said Galehot, 'I do not yet have any power over him, for I have not seen him at all since peace was made between me and my lord the king.'

[335] 'Indeed,' said the queen, 'it cannot be that you do not know very well where he is.'

'My lady,' he said, 'that is quite possible. And if he was in my tent right now, it would still need the agreement of someone other than you or me,* besides which, he is not in this land right now.'

'Then where is he?' said the queen. 'You can tell me that much.'

'My lady,' he said. 'I believe he is in my country. And rest assured that because you have begged and adjured me, I shall do all that I can to give you the opportunity to see him.'

'This much I know,' she said, 'that if you do what you can, I shall see him. I am relying on you, so do enough to make me yours* for ever more, for he is one of the men in the world that I should most like to see; not from any hope that I have of recognizing him, but because no man or woman should tire of seeing a man of valour.'

'My lady,' said Galehot, 'I know that, and you may be sure that I shall do all that I can.'

'Many thanks,' said the queen. 'Now go and arrange for me to see him as soon as you can. If he is in your country, then send someone to fetch him by night and day,* so that he is here as soon as possible.'

Thereupon Galehot left the brattice and went to the king and Sir Gawain and the other knights who were there. And the king said to him:

'Galehot, we are free of our armies, for we now have only the permanent members of our households. Do have your party draw near to ours, or I shall have mine draw near to yours, then they will be close to one another.'

'My lord,' said Galehot, 'I shall have mine move to near here, on the other side of the river, so that my tent will be opposite yours, and a boat will be made ready which will go from here to there and there to here. I shall go and do that here and now.'

'Indeed,' said the king, 'that is a very good idea.'

Then Galehot went away to his tent and found his companion very pensive, and asked him how he was. And he said: 'Very well, if fear was not oppressing me.'

And Galehot said:

'Sir, for the Lord's sake, what are you afraid of?'

'Sir,' he said, 'of being known.'

[336] 'Sir,' said Galehot, 'now do not worry, for by the

loyalty I owe you, you will never be known there, unless it is of your own free will.'

Then he told him of the offers that Sir Gawain and the king had made for him, and what the queen had said, and how the queen had pressed him regarding the good Black Knight and how he had answered her. 'And you should know', he said, 'that she desires nothing so much as to see you. And my lord the king has asked me to have my party moved towards his, so that my tent is opposite his, for we are too far from one another. Now, tell me what you wish me to do, for everything will be as you wish.'

'Sir,' he said, 'I strongly advise that you do as my lord the king asks you, for it can bring you great benefit.'

'Dear friend,' said Galehot, 'and what shall I reply to my lady regarding what I have told you?'

'Indeed,' he said, 'I do not know.'

Then he began to sigh again, and tears came to his eyes, and he turned away, and was in such a state that he did not know where he was. And Galehot said:

'Sir, do not be dismayed, but tell me outright how you wish things to be. And rest assured that it will be as you wish, for I should rather be at odds with half the world than with you alone, and it is through your love that they have mine.* So now tell me your pleasure.'

'Sir,' said the knight, 'whatever you advise, for I am in your hands from now on.'

'As God is my witness, I do not see how seeing my lady can hurt you.'

'Indeed,' said the knight, 'it would mean a good deal of trouble and joy.'

Then Galehot had some inkling of his feelings, and he pressed him so closely that he agreed to what he asked him.

'But it will have to be done so secretly,' he said, 'that no one knows about it. And do tell my lady that you have sent someone to fetch me.'*

'Leave the rest to me,' said Galehot, 'for I am sure I can see to it.'

Then he called his seneschal and ordered him, as soon as he had gone to court, to have his tent and those of his men and his iron nets gathered up, and to have everything taken to opposite the king's party, and to have camp set up so close that there was only the river between them.

Thereupon he went back again with very few companions. The queen had already come back from the brattice; and when she saw [337] Galehot coming, she sprang up to meet him and asked him how he had fared with his task.

'My lady,' he said, 'I have done so much that I am afraid your request may take from me the person I most love in the world.'

'As God is my witness,' she said, 'you will never lose anything because of me that I do not make up to you twice over. But what can you lose because of this?'

'My lady,' he said, 'the very man that you are asking for, for I am afraid that something may happen to make him angry, so that I lose him for ever.'

'Indeed,' she said, 'that I could not make up to you. But, please God, you will not lose him because of me, and he would not be courteous if he did anything to you because of my request. All the same, though, when will he come?'

'My lady, as soon as he can,' he said, 'for I have sent someone to fetch him at a gallop.'

'Now we shall see,' she said, 'for he will be here tomorrow if you wish it.'

'My lady,' he said, 'he would not be, if he set off here and now from where he is, and I wish he could be here this very night.'

While the two of them were talking together like this, Galehot's men had arrived on the other side of the river, and they began to pitch his tent opposite the king's tent. And people were looking at it in amazement, for it was very

beautiful and fine. When they were all encamped, the iron
nets were set up, and King Arthur's men were quite astonished, for they had never seen such great riches, and there
were many that day who went to see them close to.

In the evening Galehot went back to see his companion
and told him what he had found out, and that the queen was
very anxious to see him. The other felt fear and joy in his
heart at that. When they had talked together for a long while,
Galehot went, with his permission, to the king. And the
queen took him aside again and asked him if he had heard
any news of the knight. He said, not yet; and she said to him,
laughing:

'Dear friend, do not make me wait for something which
you can do quickly for me.'

'My lady,' he said, 'as God is my witness, I should be no
less glad to see him than you.'

'That is the reason', she said, 'why I am afraid because you
are not more cheerful. It is always the way that the thing one
desires is denied one the most, and there are some people
who are reluctant to let others enjoy the thing they most love.
None the less, do not be afraid, for you will never lose
anything through me that you have had.'

[338] 'My lady,' said Galehot, 'many thanks, for I believe
that you will be able to help me more than I you.'

They passed the day with such talk, and in the evening
Galehot went back to the king's tent, and the king did not
wish him to leave him. In the morning, very early, Galehot
went back to his companion and told him what the queen had
said. And what he told him comforted him greatly concerning
his fears, and he was no longer as wretched as he had been;
and there was an improvement in his body and face, which
had been pale and worn out, and his eyes, which had been
red and swollen, and he regained something of his beauty.
Galehot was delighted about that, and said:

'Sir, my lady will soon ask me about you. What shall I answer her?'

'Sir,' he said, 'whatever seems best to you, for from now on it is up to you.'

'I am certain', said Galehot, 'that she will wish to see you tomorrow, and I should certainly advise it.'

'Sir,' said the knight, 'it is a day that I should like already to have passed with honour and joy.'

Then his heart grew tender; and Galehot could see that, and he left it at that and went back to the king's tent. As soon as the queen saw him, she asked him for news; and he said:

'My lady, it is still too soon, but we shall have it by tomorrow.'

'What are you saying?' she said. 'It is up to you whether to hasten or delay it. Now, do me the same kindness you would wish me to do you, if I had him.'

Galehot began to laugh. And the Lady of Malohaut stood very close by, and watched their faces and listened to their conversation, for she was sure she knew what they were arranging, and she would have considered herself quite humiliated if she failed to find out any more in that way. Thus Galehot went to his companion in the morning and in the evening, and each time he came back the queen asked him what he had found out.

That night Galehot slept in his customary place.* And in the morning he rose very early and went to his companion, and told him that there was nothing else for it.

'Today,' he said, 'the queen must see you.'

'Sir, for the Lord's sake,' he said, 'arrange it so that no one knows anything about it apart from me and her, for there are some people at the court of my lord the king who would certainly recognize me if they saw me.'

'Do not worry,' said Galehot, 'for I shall see to it.'

[339] With that he took leave of him again, and called his seneschal.

'Take care,' he said, 'if I shortly send someone to fetch you, that you come to me and bring my companion with you, in such a way that nobody learns from you that it is him.'

'Sire,' he said, 'as you please.'

Then Galehot went back to the king's tent; and the queen asked him, what news.

'My lady,' he said, 'very good news. The flower of the knights of all the world has arrived.'

'Lord!' she said, 'how am I to see him? But I wish to see him in such a way that no one knows that it is him apart from me and you, for I do not want other people to have enjoyment from him.'

'In God's name, my lady,' said Galehot, 'that is how it will be, for he says that he would not want the people of the king's household to recognize him for anything.'

'What?' she said, 'is he known here, then?'

'My lady,' he said, 'some people might perhaps see him who would certainly recognize him.'

'Lord!' she said, 'who can he be?'

'My lady,' said Galehot, 'as God is my witness, I do not know, for he has never told me his name, or who he is.'

'No?' she said. 'As God is my witness, I am hearing remarkable things. Now I am even more impatient to see him.'

'My lady,' he said, 'you will see him this very day, and I shall tell you how. We shall go down there to amuse ourselves.' And he pointed out a place beside the meadows, covered in shrubbery. 'And we shall have as few companions as possible. And you will see him there, a little before nightfall.'

'Ah!' she said, 'what a good idea, dear friend. Please the Saviour of the world night would fall now!'

Then they both began to laugh; and the queen embraced him and made a great fuss of him. The Lady of Malohaut saw them, and thought to herself that now the affair was more imminent than it had been, and she paid close attention. And she looked at the face of every knight who went in there. The queen rejoiced greatly over the knight's arrival, and she was very impatient for the night to come, and applied herself to talking and diversions, to forget the day which irked her.

Thus they passed the day until after supper, when it was evening. The queen took Galehot by the hand, and called the Lady of Malohaut to her, and damsel Lore of Carlisle and [340] just one of her damsels who had always been with her. She went away down across the meadows, straight to where Galehot had said. When they had gone some way, Galehot looked and saw a squire, and called him and told him to go and tell his seneschal to come to him, and showed him where. When the queen heard that, she looked at him and said:

'What? Is he your seneschal?'

'No, my lady, but he will come with him.'

Thereupon they arrived under the trees, and Galehot and the queen sat down in one place, far from the others, and the ladies in another, very surprised that they were so alone. The squire went to the seneschal, and delivered his message. And the latter at once took the knight with him, and they crossed the river and went down across the meadows as the squire directed them. They were both such handsome knights that there would have been no point in looking for more handsome knights in their countries. When they approached, and the ladies looked at them, the Lady of Malohaut recognized him at once, having had him in her prison many a day. And because she did not wish him to recognize her, she bowed her head and moved close to damsel Lore. They[1] went past, and the seneschal greeted them;[2] and Galehot said to the queen:

'Here is the best knight in the world.'

'Which one is he?' asked the queen.

---

[1] i.e. the seneschal and the knight. [2] i.e. the ladies.

'My lady,' he said, 'which do you think he is?'

'Indeed,' she said, 'they are both handsome knights, but I do not see a body in which there should be half the prowess that the Black Knight had.'

'My lady,' said Galehot, 'let me tell you that he is one of these two.'

Thereupon they arrived in front of the queen. And the knight was trembling so violently that he could barely greet the queen, and he had lost all his colour, so that the queen was astonished by it. Then they both knelt down. The seneschal greeted her, and so did the other, but not very well, and he kept his eyes fixed on the ground as though ashamed. Then the queen thought that he was the one. And Galehot said to the seneschal:

'Go and keep those ladies there company, who are very much alone.'

He did as his lord ordered him; and the queen took the knight by the hand, as he was on his knees, and made him sit down in front of her, and was very pleasant to him and said, laughing:

'Sir, we have eagerly desired your presence and now, by the grace of God and Galehot here, we see you. Even so, I do not know if you are the knight I have asked for, but Galehot has told me that it [341] is you. However, I should still very much like to know who you are from your own lips, if you are agreeable.'

He replied that he did not know, and did not at once look her in the face. The queen very much wondered what could be the matter with him, until she partly suspected what the matter was. And Galehot, who saw that he was embarrassed and overwhelmed, thought that he would be more likely to tell the queen his thoughts if they were alone together. He looked up, and said very loudly, so that the ladies heard him:

'Indeed, I am very ill-bred, for all those ladies are too alone, with only one knight for company.'

Then he stood up and went to where the ladies were sitting. They sprang up to meet him, and he made them sit down again, and then they began to talk of many things.

And the queen addressed the knight and said:

'Dear sir, why are you concealing your identity from me? Truly, there is no reason for it. In any case, you can at least tell me if you are the knight who was victorious at the encounter the other day?'

'No, my lady,' he said.

'What?' she said; 'did you not have black armour?'

'Yes, my lady,' he said.

'Then was it not you to whom Sir Gawain sent the three horses?'

'Yes, my lady.'

'Then was it not you who wore Galehot's armour on the final day?'

'Yes, my lady,' he said, 'that is true.'

'Then was it not you who was victorious at the encounter on the second day?'

'My lady,' he said, 'it was not, truly.'

Then the queen realized that he did not wish to admit that he had been victorious there, and she esteemed him highly for it.

'Now, tell me,' she said, 'who made you a knight?'

'You did, my lady.'

'I?' she said. 'When?'

'My lady, do you remember that a knight came to my lord King Arthur in Camelot, who was wounded with two broken lances in the body and with a sword in the head, and that a youth came to him[1] on Friday evening and was knighted on Sunday?'

'I remember that very well,' she said. 'And as God is your witness, was it you that the damsel brought to the king, dressed in the white robe?'

---

[1] i.e. King Arthur.

[342] 'Yes, my lady,' he said.

'Then why do you say that I made you a knight?'

'My lady, because it is true, for it is the custom in the kingdom of Logres that a man cannot be made a knight without his sword being belted on, and the person from whom he receives the sword makes him a knight. And I received mine from you, for the king did not give me one. That is why I say that you made me a knight.'

'Indeed,' she said, 'I am delighted about that. And where did you go from there?'

'My lady, I went to give assistance to the Lady of Nohaut, and later Sir Kay came, who fought with me.'

'And in the meantime, did you send me any word?'

'Yes, my lady,' he said, 'I sent you two maidens.'

'By my head, that is true. And when you left Nohaut, did you meet on your way anyone who invoked my name?'

'Yes, my lady, a knight who was guarding a ford, and he told me to get down from my horse. I asked him in whose service he was, and he said that he was in yours. "Get down at once," he said.* I asked him who commanded it; and he said that there was no command but his own. And I put my left foot, which I had taken out of the stirrup, back in it, and said that he would certainly not get it[1] that day, and I jousted with him. And I am well aware that I behaved outrageously, my lady, and I ask your forgiveness. I will make whatever amends you please.'

And the queen answered him, well aware that he could not avoid being hers. 'Indeed,' she said, 'you did me no wrong, dear friend, for he was not in my service; in fact, I was very displeased with him for having said that to you, for he came to me. But now tell me where you went from there.'

'To the Dolorous Guard.'

'And who conquered it?'

---

[1] i.e. the horse.

'My lady, I entered it.'

'And did I ever see you there?'

'Yes, my lady, more than once.'

'Where?' she asked.

'My lady, one day when I asked you if you would like to go in, and you said that you would, and you seemed very downcast. And I said that to you twice.'

'What shield were you carrying?' she asked.

'My lady, first I carried a white shield with a diagonal red band, and the second time I had two bands.'

[343] 'I certainly recognize these credentials.* And did I see you there again?'

'Yes, my lady. The night you thought you had lost your nephew, Sir Gawain, and his companions, and the people of the castle were shouting: "Capture him. Capture him." And I came out, a shield with three diagonal red bands around my neck, and my lord the king was in a gallery with you. And when I went towards him, they shouted: "Capture him, king. Capture him, king." And he let me go, by his grace.'

'Indeed,' she said, 'I am sorry about that, for if he had captured you, the enchantments of the castle would have been ended. But now tell me, was it you who freed Sir Gawain from the prison, and his companions likewise?'

'My lady, I did my best to help.'

'In all the things you have told me,' she said, 'I have so far found nothing but truth. But now tell me, for the Lord's sake, who was a damsel, who spent the night in a turret above my lord the king's lodging, dressed in a white underdress?'

'Indeed, my lady, she was the maiden I treated the most despicably in the world, for my lady, the Lady of the Lake, who brought me up, had sent her to me. And she found me in that turret, and was greatly honoured on my account. When I heard the news that Sir Gawain was a prisoner, I was very upset, and left the damsel, who wished to go with me. And I asked her, by the loyalty she owed me, not to leave until she saw me or a messenger from me. And I was taken up with such weighty matters that I forgot about her and did not return to her afterwards. And she was more faithful to me than I was courteous to her, for she did not leave there again until she had word of me, and that was a long while afterwards.'

When the queen heard him talk about the damsel, she knew at once that he was Lancelot, and she enquired about all the things she had heard said about him, and she found he spoke the truth about all of them.

'Now, tell me,' she said, 'since you were made a knight and left Camelot, have I ever seen you?'*

'Yes, my lady,' he said, 'one time when you did me a great service, for I should have been killed but for you having me pulled out of the water by Sir Yvain.'

'What?' she said; 'was it you that Daguenet the Coward captured?'

'My lady, I do not know who he was, but I was certainly captured.'

[344] 'And where were you going?'

'My lady, I was following a knight.'

'And when you left us the last time, where did you go?'

'My lady, after a knight that I was following.'

'And did you fight him?'

'Yes, my lady.'

'And where did you go after that?'

'My lady, I met two great churls who killed my horse; but Sir Yvain—may he have good fortune—gave me his.'

'Ah!' she said, 'then I know who you are. Your name is Lancelot of the Lake.'

He said nothing.

'For the Lord's sake,' she said, 'there is no point in concealing it; it has been known at court for a while. Sir Gawain first brought your name to court.'

Then she told him all about how Sir Gawain had said that

it was the third encounter, when Sir Yvain said that the
maiden had said that it was 'the third'. Then she asked him
why he had allowed the worst man in the world to take him
away by the bridle.

'Because I had no control over my body or my heart.'

'Now, tell me,' she said, 'were you at the encounter last
year at all?'

'Yes, my lady,' he said.

'And what arms did you bear?'

'My lady, all red.'

'By my head,' she said, 'that is the truth. And the other
day, at the encounter, why did you do such deeds of arms?'

He began to sigh very heavily; and the queen pressed him
very hard, well aware how it was.

'Tell me,' she said, 'and without any hesitation, for I shall
not give you away. I am certain that you did it for some lady
or damsel. Tell me who she is, by the loyalty you owe me.'

'Ah! my lady,' he said, 'I can see that I shall have to say it.
My lady, it is you.'

'Me?' she said.

'Yes, indeed, my lady.'

'It was not for me that you broke the three lances which
my maiden brought to you, for I had definitely excluded
myself from the message.'

[345] 'My lady,' he said, 'for them, I did what I ought, and
for you, what I could.'

'Now, tell me, all the knightly deeds that you have done,
for whom did you do them?'

'For you, my lady,' he said.

'What?' she said, 'do you love me so much?'

'My lady,' he said, 'I do not love myself or anyone else as
much.'

'And since when', she said, 'have you loved me so?'

'My lady,' he said, 'since the day I was called a knight, but
was not one.'*

'And, by the loyalty you owe me, where did this love which you have bestowed on me come from?'

As the queen was saying these words, it happened that the Lady of the Hill of Malohaut coughed, quite deliberately, and raised her head, which had been bowed. He noticed it, immediately, having often heard her; and he looked at her, and recognized her, and he felt such fear and anguish in his heart that he could not reply to what the queen was saying. He began to sigh very heavily, and tears ran down his cheeks in such floods that the samite in which he was dressed was wet down to the knees. And the more he looked at the Lady of Malohaut, the more unhappy he became. The queen noticed this, and saw that he was looking very piteously towards where the ladies were. And she spoke to him:

'Tell me,' she said, 'where did this love which I am asking you about come from?'

He made a great effort to speak as best he could, and said: 'My lady, from the day that I mentioned to you.'

'How was that, then?' she asked.

'My lady,' he said, 'you caused it, when you made me your friend,* if your lips did not lie to me.'

'My friend?' she said, 'and how was that?'

'My lady,' he said, 'I came to you when I had taken leave of my lord the king, fully armed except for my head and hands, and I commended you to God and said that I was your knight wherever I might be. And you said that you wished me to be your knight and your friend. And I said: "Go with God, my lady." And you said: "Go with God, dear friend." That has never been out of my heart since. That was the word which will make me a man of valour, if I am to be one. Since then I have never been in such dire straits that I did not remember that word. That word has comforted me in all my troubles, that [346] word has protected me from all ills and saved me from all dangers; that word has satisfied me

whenever I was hungry, that word has made me rich whenever I was poor.'

'In faith, in faith,' said the queen, 'that was a word
fortunately spoken, and the Lord be praised for having made
me say it. However, I did not take it so much in earnest as
you did, and I have said it to many knights and only meant it
as a manner of speaking. And your thought was not unworthy,
but sweet and gracious; and it has brought you good, for it
has made you a man of valour. None the less, it is now the
custom for knights to make a great show to many ladies of
something which means very little to them in their hearts.
And your bearing shows me that you love one of those ladies
there—I do not know which—more than you do me, for you
have wept with fear because of it, and you dare not look
straight at them. I can tell that your thoughts are not so much
of me as you are making out. By the loyalty you owe the
person you most love, tell me which of the three you love so.'

'Ha! my lady, by the Lord's mercy, as God is my true
witness, none of them ever had possession of my heart.'

'It is no use,' the queen said; 'you cannot keep anything
from me, for I have seen many such affairs and I can see that
your heart is there, although your body is here.'

She said this to see how she could worry him, for she
would have been sure he had no thought of love except for
her, even if he had done nothing for her sake but the day of
the black armour; but she took great delight in seeing and
hearing his discomfort. He was so upset that he nearly
fainted, but fear of the ladies he was looking at stopped him.
And the queen feared it herself, seeing him change colour;
and she took hold of his collar to stop him falling, and called
Galehot. He sprang up and came running to her. He saw the
state his companion was in, and felt the greatest possible
anguish in his heart, and said:

'Ha! my lady, tell me, for the Lord God's sake, what is the
matter with him?'

The queen told him what she had put to him.

'Ah! my lady,' said Galehot, 'by the Lord's mercy, you could well take him from me by such distress; and that would be a very great misfortune.'

'Indeed,' she said, 'it certainly would, but do you know why he has done such deeds of arms?'

'No, indeed, my lady.'

[347] 'If what he has told me is true, it is for me.'

'My lady,' he said, 'as God is my true witness, you can certainly believe it, for just as he is more valorous than other men, in the same way his heart is truer than all the others.'

'Truly,' she said, 'you would certainly say that he was a man of valour, if you knew what deeds of arms he has done since he became a knight.'

Then she told him all the knightly deeds as he[1] himself had told them to her, and that he had admitted that he bore the red arms the year before at the other encounter.

'And let me tell you', she said, 'that he has done all this because of a single word.' Then she told him what she had said, as you have heard it.

'Ah! my lady,' said Galehot, 'have mercy on him, for the Lord's sake and because he has greatly deserved it, in the same way that I have done for you what you asked of me.'

'How do you wish me to have mercy on him?' she said.

'My lady, you know that he loves you more than anything and has done more for you than any knight ever did. And here he is and you should know that there would never have been peace between me and my lord the king, if he had not brought it about.'

'Indeed,' she said, 'I am well aware that he would have done more for me than I could deserve, even if he had done no more than bring about the peace. And I could not, with good grace, refuse him anything which he could ask me for;

[1] i.e. Lancelot.

however, he is not asking me for anything, but is very sombre and unhappy and has not stopped weeping since he began looking towards those ladies. Even so, I do not suspect him of feeling love for any of them, but perhaps he is afraid that one of them will recognize him.'

'My lady,' said Galehot, 'there is no need to talk about that, but have mercy on him, for he loves you more than himself; not that, as God is my witness, I knew anything of his feelings when he came here, except that he thought he would be recognized, and he never revealed any more to me.'

'I shall have mercy on him', she said, 'in whatever way you wish, for you have done what I required of you, so I certainly ought to do what you wish. But he is not asking me for anything.'

'Indeed, my lady,' said Galehot, 'he is quite unable to do so, for one cannot love someone without fearing them. However, I am asking you for him. If I did not ask you, then you should take steps yourself, for you could not gain a greater treasure.'

[348] 'Indeed,' she said, 'I am well aware of that, and I shall do what you ask of me.'

'My lady,' said Galehot, 'many thanks. I ask that you give him your love and take him as your knight for ever and become his faithful lady for all the days of your life. Then you will have made him as rich as if you had given him the whole world.'

'I agree to this,' she said: 'that he will be entirely mine, and I entirely his, and any wrongs and breaches of the agreement will be sorted out by you.'

'My lady,' said Galehot, 'many thanks. Now, though, an initial guarantee is needed.'

'Whatever you propose,' the queen said, 'I will do it.'

'My lady,' said Galehot, 'many thanks. Kiss him in front of me, then, as a start to true love.'

'I do not think it is the time and place for kissing at the

moment, and do not doubt that I am just as willing and eager for it as he is. But those ladies are there, who are very much wondering what we have been doing for so long, and they could not fail to see it. None the less, if he wishes it, I shall gladly kiss him.'

He was so delighted and overwhelmed that he could only answer: 'My lady, many thanks.'

'Ah! my lady,' said Galehot, 'do not doubt his wishes, for he is all for it. And rest assured that no one will notice it, for the three of us will move close together, as if we were conferring.'

'Now, why should I make you beg me?' she said. 'I desire it more than you or he.'

Then the three of them moved close together and pretended to confer. The queen saw that the knight did not dare do more, and so she took him by the chin, and kissed him for quite a long time in front of Galehot, so that the Lady of Malohaut knew that she was kissing him. And then the queen, who was a very wise and worthy woman, began to speak.

'Dear friend,' she said to the knight, 'I am yours, because of what you have done, and I am overjoyed about it. Now, take care that this thing is kept as secret as it needs to be, for I am one of the ladies in the world of whom the greatest good has been said, and if my reputation were to suffer because of you, this would be a wretched and unworthy love. And I beg that of you, Galehot, who are wiser; for if it brought me misfortune, it would be entirely due to you. And if I have good or joy from it, you will have the credit.'*

'My lady,' said Galehot, 'he could not do you any wrong. However, I have done for you what you ordered; now it would be [349] right for you to listen to a request from me, for I told you yesterday that you would soon be able to help me more than I you.'

'Tell me,' she said, 'without hesitation, for there is nothing you would dare ask me that I should not do.'

'Then, my lady,' he said, 'you have granted me that you will give me his companionship.'

'Indeed,' she said, 'if you fail to have that, you will have had a poor return for the great sacrifice that you have made for him.'

Then she took the knight by the right hand and said:

'Galehot, I give you this knight for ever, except what I have had already.* And you give your word on that,' she said. And the knight gave his word. 'And do you know', she asked Galehot, 'whom I have given you?'

'No, my lady,' he said.

'I have given you Lancelot of the Lake, the son of King Ban of Benwick.'

Thus she made him acquainted with the knight, who was very embarrassed by it. Then Galehot was more overjoyed than he had ever been before, for he had heard a good deal of rumour about Lancelot of the Lake, and that he was the best knight in the world, among the poor men; and he knew that King Ban had been a very noble and powerful man, well endowed with friends and land. In this way the first acquaintance between the queen and Lancelot of the Lake was brought about by Galehot. And Galehot had only ever known him by sight,* and that was why Lancelot had made him give his word that he would not ask him his name until he told him it, or someone else did so for him.

Then the three of them stood up. And night had already fallen, but it was light, for the moon had risen, and one could see quite clearly all down across the meadowland. Thereupon the three of them went on their own back up across the meadows, straight towards the king's tent. And Galehot's seneschal and the ladies went after them until they were opposite Galehot's tents. Then Galehot sent his companion away, and he[1] took leave of the queen, and he and the seneschal crossed over, and Galehot accompanied the queen to the king's tent. When the king saw them coming, he asked where they had been.

'My lord,' said Galehot, 'we have just been looking at those meadows with these few companions that you see.'

Then they sat down and talked of many things, and the queen and Galehot were very content. After a while, the queen stood up and went to the brattice to go to bed. Galehot accompanied her there, [350] and commended her to God and said that he would go and spend the night with his companion.

'And I shall console him, my lady,' he said, 'for I now know how. The other day, though, I did not know what to console him about.'

'Ah!' she said, 'what a good idea that is! He will be so much more content now!'

Thereupon Galehot went away and took leave of the king, and said that he should not be upset if he went to spend the night in the tent with his followers, where he had not spent the night for a while.

'And I must often do as they wish, my lord, for they love me dearly.'

'Indeed, sir,' said Sir Gawain, 'you are quite right, for anyone who has worthy followers should do them great honour.'

Then Galehot left and went to his companion, and they both lay down in one bed and talked all night long of that which made their hearts content.

Now, though, we shall say no more about Galehot and his companion, and we shall talk to you about the queen, who had gone back to the brattice very happy and content. And she had not acted as discreetly as she thought, for the Lady

---

[1] i.e. Lancelot.

of Malohaut had seen everything which she had done. When
Galehot had left, she went to a window and began to think
about that which pleased her most. And the Lady of Malohaut
moved close to her, when she saw her most alone, and said
as discreetly as she could:

'Ah! my lady, my lady, four is such good company!'

The queen heard her quite clearly, but she said nothing
and pretended that she had not heard anything. And before
long the lady said the same thing again. And the queen called
to her:

'Tell me why you said that?'

'My lady,' she said, 'by your leave, I shall say no more at
present, for it may be that I have said more than I should, for
one should not try to be more intimate with one's lord or lady
than one is, for fear of incurring their enmity.'

'As God is my witness,' said the queen, 'nothing you could
say to me would earn you my enmity, for I know you to be so
wise and courteous that you would not say anything which
went against my wishes. But say it outright, for I wish and ask
you to do so.'

'Then I shall tell you, my lady,' she said. 'I said that four is
very good company, for I saw you becoming acquainted with
the knight who talked to you down there in the orchard. And
I know very well that [351] you are the person he most loves
in the world. And you are quite right if you love him, for you
could not bestow your love better.'

'What?' said the queen, 'do you know him?'

'Yes, my lady,' she said. 'There was a time this year when
I could have kept him from you as you now would from me,
for I held him in my prison for a year and a half. And he is
the one who was victorious at the encounter, with red arms,
and at the one the other day, with black arms, and I gave him
both sets of arms. And when he was pensive by the river the
other day, and I was eager to send to ask him to do deeds of
arms, I only did it because I rather suspected that he loved

you. There was a time when I believed he loved me, but he revealed enough of his feelings to me to quite rid me of that belief.'

Then she began to tell her how she had held him for a year and a half and why she had captured him and why she went to the king's court. She told her everything up to his leaving her prison.

'Now, tell me,' said the queen, 'why you said that four is better company than three. A secret is better kept by three than by four.'

'My lady,' she said, 'that is true.'

'Then three is better company than four,' the queen said.

'My lady,' she said, 'not in this case, and I shall tell you why. It is true that the knight loves you, and Galehot knows it, and from now on they will take pleasure in it together in whatever land they are, for they will not be here for long. And you will be left all alone, and no lady but you will know of it, and you will have no one to reveal your thoughts to, and so you will bear the whole burden[1] alone. But if it pleased you to let me be the fourth in the company, then we ladies should console each other, just as the two of them will do, and you would be more content.'

'Now, tell me,' said the queen; 'do you know who the knight is?'

'No, as God is my witness,' she said, 'for you have heard how he fears me.'

'Indeed, madam,' said the queen, 'you are very observant. Anyone who wished to keep something from you would have to be very shrewd. And since it is the case that you have noticed it and are asking me for our company, you shall have it. But I wish you to bear your burden, just as I do mine.'

'My lady,' she said, 'what do you mean? I shall do unreservedly whatever you wish to have such noble company.'

---

[1] i.e. of your love.

[352] 'In God's name,' said the queen, 'and you shall have it, for I could not have better company than yours, even if it were richer. However, I shall never be able to do without you once I get to know you, for once I begin to love, no one loves more than I do.'

'My lady,' she said, 'we shall be together whenever you please.'

'Now, let me take care of it,' said the queen, 'for we shall establish the company of the four of us tomorrow.' Then she told her how Lancelot had wept when he looked at them.[1] 'And I am sure', the queen said, 'that he recognized you. And let me tell you that he is Lancelot of the Lake, the best knight in the world.'

The two of them talked together in that way for a long time, and rejoiced greatly over their new friendship. That night the queen would not allow the Lady of Malohaut to sleep anywhere but with her. And she[2] did so very reluctantly, for she was very much afraid of sleeping with such a noble lady. When they were in bed, they began to talk about this new love. And the queen asked the Lady of Malohaut if she was in love with anyone; and she replied that she was not. 'And let me tell you, my lady,' she said, 'that I have only ever been in love once, and there was no more to that than thinking.' She was referring to Lancelot, whom she had loved as much as one heart can love another, though she had never had any other joy from it. None the less, she did not say that it was him. And the queen decided to make Galehot and her lovers, but she did not wish to mention it until she knew whether Galehot had a ladylove, for then she would not request it of him.

The next day the two of them rose early and went to the tent of the king, who was spending the night there to keep Sir Gawain company. The queen woke him up and said that

---

[1] i.e. the ladies.   [2] i.e. the lady.

he was very slothful to be asleep at that hour. Then the two of them went away down across the meadows, and with them were three ladies, and some of their damsels, and they went to the place where the love had been made known. And the queen told the Lady of Malohaut that she would always like the place better because of it. There she told the Lady of Malohaut all about Lancelot's bearing and behaviour, and how he was overwhelmed in her presence. And she did not leave out anything which she could remember. Then she began to lavish praise on Galehot, and said that he was the wisest knight in the world, and the one who was best at honouring excellence.

[353] 'And indeed,' she said, 'I shall tell him, when he comes, about our friendship; and rest assured that he will rejoice greatly over it. Now, let us go, for he will soon be coming.'

Thereupon the ladies went back. And by the time they arrived, the king was up and had sent for Galehot. He came very quickly, and the queen at once told him about the friendship between herself and the Lady of Malohaut. First, however, she said:

'Galehot, tell me the truth, by the loyalty you owe me.'

'My lady,' he said, 'I shall do so, rest assured.'

'I am asking you if you are in love with any lady or damsel who possesses your love.'

'No, my lady, I give you my word, by the oath* that you have made me swear.'

'Shall I tell you', she said, 'why I ask? I have given my love according to your wishes, and I want you to bestow yours according to my wishes. And shall I tell you on whom? On a beautiful, wise, and courteous lady, who is a very noble woman, and rich, with great lands.'

'My lady,' said Galehot, 'you may certainly do as you please with both my body and my heart. But who is the one to whom you wish me to belong?'

'Indeed,' said the queen, 'it is the Lady of Malohaut. And there she is.'

And she pointed her out to him with a look. Then she told him how she[1] had spied on them, and that she had had Lancelot in prison for a year and a half, and how he had come to terms with her, and everything that she[1] had told her,[2] and how Lancelot had wept because of her.

'And because', the queen said, 'I know that she is the most excellent lady in the world, for that reason I wish to make you and her lovers, for the most excellent knight in the world certainly ought to have the most excellent ladylove. When you and my knight are in remote lands, you will lament together, and we two ladies shall comfort each other over our troubles and rejoice over our blessings. And each of us will bear his own burden.'

'My lady,' said Galehot, 'here are my heart and body: do your will with them, just as I bestowed yours where I wished.'

Then the queen called the Lady of Malohaut, and said:

'Madam, you are ready for what I wish to do with you?'

'My lady,' she said, 'that is true.'

[354] 'In God's name,' said the queen, 'I wish to give you away, heart and body.'

'My lady,' she replied wisely, 'you can treat them as though they were your own.'

The queen took her by one hand, and Galehot by the other, and said:

'Galehot, sir knight, I give you to this lady as her true, faithful lover, with all your heart and body. And you, madam, I give to this knight as his ladylove, faithful in all true love.'

They both agreed to it, and the queen got them to kiss one another. After that they arranged that they would all four speak together that night. 'And we shall organize', the queen said, 'how it can be done.'

---

[1] i.e. the lady.   [2] i.e. the queen.

Thereupon they rose and went to call on the king to go and hear mass. And he said that he was only waiting for them. Then they all went to the minster. And when they had heard mass, the meal was ready, and they sat down. When they had eaten, the king and the queen and Galehot went to sit with Sir Gawain for a long while, and then went back to where the other knights were, a great proportion of whom were wounded. They went to see them on foot, and the king held the Lady of Malohaut's hand, and the queen, Galehot's. There they settled the meeting of the four: they would talk at nightfall as they had the night before, and in that same place.

'But we shall do it differently,' the queen said, 'for we shall take my husband there, and you will have your knight ready. And he need not worry, for there will not be anyone who will recognize him, for it is no easy matter to recognize a man, if he wishes to hide his face and conceal his identity. And the more people there are, the less will be thought wrong. We shall be able to do that every day while my husband stays here, for we could not talk together more secretly, for there would be no opportunity.'

In this manner they arranged their meeting. And when vespers came, Galehot went to see his followers and told his companion what he had arranged, and he agreed to it. And when it was time for supper, Galehot ordered his seneschal that, when he saw him coming down across the meadows with the king and queen, he should cross over, with his companion. Thereupon he left with a great company of knights and went to the king, who was expecting him for the meal. After the meal, the queen said to the king:

'My lord, do let us go and disport ourselves down there in the meadows.'

And the king agreed. Then the king and Galehot and many of their companions left. The queen also went, with the Lady of [355] Malohaut, and many ladies and damsels. And when the seneschal saw them, he crossed over, and Lancelot with him, and they joined the king's party. When they had gone some way, they sat down and began to talk. And while they were talking, King Yon came to talk to King Arthur, for messages had come from his land that he must go. He called the king to one side and conferred with him for a long while. And then the queen and Galehot and the Lady of Malohaut stood up, and Galehot called his companion and the four of them went, talking together for a long time, until they came to the edge of the shrubbery. Then they sat down; and the queen showed Lancelot the lady who had had him many a day in her prison; and he was very embarrassed; and the queen said to him laughingly that he had concealed this theft* from her. They lingered there for a long while, and did and said nothing but kiss and embrace, as they were very glad to do so. And when they had sat for a long while, they returned to where the king was, and arrived back up at his tent. The seneschal took Lancelot back to their tents. And in that manner the four of them talked together every night, with no word of any other pleasure.

Thus they stayed there until Sir Gawain was much improved, and felt better than he had done; and he was very impatient to be in the country where he was as much in love as he could be, and he told the king that he would very much like to go. And the king said:

'Dear nephew, I am only staying here because of you and because of Galehot, whom I love dearly.'

'Sire,' said Sir Gawain, 'you must ask him to come away with you tomorrow, and we shall go the day after tomorrow. And if he comes, it will be a great honour for you, and if he does not come, you will see him again soon, please God, and he you.'

The king agreed to that. And the next day he asked Galehot to accompany him to his land; but Galehot said that that was impossible.

'For I have much to do in my country, my lord, which is

very far away, and I was only staying here because of you, and you because of me, I am well aware.'

'Indeed,' said the king, 'that is true. But I beg of you, dear friend, that I may see you again as soon as you can.'

And Galehot agreed. That evening the four met together. And let me tell you that there was great anguish at their parting, and they fixed a day to talk together at the first encounter to take place in the kingdom of Logres.

Thus the two knights parted from their ladies, unhappy because of the [356] parting, and happy because of the joy they expected to have at the first encounter. That night Galehot took leave of the king and queen and the Lady of Malohaut and Sir Gawain and all the others, and they were all very distressed, for they held him in high esteem. And Galehot went to his companion, and found him in a very different mood from the night before, but he did his best to comfort him. And the queen went to the king, and told him to ask the Lady of Malohaut to come away with her and to be entirely in his household from then on. 'For I like her company very much,' she said, 'and I believe she likes mine so much that she will come without much entreaty.'

'Indeed,' said the king, 'I should be very pleased.'

He went to the lady, and entreated her, until she remained, as though reluctantly. In the morning the king went away on one side and Galehot on the other, and each went away to his land. The story falls silent about the king and his party at this point, though, and says no more about them, returning instead to Galehot and his companion, although it says little about them here.

[M. LIIIa] The story says that Galehot journeyed, with his companion, until they arrived in the land of which he was the lord. This was the land of Sorelois, which lies between Wales and the Remote Isles.* This land was not Galehot's by heritage, but he had won it by force from King Gloier, a nephew of the King of Northumberland, who had been killed in the war, and had left a small, very beautiful daughter, whose mother had died in childbirth. Galehot was having her taken care of with great honour until she was grown-up, and he was going to give her in marriage to his nephew, who was very small at the moment, and he had granted him the whole of Sorelois once he became a knight. It was the most agreeable land among the islands around Britain, and the best endowed with fine rivers and forests and fertile lands. It was not very far from King Arthur's land, and Galehot very much liked staying there, for he dearly loved the pleasures of hawk and hound. And he went there more often, because the kingdom of Logres was nearer to there than to the Remote Isles, his other land.*

On the side of King Arthur's land, the kingdom of Sorelois was entirely enclosed by a single stretch of water, which was very swift-running and wide and deep, and was called Assurne. And on the other side it was entirely surrounded by the sea. Then there were castles and cities with strong walls, and agreeable [357] woods and mountains,* and there were many other rivers in the land, most of which ran into Assurne, which ran into the sea, so that no one could enter Sorelois from King Arthur's land without first crossing Assurne. It was not fresh water, for one end came out of the sea, and the other end ran into the sea.* Thus the land of Sorelois was enclosed on the side of the kingdom of Logres. And for the knight errant there were only two crossings, and there were no more as long as the adventures* lasted in the kingdom of Logres and in the surrounding islands, and they lasted, the book says, one thousand, six hundred and ninety weeks.* These two crossings were very terrible and difficult, for each consisted of a high and narrow causeway, which was no more than three toises wide, and more than seven thousand long,* and below the water, in some places, there were more than seventy toises.* That is what both the causeways were like. At the end of each one, on the Sorelois side, was a tall, strong tower; and in each tower there was a knight, the best who could be found, and ten men-at-arms with axes and swords and lances. They were in the towers in this way to win honour and renown and because they expected great rewards for it. If a stranger knight came to the causeway to cross over, he had to fight with the knight and the ten men-at-arms. If he could cross over by force, then his name was written down in the tower, and for ever afterwards he could cross without fighting; and if he was defeated, he remained in the power of the knight and the ten men-at-arms who guarded the causeway. And they had to maintain this guard for a whole year. And the story says that, at the time when Merlin foretold the adventures which were going to happen, King Lohot, King Gloier's father, who was lord of Sorelois at that time, had these two causeways made, because he was afraid his land would be destroyed. None the less, before the adventures began to happen, there many other crossings over the water, wooden ones and ferries. As soon as they began, though, these were all destroyed, so that afterwards no stranger knights ever crossed except by the two causeways.

It was in this land, which is so enclosed and unassailable, that Galehot went to stay, with his companion and the other members of his household; however, he had less of a retinue than usual, for he was keeping to himself as far as he could, so that no one should be aware of his feelings; and no one knew his companion's name except the two kings who had been his surety.

[358] Thus they stayed a long while in Sorelois, and had a good deal of sport, river-fowling and hunting. However, no sport pleased Lancelot, for he could not see her to whom he belonged completely, and he thought of nothing else. And Galehot, who was very anxious about his unhappiness, comforted him a good deal and said that he should not be dismayed, for they would soon hear some news of encounters.

Within a month of their arrival there the Lady of the Lake

sent a squire to Lancelot and sent him word to retain him in his service until he wished to be a knight. Lancelot retained him willingly and made much of him and held him very dear, because his damsel sent him word to hold him as dear as his own self. And he did so, for he did not love or listen to any squire as much, and Galehot rejoiced greatly over the squire, who was very valorous and handsome, and Lancelot's cousin, the son of King Bors of Gaunes, who had been Lancelot's uncle and King Ban's brother. And when Lancelot knew who he was,* he loved him even more, for the friendship of his kinsman made him forget a great part of his troubles, and the cousins made a great fuss of one another.

The squire was called Lionel, because of an extraordinary thing which happened at his birth, for as soon as he came out of the body of Evainne, his mother, she found a red mark on his chest in the shape of a lion, and the baby grasped it by the neck with both hands as though to strangle it. This thing was observed with astonishment. And for that reason the baby was called Lionel, and he later did many deeds of high prowess, as the story of his life reveals; and the mark on his chest lasted for a long time, until one day when he killed the crowned lion of Libya* at King Arthur's court: it had been brought to the king, because no such lion had ever been seen at his court. And Sir Yvain carried the skin of that lion on his shield,* for Lionel gave it to him when he had killed it, as the story of his deeds relates. And the mark never showed on his chest again after that. Lancelot made much of his cousin. With that, though, the story now falls silent about Galehot, and says no more about him at this point, returning instead to King Arthur, who had repaired to his land.

{Summary of pp. [359–530].}
[358–65] [M. LIVa] King Arthur goes to Carlisle, to hold court and dispense justice. Sir Gawain soon recovers from his wounds, although he is never quite the same again. The

queen and the Lady of Malohaut talk together of their loves, and plan to organise an encounter.

One evening, at table, King Arthur falls into a reverie. Kay remarks on this to Sir Gawain, who sends his cousin, Lore of Carlisle, to ask the king what he is thinking about. He replies that they should not ask, but Sir Gawain sends her to ask again. Arthur says that he is thinking of his knights' great dishonour: they swore to find the knight who bore red arms, and not to return without news of him. They broke their oath when they returned to help him against Galehot.

Gawain says that the king is quite right, and should not keep them with him. He swears not to return to court until he has found the knight. Half of the original forty questers follow his example; the other twenty are not at court. The king regrets his words, and asks the queen to persuade Gawain to stay. Nothing can persuade him, however. The queen tells him, privately, that the knight he has to find is Lancelot, and that he will find him with Galehot. The twenty knights set off, having agreed that they are also questing on behalf of the other twenty.

[366–71] [M. LVa] After riding for three days, Gawain meets four knights together. One comes to joust with him, but stops at the last minute: it is Sagremor. The others are Sir Yvain, Kay, and Girflet. Travelling together, they come to a valley, in which there is a solitary pine-tree, beside a spring. They see a squire ride up to it, with a bundle of lances, which he leaves by the tree. He also leaves a black shield with white spots hanging in the tree.

The five companions wait in concealment, and see a knight arrive and drink at the spring. He sees the shield, and begins to lament terribly. Then he becomes as happy as he was sad, and then sad again. This alternation continues for some time.

Sagremor challenges the knight to explain his behaviour. He refuses, exchanges his shield for that on the tree, and unhorses Sagremor when they joust. The same fate befalls

Kay and Girflet, and then Yvain. Gawain is about to try his hand, when a dwarf arrives, on horseback, and belabours the knight with a stick. The knight makes no attempt to resist or to escape. The dwarf then leads him away. Intrigued, Gawain decides to follow them until he finds out what is going on.

[372–93] [M. LVIa] Gawain follows their tracks until terce the next day, when he comes to a pavilion. Riding in, he sees a beautiful damsel with two attendant maidens. He greets her, and she says that she returns his greeting, unless he is one of the coward knights who let the other knight be beaten by the dwarf. Gawain asks her about the knight and his behaviour, but she will not tell him: she is convinced he is one of the 'coward knights'.

While they are speaking, the dwarf enters and kills Gawain's horse with a spear. Gawain seizes him, and threatens to kill him unless he tells him who the knight is, why he behaved so strangely, and why he beat him. The dwarf agrees, provided that Gawain will undertake to fight the knight—or a better knight—in a just cause. Gawain agrees, and the dwarf sends one of the maidens to fetch the knight.

The knight is called Hector. The damsel is the dwarf's niece, the daughter of a dead nobleman. She and Hector love one another, but the dwarf, Groadain, who is her guardian, has said that they must wait for his consent.

The lady of the land, the Lady of Roestoc, has been at war with Segurades, a redoubtable knight. He wishes to marry her, but she has refused him. Finding the war going against her, she adopted the solution proposed by her uncle: a year's respite, during which time Segurades must fight any knight she sent against him. If any of them defeated him, he and his land would be at her disposition. If, on the other hand, he remained undefeated, the lady would have to marry him. Segurades agreed to these conditions, and set guards at all the ways into the country, to keep away knights errant.

Hector and Groadain's niece were impatient to be

together, but Groadain said that they must wait until the end
of the year agreed between Segurades and the lady. His niece
asked Hector if he would fight Segurades for her. He said
that he would willingly do so, but she forbade him to fight
without her permission. He felt he could defeat Segurades,
and so avoid having to wait until the end of the year. His
ladylove forbade it, and had the black shield with white spots
made, telling him that if he disobeyed her, he would have to
carry it until he was back in her favour.

Hector dreamed that he was victorious in a knightly
encounter at the pine-tree. His lady said that that was absurd,
and that no knight could defeat Segurades, but he went there
all the same. Groadain was told, and sent a squire there first
with the shield and lances. Seeing the shield, Hector realized
that he had offended his lady, and that was the cause of his
lamentation. His rejoicing came from the thought of defeating
Segurades, and so being able to have his lady.

Groadain reminds Gawain (of whose identity he is
unaware) that he has promised to fight Hector or a better
knight, but he is afraid that he will run away, as he is clearly
the worst knight in the world. Gawain makes no reply. They
eat, and a maiden arrives with a letter for Groadain from the
Lady of Roestoc, who is a vassal of King Arthur.

The letter asks Groadain to go in haste to Arthur's court,
and bring back Sir Gawain to be the lady's champion against
Segurades. Groadain is scathing: the end of the year is so
near that he could barely reach court before then, and in any
case, Sir Gawain is hardly ever there. Instead, he will take
her the worst knight who ever carried a shield. Gawain does
not react to his insults, but Hector is displeased. They all set
off, and Hector's lady makes him promise not to fight without
her permission.

The next day, at the edge of the Lady of Roestoc's land,
they meet two knights and three men-at-arms. Groadain tells
Hector that these are Segurades's men, and that he will have

to deal with them by himself, as Gawain will be no more use than a chamber-maid. Hector obtains his lady's permission to fight, and then drives off the five opponents.

Next they meet three knights and five men-at-arms. Groadain again insults Gawain; Hector again fights and is victorious, impressing Gawain. Finally, at a bridge, they are confronted by a single knight, and thirty men-at-arms with lances. Despite the dwarf's taunts, Hector asks Gawain to help him, if need be. He then defeats the entire group unaided.

They spend the night in a castle belonging to the Lady of Roestoc, to whom Groadain sends a messenger to say that he is bringing her Hector and the worst knight in the world. He also adds a private message that the lady should prevail upon his niece to let Hector fight Segurades.

The lady comes to meet them, and tells Groadain's niece, who is her cousin, that she is counting on her help: she must let Hector fight. Hector's ladylove refuses, saying that she would not allow it even if Hector were fully armoured, and Segurades had no armour at all. The lady despairs, but her seneschal points out that another knight[1] is there to help her, and she should welcome him, for they do not know his worth. She does so, and he says that he will be glad to fight for her.

They reach Roestoc, where Gawain's composure and care of his harness create a favourable impression. Hector feels that he must be a good knight, but decides it would not be polite to ask his name. The combat is to take place in three days.

On the day, the seneschal suggests that the lady give Gawain some token, as this may inspire him in the fight. She gives him a gold chain and clasp. He tells her not to worry; overhearing this, Groadain laughs scornfully, and says that he must be drunk or stupid.

[1] i.e. Gawain.

As they go to meet Segurades, Gawain is so calm that the seneschal tells the lady he must be a man of valour, and they should have asked his name. The lady rides forward to do so, but Gawain, having overheard, forestalls her by exacting a promise that she will not ask his name for a week.*

Segurades arrives. He is a very big man, and expresses his unconcern over the coming combat. Even if Gawain, the son of Lot, were there, he says, he would be victorious. This angers Gawain, but he says nothing.

The fight is long and hard. Towards noon, Segurades begins to gain the upper hand, as this is the time when Gawain's strength always wanes.* Then it increases, and Segurades is appalled to find his opponent as fresh and vigorous as he was at the beginning of the fight. He continues to resist for a long time, however, until Gawain eventually knocks him down and removes his helm, when he surrenders.

He is led away, and the lady and most of the spectators follow, out of curiosity. Left alone, Gawain rides off towards the forest. A squire follows his tracks, and comes upon him fighting a knight in the valley. He has ripped the knight's helm off, and is hitting him with it. The knight surrenders, and Gawain sends him as a prisoner to the Lady of Roestoc.

Gawain's absence is noted. Hector and forty others are about to set out to look for him when the defeated knight arrives. He is Segurades's nephew. He describes how he ambushed Gawain, and the disdainful ease with which he was defeated. Hector and the others leave.

The squire catches up with Gawain, and persuades him to stay the night at his castle, which is not far away. They go there by back ways. Hector and the others follow their tracks until it is too dark, and then turn back. The lady blames Groadain and his insults for Gawain's departure. She decides to go to court to seek news of him, with Segurades, Hector and his lady, her seneschal, and Groadain. The latter will be dragged behind her horse at every town they come to, and this will continue until they have news of Gawain.

[394–6] [M. LVIIa] When Gawain's wounds have been tended, the squire, Helain of Taningues, asks his help. He is a nobleman, and well old enough to be a knight. Twelve years earlier, he dreamed that Sir Gawain twisted his nose, but said that he would make it up to him. He told his mother, who made him promise to be knighted by Sir Gawain, and no one else. Since then, he has been to court five times—the last time only days ago—without ever finding Sir Gawain there. The Lady of Roestoc, his suzerain, now insists that he be knighted. He asks Gawain to perform the ceremony.

Gawain does so in the morning, and delights Helain by telling him who he is. Helain asks if he may keep Gawain's armour, and give him his own. Gawain agrees. He gives the Lady of Roestoc's token to Helain's sister, who tended his wounds, and sets off for North Wales, to find Galehot.

[396–406] [M. LVIIIa] The Lady of Roestoc reaches court, and tells the king and queen her story. When she describes her anonymous champion, Guinevere says that it sounds like Sir Gawain, at which the lady is very upset.

Groadain asks the queen to intervene to end his ill-treatment. She does so, and is told by the lady that her real aim is to induce her cousin to help her uncle, Groadain, by sending Hector to look for her champion. Groadain asks his niece, but she refuses. The queen then tricks her into swearing to send Hector, but even then she will not do so. No amount of duress or persuasion can shift her, even when Hector himself asks her.

A knight with a broken arm arrives at court, with a damsel, who is carrying a strange shield. He has a message for the queen from a knight who defeated him in a joust: she did him half a service,* and he will do the same for her.

The shield comes from the Lady of the Lake. It will free the queen from her greatest sorrow, and give her the greatest joy. It is split completely in two, only the boss holding the two halves together. It shows a lady and a knight embracing, but they are separated by the split. The damsel explains: the best knight in the world asked for, and received, the love of the most noble lady. As yet, though, there is no more to their love than kissing and embracing: when it is complete, the two halves of the shield will join together.

The knight is pleased to find the Lady of Roestoc at court, as he also has a message for her. The knight who defeated Segurades sends her word that, if she needs him, he will ignore her, as she did him. He sends the knight with the broken arm as a prisoner to her seneschal, in gratitude for his courtesy, and also sends Hector a sword. He has given away the lady's token, as he feels no obligation to remember her. The lady is desolate, having fallen in love with her champion since his departure.

More pressure is put on Groadain's niece, who finally consents to let Hector go, while still refusing actually to send him. She is dissuaded from going with him. He swears to seek the knight for a year, and not to return before then without proof of having found him. The queen retains him as one of her knights, and he sets off for North Wales, where the knight with the broken arm was defeated.

[407–9] [M. LIXa] The queen has the shield hung in her chamber. Subsequently, she takes it with her wherever she goes. A squire brings Sir Gawain's battered shield to court. This causes some concern, but he brings greetings from Helain of Taningues, who sends word to the Lady of Roestoc that he has been knighted, and by Sir Gawain. He confirms that the latter was her champion.

[409–25] [M. LXa] Gawain arrives in the duchy of Cambenic. He meets a damsel, who is carrying a sword. She says that she will not stop, as she is looking for the best knight she knows of, bar one. Intrigued, Gawain wishes to know who the two knights are. She takes him to a fortified house in the forest, saying that he will find out their names inside. The sword is for the knight she is looking for.

Inside, Gawain fights, and defeats, a knight, and then a second. Still following the damsel from one room to another, he has to fight with two more. A second damsel appears, and calls on him to win her. He knocks one knight down, and then stands, raptly looking at the damsel, while the other attacks him. Only when he is wounded does he react and defeat the second knight.

He asks if he has done enough to win the damsel, and if he may now know the names of the two knights. The answer to both questions is, not yet. He is taken to yet another chamber, in which ten knights guard a bed. If he wishes to see what is under the coverlet of the bed, he must fight all the knights afterwards. He agrees, and is shown a knight lying on the bed. He is handsome and well made, but very ill: his left arm and right leg are horribly swollen.

Now Gawain must fight the ten knights. The damsel who brought him there suggests that he give up a helmful of blood instead, but he says he would rather fight forty knights, on principle.

He fights, killing one opponent and crippling two others, and gets his back against a door. Then the door opens, and the damsel he seeks to win reaches through and grasps his sword-hand. She wants the sword, and will not let go, although the others are attacking him. Rather than hurt her, he relinquishes his sword. He knocks down an opponent, whose sword he takes. The damsel returns and takes that one, also. Gawain remarks that she is less of a prize than he thought, but hands over the sword anyway. He manages to wrest another from an opponent, and asks the damsel to let him keep it: he will soon give her all the rest, if she wants them. She laughs, and stops the fighting. Gawain says that she should have let him deal with his four remaining opponents.

She says that he is her prisoner, and must ransom himself by giving the blood. He refuses, until she tells him that the sick man can only be healed by having his arm anointed with the blood of the best knight in the world, and his leg with that of the next best.

While he is being bled, and having his wounds treated, Gawain is recognized by a squire. It is his younger brother, Mordred. The sick knight, whose leg is healed by Gawain's blood, is his brother Agravain.

Agravain tells Gawain why he is there, and how he came to be sick. The damsel is the daughter of the King of North Wales. She called on Agravain to take her away, as her father wished her to marry someone else. He brought her to this house. One day, out hunting, he fell asleep in the forest. Two damsels, who had suffered from his actions, came and anointed his arm and leg with ointments. As they were leaving, they decided to at least set a limit to his sickness, by allowing the blood cure.

The damsel reproaches Agravain: she had told him to send for Gawain, but he maintained that there were many better knights. She then tells Gawain that she has a younger sister who has vowed to surrender her maidenhood to no one but him. As a result, her father has her closely guarded.

The damsel who led him to the house says that he is one of the two knights she meant, and the knight who was victorious at the encounter is the other. The sword was sent to Gawain by Agravain, to give to some worthy young knight, since the inscription on it states that, while it will continually deteriorate, its wielder will continually improve. Gawain says he knows of someone to give it to, and tells them Lancelot's name.

Gawain asks about the two damsels who caused Agravain's sickness. His brother believes they were the ladyloves of a knight whom he injured, and a damsel he offended by refusing her favours.

Gawain sets off again. He meets a knight who jousts with all comers, trying to win his lady's love. They joust several times, until finally Gawain knocks him down, breaking his arm. He takes Gawain to a crossroads, to set him on the road to North Wales. There they meet the damsel with the split shield. She will tell Gawain nothing about it, and she and the knight set off for court together.*

[425–72] [M. LXIa] Hector comes upon a damsel, who is cradling a wounded knight's head in her lap. Lost in thought of his ladylove, he nearly rides over them, but a squire strikes his horse. Hector is apologetic, and offers the damsel his services. She says she will guide him to his immediate destination: the spot where the knight with the broken arm left Gawain.

She leads him in the wrong direction, but denies that she is doing so. She tells him the wounded knight was attacked by his cousin, Guinas of Blakestan. He had lain down to sleep, quite innocently, in the same bed as Guinas's ladylove, in a pavilion. Guinas arrived, fully armed, and wounded him severely, without any warning.

They come to the pavilion in question, where they find Guinas's ladylove crying. Guinas and Hector quarrel, Hector being polite, and Guinas rude. Hector suggests that he arm, but Guinas refuses, saying that he would not even need his shield to defeat Hector. He puts on his helm, takes sword, shield, and lance, and they joust. Hector is careful not to injure him with his lance, but knocks him down, and then forces him to beg for mercy after a swordfight. Guinas says that things would be different if he were allowed to arm, and asks Hector to let him do so.

Hector agrees, having ascertained that Guinas's ladylove is crying because he is rejecting her. He reproaches him for this, and they fight again, whereupon Hector is the victor once more. The damsel who led him there tells him to cut off Guinas's head. He is only dissuaded from doing so when

Guinas's lady intervenes and persuades the damsel to relent. He makes Guinas swear to do whatever his wounded cousin wishes, and reconciles him with his lady.

Guinas gives Hector a squire as a guide. They meet the Lord of Falerne, with a large troop. He is caught in the middle of the war between the Duke of Cambenic and the King of North Wales, as he holds land from both. Hector easily defeats two of his men who joust with him, and declines the lord's offer of hospitality.

Having spent the night with the squire's father, he reaches his destination the next day. This is the place where the last news of Sir Gawain came from. He learns that Gawain took the road towards North Wales.

He sees three knights leading away a damsel, clearly against her will. She jumps from her horse and runs away, and Hector is able to catch up with the knights while they are recapturing her. He kills one, wounds another, and puts the third to flight. He takes the damsel to a castle, where they meet a squire, who tells her that her husband, Synados of Windsor, is engaged in fighting seventeen opponents with only three companions. Hector goes to help him.

Reaching the fight, he kills the leader of Synados's enemies. With his help, the four knights put the remainder to flight. They return to the castle, where they meet the rest of Synados's men, who have also been fighting. Synados persuades Hector to stop the night with him, and explains why they were fighting.

The next day, Hector comes to a strong castle, known as the Estroite Marche, around which the land has been laid waste. Going in, he finds that he cannot then leave. Everyone he sees runs away, and upon enquiring, he is told that this is because they are afraid he will ask them for lodging, and he can only be lodged in the tower of the great hall.

Reluctant to stay there against his will, Hector finds an axe, and begins to hack at the gate. A squire admonishes him not to do so, and steals his horse when he takes no notice. Hector admits defeat, and goes to the tower, where he is reproached for his conduct by the lord of the castle, who is an old man, and other knights. When he tells them that he is the queen's knight, all is forgiven. The lord of the castle tells him that he is a vassal of King Arthur, and explains the custom and the reason for it.

He has three powerful neighbours, who frequently attack him. They are the King of North Wales and the Duke of Cambenic, who are at present busy with their war, and the King of a Hundred Knights. The latter's seneschal, Marganor, is attacking him at the moment.

He has only a daughter to succeed him, and wishes her to marry a man powerful and valiant enough to defend the castle. The townspeople put pressure on him to find her a husband, and made him institute the custom: any knight passing through must spend the night in the castle, and fight for them against their enemies the next morning. On leaving, he must swear to side with them against their enemies at all times.

He tells Hector that, the previous week, Sir Yvain and Sagremor were captured by his enemies. Following the custom, they were fighting for him against Marganor, and were captured when they ventured across a small bridge over the marsh. The bridge links an area of ground in front of the castle with the land beyond the marsh, where the besiegers are encamped.

The next day, Hector goes out to fight, committing himself to go no further than the small bridge. He unhorses three knights, who are captured by the defenders. When he goes out again, a knight waits the other side of the bridge, and challenges him to fight. Neither is prepared to cross the bridge, but Hector obtains the permission of the lord of the castle to do so, it being first agreed that Hector will have nothing to fear from the rest of Marganor's men.

Marganor's plan is to have the bridge destroyed while Hector is fighting, trapping him on the wrong side of the marsh. The two knights joust, and unhorse one another. Hector recovers first, and sees the men breaking up the bridge. He attacks them, and crosses back over. Marganor reproaches him, and Hector justifies his actions. Marganor then agrees to let the fight continue. Hector is victorious.

Marganor formally accuses Hector of breaking their agreement, and challenges him to defend himself by combat. They agree to fight on the patch of ground between the castle and the bridge. Once Marganor had crossed, the bridge is to be destroyed, to safeguard Hector from treachery.

The fight duly takes place, and lasts a long time.* Twice, Hector drives Marganor to the edge of the marsh, and then lets him move away to safety. Then, having knocked him into the marsh, he pulls him out, and Marganor surrenders. They go to the castle, where Hector is welcomed, and cared for by the lord's daughter.

The bridge is rebuilt, and Hector has Marganor send for Yvain and Sagremor. From the description of his shield, they are able to tell him that the knight he is seeking is Sir Gawain. Peace is made between the lord of the castle and Marganor.

The lord mentions marriage, and Hector puts him off. During the night, the lord's daughter comes to his bedside, to ask why he will not marry her, and exacts from him a promise that he will only marry for love. She is delighted, as she expects to make him love her. When he leaves, she gives him an enchanted ring, which makes any man to whom it is given love the woman who gives it to him more and more, if he loves her in the first place.*

Hector sets off for North Wales, with Yvain and Sagremor. They see a knight abducting a damsel, and another fighting with two knights. Sagremor wishes there were a third adventure, whereupon they hear a great lamentation behind them.

Hector goes to investigate this, while Sagremor goes to help the knight, and Yvain the damsel.

Hector sees a large group of people around a bier, grieving. He asks a dwarf what is happening, but receives no answer. The dwarf says that Hector will have to strike him if he wishes to know anything, and eventually goads him into doing so. Hector learns that the dead man in the bier is Synados's enemy, whom he killed. He realizes it will mean trouble if he goes on past, but is reluctant to turn back from his quest.

Riding up to the bier, he greets the mourners. As he passes, however, the dead man's wounds begin to bleed afresh.* The dwarf cries to the mourners to seize Hector, who is attacked by some twenty knights, though none of them is fully armed. While they are fighting, a knight arrives with a damsel: it is Ladomas, the knight who was wounded by Guinas of Blakestan. The damsel who took Hector to fight Guinas tells Ladomas who Hector is, and he calls off the knights. They inform him that Hector killed his brother, Mataliz—the dead man in the bier. Ladomas tells Hector he may leave in safety, but gives him no such guarantee if they meet again.

The dwarf sends a squire ahead of Hector. The squire is to pretend to guide him to North Wales, but to lead him to a nearby spring, persuade him to dismount and drink, and then steal his horse. This he duly does, taking Hector's helm and shield as well. Hector gives chase on the squire's hack, and is led to the castle of Mataliz's father. There the dwarf and the knights accuse him of treacherously killing Mataliz. Furious, Hector kills the squire, and snatches up a shield, ready to defend himself. Ladomas arrives, and he and his father persuade Hector to become their prisoner, on condition that he will be allowed to defend himself against the charge. The story returns to Galehot.

[472-3] [M. LXIIa] Lancelot is pining: he hardly eats, drinks or sleeps. Galehot says that he will send a message to

the queen, asking her to arrange for them to see her. He sends Lionel, with instructions to tell no one, on his journey, whom he serves or where he is going.

[473–93] [M. LXIIIa] Sir Gawain meets a clerk, who is on his way to a hermitage near the castle of Leverzerp. He invites Gawain to accompany him, as the hermitage is the only shelter in the area. Gawain accepts, and is welcomed by the hermit, who asks who he is, and then whether Arthur has sent him because of the North Wales–Cambenic war. Gawain tells him his name, and that he is going to Galehot's land, looking for the best knight in the world, Lancelot of the Lake.

The hermit tells him that there is to be an encounter the next day between the Duke of Cambenic and the King of North Wales, and that the king, who is in the wrong, has the greater numbers. Also that the duke is having the better of the war, except that his son was killed.

The next day, he asks why Gawain is seeking Lancelot, and then tells him that his niece (the damsel with the split shield, who is also Lancelot's cousin) came by a short time before, and told him that Lancelot is in Sorelois. He tells Gawain how to get there, and sends the clerk to guide him as far as Leverzerp, which is on the way.

When they are in sight of the castle, Gawain sends the clerk back. As he draws nearer, he sees a great number of knights fighting, and a lone knight, watching from the sidelines. Gawain is reluctant to join in, as he does not know which side is the weaker.

Meanwhile, the clerk has circled round into the castle, and is watching, hoping to see Sir Gawain joust. He finds the duke's brother, who has just come in from the fighting, and points out Sir Gawain, saying that if he will join their side, they are assured of victory. The duke's brother goes to Gawain and asks him to join them: they are outnumbered, and in the right. Gawain agrees to help, and suggests that he ask the other lone knight, for one man of valour is a great asset.

The duke's brother does so, and is asked whether he has made the same request to Gawain. On hearing that he has, and that it is Sir Gawain, the knight laughs, and says that in that case they will not need him; it is Girflet, who assumes that this is in fact some knight passing himself off as Gawain. He tells the duke's brother that he will join the other side, and to pass that on to Sir Gawain. This he does, but without revealing either that he told the other Gawain's identity, or that he is aware of it.

Gawain goes to attack a group of fresh knights. Intercepted by Girflet, he knocks him down, and then goes on to attack the others. Girflet realizes that it must indeed be Gawain, and goes to help him. When Gawain breaks a rein, and has briefly to stop fighting, Girflet asks him who he is, and then reveals his own identity. While they are talking, the king's men regain the upper hand, but they return to the fray, and put the enemy to flight. Night brings an end to the pursuit, and Gawain and Girflet leave quietly together.

They meet two damsels, who are clearly expecting them. The knights disarm, and each asks a damsel for her love. Girflet is successful, while Gawain's damsel promises him a far more beautiful ladylove than her. He is incredulous, and wishes to know the identity of this lady. The damsel will not tell him, but assures him that her lady desires his love, and that she will take him to her.

Leaving Girflet with his new love, they ride off, and come to a fire, where another damsel and two squires are waiting. They put Gawain to bed in a pavilion.

The next day, the damsel sends the squires on to her lady with a message and says that she will take Gawain to her with all possible secrecy. They reach her aunt's house, where they are to spend the night, before travelling on to her lady the next day.

While they are there, news reaches the aunt that her husband is to be executed by the Duke of Cambenic, his lord, who believes that he betrayed his son. Her husband's accuser, the duke's seneschal, is so redoubtable a warrior that no one will act as champion for her husband, who is too old to fight. The accused, Manessel, is to die the next day, but there is still time for him to find a champion. Gawain offers his services, warning the aunt to say simply that he is 'a knight'. She goes to inform the duke.

As Gawain mounts his horse, the next day, an arrow pierces the skirt of his hauberk, and hits his horse. He duly complains to the duke, who is very embarrassed. It is discovered that the bowman was the seneschal's brother, and the duke has him hanged.

Manessel and the seneschal both swear that their cause is just, and the combat begins. The first joust is inconclusive, and the fight continues on horseback, with swords. It is long and hard.

[493–515] [M. LXIVa] Lionel happens by, on his way to court, and stops to watch the fight. Pressing forward on his horse, he upsets a knight, and they exchange rude words. Lionel says angrily that the knight is welcome to watch the fight: he knows a better knight than either of these. Gawain hears this, and also notices that Lionel refers to Galehot's wealth, when stating that the two combatants and the knight he offended, all together, would not wish to take on the knight he knows.

Gawain is preoccupied with this, and the damsel who is accompanying him calls to him, by name, to make an effort. Lionel does not believe it is Sir Gawain, who would surely not take so long to defeat one man in front of so many people. Gawain regains the upper hand.

A veiled damsel talks to Lionel, who upsets her. It is Saraide.* Wishing him to go, she calls to Gawain that Lionel could help him in his quest. Lionel hurries off, while Gawain brings the combat to a speedy conclusion. He cuts off the seneschal's head: he is in a hurry, and in any case the man's life is forfeit. He rides after Lionel, telling the damsel to wait for him there.

He meets Lionel on foot, lamenting bitterly. Seeing him, Lionel rushes into the forest, but Gawain calls him back, telling him who he is, that he knows he serves Lancelot, and that he has nothing to fear. Lionel explains that a knight on foot took his hack: he would have resisted, but a squire should not gainsay a knight. Gawain promises to recover it, or give Lionel his own horse instead.

Following the horse's tracks, Gawain finds two knights on foot, fighting. He recognizes Lionel's hack, which is tethered nearby. Ascertaining which knight took it, he demands that he come back and make amends to Lionel. The other says that he will not do so unless forced, and Gawain replies that that presents no difficulty. The third knight does not wish them to fight until he has finished fighting his opponent, but Gawain will not wait, in case the knight who took the horse should then be the other's prisoner. He offers to fight them both together. The third knight asks who he is, and the other identifies him as Manessel's champion in the recent combat, and says that he will do as Gawain wishes. Gawain tells the third knight his name.

Lionel's hack is returned to him, and he makes the knight swear never to molest an unarmed man, when he himself is armed. Gawain reconciles the two knights, who had no real quarrel, and asks Lionel about Galehot. Lionel tells him nothing, but does mention Sorelois, which leads Gawain to believe that Galehot is there. He returns to the castle, where the damsel is waiting.

They leave together the next day, and spend the night with the damsel's father. The following day, in a clearing in the forest, they come upon a lone knight, fighting vigorously against three others and five men-at-arms, although he has severely discouraged the latter. The damsel tells Gawain that the eight men serve the King of North Wales, and they should withdraw. However, she is delighted when Gawain suggests rather that he help the single knight. She pledges her love to the latter, because of his valour.

Gawain realizes that it is Sagremor, as he goes to his rescue. Together, they put the others to flight, and then exchange greetings and news. Sagremor is told that the damsel has pledged her love to him, and wishes to see her unveiled, before he accepts it. She reproaches him, but agrees, on condition that, if she does not like his face, she need not accept him, either. He laughs, and in fact each is delighted with the other.

They travel on together, and come to a fortified house. The damsel takes them inside, to a chamber, where they eat. Then she explains that the house belongs to the King of North Wales. Her mistress, who has pledged her love to Gawain, is his daughter. Now, the damsel says, she will take Gawain to see her. They pass through a stable, in which there are twenty black palfreys, then a room containing twenty goshawks, and then another stable, with twenty fine horses. These, she tells him, all belong to twenty knights, who sleep fully armed in the room next to the king's daughter, to keep Sir Gawain away.

Next she leads him to a square chamber, in which the twenty knights are sleeping. Gawain goes quietly through into the next chamber, and closes the door. Inside he finds a beautiful girl, asleep. He kisses her, and she wakes up, horrified. He tells her who he is, and she confirms this to her own satisfaction by checking his face against a likeness of him on her ring,* and then welcomes him enthusiastically. They make love, and then fall asleep.

Her father, the king, wakes in the night, and happening to open a window which looks into her room, sees Gawain in bed with his daughter. He tells the queen, and resolves to

hush the matter up, if possible. Calling two trusted chamber-
lains, he tells them to fetch a spear and a large mallet. One is
to place the spear over Gawain's heart, and the other is to
strike it with the mallet. This way, the king thinks, Gawain
will die silently, and no one else need know of his daughter's
disgrace.

They put this plan into execution, but Gawain's bare arm
happens to touch the head of the spear, as they are about to
strike. The cold steel wakes him, and he knocks the spear
aside at the last moment. He then seizes it, and kills both
men.

The queen raises the alarm, and Gawain bolts the doors to
the chamber, and then arms. The twenty knights call on the
daughter to open the door, but she refuses. At her suggestion,
she and Gawain douse the candles, and he then hides in a
recess, while she opens both doors. The knights rush in,
assume that Gawain has gone out through the king's quarters,
and rush out that way. Gawain kills the last one, and the
others come back. He waits, just inside the chamber they
were sleeping in; the doorway is narrow, and only one knight
can pass through at a time. Gawain kills the first one who
tries, and the others dare not follow.

Gawain adopts the same tactic, moving from room to room,
until he reaches the room with the horses, where Sagremor
already has two mounts saddled. More knights arrive, and
the fighting becomes fierce. From the walls, Sagremor's
ladylove calls to them to leave, and then lets down a portcullis
behind them. Shortly afterwards, she rejoins them, with two
squires and the companions' own horses. She says that the
king's daughter will be in no danger, as her father dotes on
her, but she herself will have to leave. She will go, with
Sagremor, to Agravain and her mistress's sister. She sends
one squire with Gawain, to guide him to Sorelois.

[516–24] [M. LXVa] News of Hector's captivity reaches
those variously indebted to him, and they set off to go to his

assistance. Meanwhile, a niece of Ladomas's father asks for Hector's help in freeing her sister from captivity. She wishes him to fight 'the best knight in the world'. The choice is his. Ascertaining that it is not one of Arthur's companions, Hector agrees, and the charge against him is forgotten.

Hector and the niece set off, and meet Synados and two thousand men (including those sent by the Lord of the Estroite Marche and Marganor), coming to his rescue. Hector thanks Synados and sends greetings to all those who have sent men, and to the wife of Synados and the daughter of the Lord of the Estroite Marche.

That evening, Hector asks his guide about the task facing him. She tells him about her sister, Helen, who is so beautiful that she is known as the Peerless. One Persides, a very valiant knight, and more noble than Helen, took her as his lady, against the wishes of both sets of relations. One day, an uncle reproached Persides, saying that he had abandoned knightly ways because of Helen, and was being mocked by everyone, as a result. Hearing this, Helen reacted angrily, saying that she, too, had abandoned society for Persides, which was a greater loss, as she was more beautiful than he was valiant.

Furious, Persides locked her in a tower, saying that she would never leave until her words were proved true or false. If a better knight than him ever came there, she would be free to go; while, if a more beautiful woman came, he would abandon her.

Helen has been in the tower, her sister says, for five years. In that time, Persides's relations have brought every beautiful woman they could find, but to no avail. For her part, she has been to court twenty times, hoping to find Sir Gawain, but without success.

After spending the night with another sister, the pair reach Gazewilté, Persides's castle. Hector asks to see Helen, and finds her locked up. She is the most beautiful woman he has ever seen, and he says that she must be in the right, for no man's prowess could equal her beauty. She embraces him, for luck, and he goes to meet Persides.

Hector reproaches Persides, saying that he is in the wrong: even if Helen were the wife of Sir Gawain, the best knight in the world, she would still be more beautiful than he was valiant. He suggests Persides give up the whole business and take her back, but he will not.

They fight, and Hector unhorses Persides. He again asks him to reconsider, and Persides again refuses. He kills Hector's horse. The fight continues, and Hector knocks the sword from his hand. Still Persides will not relent. Only when Hector has torn off his helm and is actually about to cut off his head does he ask for mercy.

Hector obliges him to admit that Helen was right, and says that he must go to King Arthur, taking her with him, and tell the queen the whole story.

Hector frees Helen himself, and spends the night at Gazewilté. The next day, Helen's sister directs him to North Wales, and he sets off again.

[525] [M. LXVIa] Lionel finds the queen at Logres, and is welcomed by her and the Lady of Malohaut. He tells them of his encounter with Sir Gawain. They are debating how they can arrange to see Lancelot and Galehot when news reaches court that the Irish and the Saxons have invaded Scotland. They are laying waste the land, and besieging Arebech.

King Arthur sends out word for his people to meet in two weeks at Carlisle. The queen sends word to Lancelot and Galehot to be there, incognito. She sends Lancelot a pennon to wear on his helm, and tells him what shield to carry, so that she will know him. She also says that he should do whatever he can for Sir Gawain, short of going to the encounter with him.

Arthur asks the queen whether he should send for Galehot. She subtly replies that he should wait until he sees the extent

of the problem: it would not do to appear afraid for no
reason.

[526–8] [M. LXVIIa] Gawain reaches one of the causeways which lead to Sorelois. He changes horses, and sends
his squire away on the other horse. He is challenged by a
knight, who tells him what he must do, if he wishes to cross.
He is undeterred, saying that the only thing which worries
him is that if he is victorious, he must guard the causeway
until a replacement comes from Sorelois.

At their second joust, Gawain wounds the knight badly,
and he surrenders. The ten men-at-arms attack Gawain, and
kill his horse, but make no attempt actually to harm him.*
The squire, who had lingered to watch him fight, gallops up,
snatches up the shield and lance of the defeated knight, and
attacks them, yelling to them not to kill Sir Gawain, the best
knight in the world. He kills one, and the others run away.
One of them then returns to give the keys of the tower to
Gawain. His name is written down there: he is the first knight
to cross the causeway since the peace between Arthur and
Galehot, and only the fifth ever. The previous four were
King Arthur, King Yder, Dodinel, and Meliant de Lis.

[529–30] [M. LXVIIIa] Hector hears news of a knight
making for Sorelois. He meets the squire, whom Gawain has
just sent away again. Following Gawain's instructions, the
squire ascertains that he is from King Arthur's household,
and then tells him that Sir Gawain crossed into Sorelois the
previous day.

The next day, Hector goes to the causeway. Gawain sends
a man-at-arms to ask him if he wishes to cross. He then
comes to meet him, and asks if he is one of King Arthur's
companions. Hector says that he is not, and will accept the
conditions.

They joust together, and then fight for a long time with
their swords. Around midday, they pause, and wipe their
swords. Gawain recognizes the sword he sent to Hector, and

asks who he is. Hector tells him, whereupon Gawain takes off his helm and greets him. Hector is very sorry to have fought with him, but Gawain takes the blame, and says that he is defeated. Hector cannot accept that. The men-at-arms arrive, and each knight insists he is vanquished. The men-at-arms judge that Hector is the winner, as Gawain took his helm off first. Hector is very put out, but Gawain has his name added to the list of knights who have crossed by force of arms.

[M. LXIXa] Now the story says that at the time when Sir Gawain fought with the knight of the causeway, whom he wounded, and who admitted he was beaten, and when by his prowess he had so defeated the men-at-arms that they dared not move, then a squire went straight to Sorhaut, where Galehot and his companion were, in his residence, which was outside the town. And he told them that a knight had conquered the North Wales Causeway* (but he did not know his name) and all the men-at-arms also. When Galehot heard that, he was quite astonished, and told his companion that a knight errant had beaten one of the best knights in his land and ten men-at-arms. And Lancelot said, God grant that he come there.

'Why?' asked Galehot.

'Because, sir, we have been imprisoned here for a very long while, and it has been a long time since we saw jousting or knightly deeds, and we are wasting our time and our lives. As God is my true witness, if he comes, I shall fight with him.'

Galehot began to laugh, while those who heard him said that he was not very keen on resting. Then Galehot decided that, if he could, he would quite prevent him from fighting. He had a most excellent residence on an island in Assurne; it was at least half a league into the water in every direction, and it was called the Lost Island, because it was so far into the water and away from people. He decided that he would take Lancelot there. In the evening one of his knights asked to guard the causeway: his name was Helie of Ragres and he was a very good and very bold knight. Galehot agreed to that, and that very night he took his companion away to the Lost Island. And Helie went away to guard the causeway, and found Sir Gawain there. Helie treated him with great honour when he knew that he was Sir Gawain. Sir Gawain asked him, where was Galehot; and he said that he had no news of him.

'No?' he said. 'Is he not in Sorhaut?'

[532] 'Indeed,' said Helie, 'he left yesterday night at midnight, we do not know where for.'

Then Sir Gawain was very upset, for he was afraid his quest would be prolonged.

In the morning Sir Gawain took his leave and he and Hector left, since there was a guard on the bridge. And he told the wounded knight, who was still there, to go to King Arthur's court, by his oath, and to surrender to Queen Guinevere and tell her that he[1] had found Hector, and Hector him, and that as soon as he could, he would go to court, and that Hector would have gone if he had not kept him back so that they might go together. 'And tell me your name,' he said, 'for you know mine.' And he said his name was Elinant of the Isles.

Thereupon Elinant went to the king's court, in great discomfort, and related the news. The king was delighted, and the queen had his wounds tended. And later he became a member of King Arthur's household, for he was a very valorous knight. And when the queen heard that Hector had found Sir Gawain, she was delighted. Then she told his ladylove, who was delighted and greatly comforted by it— and no one had ever made her laugh or play since.[2] The king, though, was more upset than anyone that Sir Gawain

---

[1] i.e. Sir Gawain.   [2] i.e. since Hector's departure.

had not accomplished his quest, because of the great need facing him,* for he was always at a loss without him.

[M. LXXa] Now the story goes back to Lancelot, who was in the tower on the Lost Island, very upset and pensive, and very impatient to hear what word his lady would send him. He had quite stopped laughing and playing and eating and drinking, and nothing comforted him except thinking. And all day long he was up on top of the tower, looking up and down, very downcast.

It happened, the day after Sir Gawain and Hector had left the causeway, that they were riding haphazardly, and could hear no news of Galehot, until they met a damsel on a palfrey. Sir Gawain greeted her, and she greeted him, and asked him where they were going. And they said that they did not know where to find what they were looking for.

'And what is that?' she asked.

'We are looking for Galehot, damsel,' they said, 'the lord of this country, but we cannot find him.'

'I shall direct you to him,' she said, 'if you will grant me the first boon I ask you for.' And they promised to do so. 'Swear it to me,' she said. And they swore. 'Come with me,' she said.

[533] Then they went to a very high mountain, and from there she showed them the Lost Island. 'And let me tell you that he is in there with as few companions as possible.' Then the damsel left and commended them to God, and they her. And then they made straight for the island and saw, when they were near, that it was completely covered with tall, dense forest and that nothing showed there, excepting only the battlements and the roof of the tower, which was very tall.

'Ah! Lord,' said Sir Gawain, 'what a fine and imposing fortress that is, surrounded by that swift-running, wide, and roaring water. And there is only one way by which one can enter it, for I see that the drawbridge there is raised. And I do not know by what device or ruse we can set foot in there, for those inside are hiding and concealing themselves as much as they can.'

Thus they remained at the end of the bridge and waited in this manner to see if anyone would come out. Lancelot was up in the tower, pensive, and saw the two fully armed knights at the end of the bridge. He called Galehot and pointed them out to him; and Galehot sent a squire to see who they were, and what they wanted. 'But be sure', he said, 'that you do not say that I am here.' And he went, and asked them. Sir Gawain said they were two stranger knights, and would very much like to talk to Galehot.

'My lord,' the squire said, 'he is not there.'

'I know very well', Sir Gawain said, 'that he is there. But at least tell him that, if he wishes, we will talk to him, and if he does not wish, we will not. And if he does not wish to talk to us, we shall be here a good while. And let me tell you that he will lose everything which comes out of there. And you can tell him that it is very unworthy of him to have shut himself up on account of two knights.'

The squire went back and told his lord what had been said to him. Galehot considered it very arrogant, and said that he would soon see if they captured his things so easily. Then he had two of his best knights mount up, the very best he had bar three, and sent them to the two knights. 'And if they want a knightly encounter,' he said, 'take care that they do not go away disappointed.'

When Sir Gawain saw them coming, he said to Hector:

'We must fight, it appears, for we have met with the proudest and the best knights in the world. And you should know that the best knight in Britain is waiting on that island, and because of his prowess the knights of King Arthur's household [534] have undergone many hardships and much disgrace. He is the man I am seeking, and I knew that fine words would not get me in there, unless I sent them some outrageous message, and I would rather speak than act outrageously.'

Thereupon the two knights arrived. As soon as the bridge was lowered, they came across to Sir Gawain and Hector, and said that they must give themselves up as prisoners, or fight with them.

'I would rather be a prisoner, if it meant being in there.'

'You will never come in there,' said the knights, 'but we shall put you in prison in another place.'

'I shall not surrender yet,' said Sir Gawain, 'on those conditions. None the less, if there were only the two of you guarding the bridge, I should go in there today.'

'We shall see,' they said.

Then each pair charged towards the other as swiftly as their horses could go, and they struck one another on the shields. Sir Gawain knocked his man to the ground, both him and his horse, and Hector knocked his over his horse's crupper to the ground, so that Galehot and his companions said that the two knights jousted very well. Then Sir Gawain and Hector dismounted, and attacked the knights with drawn swords, but the one that Sir Gawain knocked down was helpless, for his horse was lying on him, so that it had nearly crushed his heart in his breast. Sir Gawain grasped him, and wrenched his helm from his head and lowered his ventail and said that he would cut his head off if he did not admit he was beaten. And he did so. And Hector also attacked his man very briskly, and found that he was badly wounded, for he[1] had broken one of his ribs through shield and hauberk, and a good deal of the lance-head and shaft had gone into him. All the same, the knight did his best to stand up; and Hector went over to him as he stood up, and struck him on the head, so that he completely stunned him and knocked him down again. And he defeated him in a very short time, and he begged for mercy and admitted he was beaten and swore to be his prisoner and surrendered his sword. And they asked

[1] i.e. Hector.

the two knights, by their oath, what company Galehot had inside; and they said, wherever Galehot might be, there were some of the best knights in the world inside, but Galehot was not there. And Sir Gawain did not ask them any more. Galehot was very upset at seeing his companions captured before his eyes, and asked for his arms. And Lancelot sprang forward and said that he should not arm himself on account of those two knights. 'I shall go, instead,' he said.

[535] 'And who will go with you?' asked Galehot.

'No one,' he said, 'until I see what happens.'

'Yes, by my head,' said Galehot, 'the King of a Hundred Knights will, for you are not going alone.'

Then they asked for arms, which were brought to them. When they were armed, Lancelot put Galehot's shield around his neck and went out off the island by the bridge. And Sir Gawain told the defeated knights to go wherever they thought they would be most comfortable. 'And come back here as my prisoners in three days' time.'

'We are not going,' they said, 'for we shall not be your prisoners that long. Soon we shall be rescued.'

Then Sir Gawain was sure that it was Lancelot who was coming with Galehot's arms, and he said so to Hector.

'Ah!' he said to Hector, 'here comes the best knight in the world. You joust with the one who is carrying the gold shield with the red lion, and I shall joust with the one who is carrying the gold shield with azure crowns. And, for the Lord's sake, let all the prowess you have ever had be present right now, for there was never such great need of it.'

And Hector bore himself very stoutly, for which Sir Gawain thought very highly of him. The knights came across, and at once each pair charged towards the other. And it happened that Sir Gawain and Lancelot knocked one another to the ground, the horses on top of them. And Hector jousted very fiercely, and knocked the King of a Hundred Knights down on the ground; and he threw away his lance. When the king sprang up, Hector could not restrain his horse, and it crashed into the king. The king was very strong, but even so he could not avoid falling back to the ground; and the horse caught its feet against him, and fell over him. Hector sprang to his feet, and reached for his sword. The king did the same, and they hacked one another's shields to pieces. Sir Gawain and Lancelot were also on their feet again, and gave one another very fine blows. The fight lasted a very long time, until Sir Gawain had much the worse of it, and it was between midday and one. And Hector had the better of his fight and was doing much as he pleased with the king. And because Galehot was afraid for him,[1] he came out, for he would very much have liked to separate them, if he knew how. When he arrived, he saw that Sir Gawain was suffering badly, both he and his armour, and the king even more so. And Sir Gawain fully expected to die, for he had never before been in such straits, for in many places one could have stuck one's fists through his hauberk, and [536] there was hardly anything left of his shield. And Lancelot, for his part, was not unscathed, for Sir Gawain's good sword had hurt him badly. Then Hector went to Sir Gawain and said:

'Sir, take this one, and hand that one over to me, for I shall be able to withstand that one, but mine is troubling me. But he will not be able to withstand you.'

'No, leave yours,' said Lancelot, 'and I shall fight the two of you.'

'No, do things properly,' said Hector. 'Let us fight, all four together.'

'There will be no fourth,' said Lancelot, 'but both of you fight with me.'

Then Hector decided that it would be considered cowardice if he did not first defeat his knight; so he charged at him and pressed him very hard and struck him where he wished.

---

[1] i.e. the king.

The king's sword broke in half, and he attacked Hector with his bare hands, for he was very strong, and threw Hector down under him.* However, he was quickly on his feet again, for he was very strong and nimble. And Sir Gawain had held out for a very long time, so that the time when he habitually grew weaker* was past, and he had got his breath back a little, and his strength began to double. And he said,* since it could not be otherwise, and he could only get to know the man he was seeking by fighting the battle to the end, so be it; and from now on let each man do his worst. And he remembered the words he had heard,* and he was distressed and ashamed. Then he attacked Lancelot so violently that Galehot was very frightened, for he now saw that his companion had by far the worse of it. And he knew that, if they fought together for long, one of them must die, for Sir Gawain was now fighting so fiercely that everyone was astonished. Hector was delighted, and laughed for joy; and he said that the battle could only bring them honour, for now he could see that they had the better of it.

At that moment, by God's will, Lionel arrived. When he saw Lancelot fighting, he did not recognize him, but he did recognize Sir Gawain by his arms,* although they were badly damaged. He asked Galehot, who was on the field, who it was that was fighting with his arms; and he said, very unhappily, that it was his companion.

'It is a pity the battle started,' he said,* 'for he will pay dearly for it.'

Then he[1] went forward, and Lancelot saw him, and was very ashamed that he had not defeated the knight long since. And it seemed to him that, when he saw him, the queen could see him, and he attacked him[2] very briskly, and he[2] him, as well or better, his strength doubled and still increasing. [537] And Lionel called to him, as he valued his life, to

---

[1] i.e. Lionel.   [2] i.e. Sir Gawain.

do no more until he had talked to him. And Lancelot withheld his blow and moved back. And Lionel told him that it was Sir Gawain, and that the queen said that he should do whatever he[1] wished, and that he had suffered every kind of trouble on his account. When he heard that, he was distressed and ashamed, and threw down his sword and said:

'Ah! wretch! What shall I do?'

And he went away without another word, straight to his horse. And Sir Gawain never looked at his, but put his sword in the scabbard and ran after the knight and said:

'Ha! sir knight, tell me your name.'

And he was weeping so bitterly that he could not answer him. When Sir Gawain saw that he was not going to answer, he took a run and sprang up behind him on to his horse, fully armed, and grasped him round the body and said:

'By the Holy Cross, you will not escape me until I know your name, even if it means one of us has to die.'

Hector and the king were separated, and the king had great need of it, for he was defeated. And Galehot was very worried about Lancelot, and asked Lionel what was the matter; and he told him everything. When he had heard it, he did not know what to say or do, for he did not know if Lancelot would wish the other to know who he was, and he would not for anything give him away, nor would he for anything behave unworthily towards Sir Gawain, who had suffered so much trouble on his account. He went to Hector, and asked him who he was; and he said that he was from the land of Logres and a knight of the queen and that his name was Hector.

'And that knight,' he said, 'who is he?'*

And he said that it was Sir Gawain.

'As God is my witness,' said Galehot, 'I can well believe it, and he is a man of great valour.'

---

[1] i.e. Sir Gawain.

Thus the two of them went talking together over the bridge. And a squire brought Sir Gawain's horse after them until they reached the island. Then Galehot went to Sir Gawain, and embraced him, and said:

'Sir, you are welcome. I did not recognize you. And saving your grace, you have behaved very badly, for you have nearly caused the deaths of two of the most valorous men in the world, and for nothing, for you should have told us your name.'

'Sir,' he said, 'I could not tell it, for fear of losing this lord, whom I have sought for so long. And I was well aware that I could not deceive your great wisdom except by acting outrageously. Forgive me for it, sir.'

[538] 'Indeed, I do so completely, and we have wronged you more than you us. But do you know who that is that you are holding?'

'I know very well', said Sir Gawain, 'that he is the man I am seeking.'

Thereupon they reached the tower, and Lancelot did not wish to dismount first,* so they both dismounted together, and Sir Gawain continued to hold on to him.

'Sir,' said Galehot, 'now leave him with me, and I give you my word that I shall give him back to you, just as you have him now.'

'Willingly, sir,' he said. 'But you should know that my life depends on it.'*

Then Galehot led him[1] into a chamber. And then he went back out, and ordered that Sir Gawain and Hector should be treated with all possible honour, and had them disarmed. Then he went back into the chamber and found Lancelot grieving bitterly, and asked him what was the matter. And he said that he had lost the queen's love because he had fought with Sir Gawain. 'And from now on', he said, 'no shield will ever hang around my neck.'

[1] i.e. Lancelot.

'Now, do not worry,' Galehot said, 'for I shall extricate you from all this.'

'Ah! sir, then you will have given me life again.'

Then Galehot had him disarm and wash his face in hot water. Then he said:

'I shall have Sir Gawain come to you, and you will ask his forgiveness as though he were the Lord God Himself, and he will be more pleased than if you gave him a city. Then there will be peace between the two of you. And tell him that you are ready to do just as he pleases.'

Then Galehot went back to Sir Gawain and said, taking him by the hand, that he was to go with him, and he ordered the other knights to keep Hector company. Then the two of them went to the chamber, and Galehot asked him who he thought the knight was.

'I know for a fact', he said, 'that he is Lancelot of the Lake, the son of King Ban of Benwick, the man who made peace between you and King Arthur.'

And Galehot began to laugh.

'Truly,' he said, 'no man was ever so distressed as he has been because of you, or so ashamed. Now you will see the state his eyes are in from weeping, for you have richly deserved it.'

Then they went into the chamber. And when Galehot had said: 'Here is Sir Gawain,' he went down on his knees and asked for forgiveness. And Sir Gawain raised him up, and said:

[539]'I forgive you, sir, for truly you have done a hundred times more for me than I for you. But, for the Lord's sake, tell me your name.'

'He is the man you mentioned to me,' said Galehot.

'I should very much like', he said, 'to hear it from his own lips.'

'Tell him, sir,' said Galehot.

He was very embarrassed, and blushed; and all the same,

he told him that he was Lancelot. Then there was great joy, and they talked a good deal about many things and about Hector. And Galehot said that to his knowledge he had never seen a better or more valorous knight for his age. Then Galehot himself went to fetch him and brought him in. The King of a Hundred Knights was put to bed in a chamber, for he was badly wounded; and Galehot had Sir Gawain's wounds looked at, and Hector's also, and gave them doctors.

Three days later a maiden came to Sir Gawain in the tower, and drew him aside.

'My lord,' she said, 'your brother Agravain sends me to you with word that King Arthur is going to Scotland, where the Irish and the Saxons have invaded, and that you should not fail to go there. And send him word how you have fared in your quest.'

'Well,' he said, 'by the grace of God. Now, stay here.'*

In the evening Sir Gawain asked Lancelot for his companionship; and he willingly granted it to him, and absolutely anything he wished for. Hector, too, became part of their company, all three swearing it, because he was the queen's knight and very valorous. Afterwards Sir Gawain said that he wished to stay the whole week. 'And in the morning we shall all have ourselves bled from the right arm.' Lancelot replied that he had never been bled, but that for his sake he would be.

The next day they were bled, and Sir Gawain sent Lancelot's blood to his brother, Agravain, with the damsel. And he was completely cured as soon as he was anointed with it. Galehot had a shield made for Lancelot, as the queen had told him; and he carried the shield of one of his knights. Sir Gawain told them about the army which was going to meet the Saxons, for he thought they knew nothing about it; and he asked Galehot and Lancelot to go. And they agreed.

'But let us go', said Galehot, 'in such a way that we shall not be recognized, and all take unfamiliar arms.'

And they agreed.

They stayed in the tower the whole week. Then they set off [540] to go to the encounter, and went along, asking for news, until they met the maiden that Sir Gawain and Hector had met, when she directed them to the Lost Island. They greeted one another; and she said, God bless them.

'Damsel,' said Galehot, 'do you have any news of King Arthur?'

'Yes,' she said, 'reliable news. And let me tell you that you will hear no news of him today or tomorrow except from me. However, I shall not tell you it for nothing.'

'Indeed,' said Lancelot, 'we shall give you whatever you want for it.'

'Then you must swear to me', she said, 'that, when I call on you, you will give me what I ask of you, as far as you can, up to a league of land.'

'We shall not fail you in that,' they said.

And they all four swore it to her.

'The king', the damsel said, 'is at Arestel in Scotland. When you get there, I believe you will find him besieging the Saxon Rock.'

With that she left, and they all commended her to God, and she them. And they journeyed until they reached Arestel and found the king besieging the Rock, as the damsel had told them. It was so strong that it was safe from everything except starvation. It had been fortified secretly at the time when Vortigern married the daughter of Hengist the Saxon. From there to Arestel was at least twelve Scottish leagues, and everything in between was destroyed, apart from a castle in which there was a damsel called Canile.* She knew more about enchantments than any damsel in the country, and she was very beautiful and of Saxon descent. She loved King Arthur as much as she could love anyone, and the king knew nothing about it.

When the four knights reached the army, Sir Gawain asked

Lancelot what they were to do, for they* would not dare enter King Arthur's court without bringing reliable news of his[1] whereabouts, and he had sworn it.

'Sir,' said Galehot, 'if you please, let us leave it until after the war, and you can very well wait to enter King Arthur's residence until then. And then Lancelot will go wherever you please.'

Sir Gawain agreed to that; and he said that there were still twenty knights on the quest.

'And they gave their word', Sir Gawain said, 'that [541] we should all be at King Arthur's first encounter, if we were free to do so, and we agreed on tokens by which to recognize one another.* I shall go and see if I can find any of them, and then I shall come back to you.'

'We shall wait for you,' said Lancelot. 'Hector, you go with him.'

'Yes, indeed,' said Galehot, 'and we shall have our tent pitched out here, between the camp and Arestel, so that we are not recognized. And when we leave the camp, we shall always go out at night, so that no one will know who we are.'

They all approved that idea.

Then Sir Gawain and Hector went into the camp; and people looked at them in amazement, for they were carrying their shields back to front. Sir Gawain found his companions, with the sole exception of Sagremor, who had been kept back by his ladylove, who loved him so much that she could not do without him. None the less, he arrived before the encounter came to an end. Then his[2] companions asked him if he had had any success, and he said that he had everything he was looking for. 'However, I shall not make myself known', he said, 'until the encounter breaks up.'

Then he told Sir Yvain that they should go and lodge in twos and threes, so that they were not noticed. 'And I shall do likewise with this knight, whom I cannot desert.'

[1] i.e. Lancelot's.   [2] i.e. Gawain's.

Then Kay asked him who he was.

'Indeed,' he said, 'he is a knight who knocked all four of you down at the Spring of the Pine.'

They were quite amazed, and Sir Yvain said that he would be a good knight, if he lived. Thereupon they parted, and Sir Gawain told them to be all together at the encounter the next day. Then Sir Gawain went away to where Galehot had said that his tent would be. It was at the edge of a wood in a very beautiful spot, which was enclosed on all sides by a high palisade, and one went in through a little gate, for it was the garden of a townsman of Arestel. Inside was pitched a tent fitting for such a man,[1] and there were at least ten squires there, one of whom was Lionel, who was very valorous and sensible.

Every day King Arthur spoke to the damsel of the castle and asked her for her love; and she was not interested,* and yet had reduced him to such a state that he loved her beyond reason.

The encounter took place the day after Sir Gawain arrived. Lancelot carried the black shield with the diagonal white band;* and [542] Galehot carried the shield of the King of a Hundred Knights, and Sir Gawain carried a shield which was half white and half azure, which belonged to the best knight in Galehot's household, whose name was Galain, the Duke of Ronnes; and Hector carried a white shield with a red fesse,* which belonged to Guinier, a companion of my lord Galehot. The king himself bore arms, and they engaged the Saxons and the Irish; however, the king did not have many troops, and needed to fight well. And he fought better than he had ever done, and he did it mainly so that the maiden, who was in the castle of the Rock, should see him.

When the king had engaged in person, Sir Gawain and his twenty companions went to engage. Galehot and Lancelot

---

[1] i.e. Galehot.

had remained behind so that no one would notice them. Then they both passed in front of the building where the queen was. She and the Lady of Malohaut had gone up on to the battlements on top of the tower; and when the queen saw Lancelot, she said to the Lady of Malohaut:

'Do you recognize those knights?'

And the lady began to laugh, recognizing them at once, both by Lancelot's shield and by the pennon which she had put* on his helm. And that was the first device ever worn on a helm in King Arthur's time. Then they both looked up and saw those that they loved; and Lancelot was so overwhelmed that he nearly fell to the ground, and held on to his horse's neck. Lionel was riding beside him, armed in cap and habergeon like a man-at-arms, and keeping his head bowed, so that no one would recognize him. And when he looked up, he recognized the queen, and the queen him, and she had a damsel call him. He dismounted, and leant the lances he was carrying against the tower, and went up. He met the queen on the stairs, and she said to him:

'Be sure that the tournament takes place in front of here.'

Then she went back up. And he remounted his horse and spurred after his lord with the lances, and told him what the queen had said to him. He, however, was as pensive as could be, and replied: 'Let it be as my lady pleases.' Then, they reached the encounter, and saw the battlefield covered in mêlées; and they rushed into the fray. Then Lancelot began to fight so fiercely that everyone was taken aback. And before long Sir Gawain heard about it, who was fighting far away. He was told that a knight was doing remarkable deeds over there. He and his companions went there, [543] and immediately they chased all those on the other side as far as their lists, and many of them were lost. And when Lionel saw that, he told Lancelot to make ready to do what he had been told.

And he reined in, and said:

'Go, and tell my lady that it is impossible, unless I put

myself on the other side. But if that is what she wishes, I shall bring them all here in front of the tower.'

He went and told her that. As soon as she saw him, she went down; and when he had told her it, she went back up, saying that she wished it.

'But he is to take care', she said, 'that, as soon as he sees my cloak hanging from these battlements, with the lining outwards, he comes back on this side. And if the king suffers any loss in the pursuit, he is to be sure that it is made good.'

And he went away, and told him that. And Galehot called Sir Gawain, and said:

'Sir Gawain, I know how the king might have some of the richest men from the other side as his prisoners. If we went over to the other side and drove the king's troops to the edge of the water, without stopping, and then changed sides again, we could not fail to have them all captured or killed.'

Sir Gawain said that he would do whatever he wished.

'But how', he said, 'can I go against my uncle and my liege lord?'*

'In God's name,' said Galehot, 'for his good.'

'I will do it for that,' Sir Gawain said.

Then they went over to the Saxon side, twenty-three knights, all very valorous, and Galehot. And at once the king's troops had to give ground, once the other knights were against them. And they did not stop until they reached the edge of the water—that was where the tower stood; however, they went slowly, and they did not suffer much loss, for those on the other side were only thinking about pursuing them, for they thought they had won everything.* They were not capturing anyone, but drove them headlong into the water. The king was so grieved by it that he was nearly distracted, and he bitterly lamented the absence of Sir Gawain and his companions.

Then Lancelot looked towards the tower and saw the queen's cloak hanging down, with the lining outwards, and said that now they had stood enough. 'Now, up and at them!' he said. Then they all turned back and charged the Saxons in the rear, surrounding them, and they shook them up badly and shouted at them. They[1] were thrown into confusion, and thought they were completely surrounded, and the king's troops came back and attacked them. Lancelot, though, [544] was at the rear with his company, doing remarkable deeds, so that the queen was quite dumbfounded by it, for he was enduring a great deal to keep them near the tower. Lancelot and his men were at the point where the road crossed the ford, for they[1] all had to go back by there, and they[2] killed or knocked down so many of them in the ford that the river was completely dammed. And the queen said that all the hardship he had undergone at the other encounter was as nothing compared to what he had endured here. She very much wondered, though, who were the knights with him, who were fighting so well. Sir Gawain was doing remarkable deeds, as were Hector and the others, and no one could venture among them without being killed or knocked down, for they were all striving to fight well because of one another, so that it was wonderful to see. And because they killed so many knights in the ford, it was afterwards called the Ford of Blood, and always will be.

Lancelot endured so much at the ford, with his company, that his helm was all split and dented, and the circle was hanging down. And the queen called a damsel, and sent him a very fine helm, which belonged to the king: 'And tell him that I can no longer watch this slaughter; he is to let the pursuit begin, for I wish it.' She went and gave him the helm and told him the message the queen had sent him. And he said, many thanks. Then he laced on the helm, having taken off his own. Then he and his men drew back a little, and the Saxons crossed the ford and went fleeing away, for they were

---

[1] i.e. the Saxons.   [2] i.e. Lancelot and the others.

very much afraid and had suffered great losses, and they fled. And Lancelot and his men chased them; and in the pursuit the king's troops captured a knight called Atramont, who was the brother of Agleot, the king of the Saxons, and he was one of their best knights. At least 200 other Saxons and Irish were captured, who were all powerful men, and there were prodigious numbers of dead. During the pursuit Lancelot personally remounted King Arthur three times, for two horses were killed under him and the third fell, so that it broke its neck. And but for him the king would have had a very hard time of it, for he was alone, and his men were intent on the pursuit, which was very successful.

That day the king's enemies had a very hard time of it, and were chased as far as their lists. All day long the fighting was extremely fierce, until evening began to draw in. Then Galehot went to Sir Gawain, and said quietly that he should stay there until the troops dispersed. 'And we are going.' And Sir Gawain agreed. Then they both[1] went away right in front of the tower. The queen had come down, and they both greeted her, and she them; and she saw that Lancelot's whole arm was bloody up to the shoulder, and she was afraid that he was dying. [545] She asked them how they were; and they said, well. 'And is that arm injured?'

'No, my lady.'*

'I wish to see it,' she said.

She embraced Lancelot, armed as he was, and the Lady of Malohaut embraced Galehot. And the queen said in Lancelot's ear that she would heal him completely, before the next day, if he was not mortally wounded. And he said that he had no fear of dying as long as that was her wish. Thereupon the queen had them mount up, for she dared not keep them any longer, and she told Lionel that she wished to speak to him. The others went away to their tents, and disarmed. And by now night was beginning to fall.

---

[1] i.e. Lancelot and Galehot.

When the fighting broke up the king went away below the
Rock; and the damsel said that she wished to speak to him.
He was delighted, and waited for her; and she came down,
and went to him and said:

'My lord, you are the worthiest man living. You gave me to
understand that you love me more than any other woman,
and I wish to test whether you dare do something to prove it.'

'There is nothing', he said, 'that I should not do for you.'

'We shall see,' she said. 'I wish you to come and sleep with
me tonight in that tower.'

'That is no problem,' he said, 'if you give me your word
that I may do with you what a knight should do with his
ladylove.'

She gave him her word; and he said that he would come as
soon as he had seen his knights and eaten with them.

'You will find my messenger at the gate,' she said, 'who
will come and fetch you.'

Then the king left her, very joyful, and went to his knights.
And they saw him looking better and happier than they ever
had before. He sent word to the queen that he would not be
with her that night, and she should be very pleased, because
things had gone very well for him in the battle. And she was
by no means unhappy. In the evening Lionel went to the
queen's residence, and the queen told him that Galehot and
Lancelot should come to her there that night, and showed
him where.

'My lady,' he said, 'Sir Gawain and Hector are with them.
How will they get away from them?'

When the queen heard that, she was delighted that they
had found one another.

'But they will not be prevented from coming because of
them,' she said. 'And I shall tell you how,' she went on. 'They
must go to bed in front of Sir Gawain; and when they know
that he is asleep, they must get up, and then the three of you
will come to there.' And she showed him a garden [546]

which adjoined the bailey of the tower. 'And we shall have come out of the bailey; but they should come fully armed and mounted.'

Thereupon Lionel went away and related what he had found out, and the others were delighted. That night, when those in the king's tent were in bed, the king rose as quietly as he could. He armed, along with his nephew, Guerrehet, in whom he had confided, and went to the gate of the castle and met his ladylove's messenger. They went along until they reached the great fortress, and found the maiden waiting for them, who was very pleasant to them and had the king and Guerrehet disarmed. The king lay down in a very fine bed with her; and Guerrehet lay with a very beautiful damsel in another chamber. And when the king had lain with his ladylove for a long while and done as he wished, more than forty knights came in there, fully armed, and all holding drawn swords, and they forced open the door of the chamber. The king sprang up as best he could, for he had only his breeches, and ran to his sword, meaning to defend himself. And they brought a great many lighted candles, so that one could see very clearly; and they told him not to resist. And he did not, for he had no armour, and he could see that resistance was useless, and allowed himself to be captured. And they ran into the other chamber, and captured Guerrehet. Then they dressed them both and put them in prison in a very strong chamber which had no way in or out except a single door, and that was of iron.

Thus the king and Guerrehet were in prison. And Galehot and Lancelot had risen from their beds and had with them two squires, whom they ordered to stay there, so that if the others[1] woke up, they would think that the squires were them.[2] Then they went fully armed to the garden, and the squires lay down in their beds. They found the gate of the

---

[1] i.e. Sir Gawain and Hector.   [2] i.e. Lancelot and Galehot.

garden unlocked, and went in. The camp was only guarded in front, for in the rear, where the garden was, ran the river, which was so deep that no one would enter it, because of the mud and the marshy ground. When they were in the garden, they closed the gate and went to the bailey, and dismounted and found the two ladies waiting for them, who led their horses into a lean-to which was built against the bailey. There was no one in the bailey but the queen and her maidens. The other people were in a large building next to it, for she had deliberately had it cleared.

[547] When the two knights were disarmed, they were led into two chambers, and each lay with his ladylove, for they loved one another dearly, and they had all the joys that lovers can have. At about midnight the queen got up and went to the shield which the damsel from the lake had brought her, and felt it without a light, and found it was whole, with no split in it, and she was delighted, for now she was certain that she was loved more than any other woman.*

In the morning, a little before daybreak, the two knights rose and armed themselves in the queen's chamber. And the Lady of Malohaut, who was very shrewd, looked at the shield, and saw in the candlelight that the shield was completely joined and said to the queen:

'My lady, now we can clearly see that the love is complete.'

Then she went to Lancelot and took him by the chin and said:

'Sir knight, now you only lack a crown to be king.'

And he was very embarrassed by her, for he had been in her power many a day and had always concealed his identity from her. And the queen said, to rescue him:

'Madam, if I am a king's daughter, he is also a king's son; and if I am worthy and beautiful, he is more so.'

Galehot asked what they meant; and she told him how the shield was brought to her, and that the Lady of the Lake sent it to her, and that it had always been split until now. They looked at it for a long time in wonder; and the Lady of Malohaut said that only one thing was lacking for the shield to be as had been said:* Lancelot did not belong to the household, which the knight in question should. And the queen ordered him to stay if Sir Gawain asked him, for she was so overcome with love for him that she did not see how she could do without seeing him. However, she said it so quietly that Galehot did not hear it, for he would have been very upset. Thereupon they left, arranging to come back the following night.

In the morning, after daybreak, the people of the Rock hung the king's shield, and that of Guerrehet, from the battlements, and rejoiced in there as much as they possibly could. Then great sorrowing began in the camp; and when the queen heard about it, who was still asleep—and she was told about it in bed when she woke up—she was very worried, and grieved terribly. And she was very impatient to be able to talk to Lancelot, so that he might do something about it. Sir Gawain, however, was most anxious, and Lancelot comforted him and said that he should not be dismayed, 'for we shall all become prisoners,' he said, 'or we shall have him back.'

[548] In the evening Lionel went to the queen, and she told him to bring Lancelot and Galehot, for she had great need of them. And he went away to deliver her message. While he was with the queen, a damsel came to the tent of the four knights and told him that she was calling on them to keep their oath. It was the damsel who had told them the king was at Arestel.

'Damsel,' said Galehot, 'where do you wish us to escort you? For the Lord's sake, do not exhaust us, for we have a great deal of trouble.'

'You will soon be out of that trouble, if you will follow me, for they mean to take King Arthur out of there secretly, and take him away to Ireland. And if you will follow me, you can rescue him secretly now, for no one knows anything about it except those who are about to take him away.'

When they heard that, they leapt on to their horses, fully armed, and followed the damsel, who led them until she reached a vault. She went in, and they followed. It was already dark when they arrived there, and they could barely see. She told them that the king would be brought through there; and first of all she went to Hector.

'Guard this exit for me,' she said, 'for there are three more inside. And if they come this way, call the others.'

He stayed there; and she went a little further, and told Sir Gawain to stay there, and he did so. Then she came to another door, and went on, leaving Galehot there. And when she came to another, she left Lancelot there, and said:

'Wait for me here, for I expect to return the king and Guerrehet to you.'

Then, after waiting a long while, she came shouting 'Help! Help!' Lancelot rushed forward, and she said: 'There he is.' He rushed forward, and saw two armed knights, one in the king's armour, and the other in that of Guerrehet. He thought it was them,[1] but it was not, for she had betrayed them.[2] He saw that those two were fighting with the others and defending themselves, for there were more than twenty of them, and he ran very nimbly to help them. And the two that he was helping grasped him round the body, and threw him and themselves to the ground. And the others rushed forward, and took his sword from him by force and wrenched the helm from his head and said that they would cut off his head. And he said that, as God was his witness, that suited him, and he would not swear to be their prisoner. They took him, and led him away to prison; and they went to Galehot and had a knight arm himself in Lancelot's armour. Galehot saw him fighting, and called the others; and they came running, but

---

[1] i.e. King Arthur and Guerrehet.   [2] i.e. the four knights.

they found the doors firmly closed, so that none of them could pass his door. [549] They captured Galehot, and then unbarred the postern again, and captured Sir Gawain. However, there was a great fight first, for he certainly did remarkable deeds. Then they also captured Hector, and took all four of them away to prison. And Lancelot would not swear to be a prisoner for anyone. And they said that in that case they would throw him into a prison which he would never get out of; and if he wished, he would be untied on his oath. And he said that he desired only death, but the others[1] told him to swear; and in that way they were left in a chamber, all untied.

That night the queen was very worried, from waiting. And when Lionel saw that they were not going to come, he went to tell the queen that a damsel had led them away like that. And he told her what he had been told. When she heard it, she sighed and said: 'They have been betrayed.' And she began to grieve terribly. In the morning those in the castle hung the four shields from the battlements with the other two. When the queen saw them, rest assured that she was very distressed and would rather have been dead than alive. And it was a day of battle.

When the news reached Sir Gawain's companions, they were filled with grief. Then Sir Yvain said that now they must help the queen, for she was in great distress, and he went to her, with the permission of the seventeen,* and had her called to the stairs. And she came, delighted, when she knew it was him.

'My lady,' he said, 'I would have come to see you in there, but I cannot enter any residence of King Arthur until our quest is accomplished in full. However, I have come to comfort you; and do not be too dismayed, for, please God, you will have help. But have you heard any news of Sir Gawain?'

---

[1] i.e. his three companions.

'No,' she said.

'He is in that castle,' he said, 'with three of the best knights in the world, though I do not know who they are.'*

Then the queen fell at Sir Yvain's feet and begged him to take pity on the king's honour and on her. And he raised her up and wept himself, because he saw her weeping, for no lady was ever so loved by her husband's followers as was Queen Guinevere.

That day Sir Yvain took King Arthur's place, for what he commanded was done. And Kay the seneschal carried the great banner, as was his right. The battalions were ordered; and then the Irish and the Saxons engaged the troops of the King of Britain, thinking they had won everything because the king and his [550] companions were in prison. That day King Yder rode a horse which he thought the best in the world, and because he loved it so, he first had it covered in iron. After that he did something which people spoke ill of at first, but later it was well thought of; and it had never been seen before, and now it will always be done; for he made a banner with his arms and said that he intended to carry it where no banner could go; and he knew his horse to be so good that he wished all those who were routed to rally to him. The banner was very beautiful, for the field was white with great red circles, and the field was of cordwain, while the circles were of fine red cloth from England. In so far as these housings* were carried at that time they were always of leather or cloth, the true stories tell us, because they lasted longer.

That day the king's companions fought well, exhorted by Sir Yvain, so that no battle was ever fought so well without King Arthur himself, and there was not a single man who did not do great deeds of arms. However, all that they did was nothing compared to King Yder's deeds of prowess. He surpassed everyone, on the two sides; and because he had said that everyone should rally to his company, he endured so much that day that there was never a day afterwards that he was not crippled from it, for once he entered the battle, he never had his helm off his head, nor retreated from where he stood, nor fled. His horse was so good that it could not have been better; and the good horse endured so much under him that it had three wounds in the body and all the housing was cut to pieces, and it was so covered in blood, its own and that of others, that both knight and horse were completely red. And they were shouting everywhere that King Yder had surpassed everyone.* And he said, as he sat on his horse, the Lord keep him firm in what he had undertaken, without breaking his word or retreating, and at the end of the battle, give him death, for he would never again have such an excellent day.

King Yder withstood so much that day, and he and King Arthur's companions did such deeds of arms, that the Saxons were defeated and turned tail. A great pursuit began, and they suffered heavy losses; and King Arthur's troops chased them very vigorously. Everyone looked at Yder's horse in amazement, for no animal which had had to run all day long ever ran so fast or so easily as it ran in the pursuit. The pursuit lasted a long time, and many fell there [551] from both sides. And it happened that King Yder rode over a Saxon who had fallen, and he was holding his drawn sword, and struck King Yder's horse in the belly, so that he clove it right to the groin. And it ran a great deal after that, but all the same it fell under King Yder. He had lost a great deal of blood, and the whole pursuit went over his body, and he was left unconscious on the ground. Queen Guinevere ran there with her ladies and they brought the king away on their shoulders; and everyone thought he was beyond hope of recovery. He was carried into the queen's chamber, and the noblest ladies in the world lamented for him and regretted his loss. The king's troops had pursued as far as Mala-guienne, a very strong castle which belonged to the Saxons;

and they returned from there with great numbers of prisoners, and they had killed many. And then the army drew up nearer the Rock. However, they could not be very near it, for the Rock was high, and they could not endure the quarrels and arrows which came from up there; moreover, they could not besiege it all around, for on the other side the marsh was so wide that nothing could go there.

The army was in front of the Rock like that for a very long time, and for a very long while after that the Saxons did not dare attack the king's troops, applying themselves instead to sending for troops throughout their domain. The king's troops were also coming from all directions, for it was now known everywhere that the king was a prisoner. Thus the army was encamped in front of the Rock, and they kept watch night and day, and every day and every night 200 knights were below the gate which faced the river to guard against the king and his companions being taken away.

[M. LXXIa] Now the story says that inside there Lancelot was in such a state that he did not eat or drink, whatever comfort he was given, and he grieved so all day long that no one could comfort him. And his head was empty, and such a violent madness and frenzy went up into his head that no one could withstand him; and there was not one of his companions whom he had not given two or three wounds. The gaoler took him, and put him in a chamber by himself, and he could see that he was genuinely distracted, and he himself was very moved by it. Galehot begged the gaoler to put him with him;[1] and he would not, for he said that he[1] would kill him.

'Do not worry, my friend,' he[2] said, 'for I had rather he killed me than that he parted from me.'

The other was cruel, and would not do it. With all the talk about it, the lady of the Rock heard of it, and she went to see him[1] herself and asked the gaoler who he was. He replied

---

[1] i.e. Lancelot.   [2] i.e. Galehot.

that the others said that he did not have a pennyworth of land.

[552]'Come,' she said, 'then it would be a mortal sin not to let him go.* Open the gate down below for him.'

That was the gate which faced King Arthur's troops, and it was in the side of the Rock and just above the river. And there was a gate there which was closed in a strange way, for there was nothing to close it except air, and it seemed to all those who saw it that one could go straight in there, but no one could go in there except those inside. They went in and out whenever they wished by the power of the enchantments. The troops from inside went out by that postern to attack, with great frequency, and as soon as they could set foot inside it, they had nothing to fear from the army.

When Lancelot was put outside and Galehot heard the news, he was so grieved that he was nearly distracted, and was in such a state that he did not eat or drink. And Lancelot was in the camp, and they all feared him and ran away from him because of the extraordinary things he did. He went along until he arrived in front of the queen's residence. She was at a window, and when she saw him, she fainted, for everyone was following him,* as they do a man who is out of his mind. And when she came to, she said to the Lady of Malohaut, who was holding her in her arms, that she was about to die.

'My lady,' she said, 'what is the matter with you?'

And she told her.

'Ah! my lady,' she said, 'by the Lord's mercy, there is only one thing to be done now: hide him, for it may be that he is pretending to be mad in order to see you; and if he is out of his mind, we shall keep him until he recovers.'

The queen sent her to him; and then she rushed into a chamber, for she was afraid she would faint because of him. And when she was in there, she could not stand it, and went back out to see him. The Lady of Malohaut went to him, and made to take him by the hand; and he ran for some stones to kill her. And she began to cry out, as women do, and the queen called to him. And as soon as he heard her, he sat down and put his hands over his eyes like a man ashamed, and would not stand up for anything. The Lady of Malohaut dared not go any further; and Queen Guinevere went out, and took him by the hand and ordered him to stand up. He stood up immediately, and she led him upstairs into a chamber. Her ladies asked who he was, and there were some who said that he was one of the best knights in the world. No one could make him stay quiet except the queen; and as soon as she ordered him to stay quiet, he would not move again. Everyone was astonished by what she did with him. She sent someone to fetch Lionel, and he came; but he [553] could do nothing, for when he touched Lancelot, he attacked him. And the queen did not leave his side.

Thus Lancelot was in there and slept in with the queen. And every night she had the candles and torches put out, because, she said, the light troubled her; then she put him to bed with her and grieved so much all night long that it was a wonder she survived. However, everyone thought that it was, quite properly, for the king.

Thus the queen's grief and Lancelot's madness lasted for a long time, until one day it happened that the Saxons attacked the camp and there were many great mêlées on the two sides. Lancelot was asleep, and he had not slept in eleven days, and the queen was overjoyed. And when she heard the uproar, she got up as quietly as she could, and saw everyone on the two sides attacking, and she immediately fainted. The Lady of Malohaut took her in her arms; and when she came to, she reproached her severely and said:

'My lady, why are you tormenting yourself?'

'As God is my witness,' she said, 'because I am right to do so, for I see everyone dead, and I certainly ought to die afterwards.'

Then she grieved so much that no one could comfort or admonish her. Then she went back to Lancelot. As soon as she saw him, she fainted; and when she came to, she said:

'Ha! flower of the knights of the world, what a great misfortune it is that you are not as well as you were a short time ago! How this mortal battle would be brought to an end then!'

When he heard her regretting the loss of his deeds and his jousting and his blows, he sprang up and saw, hanging at the end of the chamber, the shield which the Maiden of the Lake* had sent to the queen. And he reached out and grasped it and looped it around his neck and took hold of the straps. And he saw a lance in a rack, old and blackened, and he ran and took it. Then he went up to a round stone pillar and struck it with the lance so hard that the whole head flew into pieces. When he had done that, he was so weak that he could not stand, but fell down and passed out. When he came to, he asked where he was; and they told him that he was in Queen Guinevere's residence. When he heard that, he passed out again; and when he came to, the queen asked him how he had been that day. And he in turn at once asked her where her husband and Sir Gawain were. And the ladies told him that they were in prison in the Rock.

[554] 'Hey! Lord,' he said, 'why am I not there, then! It would be much better for me to die now with them than here, since my lady is not here.'

Then the queen realized that he was in his right mind, and she took him in her arms and said:

'Dear friend, here I am.'

At once he opened his eyes, and recognized her and said:

'My lady, now let it come when it wishes, since you are here.'

All the ladies wondered what he was talking about, and he was talking about death. And the queen asked him:

'Dear friend, do you know me?'

'Yes, my lady,' he said, 'much better than myself.'

'And do you know,' she asked, 'how you were in prison in the Rock?'

'My lady,' he said, 'the prison in the Rock has been the death of me, for I did not eat or drink while I was there.'

The ladies all began to weep.

'Dear friend,' said the Lady of Malohaut, 'do you know me?'

'Madam,' he said, 'I know you very well, for you have done me much harm, and much honour.'

Then they all knew for certain that he was cured, and they asked him how he was and what harm he had suffered. And he said that he did not know what harm he had suffered, but he could not stand for the world. Then he looked, and saw the shield around his neck, and said:

'Ha! Lord, who put this shield around my neck? Take it off, for it is killing me.'

They took it off him; and as soon as they had taken it off, he sprang up and was just as mad as before, and went fleeing away down the hall. And when the queen saw that, she fainted.

While the queen was lying unconscious, a very tall, beautiful and noble-looking damsel came in, dressed in a silk cloth, white as snow. Behind her came three damsels and three knights and as many as ten squires. The damsel and the three maidens went up into the queen's chambers. And she had come to, and heard the clamour of people saying: 'Welcome, madam.' She wiped her eyes and went to meet her and took her in her arms and said that she was welcome. And they sat down on a couch and began to talk together. The doors of the principal chamber were closed on Lancelot, and he started to become distracted [555] and to break down the doors. Then there was no one bold enough to dare open them. The damsel asked the queen who it was; and she told her with a sigh, and she could not help tears coming to her eyes; and she said that it was a knight, and that it was a great sorrow, for he was one of the best in the world. Now he had fallen into such a great madness that no one could withstand him.

'Ah! my lady, open the door and let me see him.'

'Ha! madam,' the queen said, 'right now he is wilder than ever before.'

And she told her how he had been cured just before, and how he was mad again as soon as the shield was taken from around his neck.

'My lady,' she said, 'you will do it.* Open the door, for I should like to see him.'

Then the queen had the door opened, and Lancelot tried to spring out. And the damsel took him by the hand and called him by a name which she used to call him when she was bringing him up in the lake, for she was the one who had brought him up in the lake and had named him the Handsome Foundling. As soon as she said his name, he stood still and was very ashamed; and she told them to bring her the shield, and they brought it.

'Ah!' she said, 'dear friend, you have caused me such distress that I have come from far distant lands to deliver you.'

Then she put the shield around his neck; and he put up with whatever she wished to do to him. As soon as she had put it on him he was back in his right mind; and she took him, and laid him on a bed. He recognized her, and began to weep very bitterly; and the queen very much wondered who she could be. And when he was back in his right mind, he saw the shield around his neck and said:

'Ha! my lady, take this shield off, for it is killing me.'

'I will not,' she said. 'It will not be taken off until I wish it.'

Then she called one of her maidens, and had her get a very rich ointment out of a casket. She took it, and anointed him with it on both wrists and both temples and the forehead and the cranial suture. As soon as she had done that, he fell asleep. And the damsel went to the queen, and said:

'My lady, I am going away, and I shall commend you to God. Take care, though, that this knight is not woken up as long as he wishes to sleep; and when he wakes up of his own accord, have his bath ready and have him get into it. Then he will be completely cured. And take care that he carries no shield but this one as long as it will endure in battle.'

'Ah! madam,' said the queen, 'tell me who you are, for I think you know the knight well, since you say that you have come from distant lands, in hard stages, to cure him.'

[556] 'Indeed, my lady,' she said, 'I ought to know him well, for I brought him up when he was in great poverty, having lost his father and mother; and I did enough, with God's help, that he became a fine, big young man. Then I took him to court and persuaded King Arthur to make him a knight.'

When the queen heard that, she ran and embraced her and said:

'Ah! madam, I am pleased to see you. Now I am sure I know who you are. You are the Damsel of the Lake.'

And she replied that that was true.

'Dear lady,' she said, 'now I beg you for the Lord's sake to remain here for a while, because I ask it and for your knight's cure, for I ought to love you dearly, and you are the lady I should most honour in the world. And let me tell you that I love you so much that I could not love anyone more, for you have done me some of the greatest services which were ever done, because you sent me that shield there, which I have put to the proof so well that you never said anything to me about the shield which I have not found to be true.'

'My lady, my lady,' said the lady from the lake, 'let me tell you that you will see greater wonders involving that shield than you have yet seen. I was well aware of all that has happened to him,* and for that reason I sent him to you; for

I could see that I could not send him anywhere where he would be loved as much. And you should know that, because of the great prowess which was to be in him, I brought him up until he was as big and handsome as you saw him at court. Moreover, he never knew who he was; rather, I concealed his identity because of a knight that I loved more than any man living, for I was afraid that if he knew it, he would think something else.* So I had it said that he was my nephew. And even now, when I go back, I shall say that I have come from freeing King Arthur from prison. And he will be set free within nine days, and you should know that this man[1] will free him. Take good care, though, that he carries no shield but this one, for you will find true everything that my maiden told you when she brought it to you at Quimpercorentin. And I said something to you through her which I was very unhappy about afterwards, and I was afraid that it would worry you; for I sent you word that I was the lady in the world who knew most about your feelings and who most shared them, for I loved the person you loved. And you should know that I only love him because of the tenderness of nurturing him, and I love you because of him. However, in parting I shall tell you something, because I love you and I am going away. I ask you to retain him in your service and to take care of him, and to love above all else him, who loves you above all else, and to put aside all pride where he is concerned, for it is pointless:* [557] he values nothing compared with you. And the sins of this world cannot be committed without folly, but one has good cause for folly if one finds reason and honour in it. And if you find folly in your love, that folly is glorious above all others, for you love the pinnacle and the flower of the whole world. You can boast of that which no lady could ever boast of before, for you are the companion of the most worthy man in the world, and the lady of the best

[1] i.e. Lancelot.

knight in the world. And you have gained no small thing in the new dominion which you have, for you have gained firstly him, who is the flower of all knights, and secondly me, whatever I can do. With that, though, I must go, for I cannot linger any longer. And you should know that the greatest power there is is taking me away, that is, the power of love, for I love a knight, who does not know where I am right now. However, his brother has come here with me. In any case, I need not worry that he will be angry with me as long as that is my wish. However, one should take as much care not to upset the person one loves as one does oneself, for a person is not truly loved unless he is loved above all earthly things. And someone who is in love can have no joy except from the one he loves; therefore one should love the person from whom all joy comes.'

The two of them talked together for a very long time, until evening, and they got to know one another well and offered their services to one another, until things reached the stage where the queen could not keep the damsel there under any circumstances. When the queen saw that it was like that, she did not dare entreat her any further. So they commended one another to God, and the Damsel of the Lake mounted and went away with her company. The queen remained, very much happier than she had been for a while, and she went to Lancelot and did not move from the spot until he woke up. And when he was awake, he groaned a good deal; and she said, how was he. And he said, well, 'but I am very weak and I do not know why'. And she did not want to tell him how he had been ill until he was well on the road to recovery. The bath was made ready, and they took him to it and did all that any ladies could do for a sick knight, until he was very much recovered, while he regained his beauty and strength. Then they told him how he had been out of his mind, and that no one could withstand him, with the exception of the queen.

'And your lady was here,' the queen said, 'the Lady of the

Lake, who brought you up. And but for her, you would never have been cured.'

And he said that he rather thought he had seen her, 'but I [558] thought I had dreamed it.' And she began to laugh heartily. And he was very morose and ashamed because he was now sure that they had seen him behave badly, and he was afraid that the person he most loved in the world would hold him less dear because of it. However, there was no need for him to fear that, for she could not have done so, even if she had wished to. And when he lamented to her, she comforted and reassured him, saying:

'Do not worry about that, dear friend, for, as God is my true witness, you are more in control and more sure of me than I am of you. And I have not embarked on it* just for now, but for all the days that my soul is in my body.'

Now Lancelot was on the road to recovery, and he had everything he asked for. And he had his share of every great joy that a lover can have. The story does not tell you any more, except that he led this life for nine days. By then he was so handsome that it was wonderful to see. And during this stay, the queen became so much in love with him that she did not see how she could do without seeing him. And it distressed her to see and know that he was so eager and courageous, for she did not see how she could go on living without him, if he ever went away from court again. She would have liked him to have a little less bravery and prowess.

After nine days it happened that the Irish and the Saxons attacked those in the camp, and the alarm was raised everywhere. The king's troops had done great deeds of arms that week and were acquitting themselves very well, for troops who had no lord to lead them. And that day they defended themselves very fiercely. The fighting was already spread out again, and the clamour could be heard everywhere, for the Saxons aimed to attack the whole army and drive them back far enough that they could get the king and his companions out of the rock, and take them away deeper into their domain.

When everyone on the two sides had engaged, Lancelot, who was with the queen in her chamber, heard the clamour, and they all rushed to the windows and the battlements. And when Lancelot saw them, he was uncomfortable because he was not there, and he went to the queen, and begged her to allow him to go to the encounter. Knowing no other way to protect herself, she told him that he was not yet fully recovered. 'And our side', she said, 'have by no means the worse of it yet.'

'My lady, grant me that, if they have the worse of it, I may go.'

And she granted it, with great reluctance. He was delighted, and prayed [559] to God very humbly that their side have the worse of it, and soon.

'My lady,' he said to the queen, 'we do not know what will happen, but have some arms brought for me.'

And he was brought some excellent arms, which belonged to King Arthur himself. And when he was armed, he was extremely handsome; and there was no knight whom arms suited better than Lancelot. When Lancelot was armed except for his head and hands, a knight came in there. He had come from the battle, and he had lost his helm and was badly wounded in the head. And when he had dismounted, he went upstairs to the queen. When the queen saw that his shoulders and chest were all bloody, she was very alarmed. He knelt down in front of her, and said:

'My lady, Sir Yvain greets you and sends you word that he has been given to understand that not all the knights are in the battle. And you should know that they are badly in need of reinforcements, for our numbers are greatly reduced by the knights being sent to Arestel this morning.' (Sir Yvain had sent 200 knights there in the morning, because news had come to the camp the night before that the Saxons were going to attack Arestel.) 'So, my lady,' he said, 'he says that you should send anyone that you can send.'

'What?' she said; 'have they so much the worse of it?'

'My lady,' he said, 'they are losing everything. And the 200 knights who are guarding the gate by the river, so that the king is not taken away, are bearing the brunt of the battle. And you should know that they are badly in need of reinforcements, for they are defending themselves in the rear and on guard in front. And by now most of them are on foot, for their horses have been killed.'

'Ha! my lady,' said Lancelot, 'allow me to go there, for now the time has come.'

The queen called him into a chamber, and asked him what he expected to do against so many troops.

'My lady,' he said, 'ask the knight how much their numbers are reduced by the knights being sent to Arestel.'

She asked him; and he said, by 200. Then she repeated it to Lancelot.

'My lady,' he said, 'now ask him, if the 200 came, would they have the best of it.'

She asked him; and he told her that they would be able to defend themselves well enough.

'My lady,' he said, 'now send word to Sir Yvain that you [560] will send them quite enough knights to replace those by which their numbers are reduced. And once your pennon comes to the front there from here, you will make good all the harm they have suffered.'*

And the queen said that to the knight. Then she had a helm brought, and gave it to him in place of his own, which he had lost. And he went away overjoyed and told Sir Yvain the news which she sent him. Sir Yvain was very distressed because his knights were in such straits, and he could see that they were disheartened and worn out from fighting well. And he said:

'Ah, Lord, when will my lady's pennon come?'

Thus Sir Yvain spoke and exhorted his knights, a man who was enduring a great deal and well knew how to do so; for Sir Yvain endured a great deal, when he was in desperate straits, and otherwise he would not have been a good knight.

Lancelot had sent for Lionel, and he had him armed like a man-at-arms, as well as he could. Then two of the king's horses were brought, and both were covered in iron. Lancelot mounted the one that he was told was the better and braver and of greater endurance, and Lionel the other. And as Lancelot was about to lace on his helm, the queen took him in her arms, and kissed him as tenderly as she could. Then she laced on his helm herself, and commended him to Him who was put on the Cross, that He might keep him from death and captivity. And she had had one of her pennons attached to a lance, and had given it to Lionel. The field of the pennon was azure with three gold crowns and it had a single tongue (and all the king's pennons had three tongues, and as many crowns as would fit on; and that is how one could tell them apart).

Thereupon Lancelot and Lionel were mounted, and Lionel carried the pennon, and Lancelot carried a short, thick lance, with a sharp and bright head, and a strong, solid shaft. And thereupon they left and went spurring to the encounter. Sir Yvain saw the pennon coming, and cheered his troops, saying:

'Now, gentlemen, take heart. There is my lady's pennon. Now we shall see who is a knight, for the reinforcements have arrived.'

And the two rushed in where they saw the thickest press of Saxons, and began to shout loudly 'Clarance', which was King Arthur's battle-cry. Clarance was a very fine city which bordered on the kingdom of South Wales, and which belonged to King Tahalais, who was Uther Pendragon's grandfather. He was the head of King Arthur's line, and [561] because of that city he and all his descendants shouted

'Clarance' in all their hours of need, and they would never give up their first battle-cry, for all the high rank they achieved.

King Arthur's battle-cry was loudly shouted in an attack that Lancelot made on the Saxons and the Irish, and he struck with his lance in the thick of the fray. And when his lance broke, he knew well enough how to put his hand to his good, sharp sword, which was called Secace. This was a sword which the king only carried in mortal combat. Then Lancelot's prowess was put to the test, for he cut through Saxons and Irish and horses and heads and shields and arms and legs. He flew right and left on his horse, which was the best he could have asked for. He did not stop in any spot, he charged up and down, so that nothing escaped him, in front or behind. He was like an angry lion which rushes among the hinds, killing to right and left, not from hunger, but to display its great pride and power. That is what Lancelot did; he was a standard:* his shield was available to all, his helm appeared in every spot, his sword was at the service of everyone. And it seemed to all his enemies that all the others who were following him were the same, for it seemed to them that they only saw him, for now they saw him here, and now there, now he was on the right, now on the left. They feared him so much that, however great a number of Saxons there were, they dared not meet him; instead the most renowned gave way before him, who just before had thought they had the better of the war with King Arthur.

Sir Yvain followed him at a gallop, so pleased by the remarkable deeds he was doing that he thought he must be the crowned king of all the world. And he said that now no one should bear arms except this man, who knew how to do so properly. And all the others spurred after him, who just before had been as good as routed. And the Saxons and the Irish could not stand firm any longer, and were scarcely able to offer them[1] any opposition on the battlefield, and they[1] could see that there was little resistance left in them. And they all took heart and courage from that, so that even the most cowardly were such knights that they did greater deeds of arms than the most renowned had been doing before. Lancelot went in front, doing his remarkable deeds, and he directed his horse towards the most noble and powerful and valorous man of them all. His name was Hargadabrant, and he was half a foot and a whole hand* taller than other knights, and the point of his helm showed above the whole battle like a banner. And [562] everyone rallied to him. He was the brother of the damsel of the Rock and it was for his sake that she had betrayed King Arthur and his companions, for he aimed to take the whole of Britain, once he had the king and Sir Gawain. Lancelot went over to him, sword in hand, and the Saxon, who had seen the remarkable deeds that he was doing, dared not face him, but fled as fast as he could. However, Lancelot's horse was swifter than his, and he caught up with him on the slope of a moor, and raised his sword to strike him on the head. And the Saxon bent forward over his horse's neck and thrust his shield in the way. Lancelot struck the shield, and took off the top half, and sent it flying on to the field. The blow landed on his right thigh, and cut clean through it and the saddle-cloth down to the horse's flank, and knocked both the Saxon and his horse down all in a heap. And he rushed on past, without giving him another look, and charged to where he expected to find a mêlée. However, he did not find one, for all the Saxons and Irish had run away, as soon as they saw Hargadabrant fall, for he was their mainstay. And Sir Yvain had gone up to him, where he saw him fall, and he knew very well that it was him, but he did not think that he was so badly hurt. He stopped over him and captured him with little resistance, for he could

---

[1] i.e. Sir Yvain's troops.

no longer defend himself, and all his men had abandoned him, and were fleeing. And when he[1] had lifted him up, he saw that he was badly maimed, as his thigh was cut through, and seeing the horse cut at least half through, he began to cross himself and said that it was not wise to face the kind of man who gave such blows; for he was not a man, but a visitation and vengeance from the Lord God.

Thus Hargadabrant was captured, and Sir Yvain sent him to the tents; however, he did not live long, for he was so distressed at being mutilated that he killed himself with a knife. And Lancelot had pursued the Saxons, with few troops, for they all stayed around Sir Yvain. And when the Saxons had fled as far as the Godelonte narrows, there were never such great and remarkable deeds as Lancelot did there, for he cut so many of them to pieces that the stream which ran over the causeway changed colour. He hardly found anyone who would meet a blow from him, and more than two thousand fled into the marshes and perished there. And those who were crowded together in front went across on the causeway; but there were a great many killed in the crush. And Lancelot killed so many that his shield and hauberk and his horse were covered in blood, his own and that of others. [563] When the Saxons and the Irish were across, they bunched together on the causeway to guard the crossing, and they saw that, of all King Arthur's knights and troops, only Lancelot was pursuing them, for they saw no one else in front of the causeway. Then they were all so ashamed that they did not dare speak to one another. Lancelot was at the end of the causeway, his drawn sword in his hand, its blade all red with blood. And when he saw them all bunched together on the causeway, he was about to charge them. And Lionel took hold of his bridle, and said:

'By the Holy Cross, you will not go. Do you wish to get

---

[1] i.e. Sir Yvain.

yourself killed in a place where you can do no deeds of prowess? And if you did any, no one would ever know. Have you then not done enough, when you have achieved that which all King Arthur's troops could not do?'

And Lancelot said that he would go regardless. And Lionel held on to him.

'Go away,' said Lancelot. 'Let me go.'

'I will not,' he said.

And he swore by everything he could that he would never love him again. 'And I shall wound you, if you do not let go.'

'Then I shall let go,' Lionel said.

Then he let him go; and Lancelot charged on to the causeway, and Lionel spurred after him, and said:

'I say to you by my lady, and by the loyalty you owe her, that you are to go no further.'

When he heard that, he reined in and began to sigh very deeply. And the Saxons were already giving way before him, for they dared not meet his blows.

'Ha!' said Lancelot to Lionel, 'why did you speak so soon? You can see that they are all so routed that they would never face me.'

Then he turned away; and when he looked round, he saw Sir Yvain coming. Sir Yvain said to him:

'Sir, you are well come.'

'Indeed, sir,' he said, 'I come quite wretchedly, on the contrary, for I am returning with great dishonour.'

'Why with great dishonour?' Sir Yvain asked.

'Is it not indeed with great dishonour,' he said, 'when I dare not go forward, and yet I should gladly go if I dared?'

'As God is my witness,' said Sir Yvain, 'to go would not be bravery, but foolishness. In any case, I know you well enough that you would not refrain from doing anything out of cowardice.'

[564] And Lancelot was not content with that, but was so

very angry that he was nearly beside himself, and he did not utter a word.

Thus they went back to the army; and Sir Yvain did not speak to him again, for he could see that it did not please him. And when the Saxons had seen Sir Yvain, they had moved back on to the causeway, which they had not dared hold when Lancelot galloped on to it, and they all gave way before him. Now they did not move on account of Sir Yvain or his troops, because Lancelot was going away. Sir Yvain saw that it would not be wise to cross over the causeway, and he and his troops turned back. And when the Saxons saw them going away, they galloped after them. The others attacked them, and they withdrew on to their causeway. And when Sir Yvain turned away, then they charged again. The fighting between the two sets of troops continued like this until evening, when they withdrew on both sides because of the darkness. And Lancelot had gone to the gate above the river where the enchantment was, the one which was closed with air. And his shield had the property that no enchantment could resist it. Looking in front of the gate, he saw the 200 knights who were on guard night and day so that the king was not taken away. When they saw him coming, they recognized him and each man said: 'There is the good knight.' And they sprang up and went to meet him as soon as they recognized him, and they greeted him, and he them. Then they went back as near to the gate as they could, for they had to keep their distance because of the quarrels and arrows, which were flying thickly. Then a knight in full armour came out from inside, and he had around his neck a black shield with a diagonal band, and it was the shield which Lancelot had been carrying in the castle when he was captured. The knight asked for a joust; and Lancelot said:

'Sir knight, if you will give me a truce until I have talked to you, I shall move nearer, for I should like to talk to you.'

And the other guaranteed his safety until he had talked to

him. Then Lancelot drew near to him, and asked him where he had got that shield. And he said that it belonged to the best knight of King Arthur's household, who was up there in prison.

'And what is his name?' Lancelot asked.

'It is Gawain,' he said, 'King Arthur's nephew.'

'Truly,' said Lancelot, 'you are lying. It never hung around Sir Gawain's neck; and you do not have the man it belonged to in prison. You will regret letting him escape.'

[565] 'What?' said the knight, 'are you contradicting me? Now beware, for I no longer guarantee your safety.'

Lancelot looked at Lionel, and then took hold of the lance to which the pennon was attached, and tucked it under his arm and spurred his horse towards the knight from the castle. And the other looked up and told the archers and crossbow-men, who covered the walls, to shoot, and they did so. They wounded Lancelot's horse and Lancelot himself in many places, but he had no wound which troubled him much. And he took aim at the knight and struck him right on the throat so hard that the lance-head passed through his throat, and he knocked him to the ground. And he left the lance and pennon in his throat and spurred through the gate, and went away on without delay and rode up through the castle and found all the gates and posterns open. He did not stop until he came to the great hall and found a great many knights, who were arming themselves because of the clamour that those outside the walls had set up because the knight was knocked down. And Lancelot charged them, and cut through their arms and spines and sides, and clove them in two, and spilt the brains of everyone he could reach; and the others fled to safety in the main fortress. Lancelot dismounted, and went to where he knew the lady resided, and found her in a bed, and beside her her lover, who was called Gadresalain, and was a young knight, very handsome and of great prowess. And he was there completely without armour, for he thought

he had nothing to fear, and there were knights without
armour with him, a good many of them. Lancelot raised his
sword, and struck Gadresalain on the head, so that he clove
him to the shoulders. Then he charged the others, and cut
them all to pieces, when he caught them. They headed for
the door to flee, but he was there before them, and closed
the door in their faces and barred it firmly. Then he charged
them; and they fled into the chambers, both upstairs and
down. And he pursued them, and most of them flung
themselves out of the windows to the ground. And when he
could find no one else, he went back into the courtyard, with
drawn sword, and went towards the gaoler whom he saw,
who guarded Sir Gawain and the others; and he said that he
was a dead man if he did not tell him where to find the
armour and the prisoners in there. And the other said that he
would take him. Then he led him to a turret above the
chamber, where King Arthur and Guerrehet were in prison.
And he[1] made him open it and then had Guerrehet and King
Arthur brought out of prison. The king did not recognize
him, and wondered who he could be. Then Lancelot and the
[566] turnkey took them to the armour, and they armed
themselves swiftly. Lancelot saw a big axe, bright and very
sharp, which was hanging from a peg, and he took it and
thrust his sword into the scabbard. Then he and the gaoler
went back to where Galehot and his companions were in
prison, and set them free. And Lancelot took them to where
the king and Guerrehet were arming themselves, and they
made much of one another. And when Galehot had begun to
arm himself, he said:

'Alas! why am I arming myself, when we have lost the
flower of the knights of all the world and the person I most
loved? May God never be my witness if I want to live without
him, or if I ever again wear a helm on my head, since I have
lost him.'

---

[1] i.e. Lancelot.

Then he began to grieve bitterly. And Lancelot took off his helm, and said:

'Dear sir, do not be downcast, for I am here.'

And he[1] sprang forward and ran to kiss him. Then Lancelot laced his helm on again. And when Sir Gawain saw him, he sprang forward and said to the king:

'Sire, here is the man we have sought for so long. I have found him, and I have kept my word.'

'Ah, Lord!' said the king, 'who is he?'

'He is Lancelot of the Lake,' said Sir Gawain, 'the man who was the victor at the two encounters between you and Galehot here.'

And the king was overjoyed. And when they were all armed, the king fell at Lancelot's feet and said:

'Sir, I put myself in your power, myself and my honour and my land, for you have given me back the one and the other.'

And he immediately raised him up and he himself wept bitterly because the king was so humbling himself towards him.

Thus they were all armed. And the gaoler, who was very much afraid, helped them until they were all ready, and supplied them with their swords from where he knew they had been put when they were captured. Then they went to the great tower which stood on the great rock, but they could not go in there, for there were knights inside who had closed the doors firmly. The tower was well supplied with provisions, and no one could hold the bailey unless he held the tower. When Lancelot saw that they would not get in there in that way, he took the gaoler and told him that he guaranteed his safety, as long as he showed him the lady of the place. And the other took him to where he had found Gadresalain, her lover, and took him through into a chamber and showed her

---

[1] i.e. Galehot.

to him, and Lancelot grasped her by the hair and said that he would send her head flying.

[567] 'Ah!' she said, 'mercy, noble knight. You have already killed my lover.'

'As God is my witness,' he said, 'you are a dead woman, if you do not have that great tower handed over to me.'

She said that she would rather he cut off her head, and he would be doing something which no knight ever did before. And he raised his sword and made as if to cut it off. And she begged for mercy and said that she would have the tower handed over. Then she went below the tower and told the knights who were up there to open the tower. They said that they would not; and Lancelot swore that he would cut off her head if they did not open it to him at once. And when they saw the predicament, they were very worried and said that they would open it, as long as the king allowed them to go. And he gave them his word. Then he[1] made them all disarm, and they came out. And the king ordered Sir Gawain to go in; and he said:

'What, sire? Am I to leave you?'

'Yes, you are,' he said.

And he ordered him to enter, and there was nothing the tower would have feared.*

Thereupon they went back into the tower,* and archers and crossbowmen began to shoot from the battlements and windows. And Lancelot went to the upper gate, and showed himself. And they all began to laugh and to shout King Arthur's battle-cry, 'Clarance! Clarance!'* Meanwhile, those in the army were very worried, for they were afraid that they had lost Lancelot. The queen had heard the news that Lionel had brought her when he could not go into the castle after him; and she grieved so much over it that she was nearly overcome. And when she heard that the castle was captured,

---

[1] i.e. Lancelot.

she rejoiced as much as any lady could. And at once the castle was so full that one could not turn round. When it came to searching the chambers and cellars, Kay the seneschal went into a chamber, and found a damsel in chains. She had been Gadresalain's ladylove, and Canile had held her in prison for three years, because he had loved her. And she[1] said that she would have to die there. When Kay the seneschal had released her from prison and from the chains, he asked her where all the prisoners were. And she asked him what was happening in the town; and he said that King Arthur had captured the castle. And she raised her hands to God.

'Sir,' she said, 'has the lady of this place escaped you?'

'No,' he said, 'she is still here.'

[568] 'Sir,' she said, 'if she takes away her books and boxes you have lost everything, for, using the books she has, she could make a river flow up here.'

'Where are they?' asked Kay.

She showed him a big, very strong chest; and Kay promptly set fire to it, and burned it to ashes. And when Canile heard about it, she was so grieved that she threw herself down off the Rock, and was very badly injured. And the king was very upset about that, for he loved her very much. And she would rather have lost four such castles, if she had had them, than her good books and her boxes.

Thus the Rock was captured, and the king was inside, with a great part of his troops. And Sir Gawain came out of the tower and said to the king:

'Sire, you will lose Lancelot, if you do not take care.'

'What?' said the king.

'Indeed,' he said, 'Galehot will take him away as soon as he can, for he is more jealous of him than a knight who has a beautiful young lady. But I shall tell you what you must do.

---

[1] i.e. Canile.

You must order the gate to be closed, so that no one comes in or goes out unless I let them, and you must make me swear it, and Kay the seneschal likewise, and Sir Yvain and my brother Guerrehet. And you will have such a company there that no one will come in or go out unless you let them.'

Thereupon the king went into the great hall, and took Galehot by one hand and Lancelot by the other, and led them to the great tower, and they sat down on a couch and had themselves disarmed. Then the king called Sir Gawain, and had him swear the oath, and then Sir Yvain, who had arrived by now, and Kay and Guerrehet. And when Galehot heard it, he knew and could see what was going on, and he sighed very heavily and very anxiously deep down, for his heart told him part of what would happen. And he said it to Lancelot.

'Dear companion,' he said, 'we have come to the point where I shall lose you.'

'What, sir?' he said.

'I know for a fact', Galehot said, 'that the king will ask you to remain in his household. And what shall I do, who have devoted heart and body to you?'

'Truly, sir,' said Lancelot, 'I ought to love you more than all the men in the world, and so I do. And I shall not remain in King Arthur's household unless I am forced to do so. But how am I to refuse anything that my lady commands?'

[569] 'I shall not push you that far,' said Galehot. 'Indeed, if she wishes it, it must be.'

Thus the two of them talked together. And the king took them aside again, and they rejoiced again, more than suited the hearts of some of them. Then the king sent for the queen; and she arrived, and everyone in the tower sprang up to meet her. And she ignored all the others, and threw her arms around Lancelot's neck, and kissed him in front of all those who were in there, because she wished to deceive them all, and that no one should suspect the truth. And everyone who saw it held her in greater esteem because of it, but he was very embarrassed. And she said:

'Sir knight, I do not know who you are, which distresses me; nor do I know what to offer you, firstly for my lord's honour, and secondly for mine, which you have preserved today. But firstly for his sake and secondly for mine, I grant myself and my love to you, in the way that a faithful lady should give it to a faithful knight.'

And when the king heard that, he esteemed her highly because she had done it without instruction.

There was great rejoicing over Lancelot there. And then the queen also made much of Sir Gawain and Galehot and the other companions of the king who were with him[1] on the quest, for they were all there apart from Sagremor.* And many asked what had become of him; and Sir Gawain told how he had left him with a damsel that he loved. After that the queen told how Lancelot had been cured in her chambers of the great madness which he had contracted in the castle, and how a damsel who called herself the Lady of the Lake had cured him.

'My lady,' said the king, 'do you know who the knight is?'
She said that she did not.

'Now, then, let me tell you that he is Lancelot of the Lake, the man who was the victor at the two encounters between me and Galehot.'

When she heard that, she pretended that it came as a great surprise to her, and crossed herself very often. And after that Sir Yvain told them the remarkable deeds of arms he[2] had done all that day.

'Sire, sire,' said Sir Yvain, 'we sent to my lady, for we thought that all her knights were not in the battle. And she sent him to us, all alone, and sent us word that she would send us quite enough knights to replace the 200 who had

---

[1] i.e. Sir Gawain.   [2] i.e. Lancelot.

gone to Arestel—for I had sent 200 there. And my lady spoke the truth in that, for, as God is my witness, if the 200 had been there and he [570] had not, we should never have achieved what we have achieved now. And the Saxons would never have been put in such difficulties by the 200 as they were by him.'

'By my faith,' said the king, 'he has done greater deeds of arms in rescuing me than in all his other acts of prowess, when he has captured a castle like this, which was causing me more trouble than all the other castles in the world. And I certainly ought to love him more than all other men.'

After that Hector came before the queen and said:

'My lady, there is the object of my quest.'

And he showed her Sir Gawain; and the queen made much of him. And Sir Yvain did him great honour, for he told how he had freed him and Sagremor from the prison of the King of a Hundred Knights and how he had defeated his seneschal. And Sir Gawain told how he knocked down Sagremor and Kay and Girflet and Sir Yvain at the Spring of the Pine. Then there were many people who looked at him, for he was greatly praised; and his ladylove rejoiced more than all the others.

Thereupon the meal was ready, and they sat down. And when they had eaten, the king called the queen and said to her privately:

'My lady, I mean to ask Lancelot to remain with me and to be a companion of the Round Table, for his great prowess has been thoroughly put to the test. And if he does not wish to remain for my sake, then fall at his feet at once.'

'My lord,' said the queen, 'he is in Galehot's service,* and is his companion, and it would be a good idea for you to ask Galehot to allow it.'

Then the king went to Galehot, and asked him if he would please allow Lancelot to be in his household and to remain with him as his lord and companion.

'Ah! my lord,' said Galehot, 'I came in your hour of need with all my might, for I could not do more. And may God never be my witness, if I could live without him: how could you take away my life?'

He said that, because he did not think the queen would wish it. And the king immediately looked at the queen, and said:

'Ask him, my lady.'

And she at once fell on her knees in front of Lancelot. When Lancelot saw her on her knees, it made him very unhappy; and he did not wait for Galehot to look at him, but sprang up and said to the queen:

[571] 'Ah! my lady, I will remain with my lord at his pleasure and at yours.'

Then she stood up.

'Sir,' she said, 'many thanks.'

'My lord,' said Galehot, 'you will not have him like that, for I would rather be poor and content than rich and unhappy. Retain me with him, if I have ever done anything which pleased you. And you certainly ought to do so, both for his sake and for mine, for you should know that all the love I have for you, I have because of him.'

The king sprang up, and thanked him and said that he was retaining them, not as his knights, but as his companions and lords.

Thus the king retained Lancelot and Galehot in his service, and then after them Hector, as their companion, and in honour of the two of them. And there was such great rejoicing in the king's household that no one could describe greater to you. The next day the king said that he would hold a magnificent court in the castle of the Rock itself to rejoice over Lancelot, and he held it, very noble and rich. That was seven days before All Saint's, and there was not one day of all those seven when he did not wear his crown* and hold court more and more magnificently. On that day* the three knights were installed as knights of the Round Table. And the clerks were called, who recorded the deeds of prowess of the companions of the king's household. There were four of them, and the first was called Arodion of Cologne, and the second Tontamides of Vernaus, and the third Thomas of Toledo, and the fourth Sapien of Baudas. These four recorded all the deeds of arms that the king's companions performed, and they recorded Sir Gawain's adventures first, because he started the quest, and then those of Hector, because they were a branch of the same story, and then the adventures of all the eighteen* companions. And all that was part of the story of Lancelot, all the others being branches of that one, while the story of Lancelot was itself a branch of the Grail story, so that it was put together with it.

With such rejoicing, the king and his companions stayed in the Rock every day until three days after All Saints', and then he went away, leaving a garrison in the Rock. Then he went back to Britain in easy stages; and when he reached Cama-heu,* Galehot took leave of him and asked him to let him take Lancelot away with him to his country. However, the king agreed to it with great reluctance. And the queen wished it, and told the king that Advent would soon be beginning, and she persuaded the king to agree to it, on condition that they promised him faithfully [572] that they would be with him on Christmas Day. And he told them that he would be in the city where he made Lancelot a knight.[1] And they gave him their word. Thereupon Galehot and Lancelot left, and went away to their country,[2] and the king and his company went away to Britain.*

{Summary of pp. [572–613].}
[572–83] [M. I] Galehot and Lancelot set off. On their journey, Galehot becomes thoughtful. He realizes that, the

---
[1] i.e. Camelot.   [2] i.e. Sorelois.

first time they go to court, the queen will wish Lancelot to stay there, and he and Lancelot will be parted, since his obligations as a ruler will not allow him to spend all his time at Arthur's court. He will lose Lancelot's companionship, and the great sacrifice he made for him will have been for nothing. Distressed, he faints and falls from his horse. When Lancelot asks the reason for this, Galehot explains, adding that he does not regret anything he has done for Lancelot. Lancelot replies that he would do anything he could for Galehot, but could not refuse if the queen asked him to stay at court.

When they reach the edge of Galehot's lands, Galehot shows Lancelot a magnificent castle. He explains that he intended to wear his crown there to celebrate his conquest of Logres, and to have all the thirty-one* kings he had conquered there, each wearing his own crown. As they approach, large sections of the castle walls crash to the ground. Galehot is astonished: he thought it the strongest castle in the world, and named it 'The Proud Watch-Post'.* He decides the falling walls must be significant.

The next day, they travel to another castle, and find its walls are also down. Lancelot says that Galehot should not be dismayed: it is clearly a sign from God. The following day, they go on to the city of Caellus. There, Galehot is met by his uncle, who tells him that all his castles have collapsed. Galehot still refuses to be downcast.

That night, Galehot dreams of two lions. One of them is crowned, and they are fighting. The fight is stopped by the intervention of a leopard. In the morning, he tells Lancelot of this, and says that he wishes to send to court for the men who explained King Arthur's dream.* This will also enable them to have news of their ladyloves.

They send Lionel, who finds the king in Camelot, and discharges his messages to Arthur and the queen. Arthur sends his clerks back with Lionel, and they are warmly received by Galehot. He relates his dream, adding that a short while later (in the dream) he came upon the body of the uncrowned lion, which had been killed by the leopard.

After three days of deliberation, the clerks explain the dream—the lions are Arthur and Galehot; the leopard is Lancelot, who will cause the latter's death—and that the collapsing castles are a sign that God is punishing Galehot for his pride in attacking Arthur, the most worthy man in the world. They tell him that he will die of grief because of Lancelot, within three years. This upsets Lancelot, but Galehot comforts him.

[584–96] [M. II] King Arthur is in Carlisle, with all the Round Table knights. One day, a beautiful damsel arrives with an old knight. They tell Arthur that they are from 'Guinevere, daughter of King Leodegan of Camelide'. Arthur, they say, married her and vowed to honour her, but has not done so. They explain that, on his wedding night, Arthur left his bridal chamber, and 'Guinevere' was taken away by her enemies, who substituted the queen. The real bride was taken to an abbey, where she has been ever since. The old knight, Berthelai, offers to prove this claim in combat against any knight who wishes to dispute it. The damsel gives Arthur a letter from 'Guinevere', and tells him that if he will not take her back, he is to return the Round Table,* with as many good knights as it came to him with. She has sent an old knight as her champion as a sign of the justness of her cause. The damsel shows Arthur a ring, which seems to be the one he gave the queen when they were married. However, Gawain goes and fetches the queen's ring: the two are identical. The damsel demands a day for judgement of the case. Arthur sets it for Boxing Day, at Camelot; it is agreed that if no one defends the queen then, Arthur will accept that she is an impostor.

Berthelai and the damsel return to 'Guinevere'. He tells her that, if she does as he tells her, he will make her a queen.

She agrees, and promises to reward him well. Berthelai then enlists the support of the barons of Camelide, of whom some twenty offer their unqualified support. Saying that they must use guile rather than force, as the guilty party, King Arthur, is too powerful for them to fight, he suggests that they kidnap the king.

By a ruse, Berthelai gets Arthur alone in a forest, and he and the twenty knights capture him and take him away to the abbey, where he is given a potion, which makes him fall in love with 'Guinevere'. He is given the potion every day for two weeks, at the end of which time he is hopelessly in love with her. He says that he will make her queen, and only wonders how his wife can appear so good and yet be so treacherous. 'Guinevere' replies that those who intend evil are always more deceitful than others.

In due course, Berthelai tells the Camelide barons that King Arthur has recognized their lady as his wife. The king and 'Guinevere' tour the country, and everyone in Camelide accepts her as the true queen, since Arthur has done so.

Arthur sends a message to Sir Gawain at Camelot. He is to come to Camelide, with the companions, for Christmas. The king will hold court there, and 'Guinevere' will be crowned queen. Gawain is to bring the queen with him, to be given justice. The queen is worried, and sends a damsel to Lancelot and Galehot, to explain the situation and ask them to come and help her.

[596–603] [M. III] Lancelot and Galehot go to Camelot at once. Galehot reassures the queen, and tells her to go to Camelide with Sir Gawain and the others. If trial by combat is agreed, Lancelot will be there as her champion. If not, Galehot will have troops there to rescue her, and she and Lancelot can go and rule Sorelois together.

In Camelide, Arthur is annoyed to realize that the Round Table knights will ensure that the queen is given a proper trial, but he plans to arrange matters so that no one will dare champion her cause.

Galehot's men arrive, led by the King of a Hundred Knights. Galehot explains their presence by telling Arthur that he had heard he was a prisoner in Camelide. Arthur decrees that the queen is to be judged by Berthelai and some of the Camelide barons. After they have deliberated, Arthur himself pronounces their verdict. The queen is guilty, and is to have her hair and scalp removed, as she wore a crown to which she was not entitled; her palms are to be skinned, as she was wrongfully anointed; she is to be dragged through the town, then burned, and her ashes scattered to the winds. Arthur adds that, since they are certain of her guilt, anyone who wishes to defend her must fight the three best knights 'Guinevere' can find. Sir Gawain and Kay both offer to do so, but a furious Lancelot claims the combat, adding that he would be more than happy to fight a fourth man, if it was a certain king who is present.

[603–13] [M. IV] The combat duly takes place, and Lancelot kills each of the three champions in turn. Arthur calls 'Guinevere' and Berthelai to be judged, and the former confesses. Berthelai then reveals how he hatched the scheme, and he and 'Guinevere' are taken away and burned.

Arthur decides to hold court there in Camelide, as Christmas is only three days away. The queen tells Lancelot, in front of the king, that from now on he may consider her his. Arthur agrees that he owes Lancelot everything: peace with Galehot, rescue from the Saxon Rock, and rescue from this disgrace. He wishes Lancelot to stay with him, and says that all he has is at his disposal.

After the great court has been held, Arthur and all the others set off for Britain. When they reach Quimpercorentin, Galehot wishes to leave, but is persuaded to stay for the winter. The queen now feels her relationship with Lancelot is thoroughly justified by all he has done for her.

At the Easter court in Camelot, Arthur agrees to make Lionel a knight. As they are feasting, a damsel arrives with a lion, which has a crown growing from its head. She announces that her lady, who is very beautiful, will give her love to whoever can defeat the lion. The next day, after his knighting, Lionel fights with the lion, and strangles it.* He is made a knight of the Round Table, and the damsel takes him away to her lady, who is delighted with him.

Galehot leaves court and goes away to the Far Isles. There a damsel comes and tells him that she saw Lancelot killed in the Forest of Adventures. Galehot has just been bled, and his distress brings on a fatal illness. He dies three days later.

EXPLANATORY NOTES

3 *Galahad*: Lancelot is the young Galahad's 'surname': his epithet or nickname. The exact significance of these names is often unclear, as in this case, or that of Aramont-Hoel. The latter suggests possible conflation of two characters. In other instances, such as Sagremor the Impetuous, it is clearly a nickname, while in such as Yvain the Tall, it distinguishes one Yvain from another (cf. n. to p. [197], Kennedy). The name Galahad does not seem to have any significance here, with regard to the Holy Grail. It should also not be confused with that of Galehot, who is another character altogether.

explain later: there is in fact no subsequent explanation.

Berry: one of the old regions of France, capital Bourges. Situated in the centre, it is now divided into several *départements*.

feudal service: in feudal society, the vassal held his land in fief from an overlord (who was usually himself a vassal, and so on, up to the king, and sometimes beyond, as a king might hold land from another king), to whom he owed service, essentially of a military nature. In turn, the overlord was expected to protect his vassals' interests, to administer justice in disputes between vassals, and so on.

4 *became his man*: Aramont pays homage to Uther, and so becomes his vassal; cf. the previous note.

Logres: the kingdom of Uther Pendragon, then of Arthur, and apparently the same as Britain. Also the name of a city.

5 *leagues*: not nautical leagues, but an old measure of distance. It varied considerably from one country to another, cf. 'English leagues', p. [7]. Possibly about three miles, but perhaps as little as half that.

from the forest: I have elected to read *de vers*, rather than *devers*; the sense of the latter would be the opposite: 'had moved towards the forest'.

6 *the foragers*: that is, Claudas's foragers, scouring the countryside for food for his troops.

8 *clear evidence*: this is to be a king travelling with his wife and son, and only one retainer.

9 *the night of the Assumption*: this would make the Assumption (15 August) a Friday; subsequently, Claudas refers to it being on a Sunday. Is it possible that the feast was celebrated on the nearest Sunday to 15 August? Later in the text, there is a reference to the week of the Assumption.

    three leagues: that is, the time it would take to go three leagues.

    worthy: the terms *preu* and *prodome* cause great difficulty in translation. Their sense covers good qualities of every sort, from religious to military excellence, hence the various terms I have used to render them: 'worthy, valorous', and 'man of worth, worthy man, man of valour'.

10 *footservant*: there is an inconsistency here. The king stated that he would take only one squire, and subsequently we only hear of one. Here, however, there is a servant, and a squire, and if *garçon a pié*, which I have translated 'footservant', were taken to mean literally a servant on foot, there would be three attendants.

11 *in front of all my barons*: the barons are to be witnesses to a formal ceremony.

12 *hurled him down dead*: note that Banin is using a lance, although he is on foot. The lance of this period was not much different from a long spear.

13 *alures*: these are the walkways around the inside of the walls, from which the defenders could shoot and hurl missiles at attackers.

    drawbridge: it was not uncommon to find small drawbridges inside castles, isolating sections of the defences. In this way, the defenders could make a progressive retreat, even if the attackers got inside the walls.

    the small castle: the layout of Trebe's defences is not altogether clear. There is a small castle, probably protecting the gates, and a main fortification, comprising, at the very least, tower and bailey.

14 *as a traitor*: this might mean that Banin will not desert one lord for another, since, although he subsequently does so, he has an ulterior motive. Alternatively, it may simply mean that he will not give up until he has done all he can.

16 *accuse of something*: this is a deliberate, amd almost verbatim, repetition of a formal agreement, here ratified in front of witnesses.

his liege lord: here we have a deliberate repetition of what is a formal accusation; cf. the previous note.

fiefs: while *honor* can mean 'honour' or 'land', in this case the seneschal was promised the kingdom of Benwick.

17 *he has only you*: the judicial duel is to be single combat between the two parties, with no involvement of champions or friends; cf. the note to p. [25–9].

take this: I have assumed that Claudas gives the seneschal some symbol of office.

prowess and loyalty: these were the essential qualities in a judicial combat, where the rightness of a man's cause was considered as important as his fighting ability. Indeed, it was theoretically more important, since it was assumed that God would help whoever was in the right.

19 *stopped up*: tears were believed to come directly from the heart, and are sometimes called the 'water of the heart' in this text. Presumably the inability to let them out was believed to be dangerous.

Kingdom of Adventures: doubtless the same as Logres (cf. the note to p. [2]), which is later called the Adventurous Perilous Kingdom. See Kennedy's note in vol. ii of her edition for a discussion of these lines.

23 *the world*: that is, the secular world, society.

25 *in his place*: to have a champion fight in one's stead in a judicial combat was commonplace, and essential for women. Cf. later, the fight between Lancelot and Kay, as the champions of the

Lady of Nohaut, and the champions of the King of Northumberland.

26 *a vassal of the late King Bors*: Pharien is Claudas's vassal, but has apparently never renounced his homage to King Bors. The technicalities of the feudal bond are an essential feature of the action in this part of the text.

Gaunes and Benwick: Lancelot, the heir to Benwick, is believed to be dead.

for fear of his life: Claudas is afraid that Dorin, thwarted in his desire to be liberal and extravagant, will kill him, and take the throne, in order to have a free hand.

over two years: that is, before the events just related. This is not the only such backward shift in time in the text.

Heliabel: for Helen, cf. the summary of pp. [516–24]; Heliabel is the sister of Perceval, the original Grail-hero.

Little Ireland: I would conjecture that this might mean the Isle of Man.

27 *Galone*: this may be a corruption of *Galvoie*: probably Galloway, rather than Galway.

tutor: I have used this word to translate *maistre* (Latin *magister*). A more exact term might be 'governor', in its archaic sense; that is, the male equivalent of a governess: a man who is responsible for every aspect of a child's upbringing.

29 *full of joy*: this *joie* is probably that which will stem from Lancelot's love for Guinevere.

30 *source*: I would take this source of joy to mean Guinevere, cf. the previous note.

31 *a friend*: the Old French word *ami* can also mean a kinsman, which may well be the sense here; cf. also the note to p. [165].

32 *disgraced*: failure to appear on the appointed day would be tantamount to an admission of guilt, or of having made a wrongful accusation.

38 *give away his own*: I take this to mean that a king's son should not be limited in his generosity.

39 *Saraide*: the damsel's name is twice given as Saraide here, after which she is just called 'the damsel'. Later on, however, the same damsel is called Celice, cf. the note to pp. [493–515].

   the feast of Mary Magdalene: 22 July.

42 *his wife*: she, it will be remembered, had an affair with Claudas, which Pharien knows about.

46 *decides not to kill him*: this incident, vividly depicted, must have made an impression on contemporary audiences, for it is related, sometimes with near verbatim reproduction of the dialogue, in the other great prose work of Old French literature, the prose *Tristan*.

47 *the Watch*: this institution is referred to in other texts, notably Chrétien de Troyes's *Perceval*, but it is not clear what it is. It would seem to be separate from, and less prestigious than, the Round Table, and in this text it is said to comprise 150 knights.

48 *near home*: there would be little chance of a kill near human habitation.

53 *knights*: in Old French, as in Modern French, 'horse' is *cheval*, 'knight' is *chevalier*.

   arms: here, the word 'arms' means weapons and armour. It often has the sense of the 'coat of arms', or cognizance, of a knight.

   hangs around his neck: the shield was normally carried on a strap which went around the neck; there were also arm-straps on the back, which were generally used only in combat.

56 *to the Lord God and to Our Lord*: this is apparently a distinction, not always made, between God and Jesus.

   John the Hyrcanian: John Hyrcanus I, high priest of the Jews 135–105 BC, third and youngest son of Simon Maccabaeus, himself the youngest brother of Judas.

   Judas Maccabaeus: see 1 Maccabees 3–9.

57 *called Wales in his honour*: Gales, 'Wales', from Galahad.

   Alain the Thickset: Pelles and Alain are the father and uncle (or uncle and father, in some texts) of Perceval, the original Grail-winner. It would appear that in this, the non-cyclical Lancelot, Perceval was still regarded as the Grail-hero, and had not yet been supplanted by Galahad.

59 *silver boss*: the shield was made of planks, glued together and covered with leather, which was usually painted, often with the 'arms' of the knight. A central, reinforced boss would help to protect the knight's shield-arm.

the damsel's lover: the 'damsel' is the Lady of the Lake. Her lover is a shadowy figure, who is only mentioned here and on p. [107], although she alludes to him on p. [556].

protecting the boys: this is Saraide; cf. the summary of pp. [57–70].

60 *Floudehueg*: this port has been variously identified with Hudan Fleot, formerly near West Hythe, and with Weymouth.

61 *coif*: the coif was a hood of chain-mail, attached to the hauberk and worn beneath the helm. The Old French word used here is actually *ventaille*, which at this time would normally mean a flap of mail tied up to cover the lower part of the face. If this were the meaning here, the sword would certainly have killed the knight, besides which the sense of *ventaille* in the *Lancelot* often seems to overlap with that of *coife*, 'coif'. I have therefore used whichever word seemed appropriate to translate *ventaille* (it should be noted that the sense of 'ventail' does not correspond to the definition given by the *OED*), while always rendering *coife* by 'coif'.

his name: in fact, the knight's name is only given in the longer, cyclic version.

62 *friends*: cf. the note to p. [42].

my vassal: if the man were Arthur's vassal, the king could not fight with him, unless a dispute had caused the man to renounce the feudal tie.

69 *he is very handsome*: the emphasis on the youth's good looks, already noted by Arthur and Yvain, is a feature of this whole episode. The admiration they provoke in the men at court, which may at first seem slightly odd to the modern reader, is

essentially a reflection of the idea, current in medieval times, and implicit in the words of the Lady, on p. [154], that the inner self should correspond to the outer, and that a man or woman of great physical beauty may be expected to possess outstanding inner qualities to match.

73 *asked the youth*: Yvain has, of course, already told him, and is about to do so again. However, the emphasis here is presumably on firsthand acquaintance with the facts, questioning the knight himself. Yvain's retelling of the conditions is given a 'rubber stamp' of authority by the knight's presence.

set up: tables in the Middle Ages frequently consisted of large boards on trestles, which were set up, or 'laid', before the meal, and cleared away after it.

74 *in front of the knight's squires*: an oath was sworn by something holy (here, the church), and before witnesses (here, the knight's squires).

78 *a thing which it is reasonable to ask*: it was traditional, at least in the romances, to grant the first request of a newly made knight.

his cousin, Sir Yvain: Gawain and Yvain are cousins because their fathers, Lot and Urien, are brothers, cf. p. [181]. Gawain is Arthur's nephew on his mother's side.

80 *by another hand than that of the king*: the bestowal of the sword is the final act in the knighting ceremony and, as such, more important even than the accolade. As is made clear in the story, the knighting is not complete until this act has taken place. The youth, of course, wishes to have his sword officially given to him by the queen.

he did not fail to recognize her: I would interpret this as meaning that he had no difficulty in spotting the queen among all the ladies present: in other words, his eye was drawn to her at once.

81 *dear friend*: the Old French word *ami(e)* can denote any degree of friendship, right through to the intimacy of 'lover' (a sense it has frequently in the romances). The queen uses it here in a neutral sense, as a form of address which occurs often in the text, while the youth reads into it a greater degree of intimacy.

82 *none*: the day is divided according to the canonical hours. Those mentioned most often are: prime (6 a.m.), terce (9 a.m.), none (3 p.m., not noon), and vespers (6 p.m.). The sense of none, in particular, became very fluid, corresponding rather to 'early afternoon'.

83 *make up to me*: the hardship is caused by the knight's interruption of Lancelot's thoughts, when he is doubtless thinking about the queen. This motif recurs in the romance.

85 *at the edge of the forest*: this seems directly to contradict the earlier statement, that the pavilion was 'in the middle of a wide open space', but the phrase 'at the edge of the forest' might be interpreted fairly loosely.

96 *peacefully*: this might possibly mean without death or injury, or it might refer to relations between Lancelot and Kay.

100 *straps*: these are the fighting-straps; the forearm was slipped through them, or through one of them, while the left hand held the other; cf. the note to p. [148].

105 *conditions*: I have used the word 'conditions' to translate *covine*, the sense of which is often close to 'customs', and seems to embrace the entire situation inside the castle, particularly the enchantments.

107 *swore to be his prisoner*: when a knight was defeated in combat, it was customary for him to give himself up as a prisoner of the victor. He would then do whatever the victor asked of him, to discharge this obligation. Thus, in the romances, we often see defeated knights sent to a lady, or to King Arthur, who not infrequently makes them members of his own household. In reality, a simple ransom was the norm.

108 *his prisoner*: removing the defeated man's headgear is, of course, a preliminary to cutting off his head, should he fail to co-operate.

109 *begin again*: the text might be interpreted 'you will be able to carry on where you left off', but we shall see on p. [188] that this is not the case.

110 *red band*: I have not generally used the proper heraldic terms (here, 'bend'), on the principle that they might be unfamiliar

to some modern readers, whereas the Old French equivalents would have been perfectly familiar to the contemporary public.

112 *trying the adventure again*: in other words, he will release them, thus removing the obstacle just mentioned by the other knight.

116 *lord of the castle*: not, it would seem, the spokesman who talked to Lancelot earlier (p. [189]).

117 *his great sorrow*: that is, the capture of the Dolorous Guard, and with it the end of the 'customs' and the loss of his seat of power; cf. the note to p. [200].

exerted himself: I have chosen to read *vistoier*, with Micha, rather than *justoier*, with Kennedy. The two readings would be effectively identical in manuscript, but the meaning is not absolutely clear in either case.

120 *halls*: Old French *palais*, a great hall, or 'palace'.

121 *what arms he bore*: here, 'arms' means the coat of arms, or cognizance. This would most obviously be worn or carried on the shield, but might also be found on a surcoat (over the hauberk), and even on the horse's trappings. Banners bearing the coat of arms were also carried in battle.

122 *is he your brother, then?*: Kennedy's original punctuation would have Arthur speaking to the young man, i.e. 'What? is Aiglin your brother, then?' She shares my view that the sentence should be repunctuated.

Yvain the Bastard: a number of Yvains appear in Arthurian literature, chief among them being Yvain, the son of Urien (also called Yvain the Tall, in this text), Yvain the Bastard— generally taken to be the illegitimate brother of the aforementioned,—Yvain of the White Hands, and Yvain of Leonel. It is probable that some of these were originally the same person, cf. the note to p. [299].

124 *clerk*: a man of learning, frequently—but not necessarily—a member of the clergy.

125 *galleries*: these are open galleries, or balconies, usually on an upper floor, and looking out on the streets, or the countryside; they sometimes also have a view into the great hall.

126 *the castle hill*: that is, the Dolorous Guard. It is conceivable that *l'angarde* here is an error for *la garde*, 'the Guard'.

127 *the others*: presumably, this refers to Brandin's other castles. It would seem that he rules his land by force.

131 *in good faith*: this may be ironic, or it may mean that the companions accepted his offer in good faith. The reply that they have what they were promised is, of course, only partly true: they were also told that they could return to the Dolorous Guard every day, if they so wished.

132 *the son of King Arthur*: Lohot is a shadowy figure in Arthurian romance. He is mentioned in Chrétien de Troyes's *Erec* (the earliest surviving Arthurian romance), and in Ulrich von Zatikhoven's *Lanzelet*; in the latter he is the son of Guinevere and Arthur. He also appears in some of the prose romances, notably *Perlesvaus*, in which he is killed by Kay. In Welsh tradition, Arthur has a son called Llacheu, but Rachel Bromwich, *Trioedd Ynys Prydein*, considers it unlikely that there was any early association between the names and characters of Llacheu and Lohot.

135 *false postern*: a small, concealed door or gate, which may be used for secret comings and goings.

138 *thought to be a knight*: it will be remembered that Lancelot's knighting was only completed when he received a sword from the queen. The reference here is to the day King Arthur 'knighted' him.

139 *chalice*: it would seem that the hermit went to administer Extreme Unction to the two knights.

140 *Welsh ditches*: possibly bank and ditch earthworks.

    us: this would seem to mean just the hermit himself.

142 *lost them*: he is afraid that he will now be unable to exchange the lord of the castle for Sir Gawain and the others, and possibly also that they will be killed in retaliation.

145 *badly served*: this is a reference to their combat as champions of the Lady of Nohaut, and his suggestion that they fight to decide who should undertake it, cf. p. [176].

on his shield: it was apparently not uncommon for a shield to be used as an improvised stretcher.

hermit-knight: the hermit, it will be remembered, was a knight before he became a hermit.

opened: presumably so that they could go inside for the swearing of the oath.

returned: presumably from the chapel.

tokens: the lord gives the hermit some means of identication—either a token, such as a ring, or perhaps a 'password'.

146 *a prisoner*: the damsel was told not to leave before she saw the knight again, p. [205].

151 *sounded in the new day*: the watchman blows a horn to herald the beginning of each new day.

left his squires: cf. p. [178].

153 *encounter*: here and subsequently, this term has a military sense, a coming together for combat.

154 *the feast of Our Lady*: 8 September, the Nativity of the Blessed Virgin Mary.

impossible: Gawain clearly considers his pledge to be as binding as an oath.

gauntlets: strictly speaking, *manicles* would in this case be chain-mail mittens.

155 *Godoarre*: it is possible that this represents a deformation of Cotoatre, which occurs in Chrétien de Troyes's *Perceval*, and has been identified with the Forth.

157 *the knight's death*: that is, the impending death of the captive knight.

158 *brattice*: a (temporary) tower or other fortification made of wood.

159 *serious business*: Kennedy's text here follows the base manuscript *se por vostre affaire n'est*, 'except on your business', but the editor points out that this reading, an isolated one, seems weak, although difficult to explain as a mechanical error. I have based my translation on the reading *se por haut affaire non*, which occurs in one manuscript. The others, which do not

have the term *affaire*, but use a variety of phrases including the term *honte*, contain the idea of a defence of one's honour, a very grave matter.

160 *better than the knight himself*: this refers to the adventure Lancelot took on as soon as he was knighted, pp. [150, 160–1]. Below, the 'dead man' is the man who inflicted the wounds on the 'wounded man', the knight who came to court.

Sir Gawain and four like him: throughout (Old French) Arthurian romance, until the prose *Tristan*, Gawain is the yardstick by which other knights are measured. His valour is traditionally equalled only by his courtesy. It is common for the hero of a romance to fight with him: these combats, in which the protagonists generally do not recognize one another, are usually inconclusive, and brought to an end when the identity of one or both is revealed. This motif is not neglected in this text, as we shall see.

165 *he went on*: the second sentence here is attributed to Gawain in some manuscripts.

166 *I can well believe it*: this remark reflects the lady's noble looks, and the views described in the note to p. [156]. The king's statement that he would have gone to fetch her himself, had he known who she was, is a mark of the courtesy due to a great lady.

167 *Orkenise*: perhaps the same as *Orcanie* (or Orkney), which occurs in Chrétien de Troyes's *Perceval*, where it is also possible to go there without crossing the sea.

for gain: a knight captured in a tournament, or even in battle, was usually ransomed, if only for the price of his horse and equipment. It was possible for a skilled exponent of the tournament art to make large sums of money in this way.

knights bachelor: a *bacheler* is generally taken to be young, landless, and unmarried (cf. Mod. Eng. 'bachelor'). The latter two states would often coincide, in a society where most marriages were essentially property deals.

168 *had not shown themselves*: that is, they avoided revealing their presence to King Arthur, thereby circumventing his announcement (p. [230]).

lists: normally, the 'lists' at a tournament comprised a large marked area, in which the fighting took place. A knight outside this area would be 'safe'. The tourney itself might be between two sides, with or without specified numbers of participants, or it might be a sort of general free-for-all. In the latter case, knights would probably tend to group themselves with another who was performing particularly well, or known for his prowess, especially if their motive was profit (cf. the note to p. [230]). In some instances, the word 'lists' is used to denote the area outside, rather than inside, the boundaries, or even the boundaries themselves.

with bodies and faces: this seems slightly curious for two knights on horseback, but might be explained if the practice was to lean well out of the saddle towards the opponent.

a new knight: a shield of a single colour was a mark of a new knight.

169 *both sides of the hauberk*: as on p. [149], this would appear to mean the front and back of the hauberk, and I have translated accordingly, but as the mail of the hauberk might be double (or even triple) thickness, it is possible that it means 'both thicknesses'.

the exposed hauberk: the king's lance misses the other's shield and strikes the hauberk directly.

170 *in no pain*: we may deduce that his well-being is due to the queen's presence.

at the encounter: cf. the damsel's words, p. [219].

171 *master*: this (Latin *magister*) was a common form of address for learned men of all denominations.

172 *he*: I take this to mean Arthur, but it could refer to Gawain.

could bear arms: I take this to mean that Arthur here has so many men that they cannot all take part at once.

the Monday before Advent: this would probably be in some ten weeks' time, although the chronology in this section of the text is rather vague. Gawain is here speaking as Arthur's chief warrior, the first knight of the Round Table.

173 *It is him*: that is to say, they are both looking for the same man.

174 *freed me from this quest*: cf. p. [220]: Gawain only vowed to find out the knight's identity.

176 *down in the town*: this would seem to mean inside the walls of the Dolorous Guard, but outside the citadel itself.

knew it as well as he did: I take this to mean that he believes the queen knows that he was responsible for the fact that she was kept waiting.

178 *opened a window*: presumably by opening the shutters, or pulling back drapes.

179 *that ring on your finger*: clearly the ring given him by the Lady of the Lake (p. [154]); this is presumably how the maiden recognized his hard.

184 *treacherously*: the knights have attacked him, two to one, and with no warning or justification given.

186 *Danish axes*: long-handled war-axes.

the castle: the brattice and gate mentioned previously.

188 *said the other*: we shall see that this knight has a particular reason for helping Gawain, unlike the others, who merely respect him as the nonpareil among knights.

191 *conquered the fief*: or possibly 'won the honour'?

193 *for an armed knight to cross*: the weight of full chain-mail, plus sword, shield and helm, would scarcely be conducive to making even a short jump of this nature.

held on to him: it is not altogether clear who is doing what, here. Since the 'axeman' was on the far side of the well, though, I assume it is Lancelot who would have fallen in, had he not grabbed hold of the other man.

louder than the last: this demonic arrangement bears a curious resemblance to a church organ.

194 *as level as the middle of the chamber*: the well has disappeared.

had had the red shield made: this is a variant reading. The text has 'he had made'.

196 *three knights*: the third knight is the one who stopped fighting
Keheriet and gave him a horse.

a fair offer: that is, to fight for the maidens, three against three.

197 *I defy you*: this defiance is a formal challenge: it was normal for
a combat to be preceded by some declaration of hostilities; cf.
the note to p. [243].

198 *However*: I take this to mean, approximately, 'although there
were only two of them . . .', but cf. the note below, concerning
an inconsistency here.

he said: I take this to be Brehu speaking, but it could be
Keheriet.

knocked down: there is a marked inconsistency in this section of
the text. We were told that Gawain and the anonymous third
knight each killed an opponent, but here we have a reference
to a knight whom Gawain merely unhorsed. Furthermore, this
unhorsed knight is clearly the one who is sent as a prisoner
with the damsel.

199 *poor men*: landless knights, to be contrasted, like the knights
bachelor (cf. the note to p. [230]), with the 'barons', men of
substance.

he is our equal: Kennedy takes *parent* here to mean 'equal,
peer', and Agravain's words would seem to support this. While
I know of no other instance where the word has that sense, the
alternative 'he is our kinsman' would be quite untrue.

201 *break my oath*: cf. p. [240].

who had stayed: this is the other maiden, who has been travelling
with Gawain since they met on the road, for the second time,
p. [234]. (It is the maiden who was left in the Dolorous Guard
who has stayed with Lancelot.)

Carlisle: *Cardue(i)l* is generally taken to be Carlisle, although
once in this text it is said to be in *Gales* (p. [296]).

207 *what they were used to seeing*: King Arthur's knights are accustomed to having a steady stream of 'adventures' come to court.
This, of course, is in no small measure due to Arthur's

reputation for providing assistance to all who need it (cf. p. [150]).

210 *counsel*: here, and in subsequent references to the Flower, the approximate meaning of 'counsel' is 'help and guidance'.

211 *surcoat*: a sleeveless over-tunic.

The devils of hell make you look at ladies: that is to say, 'you have no business looking at ladies'.

where I have promised: that is, somewhere where he will not dare follow.

215 *there*: I take this to mean the far bank, where the queen is.

delayed too long: Yvain intended to go hunting with the king, but arrives too late.

217 *two or three*: clearly, we are to understand that Daguenet's claims are groundless.

218 *I well believe it*: is this an oblique reference to Yvain's famous courtesy?

Against Daguenet?: Yvain is asking the queen to be *his* surety in the matter: if Daguenet makes a fuss, Yvain will refer him to the queen. Technically, having stood surety for Lancelot, Yvain would become Daguenet's prisoner if the former left.

219 *And what do you want?*: Kennedy, using a manuscript in which this question is followed by 'he said', attributes it, not to Daguenet's knight, but to the other, and distributes the remaining dialogue accordingly. To my mind, it is clearly the other knight who makes the demands here. Lancelot's role as the non-aggressor is confirmed in the preliminaries to the fighting, and by his return of his opponent's horse; cf. the fight with Alybon, pp. [179–80]. This is not the only instance in the text of a superfluous 'he said'.

221 *he knocked to the ground*: the text is slightly ambiguous here. I take it to mean that the giant broke off part of the knight's shield with his club.

224 *or: his horse*: I have added these words.

right: most of the MSS have the more usual 'it is time'.

a long time ago: it appears to be some five or six months since the incident referred to, but the chronology here is very fluid.

225   *relatives*: cf. the note to p. [42].

226   *greatly upset*: this sentence is very elliptical: I understand '. . . upset [and would have been pleased] if he could have . . .' Kennedy understands the unstated element as [that he might have done otherwise].

227   *toises*: a toise equals 6.395 feet, or about 2 metres.

228   *your land*: the damsel is clearly Arthur's vassal, so that her land is also his land.

229   *kings and barons*: presumably the leaders of the ten thousand men.

       a company formed: the terms 'company' and 'battalion' are used here simply to denote divisions of a body of armed men, and do not correspond to their modern military equivalents.

230   *the others*: probably 'they' are Galehot's men, and 'the others', Arthur's.

231   *They forced them*: probably, it is Gawain and the king's men who are driven across the ford.

232   *a knight in prison*: this unnamed knight is, of course, Lancelot. The link here is made only indirectly, by the reference to the lady and the description of the gaol. It is interesting that this description differs slightly from the one above.

       a large stone's throw: that is, the distance one can throw a large stone, rather than a long stone's throw.

234   *three days from tomorrow*: apparently, the fighting takes place on every third day; cf. below.

235   *ill as he was*: Gawain's inability to take part in the battle seems to be a variation on the tradition whereby, when some crisis occurs at Arthur's court, Gawain is absent, thus escaping blame. The crisis is normally resolved by a newcomer to the court.

       braggarts: these *parleor d'armes* are the men who 'talk a good fight'.

in the chest: the 'Red Knight', it will be remembered, has no shield at the moment.

237 *failed him badly*: since Arthur's men seem to have given a good account of themselves, and since he has so few men, this would seem to mean 'failed to turn up'. However, what the worthy man subsequently tells him seems to imply that the failure lies in their actual performance in battle.

adultery: Arthur was engendered by Uther Pendragon, to whom Merlin gave the form of the Duke of Tintagel, Ygerne's husband. Uther and Ygerne were subsequently married, after the Duke's death.

239 *folly*: the variant readings are generally more vehement, speaking of 'crimes' or 'sins'.

240 *done great honour*: the honour done to these great barons might include the granting of fiefs, although it seems to have a wider sense here; cf. the note to p. [11].

242 *heard the rights and wrongs*: that is, administered justice.

more: that is, a more favourable judgement.

down there: this doubtless refers to the seating at a meal, where the king and other important people would sit at the 'high table', literally raised up above the others.

poor men: cf. the note to p. [254].

lies: one would expect some qualifier here, such as 'often', corresponding to that in the second part of the phrase.

243 *the true witness*: that is, the man Arthur will have sought out to advise him on the merits of the local people.

247 *the royal crown*: I can only assume this means (the art of) kingship.

and which: we would expect '. . . from God, *who* put . . .'

they: the text has 'he'; the editor agrees that a correction is needed, and I have adopted a variant reading.

249 *fifteen years*: in Exodus 16:35 it is forty years; many of the MSS have forty-five years.

252 *showed*: I have added this word from the variants.

255 *Carlisle in Wales*: cf. the note to p. [256].

    serving with the others: Gawain is waiting on the king.

256 *to make the great find*: that is, to find the knight.

257 *last of all*: the others are committing themselves, in advance, to being bound by the terms of Gawain's oath.

258 *unless death took him*: it is not clear whether this refers to death taking Gawain, or any one of his companions.

    exemption from your oath: Arthur thinks Gawain's oath should have allowed the knights to return for the encounter, whether or not they have found the knight.

    Yvain of the Little Lion: this character, sometimes called 'Yvain of Lionel/Leonel' (cf. p. [204]), as opposed to 'of the *lionel*, or little lion', is very possibly an *alter ego* of Yvain (the Tall), the son of King Urien, who is the hero of Chrétien de Troyes's romance *Yvain*, or *The Knight of the Lion*; cf. the note to p. [197].

    Brandeliz: or Bran of Liz. This character first appears in the First Continuation of Chrétien de Troyes's *Perceval*, where he is the uncle of Gawain's illegitimate son. It is interesting that in this text he is always called *Sir* Brandeliz.

    Braveheart: the form of this name in most of the MSS is *Cors Hardiz*, which suggests physical bravery, while a number of MSS give *Cuer Hardiz*; 'Braveheart' would convey the sense of both these forms.

    the Ugly Hero: this character often features in lists of knights, usually as the counterpart of the better-known Handsome Coward, who plays a role in several romances.

260 *give him back to me*: that is, she must not actually let him go.

261 *uphold her cause*: that is, fight for her in judicial combat; the 'he' in the next phrase is the neighbour.

262 *hold it against her*: the lady is making out that she was afraid Arthur would object to her holding one of his men a prisoner.

265 *surcoat*: a sleeveless tunic worn over the armour, carrying the coat of arms; not the same as the surcoat mentioned in the note to p. [262].

houses: Arthur's subjects erect temporary dwellings at the spot where the battle is to take place.

266 *lists*: see the note to p. [230].

268 *by himself*: such extraordinary feats of arms, common in this text, might have been possible in reality, where the numbers of combatants were generally small, and battles did not involve the sort of numbers present here.

strong: the base MS of Kennedy's edition gives *fres* (not an isolated reading), that of Micha *fors*; *fres* might arise from a misreading of *fors*, but in many contexts has a similar meaning, 'fresh, hence strong.' On these grounds, the translation 'strong' seems justified.

269 *kinsman*: cf. the note to p. [242].

could ever die: that is not to say that Gawain is so valorous that he cannot die, but that no one more valorous will ever die; compare the lady's words, a few lines below.

rejoiced: in contrast to the men of valour, who are all distressed.

270 *three days from today*: cf. the note to p. [281].

272 *forty thousand*: these figures would mean, approximately, that Galehot has 120,000 men, against Arthur's 80,000 plus. However, it was earlier stated that Galehot had twice as many men as in his previous army, which was said on p. [275] to consist of at least 100,000 mounted men (it is possible that footsoldiers are discounted in these figures). He ought now, therefore, to have 200,000 or more.

273 *habergeon*: unlike a hauberk, this had no sleeves, and often reached only to the waist.

274 *forty*: some MSS have 'sixty', which would make a better progression.

275 *down to his hand*: that is to say, he struck with his broken lance until there was only enough of it left to hold in his hand.

276 *sought*: I take this to mean that the lady suspects that Lancelot loves the queen, and now expects to have her suspicions confirmed.

277 *renown at arms*: many of the MSS here have 'love's prize', which I take to mean the love of ladies, given to renowned knights.

arrive in time: this merely indicates their impatience, rather than any fear that they will be too late for the battle.

278 *very tight*: this passage is confused, and surely corrupt, as Kennedy, who discusses the problem at length, points out. The horse that the squire brings must in fact be the first of Sir Gawain's three: it is only when the knight mounts it that the Round Table knights notice Gawain's arms, and he has three killed under him after this, the third of which is said to be 'the last of his horses'.

all day: that is to say, apparently quite unwearied by his previous exertions.

279 *iron and wood*: that is, armour and shield.

280 *too old*: Hervi, it was revealed on p. [55], was in the service of Uther Pendragon, Arthur's father, before serving Arthur. We learn later that he is over 80.

281 *force*: or 'banner', but 'force' seems more likely in this context, and below.

Hervi: it was common for a leader's name to be the battle-cry of a group of men.

282 *armed as he was*: that is, in habergeon and steel cap, and carrying only a staff; cf. p. [310].

283 *like a standard*: that is to say, he is like a rallying-point for his side.

284 *weary you*: the idea seems to be that the Black Knight is to be allowed to go on fighting as long as he can; thus he is not to be captured, or driven from the field while on foot, and Galehot will provide him with fresh mounts. Galehot's motive is apparently to see whether he can continue his prodigious feats of arms all day long.

engaged: as Galehot's troops are apparently on a hill, it may be that some of them are concealed behind the brow of the hill.

288 *a small stone's throw*: cf. the note to p. [279].

291 *unworthy*: it is clearly a sign of honour for the knight to sleep in a higher bed than the others.

in the bed: I have added these words, which are required by the context. It was not uncommon for men to share a bed (cf. p. [227]), but that is clearly not the case here.

293 *a day of battle*: the fighting seems to be on pre-arranged days, as in the first encounter.

too big and wide: Galehot, it will be remembered, is the son of a giantess, and 'at least six inches taller than any knight known', p. [264].

294 *passage*: as the boundary of the lists here seems to coincide with the river (cf. Arthur's orders, above), this may mean a ford.

is it enough?: I take this to mean 'is it enough merely to ask?', but the sense is by no means clear. It could be that Lancelot is asking whether Galehot feels he is sufficiently master of the field.

295 *put his hands together*: while this might be a sign of entreaty, it was also a symbolic gesture of paying homage. The vassal placed his hands together, and the overlord placed his around them.

296 *reliable word*: Arthur would presumably send some 'password' by which the queen would know the message genuinely came from him, and was not an enemy ruse.

297 *I now see*: this is a difficult passage, and perhaps corrupt. I interpret 'in the way I now see' as meaning 'in these circumstances': as opposed to, for instance, an acquaintance made where Galehot was victor and Gawain and Arthur vanquished.

299 *for anything*: that is, if he had known that they were to sleep in with him. They, of course, stated that they would sleep elsewhere, but in fact slept in the same tent as the knight.

302 *keep your word*: this refers to Gawain's previous adjuration.

nothing of him: in other words, Galehot is saying that he is quite unable to show the knight to them, as he knows nothing of his identity or whereabouts.

my lord: whether Galehot is using this term to mean Arthur or, less probably, Lancelot, he appears to be dissembling.

303 *the oath*: this refers to the adjuration 'by the person you most love'.

304 *someone other than you or me*: that is, Lancelot.

305 *yours*: this might be interpreted as 'your friend', 'grateful to you', 'in your debt'.

night and day: that is, travelling night and day.

306 *it is through your love they have mine*: that is to say, Galehot has bestowed his love on King Arthur and his people only because Lancelot loves them, and he loves Lancelot.

sent someone to fetch me: presumably, so that she will not know he is near at hand.

309 *in his customary place*: I take this to mean in the king's tent.

314 *he said*: this is not an exact report of their conversation; cf. pp. [179-80].

315 *credentials*: that is to say, she believes he is telling the truth, because he is able to give her these details.

316 *have I ever seen you*: the question seems slightly odd, as the queen has already ascertained that she saw Lancelot at the Dolorous Guard. It is there we would expect her to mention, rather than Camelot.

317 *but was not one*: cf. p. [342] and the note to p. [209].

318 *your friend*: cf. the note to p. [165].

322 *credit*: in both cases, the blame or credit will attach to Galehot, for having brought Lancelot and the queen together.

323 *what I have had already*: that is, presumably, his love.

by sight: not in the usual sense, of having seen someone, but not met them, but meaning that he had met and would recognize him, but did not know who he was.

328 *the oath*: this refers to the adjuration 'by the loyalty you owe me', cf. the note to p. [334].

presumably that of the Lady of Malohaut, who 'stole'
...elot from her.

Remote Isles: the location of Sorelois, and to some extent
...ne description, call Anglesey to mind. It is open to question,
however, whether the geography of the text corresponds to any
kind of reality.

333 his other land: the Remote Isles and Sorelois are Galehot's own
lands, as opposed to those which belong to his vassals, such as
the King of a Hundred Knights.

mountains: the text seems garbled here, and I have interpreted
it with a degree of freedom.

into the sea: in other words, Assurne is a strait, separating
Sorelois from Logres, although the author talks of it as if it
was a river, cf. the note to p. [356].

adventures: Arthur's reign is often associated with a period of
so-called adventures. Sometimes these are linked to the Grail,
cf. the note to p. [14].

one thousand, six hundred and ninety weeks: that is, thirty-two
and a half years.

seven thousand long: that is, nearly 8½ miles.

seventy toises: there is no mention that the causeways can only
be crossed at low tide, but that seems the most likely case.

335 who he was: it seems curious at first sight that Lionel is
presented here almost as a new character, and as though he
and Lancelot had never met. It is, after all, only some two
years since Lancelot left the Lake. However, Lancelot only
learnt of their kinship when they parted, and has since
discovered his own identity. This is therefore his first opportunity to enjoy Lionel's company in the full knowledge of their
relationship. At the same time, the restatement of Lionel's
identity would serve as a reminder to the public, after his
lengthy absence from the narrative.

the crowned lion of Libya: three MSS later give an account of
Lionel's fight with the lion.

on his shield: cf. the note to pp. [603–13].

340 *for a week*: it is part of the Arthurian romance tradition that Gawain never refuses to reveal his name, even when to do so may be dangerous for him.

wanes: another tradition concerning Gawain. The exact link between the increase and decrease in his strength and midday varies from text to text. It has been suggested that this trait is a relic of solar mythology, while it is given a Christian explanation in the *Mort Artu*.

341 *half a service*: this refers to the queen telling Gawain that he might find Lancelot with Galehot, but not telling him where they might be found.

345 *together*: the action in this section is related retrospectively, as these characters have already been shown arriving at court.

348 *a long time*: curiously, Hector's sword is said here to improve constantly—the opposite of what was stated earlier; cf. the summary of pp. [409–25].

in the first place: the ring does not appear to have any effect on Hector, who already has a ladylove.

349 *afresh*: it was a widely held belief that a dead man's wounds would bleed in the presence of his killer. There is an incident similar to this in the First *Perceval*-Continuation.

352 *Saraide*: cf. the summary of pp. [57–60] and the note there; here the damsel is called Celice.

354 *on her ring*: there is a similar episode in the First *Perceval*-Continuation, in which a damsel, who has made the same vow, compares Gawain's face with an embroidered likeness of him.

358 *to harm him*: there are marked similarities between this and a passage in Chrétien de Troyes's *Lancelot* (lines 2209–550).

359 *Causeway*: earlier the crossings were called the North Wales Bridge and the Irish Bridge.

361 *the great need facing him*: that is, the invasion by the Saxons and Irish, which must be dealt with. Gawain is traditionally Arthur's right-hand man, chief among his knights.

366 *under him*: it would seem, from the romances, that it was not uncommon for knights on foot to resort to wrestling.

grew weaker: cf. the summary of pp. [372–93] and the note to p. [388].

he said: Gawain is apparently not speaking aloud.

the words he had heard: presumably this refers to Hector's tactful but transparent offer of help, and Lancelot's suggestion that he should fight both men together

by his arms: Lionel, it will be remembered, met Gawain previously and was told who he was: cf. the summary of pp. [493–515].

he said: the text is thoroughly ambiguous here. It could be Galehot who is speaking, afraid that Lancelot will be injured or killed; or it could be Lionel, referring to Gawain (Micha's interpretation) or Lancelot, and fearing the same. My own view is that the speaker is probably Lionel, referring to Lancelot, and meaning that he will regret it, when he hears the queen's message that he must do all he can for Gawain.

367 *who is he?*: a slightly curious question, since Lionel has just told him that it is Gawain, but it may be that Galehot wishes for confirmation of that.

368 *first*: I have added this word, found in Micha's edition, as it makes sense of a somewhat cryptic passage.

depends on it: I take this to be meant figuratively: Gawain is desperate not to 'lose' the object of his quest.

370 *stay here*: several MSS add the words '(for) today/tonight', which makes rather better sense.

Canile: the damsel is actually called Gartissiee here, and Canile on pp. [567–8]. However, unlike the Saraide/Celice inconsistency mentioned previously, this could be due to copying error/variation, and I have preferred to regularize the name.

372 *they*: probably Gawain is here associating Hector with his actions, although he might be referring to all the questers.

recognize one another: they had agreed to hang their shields back to front.

373 *not interested*: this contradicts what was said on p. [504].

white band: this was the shield the queen said that he should carry; cf. the summary of p. [525].

fesse: a broad horizontal bar across the centre of the field.

374 *put*: or rather, 'caused to be put', since the queen sent the pennon to Lancelot, cf. the summary of p. [525].

375 *liege lord*: Gawain's uncle and his liege lord are, of course, one and the same: Arthur.

won everything: I take this to mean that, with their enemies hemmed in by the river and in full flight, the Saxons are not bothering to capture individuals, as they expect to round up or destroy the whole force.

377 *No, my lady*: the blood which covers Lancelot's arm is, of course, that of his enemies, not his own.

380 *any other woman*: cf. the summary of pp. [396–46] for details of the shield.

381 *as had been said*: cf. the preceding note; the queen was told that at the time the shield became whole, she would be freed from the greatest sorrow she ever had and would have the greatest joy she ever had; this would not happen, though, until the best knight outside King Arthur's household became part of that household.

383 *seventeen*: that is, the original twenty knights who resumed the quest, less Gawain, who is in prison, Sagremor, who has not yet arrived, and Yvain himself. Gawain's other brother, Guerrehet, a member of the first quest, did not take part in the second.

384 *I do not know who they are*: Kennedy's text should read *sai*, not *sait*, here.

housings: this suggests that the 'banner' is placed on the horse.

surpassed everyone: I have here rejected the reading of the base manuscript, taking up Kennedy's suggestion that it might result from a scribal error (a misinterpretation of the reading on which I have based my translation, *crioient amont et aval li rois ydiers a tot veincu*), even though it is supported by a manuscript from a different group.

1 *let him go*: as Lancelot is not rich, they will get no ransom. As he is mad, he is no danger to them.

following him: I have interpreted *seust* ('follows'), rather than *seüst* ('would have known'). Kennedy would interpret 'would have known him to be someone out of his mind'.

389 *Maiden of the Lake*: the Lady of the Lake, as she is more usually called.

391 *do it*: that is, presumably, open the door. Micha's text reads simply: 'My lady,' she said, 'have the door opened, for . . .'

392 *happened to him*: that is, she knew it in advance.

393 *something else*: presumably, the Lady was afraid her lover would think she was bringing up the young Lancelot to take his place.

it is pointless: Micha's text runs better: '. . . where he is concerned, for he wishes for, and values nothing . . .'

395 *it*: that is, their love-affair.

397 *they have suffered*: the text puts this more actively: 'they [the enemy] have inflicted'.

399 *standard*: cf. the note to p. [318].

400 *hand*: a palm's width, or four inches: still in use as the standard unit of measurement for horses.

407 *feared*: I understand an unstated element here, along the lines of ('if the knights had not been forced to surrender it.').

into the tower: this does not seem altogether clear (cf. the following note), and it may be that *tor* is an error for *cort* (the reading of at least one manuscript): 'they went back into the courtyard'.

Clarance: it is not quite clear who is doing what, and where, in this passage; it is presumably Arthur's troops (the 200 knights on guard outside the gate) who are shouting, as the sight of Lancelot tells them the Rock has been captured.

410 *apart from Sagremor*: there is an inconsistency concerning Sagremor: it was stated on p. [541] that he arrived before the end of the fighting, yet here he is still absent; cf. also the note to p. [571].

411 *he is in Galehot's service*: or perhaps 'he belongs to Galehot', but Lancelot is not strictly Galehot's man, as he has never done him homage.

412 *wear his crown*: crown wearing was a solemn and formal affair, and normally took place only at the king's great courts.

that day: probably All Saints' is meant.

413 *eighteen*: this would appear to exclude Sagremor, since Hector was not one of the original twenty questers.

Camaheu: it is not clear whether Camaheu is in Britain.

Britain: this corresponds to the end of vol. viii of Micha's edition. The remainder of the text corresponds to chapters I–IV of his vol. iii, while the material in it corresponds approximately to chapters I–IX of the cyclic version, as found in his vol. i, although Galehot does not die until Chapter XXXV, at the end of that volume.

414 *thirty-one*: Galehot had meant this to include Arthur; cf. pp. [263–4].

The Proud Watch-Post: the name, *L'Orgueilleusse Angarde* is reminiscent of the *Dolereuse Garde*.

dream: cf. pp. [260–2].

415 *Round Table*: this explanation of the origin of the Round Table—that it was a part of Guinevere's dowry—differs from those given by Wace (*Brut*, 9747–60) and Robert de Boron (*Merlin*, pp. 95–8). It is important, in that Lancelot is saving not only the queen, but also the Round Table itself.

418 *strangles it*: it is said here that Yvain wore the lion's skin on his shield, whence his epithet, 'The Knight of the Lion'. While this explanation is quite at variance with that given in Chrétien de Troyes's *Yvain*, which would have been well known to the contemporary public, it forms part of a subtle interplay between that work and our text, helping to underline the main themes of the making of a name and the knightly lover. See E. Kennedy, *Le rôle d'Yvain et de Gauvain dans le* Lancelot *en prose (version non-cyclique)*, in *Lancelot—Yvain—Gauvain* (Paris, 1984), pp. 19–27.

THE WORLD'S CLASSICS

A Select List

BEN JONSON: Five Plays
Edited by G. A. Wilkes

LEONARDO DA VINCI: Notebooks
Edited by Irma A. Richter

HERMAN MELVILLE: The Confidence-Man
Edited by Tony Tanner

PROSPER MÉRIMÉE: Carmen and Other Stories
Translated by Nicholas Jotcham

EDGAR ALLAN POE: Selected Tales
Edited by Julian Symons

MARY SHELLEY: Frankenstein
Edited by M. K. Joseph

BRAM STOKER: Dracula
Edited by A. N. Wilson

ANTHONY TROLLOPE: The American Senator
Edited by John Halperin

OSCAR WILDE: Complete Shorter Fiction
Edited by Isobel Murray

VIRGINIA WOOLF: Mrs Dalloway
Edited by Claire Tomalin

A complete list of Oxford Paperbacks, including The World's Classics, OPUS, Past Masters, Oxford Authors, Oxford Shakespeare, and Oxford Paperback Reference, is available in the UK from the Arts and Reference Publicity Department (BH), Oxford University Press, Walton Street, Oxford OX2 6DP.

In the USA, complete lists are available from the Paperbacks Marketing Manager, Oxford University Press, 200 Madison Avenue, New York, NY 10016.

Oxford Paperbacks are available from all good bookshops. In case of difficulty, customers in the UK can order direct from Oxford University Press Bookshop, Freepost, 116 High Street, Oxford, OX1 4BR, enclosing full payment. Please add 10 per cent of published price for postage and packing.